D1272986

# Farwell's Rules
# of the Nautical Road

# Farwell's Rules of the Nautical Road

Originally known as The Rules of the Nautical Road
by Captain Raymond F. Farwell

Seventh Edition prepared by
Captain Richard A. Smith, Royal Navy

**Naval Institute Press**
Annapolis, Maryland

**Library of Congress Cataloging in Publication Data**

Farwell, Raymond Forrest, 1893–
    [Rules of the nautical road]
    Farwell's rules of the nautical road.—7th ed. / prepared by
Richard A. Smith.
      p.    cm.
    Includes index.
    ISBN 1-55750-772-4 (acid-free paper)
    1. Rule of the road at sea.   2. Inland navigation—Law and
legislation—United States.   I. Smith, Richard Arthur, 1940–
II. Title.
K4184.F37   1993
343.09′66—dc20
[342.3966]                          93-34973
                                           CIP

# Contents

# Preface to the Seventh Edition

This book was first published in 1941 as *The Rules of the Nautical Road,* by the late Captain Raymond F. Farwell, U.S. Naval Reserve. Since its first publication, numerous statutory and regulatory changes have been made in both local and international nautical rules. Such changes automatically necessitate revisions of any authoritative texts pertaining to this subject, and hence the book has been revised whenever occasion demanded.

Over the years, common usage has made Captain Farwell's name synonymous with the book itself; accordingly, since the Fourth Edition it has been titled *Farwell's Rules of the Nautical Road.*

The welcomed alignment of the rules of the road, brought about by the International Regulations for the Preventing of Collisions at Sea 1972 and the Inland Navigations Rules Act of 1980, has evolved further with a series of amendments and other developments during the subsequent decade. The seventh edition of *Farwell's* acknowledges this progress with an approach different to previous editions. Gone is the extensive side-by-side treatment of the rules governing both the International and Inland waters; the differences between the two regimes are greatly reduced. Such differences that do remain, both in the regulations and the findings of the courts, are explored in appropriate chapters for both open and restricted waters. Some simple diagrams to aid understanding of collision cases have been incorporated, and the appendix provides the ready reference to the rules themselves.

Commander Frank E. Bassett helped launch this edition but was unable to complete it due to other commitments. Full recognition is hereby given to his valuable contribution. Equally, the generous access to its research facilities granted by the Institute of Maritime Law, University of Southampton, is gratefully acknowledged.

The root cause of many a collision is either standing too close to danger or misapplication of the rules: perhaps through carelessness and confusion. The primary purpose of this book is to illustrate all causes of collision and by so doing, bring about a heightened awareness of the risks and a better understanding of the rules so that some calamities may be avoided.

Richard A. Smith

# Preface to
# the First Edition

Marine Collision Law has too long been a specialty of judges on the admiralty bench and of a very limited number of admiralty lawyers at the bar. It should, of course, be instead a specialty of the mariner on the bridge. The present book is planned to satisfy the needs of classes in seamanship such as those at the Naval Academy and at Naval ROTC colleges, and at the same time to serve as a useful handbook on the subject for the officers at sea in the actual practice of navigation. To this two-fold end an adequate amount of case material has been included, and in addition an index sufficiently comprehensive so that ready references may be made to any desired rule.

To the man on the bridge it may be superfluous to say that a collision situation is neither the time nor the place for him to look up the law that determines his proper action. But it must be pointed out that the alternative is such a thorough understanding of his duty in every situation that his action will almost instinctively be the proper one from the standpoint of both law and seamanship. It is said that Admiral Knight required his officers to read through the rules of the road each time before getting under way. Certain it is that the complexity of rules effective under American law makes frequent study of them both desirable and necessary.

As teacher and practical mariner of some experience, the writer believes that a clear, definite, positive knowledge of the principles here presented should be an essential part of the professional equipment of every man on the bridge engaging in the practice of navigation. Court decisions in an overwhelming number prove that nearly all marine collisions follow violations of the rules of the road. The inference is that the rules, if implicitly obeyed, are practically collision-proof. It is the writer's opinion that most of this seeming disregard of the law is due to misunderstanding of the rules as interpreted by the courts. The rules will not be better obeyed until they are better understood. Such a better understanding by the mariner is the primary purpose of this book.

University of Washington                                     Raymond F. Farwell
December 15, 1940                                    Captain, U.S. Naval Reserve

# Farwell's Rules
# of the Nautical Road

# 1

# Collision Regulations: Growing International Conformity

### Background to the International Rules

The industrial revolution of the eighteenth and nineteenth centuries and the upsurge in international commerce that resulted led to a number of international treaties related to shipping, including safety. In the twentieth century the flow of such treaties markedly increased, considerably improving the standards of safety at sea. The topics covered included load lines, tonnage measurement, signalling, limited liability, pollution, training, and, the subject of this book, the prevention of collisions.

The International Regulations for Preventing Collisions date back to rules introduced in 1863 by Great Britain and France, and similar rules adopted by the United States in 1864, which in turn were adopted, with amendments, before 1886 by the United States, Great Britain, France, Germany, Belgium, Norway, and Denmark. These early rules were modified at a conference of representatives of the maritime nations of the world at Washington, D.C., in 1889, and subsequently adopted by the respective nations concerned. In the United States that became effective in 1897. Amended slightly in 1910, unsuccessful attempts were made to amend them further in 1913–1914 and 1929.

In 1948 at London, the International Conference on Safety of Life at Sea (SOLAS) proposed a revision of the 1889 International Rules. Raymond Farwell himself was, of course, a leading participant in this conference, and although not all of his personal proposals won acceptance, the final revision was passed by the maritime nations and came into force in 1954.

The 1948 rules, unlike the 1889 rules, were of short duration. They were reconsidered and revised again at a similar conference of the same name and scope held in London in 1960. These rules were made effective in 1965.

The most recent International Conference was held in London in 1972. The revision was a major one, making the rules more comprehensive and resulting in a completely new format. They became effective in 1977, with further amendments coming into force in 1983, 1989, and 1991. Four years should elapse between successive amendments.

**International Maritime Organisation**

The growing and accelerating pace of international cooperation evident at the 1948 SOLAS Convention led to the creation of a permanent international maritime body to deal with still more internationally developed treaties. The International Maritime Organisation (IMO) came into existence in 1959 (until 1982 it was called the Inter-Governmental Maritime Consultative Organisation—IMCO), responsible for ensuring that conventions were kept up to date and for the task of developing new conventions as and when the need arose. The creation of IMO coincided with a period of tremendous change in world shipping, not least in technology that has had a bearing on the practical application of the rules of the road.

Conventions and other multilateral instruments create international treaty obligations. Governments that ratify or accept them agree to bring their laws and measures into conformity with the provisions of such treaties. The purpose of IMO's instruments is to establish standards that are acceptable to as many countries as possible and can be implemented in the same way, thereby eliminating differences between national practices. Relevant to the caliber of those who have to apply the Rules is the International Convention on Standards of Training, Certification and Watchkeeping for Sea-Farers (STCW 1978).

Nonetheless, the 1972 International Collision Regulations (ColRegs) recognized that local circumstances might require special rules to be adopted for waters other than the high seas. Many countries have local rules, not the least the United States.

**Background to the Inland Rules**

The rules for the preventing of collisions on the inland waters of the United States were enacted in the Inland Navigational Rules Act of 1980. They became effective in 1981. The act makes the international rules nonapplicable to vessels inshore of the lines of demarcation between the inland waters of the United States and the high seas.

Prior to this act different statutes subdivided U.S. inland waters into three sections, with a distinct set of rules for each, and the statutory rules were supplemented in each case by a corresponding body of pilot rules, formulated and issued by the Commandant, U.S. Coast Guard. The three sections of inland waters referred to were (1) the Great Lakes and connecting and tributary waters as far east as Montreal; (2) the Red River of the North, and certain other rivers and their tributaries whose waters flow into the Gulf of Mexico; (3) all other inland waters of the United States. In each of these sections, the pilot rules, except where they were in conflict with the statutory rules, had coextensive jurisdiction with them, and the mariner had therefore to be equally familiar with both. To add to the complexity, Rules and Regulations of the Corps of Engineers, Department of the Army, supplemented the pilot rules for the "Great Lakes." They, too, when not in conflict with the statutory rules, had coextensive jursidiction with them, in the same manner as did the pilot rules. There were also special navigational light requirements for small commercial and recreational vessels of not more than 65 feet in length found in the 1940 Motorboat Act. While these seven sets of rules were alike in many respects, there were significant differences between them, as well as between the international rules, that tended to generate confusion among mariners.

An attempt to unify the various laws, rules, and regulations that affected the navigation of vessels on the waters of the United States was made during the early 1960s. It was then decided that unification of the inland rules into a single system should be deferred until the international maritime community further developed the international regulations. The latter was completed by the entry in force, in 1977, of the International Regulations for Preventing Collisions at Sea, 1972. Since then, the Coast Guard actively pursued the unification of the inland rules and regulations. To assist in developing the best possible set of rules, the Coast Guard established the Rules of the Road Advisory Committee, whose membership was composed of a cross section of maritime interests that used or were familiar with the inland waterway systems. After deliberations and discussions over a period of eight years, the Advisory Committee developed a proposal to unify the inland navigation rules. That proposal was the basis of the Inland Navigation Rules Act of 1980.

Simply stated, the act established a unified system of local or special navigation rules applicable to U.S. domestic waters, as consistent as possible with the international system of navigational rules. In certain instances the international rules were considered inappropriate for specific waters of the United States because of local problems, and as a result, some previous domestic rules and practices have been adapted. Thus, reference will still be found in the act to the Western Rivers and the Great Lakes.

Despite the differences that remain between the inland rules and international regulations, the Act of 1980 was a major advance along the road to revision and unification, a matter that received considerable support in previous editions of this book. The power granted to the secretary of transportation to issue regulations and establish technical annexes to the act has provided the flexibility to meet changing conditions and prevent the United States rules from becoming unduly out of line with international practice.

## Ships' Routing

The practice of following predetermined routes originated in 1898 and was adopted, for reasons of safety, by shipping companies operating passenger ships across the North Atlantic. Related provisions were subsequently incorporated into the International Conventions for the Safety of Life at Sea.

The 1960 Safety Convention referred to the same practice in converging areas on both sides of the North Atlantic. The contracting governments undertook the responsibility of using their influence to induce the owners of all passenger ships crossing the Atlantic to follow the recognized routes and to do everything in their power to ensure adherence to such routes in converging areas by all ships, so far as circumstances permit.

In 1961 the Institutes of Navigation of the Federal Republic of Germany, France and the United Kingdom undertook a study of measures for separating traffic in the Strait of Dover and, subsequently, in certain other areas where statistics indicated an increased risk of collision. Their studies resulted in proposals for the separation of traffic in those areas as well as for certain basic principles of ships' routing. These proposals were submitted to the IMO, the specialized agency of the United Nations responsible for maritime safety and efficiency of navigation, and were generally adopted. This initial step was further developed by IMO, and the basic concept of separating opposing traffic was applied to many areas throughout the world.

The increase in recent years in the size and draft of ships, particularly oil tankers, produced problems in certain shallow-water areas and led to the establishment of deep-water routes.

Similarly, the hazards to navigation in certain areas and the associated dangers to the marine environment and ecology resulted in the establishment and adoption by IMO of "Areas to be Avoided" by certain ships.

Rule 10 of the International Regulations for Prevent Collisions at Sea, 1972, as amended, prescribes the conduct of vessels within or near traffic separation schemes (TSS) adopted by IMO. The purpose of ships' routing is to improve the safety of navigation in converging areas and in areas where the density of traffic is great or where the freedom of maneuver is inhibited by restricted sea room. Routing measures are shown on charts in Figures 1 and 2, and are in the main self-evident, providing Rule 10 is properly understood.

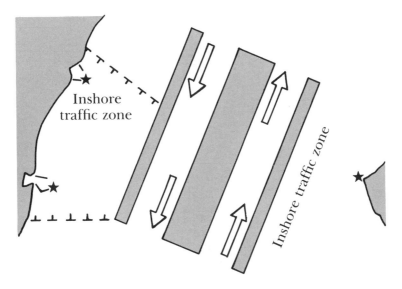

**Fig. 1.** The separation of through and local traffic by providing inshore traffic zones.

## Vessel Traffic Management

Vessel traffic services (VTSs) have been established in principal ports and their approaches, both to reduce the risk of collision and to expedite the turnaround of ships.

Where VTSs exist they may provide from one or more traffic centers a number of services, including information to ships operating in the area on the arrival, berthing, anchoring, and departure of other vessels, as well as details of any navigational hazards, weather, and port operations. These services also usually include designated points along the approach routes to which ships should report as they pass to enable traffic centers to keep track of all shipping movements. In some places radar surveillance is also used to present a continuous picture of the traffic situation to traffic centers.

In 1972 the Ports and Waterways Safety Act was passed by Congress and amended by the Port and Tanker Safety Act of 1978. The act as amended authorizes the secretary of the department in which the Coast Guard is operating to establish and operate vessel traffic services for navigable waters of the United States, as well as to exercise control over environmental quality in the same waters. The U.S. Oil Pollution Act of

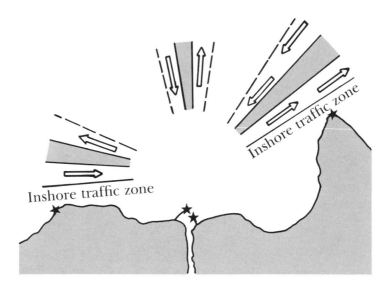

**Fig. 2.** Sectorial division of adjacent traffic separation schemes at approaches to focal points.

1990 revitalized the establishment of VTS systems designed to enhance protection of the environment by preventing vessel collisions and groundings. In some respects the acts are complementary to the traffic separation schemes of the international rules, and the systems of both dovetail neatly at the boundaries of the high seas.

**Differences Between the Rules**
Essentially the inland rules follow the same format as the international rules with some minor editorial changes. They are divided into five parts containing 38 rules as follows:

*Part A—General*
Contains rules on applicability, responsibility, and definitions. This part includes Rules 1 through 3.

*Part B—Steering and Sailing Rules*
Contains three subparts for the conduct of vessels in any condition of visibility, in sight of one another, and in restricted visibility. Subparts I, II, and III include Rules 4 through 10, 11 through 18, and 19, respectively.

*Part C—Lights and Shapes*
Contains rules on applicability, definitions, visibility of lights; and lights for power-driven vessels under way, vessels towing and pushing, sailing vessels under way, vessels under oars, fishing vessels, vessels not under command, anchored vessels, vessels aground, and seaplanes. This part includes Rules 20 through 31.

*Part D—Sound and Light Signals*
Contains rules and definitions concerning equipment for sound signals, maneuvering and warning signals, sound signals in restricted visibility, signals to attract attention, and distress signals. This part includes Rules 32 through 37.

*Part E—Exemptions*
Provided certain exemptions that permit a smooth transition period. This part consists of Rule 38.

In addition, there are five annexes, the equivalent of Annex V not being found in the international regulations, as follows:
Annex I—Positioning and Technical Details of Lights and Shapes
Annex II—Additional Signals for Fishing Vessels Fishing in Close Proximity
Annex III—Technical Details of Sound Signal Appliances
Annex IV—Distress Signals
Annex V—Pilot Rules
A close study of the international and inland rules reveals a remarkable degree of unanimity. Nonetheless, variations exist, and the following section highlights those differences. Only the main points are covered here, but discussion in specialized chapters will explore the rules in more detail. As ever, it is only by examination of the rules themselves, conveniently laid out side by side, that immediate comparison is possible.[1]

## PART A—GENERAL

*Application*
RULE 1. The inland rules constitute special rules within the meaning of Rule 1(b) of the international regulations. They apply to all vessels of all nations when on the navigable waters of the United States, shoreward of the ColRegs demarcation line. These rules also apply to U.S. vessels when on the Canadian waters of the Great Lakes to the extent that there is no conflict with Canadian law. All vessels complying with the

---

[1] See Appendix; also Navigation Rules: International—Inland (COMDTINST M16672.2B).

construction and equipment requirements of the ColRegs are also in compliance with the inland rules. Vessels unable to fully comply with the rules require certificates of alternative compliance.

Traffic separation schemes adopted by IMO for use on international waters do not appear in the inland rules, but vessel traffic services may be in effect in certain national areas.

*General Definitions*

RULE 3. The international term of a "vessel constrained by her draft" is not included in the inland rules. Additional definitions in the inland rules delineate some U.S. inland waterways.

## PART B—STEERING AND SAILING RULES
*Conduct of Vessels in Any Condition of Visibility*

RULE 8. The international rules contain a general paragraph on the duties of a vessel required not to impede the passage or safe passage of another vessel. This is not present in the corresponding inland Rule 8 but is effectively covered in part elsewhere, particularly in Rule 9 covering downbound vessels.

RULE 9. This rule covering narrow channels is identical in both regimes except for two important differences. Firstly, in inland waters a vessel proceeding downbound with a following current in specified waters has right-of-way over an upbound vessel and the obligation to *propose* the manner of passing. Secondly, a vessel overtaking another in inland waters shall indicate her *intention*, though the overtaken vessel still has to agree. Under the international rules this signal of intent to overtake is only necessary if the vessel to be overtaken has to take action to permit safe passing: not so for the inland rules. Also the sound signals are different, not only in their characteristics, but also their meaning under inland rules (see Rule 34).

RULE 10. The international rule seeks to be universal in its coverage of traffic separation schemes and is fairly comprehensive. The inland rule equivalent is short, leaving the specifics to the actual regulations for each area.

*Conduct of Vessels in Sight of One Another*

RULE 14. The head-on situation is virtually the same under both sets of rules except that the inland rules make provision for an agreed passage other than port-to-port. Also repeated here is the right-of-way for a downbound vessel with a following current in specified inland waters.

RULE 15. The action to take in a crossing situation is consistent in both international and inland waters. The inland rules additionally spell out that a vessel crossing in specified waters shall keep out of the way of a power-driven one ascending or descending the river.

RULE 18. This rule establishes a hierarchy of precedence between vessels of different categories. The one difference between the rules is the inclusion of a vessel "constrained by her draft" on the high seas.

*Conduct of Vessels in Restricted Visibility*

RULE 19. There are no differences between the rules for action by vessels not in sight of one another in or near an area of restricted visibility.

## PART C—LIGHTS AND SHAPES

RULE 21. The inland rule is the same as the 72 ColRegs with two exceptions: one, it states that a vessel less than 12 meters in length may place her masthead light and, if fitted, her combined sidelight as close to the centerline as possible; and two, it adds a special yellow flashing light to be placed at the head of a tow being pushed ahead.

RULE 22. Apart from the inland addition of the special flashing light, this list of the range of visibility of lights required for vessels of different lengths is identical in both sets of rules.

RULE 23. There are very similar rules for the lights of power-driven vessels under way, but the inland version allows a modest degree of freedom for the positioning of the masthead light in vessels less than 20 meters in length. On the Great Lakes the second masthead light can be combined with the sternlight, a special rule to take account of the low-lying fogs prevalent in the area.

The international rule is in accord with the inland rules for the lights of power-driven vessels less than 12 meters in length, but then goes on, alone, to create a subdivision for such a vessel, this time less than 7 meters in length, whose maximum speed does not exceed 7 knots, who need only show sidelights if practicable. This is followed by an exemption for vessels under 12 meters in length on the placement of the masthead or all-round white light, provided the sidelights are combined in one lantern. These latter provisos are very similar to the relevant parts of Inland Rules 21(a) and (b). It seems a pity they are not located more adjacent to each other in the respective rules.

RULE 24. A tug pushing ahead or towing alongside in inland waters shows two towing lights in a vertical line aft in lieu of a sternlight. The vessel(s) she is pushing will display the additional special flashing light required by the inland rules.

An inconspicuous partly submerged tow is treated similarly under both sets of rules, though the prospect of lengthier tows on the high seas allows for the provision of a second daymark on tows of over 200 meters. The inland rules suggest that a towing vessel can illuminate inconspicuous tows with her searchlight to warn an approaching vessel. Both rules reinforce this for unlighted or emergency tows.

Vessels pushing ahead (other than a composite unit) on stretches of the Western Rivers and other specified waters are not required to display masthead lights.

RULE 25. The one minor difference for sailing vessels is that a vessel under sail, when also being propelled by machinery, must show a conical shape, regardless of size, on the high seas, whereas it is optional in inland waters if under 12 meters in length.

RULE 28. Only the international rules provide for a vessel constrained by her draft.

RULE 30. The inland rules exempt vessels less than 20 meters in length from showing anchor lights or shapes, in designated special anchorage areas.

## PART D—SOUND AND LIGHT SIGNALS

RULE 34. The underlying philosophy for sound signals differs markedly between the two sets of rules. The long-established signals of "intent" and "assent" are enshrined in the inland rules; they are very different from the signals of "action" in the international rules. However, at least the three-short-blast signal means the same thing under both rules! Nonetheless, not too much should be read into these different approaches: the aim is still the same—to pass each other safely in accordance with the rules for the head-on, crossing, or overtaking situations. The latter situation illustrates most markedly the different sound signals required either side of the demarcation line.

Whistle signals may be supplemented by light signals under both sets of rules. The inland rules allow a yellow all-round light to be used in lieu of the international white one, but cuts back the visibility range for both from 5 to 2 miles. The inland rules also allow agreement reached by radiotelephone, as prescribed by the Bridge-to-Bridge Radiotelephone Act, to obviate whistle signals.

Finally, the inland rules require a power-driven vessel leaving a dock or berth to sound one prolonged blast.

RULE 35. Sound signals in restricted visibility are identical in both sets of rules, other than there being no category of a vessel constrained by her draft under inland rules, nor any need for vessels under 20 meters in length or certain other nondescript craft to sound signals in special anchorage areas.

RULE 37. Distress signals for inland waters are the same as for international waters with the addition of a high-intensity white light flashing at regular intervals from 50 to 70 times a minute.

## PART E—EXEMPTIONS

RULE 38. Most of the exemptions in this rule have now expired. However, some vessels under 150 meters and others less than 20 meters enjoy certain permanent exemptions for the repositioning and specification of lights, if constructed under previous regulations.

## ANNEX 1—POSITIONING AND TECHNICAL DETAILS OF LIGHTS AND SHAPES

The differences that arise between the two sets of rules in this technical annex are mainly ones of detail more of importance to the ship- or boat-builder than to the mariner. Nonetheless, for the sake of completeness the differences are:

- The Inland Annex spells out what "practical cut-off" means for vessels over 20 meters in length.
- The Inland Annex prescribes slightly smaller dimensions than the International Annex for positioning of masthead lights.
- The Inland Annex (consistently) avoids mention of the International Annex reference to Rule 28 (vessel constrained by draft).
- The Inland Annex uses a different formula for the positioning of sidelights of power-driven vessels than the International Annex, but the intent is the same.
- The Inland Annex specifies a different maximum horizontal distance apart (50 meters) of masthead lights than the International Annex (100 meters). Additionally, vessels between 50 and 60 meters in length operating on the Western Rivers have a minimum distance apart of 10 meters.
- The Inland Annex requires the masthead or all-round light in power-driven vessels of less than 12 meters to be screened to prevent spillage of light onto the deck forward of the helmsman.
- The International Annex frowns on variable control of luminous intensity of lights.
- The Inland Annex is adamant that the all-round white light in lieu of the second masthead and sternlights may not be obscured at all.
- The Inland Annex legislates for the vertical sectors of lights on unmanned barges.

## ANNEX II—ADDITIONAL SIGNALS FOR FISHING VESSELS FISHING IN CLOSE PROXIMITY

There are no differences between the Inland and International annexes.

## ANNEX III—TECHNICAL DETAILS OF SOUND SIGNAL APPLIANCES

The International Annex has a greater spread of the fundamental frequency for sirens than the Inland Annex. The latter gives a fuller table (including provision for vessels between 12 and 20 meters) laying down frequency against length of vessel than the International Annex, but there are no basic differences. The Inland Annex goes into greater details for combined whistle systems and allows a tug whose normal trade is pushing ahead or towing alongside to use a whistle whose characteristic falls within the limits of her longest customary length of vessel and tow. Finally, in a footnote, the Inland Annex recommends the use of a power-driven bell striker to ensure constant force.

## ANNEX IV—DISTRESS SIGNALS

The Inland Annex adds a high-intensity white light flashing at regular intervals between 50 to 70 times per minute.

## ANNEX V—PILOT RULES

Not found in the international rules, this Inland Annex requires the operator of a self-propelled vessel 12 meters or more in length to carry on board for ready reference a copy of the inland rules. Also exemption from light and shape requirements is allowed when passing under bridges. Provision is further made for a blue flashing light for police vessels and an alternately flashing red and yellow light signal for vessels engaged in public safety activities. Finally, the requirements for barges at bank or dock are spelled out. So too are the yellow and red lights for dredge pipelines that might be encountered on inland waters.

## INTERPRETIVE RULES

Both the international and inland versions of these rules are those adopted by the USCG and concern only the definition of a composite unit. There is no difference between the published interpretive rules. However, IMO in the past has issued *guidance* for the uniform application of certain rules. In the main the guidance has been overtaken by amendments to the international rules, but those still relevant include:
- clarification of application of the word "underway."
- clarification of the transference within a lane in a traffic separation scheme.

Some governments have not brought the above *guidance* to the attention of their mariners. Some have, even though others consider that the interpretations may not hold up in court. Possibly so—but no reason for not telling the high seas mariner?

## THE EXTENT OF THE COLLISION PROBLEM
### Statistics

The discussion in subsequent chapters on the principles of marine collision law would be well served by gaining an understanding of the width and breadth of the collision problem itself. There has occurred a global

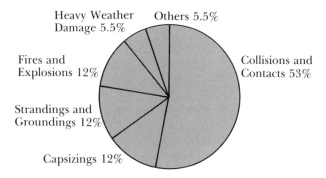

**17 Total Losses and Serious Casualties**

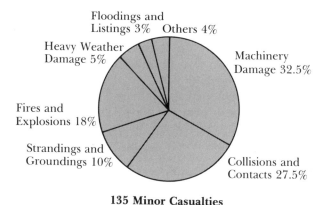

**135 Minor Casualties**

**Fig. 3.** Extract from British Marine Accident Investigation Branch's (MAIB) brochure.

rise in the amount of cargo carried over the past few decades with the overall number of ships doubling, though the increase has been almost entirely restricted to vessels over 10,000 gross tons.[2] Tankers fall into this category with their tonnage alone increasing sevenfold. The magnitude of the ecological impact from some of our more recent ship disasters, especially with this latter category of vessels, and the attendant media attention tend to obscure the evidence that the vast bulk of waterborne transport is conducted safely. Although no figures are readily available to compare

[2] K. H. Kwik, "Collision Rate as a Danger Criterion for Marine Traffic," *Journal of Navigation* (published by Royal Institute of Navigation), 39 (1986), 203.

the number of collisions with the number of uneventful passages, a recent European probability assessment would seem to support this.[3] However, it is not the safe voyages that demand our attention but the lessons to be learned from those that went wrong.

Several countries investigate accidents at sea and on board ships of their flags. Investigations aim to determine what caused an accident in order to prevent its happening again, an important contribution to improving safety at sea. A diagram of one country's annual findings is shown below (see Figure 3). Note the large percentage of collisions and contacts (i.e., striking another vessel not under way).

Worldwide data on collisions, however, is incomplete because there is no uniform global accounting system in place. Sometimes figures are available only for total losses, or only when a formal investigation is held or when collisions culminate in court action, though in some countries the system allows access to all known casualties. Although IMO has begun to address the matter of issuing statistics for serious casualties, presently a variety of sources, none operating with the same ground rules, provide the only input. However, some worthwhile indicators have emerged from the study of the limited information that does exist. One such indication of the size of the problem, compiled mainly from *Lloyd's Register of Shipping*, is shown below (see Figure 4). This graph depicts the total loss worldwide resulting from collisions of vessels of 100 gross tons or more. From it can be seen that the number of losses is stabilizing after an upsurge in the late seventies.

The geographical distribution of total losses is similarly published annually by *Lloyd's Register of Shipping*. Based on this, other published data, and responses to requests for further information, a statistical survey of worldwide collisions in open waters was reported on in 1982.[4] A comprehensive breakdown of regional totals was compiled, and the table following is an extract from it. Study of the table reveals that the number of collisions off northwest Europe has dramatically declined, in contrast to those off the eastern Asian seaboard. The reduction in incidence of ships lost to collision off the former region is due partly to the effectiveness of traffic routing measures. Some decrease in losses off northeast Asia has since occurred, but the remaining high incidence has been mainly attributed to high traffic density, intense fishing activity, and the frequency of fog in the summer.[5] The other trend discernible from the

---

[3] The European Economic Community (1987), "Committee on Science and Technology Project 301 (*COST 301*)."

[4] A. N. Cockcroft, "The Circumstances of Collision," *Journal of Navigation*, 35 (1982), 100.

[5] A. N. Cockcroft, "Routing and the Environment," *Journal of Navigation*, 39 (1986), 223.

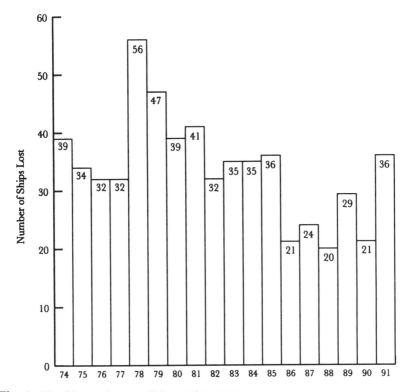

**Fig. 4.** Total losses from collision 1974–1991.

table (see Figure 5) is the reduction in the proportion of collisions in restricted visibility.

## Analysis

Analysis of incomplete statistics is limited. Nonetheless, some general pointers can be derived from what is available, always bearing in mind that few reports cover matters such as commercial pressures or fatigue.

In open and coastal waters three times the number of collisions occur in darkness than occur in daylight. In restricted visibility, hardly surprisingly, there is no apparent difference as to whether it is day or night. A breakdown of the number of collisions in terms of the difference between the ships' initial courses in both clear and restricted visibility was compiled in Cockroft's 1982 paper[6] and is shown below (see Figure 6).

[6] Cockroft, "Circumstances of Collision."

| Region | 1956–60 | 1961–65 | 1966–70 | 1971–73 | 1976–80 | Total |
|---|---|---|---|---|---|---|
| Southern North Sea | | | | | | |
| Dover Strait | 201 | 198 | 156 | 85 | 62 | 702 |
| English Channel | (118) | (142) | (96) | (42) | (33) | (431) |
| E Coast UK | | | | | | |
| E Coast N | 27 | 22 | 20 | 18 | 11 | 98 |
| America | (16) | (14) | (12) | (9) | (5) | (56) |
| Malacca and | | | | | | |
| Singapore Straits | 9 | 40 | 138 | 213 | 150 | 550 |
| Korea and Japan | (5) | (13) | (84) | (96) | (55) | (255) |
| SW Pacific | | | | | | |
| World Total | 359 | 397 | 453 | 454 | 356 | 2019 |
| | (189) | (232) | (245) | (207) | (139) | (1012) |

Notes:
1. Figures in parentheses represent numbers of collisions occurring in restricted visibility
2. World total is sum of regional figures shown plus those of rest of world
3. Adapted from Cockcroft, AN (1982) The Circumstances of Sea Collisions, Journal Royal Institute of Navigation Vol 35, 105
4. Cockcroft, A.N., "The Circumstances of Collision," *Journal of Navigation*, 35 (1982), 100.
5. Cockcroft, A.N., "Routing and the Environment," *Journal of Navigation*, 35 (1986), 223.

**Fig. 5.** Some regional totals and trends in collisions.

From the left-hand chart it would appear that there is a slightly greater risk for vessels proceeding in the same general direction than for those closing from the bows in clear weather. In restricted visibility (right-hand chart) there is a dramatic increase in the proportion of collisions with vessels approaching from ahead. For all conditions of visibility the lowest incidence is with vessels closing at broad angles.

Another analysis[7] over a long period showed not unsurprisingly that smaller ships usually came off worse in any collision; that the age of ships had a relatively small effect on collision loss ratios (in contrast to wreck loss ratios); and that the loss ratio for collisions showed only small differences between various flag states (though again in contrast to wreck loss ratios).

### Causes of Collision
Later chapters will suggest causes for collisions in each type of approach situation. In some cases the cause may never be fully known, as in, perhaps, the worst peacetime loss of life ever recorded. The inter-island ferry *Dona Paz* collided with the tanker *Vector* in Philippine waters in

[7] A. N. Cockcroft, "Factors Affecting Shipping Losses by Collision and Wreck," *Journal of Navigation*, 39 (1986), 375.

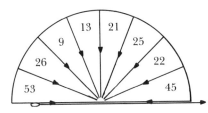 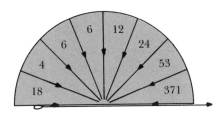

**Fig. 6.** *Left:* Numbers of collisions in clear visibility in relation to sectors of course difference. *Right:* Numbers of collisions in restricted visibility in relation to sectors of course difference.

1987. Both ships were enveloped in flames and 4,021 lives were lost.[8] Nonetheless, sufficient is known in most cases to allow some generalizations to be made.

One study[9] suggests that incompetence in collision situations is only rarely related to a lack of knowledge. More often it is a lack of practiced skills, that is procedural competence, that leads mariners into a collision. The conclusion reached is that time at sea practicing the art is more critical in avoiding collisions than increasing the amount of knowledge. The study showed violations of the rules arose more from improper weighing of, or even disregard for, the unpredictable elements in a given situation rather than from outright mistakes. Watch keepers were exhibiting a tendency to delay decisions until more information became available to them. Thus chances for collision increased as the balance between increasing certainty and decreasing maneuvering room tilted toward the latter.

Providing more information earlier to the watch keeper is not necessarily the solution to this problem and is certainly not a panacea. To be so it must be shown that not only was it the lack of information given to the watch keeper that brought about a collision but that he or she would have in fact used it were it available. In about half the collisions in this study it was considered that sufficient information *had* been available to the watch keeper. Additionally, in many others although the information was available, it had not been communicated. This begs the question that if watch keepers do not make use of all the intelligence that is now available to them, would they be swamped by even more information? In this regard, IMO has adopted a policy that new proposals for fitting

[8] *Marine Casualties,* Lloyd's Nautical Year Book, 1989.

[9] D. T. Bryant, A. F. M. De Bieve, and M. B. A. Dyer-Smith, "Marine Casualty Investigation Methods and the Human Element" (paper presented at joint seminar by the Royal Institute of Navigation and the Nautical Institute, *Navigation and the Human Factor,* 1987.

extra equipment must show a "clear and compelling need." Perhaps the solution lies in improved display of information through better human-machine interface.

Another study by one underwriters' association[10] concluded that the majority of collisions affecting their ships were caused by basic errors of "navigation" usually with one of the vessels moored or at anchor. Only in 21 percent of the collisions were both ships under way. Contributing factors to the collisions, in order of frequency, were:
- inefficient watch keeping;
- excessive speed;
- lack of assessment of the situation;
- lack of early positive action;
- passing or overtaking too close;
- failure to observe traffic schemes;
- incorrect lights or signals:
- mechanical failure;
- negligent maneuvering.

With respect to watch keeping, it was considered that the expertise and care of those on watch were more crucial than the number in the crew. Perhaps so, but the latter factor can have a crucial impact on the efficiency of watch keeping as well as on the overall fatigue level when extra personnel are required for tricky conditions.

Cockroft's paper[11] noted that in clear visibility collisions were partially brought about, in the head-on situation, by bad lookout, the presence of a third vessel, or a late starboard turn by one ship canceled out by port helm action by the other one. For crossing and overtaking situations a major cause of collisions was bad lookout by the give-way ship. In some crossing collisions, trouble arose when initial courses were altered for navigational purposes around headlands or through confined waters. Quite a few overtaking collisions occurred from steering gear failure when passing close. In restricted visibility, the major contributory factor was poor radar lookout, allied to unsafe speed and associated with lack of bold helm action until too late. For all conditions of visibility there is an underlying trend of getting into close quarters unnecessarily.

A disturbing feature of many casualty reports is the absence of anxiety or anticipation until shortly before the occurrence of the casualty, by which time it was too late. It is probably true to say that the majority of collisions, especially those in open waters, could have been avoided—even

---

[10] "The Causes of Collision at Sea" (1989), The Steamship Mutual Management Report, 1988.
[11] Cockcroft, "Circumstances of Collision."

when one ship had failed to observe the ColRegs—had alertness and prudence been displayed in the conduct of the other ship. Furthermore, while mistakes or errors of judgment can be made, casualties seldom stem from one individual error but rather from an accumulation of them—especially, perhaps, of those of omission.[12]

## Conclusion

There is not enough public information available on collision causes to make other than broad generalizations. A need exists to create a standard worldwide compilation with a methodology that spans existing gaps in knowledge and overcomes prejudices and assumptions.[13] The fitting of systematic data-recording devices would make a sound start to this process.

There is no doubt, however, that human factors are involved to a very considerable degree in most collisions. IMO has resolved:

. . . the great majority of maritime accidents are due to human errors and fallibility,

and concluded that:

. . . the safety of ships will be greatly enhanced by the establishment of improved operating procedures.

## SUMMARY

For over a century countries have sought to standardize common navigation rules—with steadily increasing effect. The International Rules for Preventing Collisions at Sea 1972 marked the most recent accomplishment, a remarkable degree of international consensus. Additionally, the need to keep pace with rapidly changing circumstances was acknowledged by the introduction of a continuous process of amendment.

The international rules apply to all vessels on the high seas and in all waters connected therewith navigable by seagoing vessels. Should an appropriate authority introduce special rules for waters connected with the high seas, these rules must conform as closely as possible to the international rules. With the enactment of the Inland Navigational Rules Act 1980, the U.S. rules closely parallel the international rules along with the same ability to refine the rules over the years with appropriate amendments and additions.

Some differences remain where it is felt that the special circumstances or common practices of operating on U.S. waters dictated the retention

---

[12] "Marine Casualty Report Scheme Analysis" (1972), Chamber of Shipping, London.

[13] But see Kwik, "Collision Rate as Danger Criterion," 204, who argues that the statistical approach based solely on historical data has several serious shortcomings, and who favors a mathematical model approach.

of previous special rules. The most significant of these between the two sets of rules concerns whistle signals. The inland signals are ones of intent and reply, while the 72 ColRegs are action signals. This dichotomy could still lead to problems when two vessels are approaching each other on either side of the demarcation line marking the boundary of the two jurisdictions. It is in such waters that the risk of collision between ships is at its greatest.

Nonetheless, the limited data available do seem to indicate the number of collisions at sea has stabilized, due, in part, to the introduction of routing measures. Even so the occurrence of collision is unnecessarily high, with the prevalence of human factors being the major feature.

# 2

# Principles of Marine Collision Law

## Jurisdiction in Collision Cases

Jurisdiction over cases of collision between vessels on public navigable waters is placed by the Constitution of the United States in the hands of federal courts, sitting as courts of admiralty. Public navigable waters may be defined as waters used, or capable of being used, in interstate commerce. The definition excludes from federal jurisdiction collisions occurring on a lake wholly within a state, but includes cases on a navigable river that flows in or between two states or empties into the sea or an inlet of the sea. A collision case ordinarily begins in the federal district court, from which it may be appealed to the circuit court of appeals and on proper grounds to the United States Supreme Court.

State courts have exclusive jurisdiction over a collision on a lake completely surrounded by territory of the state and concurrent jurisdiction over one occurring on any portion of public navigable waters within the state. Thus, a collision that takes place on Puget Sound may by mutual consent of the parties be adjudicated in a damage suit between the vessels' owners in the Superior Court of the State of Washington. However, such cases are actually tried, in an overwhelming majority, in the federal courts, because usually at least one of the litigants regards certain admiralty principles peculiar to these courts as favorable to his or her side of the case. Cases of collision on public navigable waters, unless action has already been started in a state court, may always be taken to a federal court by either party.

For collisions that occur outside the inland and territorial waters of the United States, action may be brought in other countries. An international convention suggests where such cases can be settled.[1] There is, however, a distinction between choice of jurisdiction and choice of law. A national court can, and often does, decide questions of foreign law on the basis of expert evidence from foreign lawyers. The general rule is that the procedures in collision cases are governed by the law of the court where the case is tried (*lex fori*), while the liability is governed by the law of the place of collision (*lex loci*). To illustrate, in an investigation of a collision that occurred totally in the waters of another country, Judge Krupansky of the District Court of Ohio said, "the rights and liabilities arising as a consequence of the collision were governed by the law of Canada." In coming to its findings the U.S. court considered and made determinations based on Canadian legislative acts.[2]

After a collision has occurred on the high seas, an action may be brought in the country of either the plaintiffs or the defendants or in any other country where the law permits such action to be brought. Generally speaking, most courts will allow an action to be brought if the defendant vessel is in a port of their country at the time.

A valid judgment by a foreign court, delivered abroad before action is brought in another country and given in the presence of both parties, is final and conclusive and a bar to further proceedings between the two same parties in the other country, except possibly for the enforcement, extension, or registration of that judgment. Also, provisions exist in other countries for the arrest of a ship, under certain circumstances, in the jurisdiction of another state not involved in the collision litigation.[3]

## Legal Personality of a Vessel

In American admiralty cases, an important principle applied by the federal courts is the legal personality of the vessel, which is assumed to make the vessel herself the wrongdoer when collision follows a violation of the rules of the road. The action may be, and commonly is, between John Doe and the steamer So-and-So, or it may be between the two vessels. The vessel sued or "libeled" is held until the claims against her are satisfied, unless the owners obtain her release by paying into the court an amount equal to her appraised valuation, or post a bond double the amount of existing liens. If a judgment is obtained against her, the vessel may be sold at public auction by the marshal in order that the proceeds of the sale may place funds in the registry of the court for satisfaction

---

[1] International Convention on Certain Rules Concerning Jurisdiction in Matters of Collision, Brussels, 10 May 1952.

[2] The *Steelton* [1979] 1 Lloyd's Rep. 431.

[3] International Convention for the Unification of Certain Rules Relating to the Arrest of Sea-Going Ships, Brussels, 10 May 1952.

of the judgment. A final recognition of the vessel's personality is seen in the fact that a marshal's sale, properly conducted, divests her of all maritime liens against her, and starts her out with her new owners free of any old claims against her. She thus literally receives a new lease on life.

## Division of Damages

Originally, a principle of admiralty courts was the doctrine of equal responsibility for unequal fault. When two vessels were in collision and both of them had violated a rule, the liability of each vessel was 50 percent of the total loss, regardless of her degree of guilt. One vessel may have been guilty of what seemed to be only a minor infraction and the other may have violated several rules and been flagrantly and deliberately negligent. The courts were concerned with the *fact* of fault but not, in most cases, with its amount:

> Damages from collisions between vessels both at fault must be equally divided, irrespective of degree of fault.[4]

This rule was an ancient form of rough justice, a means of apportioning damages where it was difficult to measure which party was more at fault.

The Brussels Collision Liability Convention of 1910 subsequently provided for the apportionment of damages on the basis of degree of fault whenever it was possible to do so. The United States was virtually alone among the world's major maritime nations in not adhering to the Convention—a fact that encouraged transoceanic court forum shopping. While the lower federal courts followed the old equally divided damages rule, they did so only grudgingly, and in 1975 the Supreme Court divested themselves of this vestigial relic and substituted a rule of comparative negligence:

> We hold that when two or more parties have contributed by their fault to cause property damage in a maritime collision or stranding, liability for such damage is to be allocated among the parties proportionately to the comparative degree of their fault, and that liability for such damages is to be allocated equally only when the parties are equally at fault or when it is not possible fairly to measure the comparative degree of their fault.[5]

If one vessel is solely at fault, she is liable for the total damage to the other, subject only to the provisions of the Limited Liability Acts, which limit the liability of a vessel of her value after the collision, plus earnings for the voyage, collected or collectible. If neither vessel is at fault, we then have that extremely rare species of collision characterized by the courts as inevitable accident, and each vessel, of course, bears her own loss, be it great or small. It is evident, therefore, that in a collision between

---

[4] The *Marian* (1933) 66 F.2d 354.
[5] U.S. v. Reliable Transfer Co., Inc. (1975) 44 L. Ed. 251. *See also* Prudential Lines v. McAllister (1987) AMC 231.

vessels A and B, we have four possibilities as to liability as determined by our admiralty courts: A solely liable; B solely liable; A and B both liable, in which case the damages are proportioned to degree of fault; and neither liable.

## Inevitable Accident

Many instances of the first three possibilities for division of damages will be found in succeeding chapters. Examples of the fourth category are not only rare, representing about 1 percent of all cases recorded, but also date in the main from decisions made in the latter part of the last century and the early decades of this century. Modern technology, forecasting, and accountability have markedly reduced any grounds for justification of inevitable accident. Nonetheless, the possibility, under common law, exists that an accident could be said to be inevitable if it was not occasioned in any degree, either remotely or directly, by the want of such care and skill as the law holds every mariner bound to exercise.

Similarly, under the maritime law:

> An inevitable accident is something that human skill and foresight could not, in the exercise of ordinary prudence, have provided against.[6]

> The term "inevitable accident" as applied to a collision means a collision which occurs when both parties have endeavored by every means in their power, with due care and caution and a proper display of nautical skill, to prevent the occurrence of the accident, and where the proofs show that it occurred in spite of everything that nautical skill, care, and precaution could do to keep the vessels from coming together.[7]

The matter of establishing the vessel's innocence by satisfactory proofs is even more emphatically stated in a later decision holding that:

> To sustain the defense of inevitable accident in a suit for collision, the defendant has the burden of proof and must show either what was the cause of the accident, and that cause was inevitable, or he must show all the possible causes and in regard to every one of such possible causes that the result could not have been avoided.[8]

It is not enough for a vessel to show that all that could be done was done as soon as the need to take action to avoid collision was determined. The point is whether actions should not have been taken earlier. When two ships are shown to have been in a position in which collision became

---

[6] The *Drum Craig* (1904) 133 F.804; the *Pennsylvania* (1861) 16 L. Ed. 699.

[7] New York and Oriental SS Co. v. NY, NH and H Ry Co (N.Y. 1906) 143 F.991; the *Mabey* and *Cooper* (1872) 20 L. Ed. 881.

[8] The *Edmund Moran* (CCA N.Y. 1910) 180 F.700, adopted from the *Merchant Prince* (1892) P 179, 189; *see also* Southport Corporation v. Esso Petroleum Company Ltd. [1955] 2 Lloyd's Rep. 655.

inevitable, the question is, by whose fault did the vessels get into such a position?[9]

In the light of these interpretations of inevitable accident, it will readily be understood that most of the cases determined by the courts have been due either (1) to *vis major,* or superior force of the elements, or (2) to a mechanical failure, in a collision situation, of steering gear or other machinery that due diligence could not prevent. The few cases that remain may for want of a better term be classed as miscellaneous, due either to a special combination of circumstances, or to causes that could not be ascertained from the evidence and were therefore not chargeable to either vessel.

The doctrine of inevitable accident cannot be invoked where legal fault, which could have contributed to the collision, can be imputed to either vessel. The defense of inevitable accident is never an easy argument to mount. The whole sequence of events that led up to the collision will be examined, and the defense will fail if negligence is shown at any point. The paucity of modern, successful claims of inevitable accident no longer merits a separate chapter devoted to this difficult-to-sustain defense. Where it has been used, unsuccessfully, mention will be made in the appropriate chapters that follow. Thus, any reader seeking further treatment of this subject should consult an earlier edition of *Farwell's.*

## Limited Liability of Vessel

The principle of limited liability is a very old one, and was originally based on the high degree of risk that was inherent in any maritime venture. The theory was, and to some extent still is, that capital would be discouraged from investing in a business where an absentee agent, the master, might by his or her negligence involve the owners in enormous losses through disaster to a ship and her cargo, unless the amount of that loss could be limited somewhat in accordance with the old common-law principle. As described by Justice Holmes in the Supreme Court in a case just after the First World War:

> The notion, as applicable to a collision case, seems to us to be that if you surrender the offending vessel you are free, just as it was said by a judge in the time of Edward III: "If my dog kills your sheep and I, freshly after the fact, tender you the dog, you are without recourse against me.[10]

Under the original statute of 1851 and its later amendments, the law in the United States now provides that where a vessel is at fault without the privity or knowledge of her owners, the limit of her liability is the

---

[9] R.G. Marsden, *Collisions at Sea,* 11th ed. (London: Stevens, 1970), 8, 9.
[10] Liverpool, Brazil, and River Plate Stream Navigation Co. v. Brooklyn Eastern District Terminal (1919) 64 L. Ed. 130.

value of the vessel at the expiration of the voyage, plus any earnings that have accrued or are collectible for the transportation of passengers or cargo. Under a usual form of contract providing that, once the voyage has begun, freight is payable, ship lost or not lost, it frequently happens in the case of a commercial vessel that although the vessel herself is a total loss, these earnings, technically known as "pending freight," may amount to a considerable item. Pending freight is added to the value of the vessel at the end or breaking-up of a voyage, and therefore her value after the accident causing the liability determines the limit, and not her value before the accident as in English law. This value, including pending freight, may be levied for faulty damage to the other vessel or her cargo or for injury to personnel on either vessel. The Harter Act and the later Carriage of Goods by Sea Act, however, excuse the vessel in a faulty collision from liability for damage to her own cargo. It will be seen that where a vessel that is solely at fault in a collision is totally lost and there is no pending freight, the injured vessel can recover nothing for damage either to herself or to her cargo.

An amendment to the Limited Liability Acts, patterned after the English law and passed 29 August 1935, changes the liability for death or personal injury to a maximum of $60 per gross registered ton where the remaining value of the ship is less than that amount. An increase to $420 was proposed in 1984. The liability for damage to vessels or cargoes was not affected by this amendment. However, the Convention of Limitation of Liability for Maritime Claims, 1976, held under the auspices of IMO (International Maritime Organization) provides for the calculation of general limits in accordance with a rather complicated version of the English law. In essence, the size of the "limitation fund" does not increase in the same amount as the tonnage of the ship does, but is progressively reduced instead. The result would be that owners of larger ships would provide a smaller fund than the tonnages of their vessels warrant under the present straightforward English application of a multiplier of the registered tonnage. There are other innovations agreed upon by the convention that if made part of national laws, could align practice in this branch of the law in various countries. LLMC 1976 gained IMO endorsement in 1984.

One fundamental principle that is likely to remain unchanged in all jurisdictions is that the privilege of limiting liability is available only to the shipowner who is in no way to blame for the damage. The term "privity or knowledge of the owners" refers to cases in which damage and consequent liability are incurred through circumstances not beyond the control of the owners or managers. This is a harsh test and not excused by showing that acts were not the sole or next chief cause of the mishap. Rather, "They must show that they are themselves in no way in fault or privity to what occurred."[11]

If such guilty knowledge can be attributed to the owners or managers, limited liability cannot be invoked, and the injured vessel or cargo owners may bring all the offending owners' resources into that suit. One excellent illustration is the case of the USS *Chicago* and the British freighter, *Silver Palm*, which were in a collision in a fog off the California coast in October 1933. The vessels sighted each other a minute before the collision, and both commanding officers ordered their engines full speed astern. The *Chicago* was practically brought to a standstill, but the *Silver Palm*, unknown to her master, had an early type of diesel engine that could not be reversed at speeds higher than 6 knots until the fuel was shut off and the vessel had lost a substantial part of her headway, the result being that she struck the *Chicago* while still making excessive speed. When the government showed that this defect was known to her owners, but they had not warned the master, who was making his first voyage on the vessel, of the conditions, both the district court and the circuit court of appeals denied the *Silver Palm*'s petition for limitation of liability, thus opening the way for the United States to levy the entire fleet of her owners, if necessary, to make up the difference between the value of the damaged *Silver Palm* and the amount of the judgment.[12]

"Turning a blind eye" to practices of masters can equally frustrate any attempt by owners to limit their liability. The master of the *Lady Gwendolen*, regularly carrying stout from Dublin to Liverpool, went up the River Mersey at full speed, relying entirely on radar. Following a collision, the court found that the cause was inadequate use of radar and excessive speed. Furthermore, because the directors of the company had not stopped the practice, they were consequently not entitled to limitation.[13] Failure to ensure that a proper logbook is kept also provides grounds for denial of limitation of liability.[14]

Recent cases continue to reinforce this rule in other countries. On 27 June 1970, a collision occurred between a racing dinghy and an unmanned barge that was being towed by the tug *Kathy K* in English Bay, Vancouver. The crew of the sailboat was killed. Although both vessels were at fault, the owners and the operator of the tug were unable to

---

[11] Standard Oil Co. of New York v. Clan Line Steamers Ltd. (1924) AC 100.

[12] Decided 28 October 1937. The circuit court found both vessels at fault, thus halving the damage that could be collected under the district court decision. Certiorari denied (1938) 82 L. Ed. 1539.

[13] The *Lady Gwendolen* [1965] 1 Lloyd's Rep. 335.

[14] The *Dayspring* [1968] 2 Lloyd's Rep. 204.

limit their liability because it was shown that they had failed to do the
following:

- discuss the length of tow ropes to be used in Vancouver harbor;
- supply the *Kathy K* with copies of the Collision Regulations or the harbor regulations;
- see that she had the minimum crew of three persons as required by her inspection certificate;
- see that the master was sufficiently experienced;
- see that the vessel was equipped with a whistle control on the flying bridge; and
- see that she had an alternative means of sounding the whistle if the electrical system failed.

The Canadian Supreme Court found that the owners "were actually
privy to the fault and negligence" and that the operator's acquiescence
"in the tug and tow being left in such inexperienced hands created a
situation exposing other traffic in the bay to potential dangers which in
fact ensued."[15]

So too fared the owner of the vessel *Blue Waters* that negligently collided
with and sank a properly anchored and lighted vessel. The *Blue Waters*
could not limit her liability under the Canada Shipping Act because the
crewmen in charge at the time of the collision were inexperienced and
had been employed by the owner, who knew of their inexperience and
knew that they would be in charge at sea, thus endangering other
shipping.[16]

On another occasion the Supreme Court of Canada found that "no
actual fault" could be attributed to the owners because the experienced
master of a tug was "so unpredictably careless as to overestimate the
height of the tide."[17]

Failure to provide copies of local regulations was also the cause for
the English Court of Appeal to deny limitation of costs to the owners of
a motor vessel involved in a collision in the River Thames:

> The managing owner ought to have foreseen that, without specific instruc-
> tions, the Master, however competent, might fail to have the Port of London
> River By-laws available.[18]

One of the more interesting problems of limitation of liability arises
when by negligent navigation a tug causes her tow to collide with another

---

[15] The *Kathy K* [1976] 1 Lloyd's Rep. 154.
[16] Vaccher v. Kaufman [1981] 1 SCR 301 (1981) 121 D.L.R. (3d) 1 (1981) 35 N.R. 334
(Sup. Ct. of Canada).
[17] The *Chugaway II* [1973] 2 Lloyd's Rep. 159.
[18] Rederij Erven, H. Groen & Groen v. the *England* owners and others [1973] 1 Lloyd's
Rep. 373.

vessel. The tug's limitation fund may be trifling compared to that of her tow. The tug owner is able, in some countries, to limit liability to a sum based on the tonnage of the tug alone, which may not be sufficient to satisfy the claim in full.

In some cases, an American judge may put together the tonnage of the tug and tow to raise the amount of the limitation fund. In one case judged in the United States a tug, a barge, and a derrick lighter working together had anchored separately at a good distance from each other. The barge broke ground during a storm and collided with a gas well structure. The tonnage of all three vessels was used when calculating the limitation fund. However, a vessel hiring a tug is not regarded as being involved in such a "common enterprise," and if the tug's action alone causes damage, American practice would be in line with English practice where the liability would be limited to the tonnage of the tug. As was said by Lord Denning, "there is not much room for justice in this rule . . ."! The rule has its critics on both sides of the Atlantic, and although English judges cannot get away from it—but do try to mitigate its harshness—in some circumstances, such as that outlined above, American judges can be more flexible.[19]

Current attitudes are less favorable on the right to limit. Most earlier cases in which owners were held unable to limit were concerned with the fault of the owners leading to the ship itself or its tackle being in some way unsafe. The assumption seems to have been that shipowners discharged their other responsibilities by appointing a competent master and leaving navigation (including provision of charts) to him. Only comparatively recently has their duty been extended to cover the supervision of day-to-day activities. The judgment in the case of the *Lady Gwendolen* mentioned earlier perhaps marked the change where the owner must have done something in this regard and not have left such matters to the discretion of the master.[20] Where some measure of supervision had been exercised, then the owners were often held entitled to limit.[21] However, in the case of the *Marion*, although the owners had exercised supervision in various ways, the decision was that supervision was not adequate in the circumstances:

> It seems to me that any company which embarks on the business of shipowning must accept the obligation to ensure efficient management of its ships if it is to enjoy the very considerable benefits conferred by the statutory right to limitation.[22]

[19] Synopsis from "Mariner at the Bar," *Seaways Bulletin* October 1977.

[20] The *Lady Gwendolen* [1965] 1 Lloyd's Rep. 294; also the *England* [1973] 1 Lloyds Rep. 373.

[21] The *Garden City* [1982] 2 Lloyd's Rep. 382.

[22] Grand Champion Tankers Ltd. v. Norpipe A/S (the *Marion*) [1984] 2 W.L.R. 942.

This decision arose from a case of a master using an out-of-date and uncorrected chart, even though a more recent chart was on board. Thus, although the ship was correctly equipped in this respect, the owners' fault consisted in their failure to maintain effective supervision. Namely, they did not ensure a proper system for keeping charts on board up-to-date and the managing director failed to have had brought to his attention a marine inspectorate report referring to the unsatisfactory state of the ship's charts. The owners were held not entitled to limit.

This stringent examination of owners' discharge of their responsibilities is likely to be modified by those countries that have acceded to the 1976 Liabilities Convention, which came into force December 1986.[23] Essentially, this convention entitles owners to limit their liability except where it is proved that a loss resulted from their personal acts or omissions committed with the intent to cause such loss, or recklessly and with knowledge that such loss would probably result. The effect, therefore, should be to confirm the previous assumption of shipowners and to reverse the direction that followed from the *Marion* judgment.[24]

**Statutory Duty**

In what became known as the *Pennsylvania Rule* the U.S. Supreme Court held that a vessel that had violated a navigational statutory duty must clearly show not only that its statutory violation did not cause the accident but that the violation could not have contributed to or caused the accident.[25] Thus, although the ruling obligates a statutory offender to prove causation, it does not *ipso facto* impose liability.[26] In a small-boat collision the appellant sought to reduce his liability for causing the collision by showing that the other craft into which he turned at close quarters had not kept a proper lookout and therefore under the *Pennsylvania Rule* had to prove that such negligence was not a cause of the accident. The U.S. Court of Appeals found the appellant's boat operator solely at fault for his sudden turn and that the navigation rules requiring maintenance of a proper lookout were not in this case a statutory requirement, violation of which shifted the burden of proof.[27] Similarly, when a downbound overtaking tug was solely at fault for colliding with the overtaken vessel, the former's negligent navigation did not require under the *Pennsylvania*

---

[23] International Conference on Limitation of Liability for Maritime Claims (LLMC) 1976.

[24] FMBR "Limitation of Shipowner's Liability" *Lloyd's Maritime and Commercial Law Quarterly* (1984), 364.

[25] The *Pennsylvania*, 86 U.S. 125 (1873).

[26] Otto Candies v. *Maldine D.* 1987 AMC 911.

[27] White Cloud Boat Co. Inc. v. Dick, U.S. Ct. of Appeals, 9th Cir., 6 April 1987, AMC 2216.

doctrine that the other vessel be held partly at fault for violating a navigation rule.[28]

### Liability of the Mariner

Apart from the owners, the master, officers, and crew of a vessel are clearly liable for their actions. Until recently, prosecutions for infringement of the International Regulations for the Prevention of Collision at Sea were few. Judgment on members of ships' crews was usually confined to those arising from collision cases that ended up in court, though inquiries by national boards of inquiry could and did result in the loss or suspension of qualifications. However, for those infringements of the collision regulations that did not result in a collision, it was difficult to establish intentional or careless conduct on the part of shipmasters. The advent of traffic separation schemes (TSS) governed by the international rules has removed some of this difficulty. A vessel navigating contrary to the rules simply needs to be plotted and identified. The surveillance of traffic separation schemes has led to an increase in the number of masters brought before the courts for contravening the rules. Offenders who are not under the jurisdiction of the littoral states are reported to their flag nation, who follow up substantiated allegations in their own court or disciplinary system. The penalties can be steep, involving heavy fines and, on occasion, the arrest of the offending vessel.[29]

Generally it has been upon the master of a vessel that these sanctions have been imposed, sometimes under questionable grounds. Traditionally it has been considered that the master alone controls the vessel and he or she alone can be prosecuted; much modern legislation still homes in on this point. But the wealth of complex new legislation covers so many activities, some of which impact on the rules of the road, that it is difficult for one person to "master" them all. Yet failure to do so can lead that master to criminal prosecution. There can be no doubt that the master is responsible for everything that happens in the ship. But that he or she therefore "carries the can" for anything that goes wrong on board is true in civil law, it is not necessarily so in criminal law. Yet in many cases where the person who ought to be prosecuted for the infringement of a rule is the actual wrongdoer, it has often been the master who ended up in court.

Usually it has been only when an incident has occurred that the risk of prosecution arises. Often the circumstance has been a collision, though

---

[28] Alter Barge v. TPC Transport, 1987 AMC 1788.

[29] For example, since the entry into force of the 1972 ColRegs up until the end of 1982, 1,539 reports of violations of the Dover Strait TSS were sent to foreign flag states. As a result, 446 fines were imposed, 127 warnings issued, and 31 masters suspended or dismissed.

increasing shore surveillance, as mentioned earlier, leads to prosecution for other reasons, perhaps too simplistically leveling the charges at the master. In one case where a master turned in sick, having properly delegated part of the job of running the ship, it was the master who was found to have neglected his duty when the anchor watch was not correctly kept, because

> the Master could not evade his responsibility since the duty was his and his alone.[30]

Such a decision raises serious implications for the safe running of a ship. No master can do everything: it is a team effort that runs a safe ship. Considered delegation to properly qualified subordinates is essential in all manner of works, not least in that of keeping the navigational watch. Default by such a subordinate should not automatically lead to the conviction of the master for default of his or her duty. Perhaps appreciation of this viewpoint is growing. In August 1980 the *N.F. Tiger* was at sea in the English Channel. Her master was on the bridge and ordered a course to be steered that would have resulted in his vessel crossing the traffic lane in accordance with the International Regulations for the Prevention of Collisions at Sea 1972. About five minutes later, he properly handed over the watch to his chief officer, a qualified master mariner, and left the bridge. While he was away the vessel altered course to one that was in breach of the 1972 Regulations. When the master was subsequently arraigned, the allegation against him was dismissed because the justices were not satisfied that the master had actual knowledge of the infringement or had been deliberately negligent. This judgment was upheld on appeal.[31] Six years later, a hearing into alleged negligent navigation resulted in charges being proven against the officer on watch of the British ferry *St. Anselm,* and not the master, for failing to keep well clear and failing to keep out of the way of the Panamanian car transporter *Sirius Highway.*[32]

U.S. penalty provisions cover both violations of the international rules (33 U.S.C. 1608) and inland rules (33 U.S.C. 2072). More generally, any vessel under U.S. jurisdiction operated negligently is liable (46 U.S.C. 2302), while more specifically an infringement of the Bridge-to-Bridge Radiotelephone regulations attracts a civil penalty (see 26.10).

### Naval Vessel Not Subject to Lien

The doctrine of personality of the vessel is modified with respect to navy and other publicly owned vessels, in that it is contrary to public policy

---

[30] Hodge v. Higgins [1980] 2 Lloyd's Rep. 589.

[31] Secretary of State for Trade v. Ewart-James (the *N.F. Tiger*) [1982] 2 Lloyd's Rep. 564.

[32] Lloyd's List 8 February 1988.

to permit such vessels to be libeled and taken into custody of the marshal and thus held out of service. Nevertheless, the old theory that "the King can do no wrong" is never used as a defense in cases of collision between a ship of the United States Navy and a merchant vessel, even in time of war. Instead, under a special statutory provision, the government permits itself to be sued as an owner *in personam,* and the damage sustained by both vessels is adjudicated exactly as it would be done were the action *in rem* between the vessels themselves. Indeed when the collision occurred because the naval vessel was patrolling without light and fog signals, due to actual war conditions, so scrupulously has the United States accepted its responsibility that it has paid the losses in full.[33]

As for other government-owned vessels, apart from obvious cases, a divided panel recently held that, since a privately owned vessel serving as a United States Coast Guard auxiliary was deemed to be a "public vessel" for whose faults the government was responsible under the Public Vessels Act, the government as owner *pro hoc vice* was entitled to limit its liability for such fault in accordance with the Limitations of Liability Act.[34]

### Rules of the Road Are Mandatory

At the beginning, it will be well to have in mind certain general principles that govern the action of the courts in determining collision liability. The first of these is that the rules of the road applicable to a particular case are in no sense optional, but are for the most part absolutely mandatory. To avoid liability for a collision, the requirements *must* be obeyed. The courts will excuse a departure from the rules on two grounds only, and one of these—to avoid immediate danger—is provided for by the rules themselves.[35] Departure from the rules for any other reason, or for no reason at all, must be justified on the ground that while there was a technical violation, the circumstances were such that it could not possibly have contributed to the collision. As said by the Supreme Court, not only once but in substance many times:

> But when a ship at the time of collision is in actual violation of a statutory rule intended to prevent collision, it is no more than a reasonable presumption that the fault, if not the sole cause, was at least a contributory cause of the disaster. In such a case the burden rests upon the ship of showing, not merely that her fault might not have been one of the causes, or that it probably was not, but that it could not have been.[36]

---

[33] Watts v. U.S. (1903) 123 F. 105.

[34] Dick v. United States, 671 F.2d 724 [1982] AMC 913 (2d Cir. 1982).

[35] Special Circumstances, Rule 2, International Regulations and Inland Rules.

[36] The *Pennsylvania* (19 Wall) 125 (1875).

It will be recognized that a disregard of any rule on the basis of convenience, courtesy, good nature, or disbelief in its efficacy places the navigator under a burden of proof that it is almost impossible for him to carry.

## Obedience Must Be Timely

In the second place, not only must the rules be obeyed, but the action prescribed by them must be taken in ample time to carry out their purpose. It must be remembered that the rules are intended not only to prevent collision but to prevent serious and imminent risk of collision. This precept applies with particular force to the use of sound and/or radio signals, which should always be given in time to be corrected if misunderstood, or as one judge expressed it "in time to maneuver out of a misunderstanding." Obedience to the letter of the rule is not obedience to the spirit of the rule unless it is rendered *before* the vessels are in dangerous proximity, in a sufficiently timely manner so that each vessel is aware of the other's intentions in time to conduct herself in accordance with them and aid in carrying them out.

## Rules Apply Alike to All Vessels

A third principle that must be remembered is that the rules apply with equal force to all vessels on public navigable waters, without regard to flag, ownership, service, size, or speed. A so-called "stand-on" vessel is as much under the obligation to hold course and speed as is the "giveway" vessel to keep out of her way. No rights or exemptions, except those conferred by the rule, or amendments thereto, apply under American law to naval vessels, passenger liners, ferries, or towboats with tows, and the same steering and sailing rules govern the USS *America* and a 30-foot trawler. To give the rules their maximum effectiveness, this is, of course, precisely as it should be.

Yet there has been a modern challenge to this seemingly commonsensible principle in the aftermath of a collision between two pleasure craft on the Amite River, Louisiana, leading to the death of one occupant. It was submitted that admiralty jurisdiction of the federal judiciary did not extend to this collision because the boats were not engaged in commercial activity and the waters were seldom used by commercial vessels.[37] Although the district court agreed that the subject matter was outside their jurisdiction, the Fifth Circuit Court of Appeals reversed this opinion, holding that regardless of purpose, two boats using navigable waters are engaged in maritime activity, a decision subsequently affirmed by the

---

[37] Based on Executive Jet Aviation, Inc. v. City of Cleveland, 409 U.S. 249 [1973] AMC 1 (1972).

Supreme Court.[38] No doubt practicing mariners of all types will agree that the Court of Appeals correctly relied on the fact that navigational rules govern all vessels on navigable waters and that uncertainty would be caused by denying admiralty jurisdiction. A contrary rule would have had chaotic effects on United States maritime law.[39]

## Rules Modified by Court Interpretation

A fourth principle of the rules too often overlooked by mariners in their seagoing practice of collision law is that to avoid liability they must know not only what the rules applicable to a given situation provide but what the federal courts have interpreted them to mean. Judicial interpretation has, in the history of the rules, performed three important functions. First, it has determined the legal meaning of certain phrases not defined in the rules themselves, such as efficient whistle or siren, flare-up light, proper lookout, special circumstances, immediate danger, ordinary practice of seamen, and risk of collision; it is in accordance with the meanings thus established that these terms are construed in collision cases. Second, it has filled certain gaps in the rules, sometimes modifying the statute to do this. For example, Article 28, in the old Inland Rules, provided that three short blasts, when vessels were in sight of each other, meant, "my engines are going at full speed astern," while the courts required the same signal to be given when the engines were going at less than full speed astern or when one engine was going ahead and the other astern, with the vessel actually making sternway.[40] Again, the courts have determined the proper signals when vessels approach each other in a collision situation stern first, a point on which the rules are silent. Third, judicial interpretation has been used not only to eliminate the old Pilot Rules found contradictory to the old Inland Rules, but to reconcile occasional inconsistencies or conflicts in the latter. This is illustrated in the treatment by the courts of the apparently inconsistent sections of old Article 18, Inland Rules, in which Rule III required the danger signal by an approaching vessel when she failed to understand the course or intention of the other *from any cause,* and Rule IX of the same article provided that in fog, when vessels cannot see each other, *fog signals only must be given.* The courts decided, in effect, that the danger signal in inland waters

---

[38] Foremost Insurance Co. v. Richardson, 102 S. Ct. 2654 [1982] AMC 2253, rehearing denied, 103 S. Ct. 198 (1982).

[39] Nicholas J. Healy, "U.S. Admiralty and Shipping Law—Recent Developments," *Lloyd's Maritime and Commercial Law Quarterly* (1983), 610.

[40] The *Sicilian Prince* (CCA N.Y. 1903) 144 F. 951; the *Deutschland* (CCA NY 1904) 137 F. 1018; the *San Juan* (Calif. 1927) AMC 384.

must be included as a fog, as well as a clear weather, signal.[41] Most of these interpretations have subsequently found their way into the body of the rules.

Whatever mariners think of the legal setup, which has the effect of giving the courts more authority over the rules of the road than the Commandant, U.S. Coast Guard, who enforces them through the local inspectors, they must obey the law as they find it—and that means in practice, as the admiralty judges interpret it. Notwithstanding the fact that in the United States we do not have special admiralty courts, but any federal judge may be required to hear a collision case, it will be found that the decisions have been, as a whole, sound in seamanship as well as in law. The most experienced judges are not infallible, of course, and not infrequently circuit courts of appeal, co-ordinate in rank, will differ on some disputed point of collision law and the issue must be settled by the Supreme Court. The basic rules have existed in substantially their present form for so many years that most doubtful questions have long since been decided by that august tribunal, and the law for the most part may be regarded as pretty well settled. It remains only for mariners to familiarize themselves with the gist of the important ruling decisions, many of which are set forth in textbooks dealing with the subject.

The international character of the Collision Regulations requires that they should be understood by the seamen of different nations in the same sense. It is therefore of importance that the construction placed on them by courts of different countries should be uniform. This has been distinctly recognized in the United States:

> The paramount importance of having international rules, which are intended to become part of the law of nations, understood alike by all maritime powers, is manifest; and the adoption of any reasonable construction of them by the maritime powers . . . affords sufficient ground for the adoption of a similar construction . . . by the courts of this country.[42]

### Rules Apply According to Location of Vessel

A fifth principle to be borne in mind by mariners is that they must always be careful to observe the particular rules that apply in the locality of their vessel during the approaching situation. There are important differences in the rules to be followed on the high seas and those of many local waters throughout the world. The inland waters of the continental United States are governed by a set of special rules laid down in the Inland Navigation Rules Act of 1980. While as consistent as much as possible with the international rules, there are major differences in the

---

[41] The *Celtic Monarch* (Wash. 1910) 17 F.1006.
[42] The *Sylvester Hale*, 6 Bened. 523.

special rules applicable to United States domestic waters. The significant point to which attention is drawn here is that obedience to the wrong set of rules, where they are in conflict, constitutes just as serious a breach as does the deliberate disregard of the law altogether. To illustrate: the use of a single short blast of the whistle by a stand-on vessel holding her course and speed when crossing at a distance within half a mile is proper in inland waters, as provided by Rule 34(a)(i), but might make the vessel liable for a collision if she used the same signal on the high seas, where one short blast indicates a change of course to starboard.

**Customs of Navigation**
In some parts of the world there have developed over many decades, customs of navigation to cover local situations not covered by statutory rules of navigation. In the main these are in the process of being encapsulated in local rules—but not everywhere. There thus can be a statutory void that the local custom fills. Admiralty courts have recognized some of these customs as having the "force of law" and constituting the appropriate standard of navigational conduct in that locality. In U.S. inland waters the "point-bend" custom of the Mississippi River is a prime example. Although not a statutory rule of law, the point-bend custom has been accorded long-standing judicial recognition. The custom has become so firmly entrenched that courts have been reluctant to excuse noncompliance with it even when "special circumstances" exist. However, recently some admiralty courts have attempted to restrict the applicability of the custom in circumstances where it would create a significant navigational hazard. Thus, while the custom remains viable in the courts, it alone is not necessarily a satisfactory standard of navigational conduct, and its applicability should be tempered by principles of good prudence, good seamanship, and common sense.[43] The point-bend custom may have the "force of law," but that custom is not a "rule of law."[44]

**SUMMARY**
Federal courts, sitting in admiralty, have jurisdiction over collisions occurring on public navigable waters, which have been held to be waters navigable, though not necessarily navigated, in interstate commerce. State courts may have concurrent jurisdiction, when provided by local statute, over certain cases on public navigable waters within a state. Admiralty law permits action to be brought against a vessel *in rem* (against a thing) or against her owners *in personam* (against a person). Whenever both

---

[43] Robert T. Lemon II, "The Mississippi River Point-Bend Custom," *Journal of Maritime Law and Commerce* 19, no. 3, July 1988.
[44] Canal Barge Co. v. China Ocean Shipping Co. (1986) AMC 2042.

vessels in a collision are at fault, under United States law the liability must be apportioned between them. A vessel may be sold at auction to satisfy a judgment against her, but the right to collect for damage may be modified by the provisions of the Limited Liability, Harter, and Carriage of Goods by Sea acts. As a matter of public policy, naval and other publicly owned vessels cannot be libeled, but the government permits itself to be sued *in personam* for faulty collision damage by a public vessel.

Vessels on the high seas are subject to the international rules; when in specified inland waters, various local rules, which differ in important respects, govern their action in collision situations. The rules are mandatory, must be obeyed in a timely manner, apply alike to all vessels, must be understood in the light of court interpretation, and have application within fixed geographical limits. While uniformity of the rules has been greatly advanced, the mariner must observe the differences in requirements according to the immediate location of his vessel.

# 3

# Lawful Lights

**The Function of Running and Riding Lights**
The importance of proper running and riding lights on vessels using public navigable waters can scarcely be overemphasized. During the hours of darkness it is the function of these lights in clear weather to give such timely and effective notice to one vessel of the proximity of another that all doubt as to her character and intentions will be satisfactorily settled before there is any serious risk of collision. Even in restricted visibility, with the mariner's safety in an approaching close-quarters situation dependent upon radar and sound rather than upon sight, it is often the welcome glimmer of these same lights through the haze that finally enables each fog-enshrouded vessel to feel her way safely past the other. To the student of collision law it is significant that twelve of the thirty-eight international regulations and eleven of the thirty-eight inland rules relate wholly or in part to lights, and that both sets of rules are supplemented by annexes that go into great detail as to the technical specifications of lights and also provide additional lights for vessels engaged in fishing. In cases of collision the courts are as certain to hold a vessel at fault for improper lights as for a violation of signal requirements or for failure to maintain a proper lookout.

**Lights at Anchor Must Conform**
It is evident from the court cases that mere volume of light, even for a vessel at anchor on a clear night, does not constitute the due notice to which approaching vessels are entitled or satisfy the requirement for regulation lights. In an interesting decision affirmed by the circuit court of appeals, the large seagoing tanker *Chester O. Swain* collided with the government cotton carrier *Scantic* on the Mississippi River anchored 600

feet off the docks at New Orleans, and the latter vessel was found equally at fault with the *Swain* because of the irregularity of her anchor lights. It appeared that on the day preceding, fire had spread from a cotton warehouse to the *Scantic* and her cargo, damaging the vessel's running lights before it could be extinguished. The *Scantic* was shifted from her pier to a temporary anchorage across the river from the regular anchorage, so that if the fire in her cargo again broke out, as sometimes happens with cotton, it would not result in damage to other vessels at anchor. The lights were not repaired during the day, as they might have been; according to the testimony, the following lights were shown by the *Scantic* as soon as darkness fell: an oil lantern lashed to the jack staff; an oil lantern on an awning spreader aft; four sets of cargo cluster lights (each containing four large bulbs), one at the center of the bridge, one on the forward part of the boat deck to light No. 3 hatch, one at the after end of the boat deck to light No. 4 and No. 5 hatches, and one on the starboard side near No. 4 hatch to light the pilot ladder that led down to a motorboat tender standing by to render aid in case of the fire's recurring. In charge of a pilot, the *Swain*, proceeding down the river from Baton Rouge with a load of oil, rounded Algiers Point and crossed over to within 600 feet of the left bank, when the lights of the anchored vessel were first sighted against the background of city lights about 1,500 yards ahead. Instead of maneuvering promptly to avoid collision, the *Swain* first continued ahead, then stopped, then backed, then stopped and drifted helplessly into the mass of lights that marked the *Scantic*. The tanker was held at fault for her vacillating conduct and for the lack of vigilance of her lookout, but in also inculpating the *Scantic* the circuit court held that:

> while the lights she [the *Scantic*] installed ought to have been discovered by the *Swain* in time to prevent the collision, it cannot be said that better and more conventional lights would not have got the attention of the *Swain* sooner than those which the *Scantic* rigged and would not have averted the trouble.[1]

The importance of having anchor lights conform to the specific requirements was brought out in a number of early cases in which incorrect lights, though visible, proved misleading to approaching vessels. In one such case, a 75-foot dredge in New York harbor exhibited two white lights at anchor instead of the stationary single light and was mistaken by an approaching tug with tow for a tug under way and being overtaken. The tug did not discover her error until within 300 feet of the dredge, when she avoided collision herself by a hard-over helm but was unable to pull her tow clear. Although the tug was held at fault for failure to

---

[1] The *Chester O. Swain* (CCA N.Y. 1935) 76 F.2d 890.

discover sooner that the dredge was stationary, nevertheless the dredge shared the damages because of technically improper lights.[2]

Notwithstanding this, it seems that a ship will not necessarily be held at fault for a collision caused by improper lights, if her own regulation lights have recently been destroyed. A steamship at anchor with her masthead light up instead of her proper riding lights, was held free from blame in an English court. Her riding light had been broken shortly before the collision in a previous collision for which she was not at fault.[3]

Today the availability of modern highly suitable replacement lights is less likely to lead to exculpation. The anchored Liberian tanker *Coral I* had run out of fuel for her generator and relied on oil lamps, instead of the more capable and readily available butane gas lamps, to illuminate her at anchor. Although the other ship's lookout was defective, the *Coral I* took 60 percent of the blame.[4]

## Lights Under Way Must Conform

The tragic collision of the USS *S-51* and the steamship *City of Rome* off Block Island 23 September 1925 affords a striking example of the importance attached by the courts to proper running lights under way. It also indicates the strictness with which the exemptions authorized for vessels of special construction by Rule 1(e), of both international regulations and inland rules, regarding lights, will be construed. This collision, which attracted unusual public interest because of the protracted but futile efforts that were made in the face of Atlantic storms to rescue possible survivors in the sunken submarine, happened on a clear night, and the masthead light of the *S-51* was under continuous observation from the *City of Rome* after being reported by her lookout twenty-two minutes before the collision. It was first made out as a faint white light broad on the starboard bow, and its bearing did not appreciably change until shortly before the collision, when it was observed to be closing in on the steamship's course and to be growing brighter. According to the testimony brought out at the trial, the captain of the *City of Rome* had been watching the light for some twenty minutes without taking any action, although in some doubt as to its character. He concluded at this point that he was overtaking a small tug or fishing vessel and ordered the course changed to the left to give it a wider berth. But a few seconds later the red sidelight of the submarine appeared a little to the right of the white light, indicating for the first time that she was

---

[2] The *Arthur* (N.Y. 1901) 108 F.557.
[3] The *Kjobenhavn* (1874) 2 Aspinall MC 213.
[4] The *Coral I* [1982] 1 Lloyd's Rep. 442.

not an overtaken vessel but was crossing the course of the *City of Rome* from right to left, as she had a right to do under the rules. Although the liner's rudder was ordered put the other way immediately and a few seconds later the engines were reversed, it was then too late to avoid the collision. The submarine sank very quickly, and of the three survivors picked up none had been on deck during the approaching situation or could give evidence as to the navigation of the submarine. However, notwithstanding that the *City of Rome* was flagrantly at fault for failure to reduce her speed when in doubt regarding the movements of the other vessel and for failure to signal her change of course to the left by two short blasts as required under the then effective international rules, both the district court and the circuit court of appeals found the *S-51* at fault for improper lights. Referring to Article 2 of the 1889 International Rules, then in force, the court said:

> The *S-51* was 240 feet 6 inches long; her beam 25 feet; her surface displacement upwards of 1,000 tons; her forward white light was not 20 feet above the hull but was only 11 feet 2 inches above the deck; the sidelights were fixed in a recess on the chariot bridge 7½ feet above the hull; they were not fitted with inboard screens projecting at least 3 feet forward from the lights. There is also testimony that the red light was so constructed and in such close proximity with the masthead light, only 3½ feet apart, that the visibility of the relatively dim red light was materially reduced by the greater brilliancy of the white masthead light.

To the student of collision law, a very significant feature of this case was the comments of both trial and appellate courts on the government argument that it was not practicable to have *S*-boats comply with the literal provisions in regard to lights, and moreover as a special type of naval vessel such craft were not under compulsion to comply. The district court said:

> I cannot accept the view that submarines running on the surface through traffic lanes are immune from the usual requirements regarding lights. . . . The obvious answer to the contention that the nature of their construction and operation makes it impractical for them to comply with these rules is that if this be so they should confine their operation to waters not being traversed by other ships. The fact that they are more dangerous should not be a reason for their disregarding rules which other ships must observe. . . . The testimony conclusively shows not only that the failure of the *S-51* to show proper sidelights might have contributed but that it was a principal cause of the disaster.

In confirming the decision of the lower court to hold the submarine equally at fault with the liner, the circuit court of appeals added:

> There remains only the contention that the submarine was not subject to the ordinary rules of the road. It does not appear that it was impossible for her to comply with these, but it would make no difference if it did. . . . It is apparent that the rules regulating lights were meant to apply to ships of war; Article 13 would be conclusive if the preamble alone were not

enough. If unfortunately it is impossible to equip submarines properly, they must take their chances until some provision has been made for them by law. We have no power to dispense with the statute nor indeed has the Navy. As they now sail they are unfortunately a menace to other shipping and to their own crews, as this unhappy collision so tragically illustrates. We cannot say that they are not to be judged by the same standard as private persons. The safety of navigation depends upon uniformity; only so can reliance be placed upon what masters see at night.[5]

To illustrate the international character of court findings, a similar collision occurred between HM Submarine *Truculent* and a merchant ship in the Thames estuary, with equally tragic loss of life in the submarine. The masthead light of the submarine, like that of the *S-51,* was improperly placed according to the existing rules (also the 1899 ones), and was held to have contributed to the collision and damage. Evidence was accepted showing that the difficulties, in the case of submarines, of complying with the requirement for a masthead light were great, if not insuperable, and that the positioning of lights in submarines of all navies was similar but:

. . . these considerations afford no answer to the charge that the steaming light of HMS *Truculent* constitutes a breach of the regulations.

It was further held that if it was really impossible in the case of a submarine to fit a masthead light that complied with the rules, then there was a duty to issue a warning to mariners of the fact.[6]

Due warning, in the format of Notices to Mariners, was issued in 1953. The next revision of the international rules, effective 1 January 1954, provided the basis for the legal exemptions referred to in the *S-51* case. Subsequent revisions of the rules have maintained the exemptions for naval or military vessels unable to comply, and Rule 1(e), International and Inland Rules, extends them further to any vessel of special construction or purpose approved by her government. Exemptions in the United States are issued by the secretary of the department in which the Coast Guard is operating, for USCG and commercial vessels, and by the secretary of the navy for naval vessels, as certificates of alternative compliance. Similar exemptions for foreign warships are to be found in national notices to mariners and in the appropriate sailing directions. All these vessels must be certified as being unable to comply with the requirements regarding lights and *must be in the closest possible compliance* with the literal requirements of the rules. Should a collision such as was cited occur, it undoubtedly would still be indefensible, on the grounds of inadequate compliance. The variation in the number or position or character of the

---

[5] Ocean SS. Co. of Savannah v. U.S. (CCA N.Y. 1930) 38 F.2d 782.
[6] The *Truculent,* Admiralty v. SS *Devine* [1951] 2 Lloyd's Rep. 308.

lights required to be shown cannot be misleading.[7] On the contrary, the obvious intention of the authorized exemptions is to recognize the inability of certain vessels to comply with the literal requirements, while requiring that the nature and spirit of the lighting requirements of the rules be maintained. Thus, it may be presumed that the courts will be extremely critical of any unnecessary departure from the literal requirements or failure to give proper notice of the character and position of the lights carried by such vessels of special construction.

Improper lights contributed to the tanker *Frosta* being held solely to blame for a collision with another tanker, the *Fotini Carras*, in the Indian Ocean in December 1968. The *Frosta* was overtaking the *Fotini Carras*, about 500 yards off, when her steering gear jammed. Among other actions, she promptly exhibited her not-under-command lights but failed to extinguish her masthead lights. Mr. Justice Brandon held that the *Fotini Carras* was not at fault because, among other factors, her chief officer, who was on watch

> . . . would at this stage be concerned mainly with judging the heading of the FROSTA and the extent to which she was closing FOTINI CARRAS and that, while doing so, he might well not notice that not-under-command had been switched on above the bridge of FROSTA so long as the masthead lights continued to show. . . . I am not prepared to find the chief officer was at fault in not noticing the not-under-command lights before he took action for other reasons.[8]

### Improper Lights May Be a Fault in Naval Vessels

In the United States the courts have held all vessels to a strict observance of the rules even in time of war. Thus, when the armored cruiser *Columbia* sank the British freighter *Foscolia* off Fire Island during the Spanish-American War, the *Columbia* was held solely liable for the loss, the court finding that even a vessel of the navy in time of war cannot be excused for masking her lights, orders of the squadron commander notwithstanding, since there is no statutory authority for such an order.[9] Similarly, in a collision off the East Coast in 1918 between the privately owned cargo steamships *Proteus* and *Cushing*, both vessels, because of danger from hostile submarines, and under authority of the Navy Department, were proceeding without lights, and both were held at fault because they did not turn on their lights in time to avoid collision,[10] and in still another

---

[7] The Peruvian submarine *Pacocha* was sunk by a Japanese tuna boat at night off Lima in 1988. It is believed the *Kyowa Maru* may have mistaken the lights of the submarine for a small boat and hit the stern.

[8] The *Frosta*, Q.B. (Adm. Ct.) [1973] 2 Lloyd's Rep. 348.

[9] Watts v. U.S. (N.Y. 1903) 123 F.105.

[10] The *Cushing* (CCA N.Y. 1923) 292 F.560.

case, less than three weeks later, the U.S. Navy tanker *Hisko*, running without lights, was held solely at fault for sinking the cargo steamship *Almirante*, which was showing proper sidelights, though no masthead light.[11]

During the 1939–45 war, Allied convoy orders had statutory force and, for nations affected, overrode all contrary provisions contained in the international regulations.[12] Vessels remained otherwise bound to comply with the remainder of their obligations, including the duties of good seamanship, which were not affected by the convoy orders.[13]

## General Characteristics of Sidelights

The precise nature of the lights required in inland waters was not always clear from the wording of the rules, as indeed had been the case previously on the high seas. Earlier rules dictated some compromise since the sidelights, mounted at the sides of a ship, would have to shine across the projected fore-and-aft line of the vessel at some point in order to be visible from ahead, or else there would be a theoretical "dark lane" ahead that could result in vessels meeting exactly end on being unable to see each other's sidelights. The revised international regulations and inland rules cover this eventuality by allowing a practical cut-off outside the prescribed sector. The full details concerning arcs of visibility, contained in Annex I to the 1972 International Rules, are shown below. Similar specifications are contained in Annex I to the Inland Rules.

9. Horizontal Sectors

(a) (i) In the forward direction, sidelights as fitted on the vessel must show the minimum required intensities. The intensities must decrease to reach practical cut-off between 1 degree and 3 degrees outside the prescribed sectors.

(ii) For sternlights and masthead lights and at 22.5 degrees abaft the beam for sidelights, the minimum required intensities shall be maintained over the arc of the horizon up to 5 degrees within the limits of the sectors prescribed in Rule 21. From 5 degrees within the prescribed sectors the intensity may decrease by 50 percent up to the prescribed limits; it shall decrease steadily to reach practical cut-off at not more than 5 degrees outside the prescribed sectors.

Previously, vessels that did operate solely on the inland waters of the United States were governed to a certain extent by court interpretations. An analysis of early collision cases involving improper sidelights, mostly concerning sailing craft and steamships around the turn of the century,

[11] Almirante SS. Corp. v. U.S. (CCA N.Y. 1929) 34 F.2d 123.
[12] The *Vernon City* (1942) 70 Ll. L. Rep. 278.
[13] The *Scottish Musician* (1942) 72 Ll. L. Rep. 284.

shows that out of the confusing phraseology of the rules, the courts have reached the following definite conclusions:

(1) A vessel in collision is liable if any obstruction prevents the sidelights from being visible to a vessel closing from ahead.[14]

(2) A vessel in collision is liable if the inboard screens are not of the prescribed length and if the sidelights are seen excessively across the bow.[15]

(3) A vessel in collision is liable if both sidelights are visible from a point on her own bow, i.e., both can be seen from the stem of the vessel.[16]

In a crossing collision between two steamers off the New Jersey coast on a clear night, the stand-on vessel had her sidelights set in the rigging in such a manner that they crossed at her stem, and her green light could be seen by the burdened vessel 3 points across the bow. In finding her at fault for improper lights, the Supreme Court made the following emphatic comment:

This rule in regard to setting and screening the colored lights cannot be too highly valued, or the importance of its exact observance be overstated. Better far to have no sidelights than to have them so set and screened as to be seen across the bow. In that situation they operate as a snare to deceive even the wary into error and danger.[17]

Modern vessels have far less cluttered superstructure than the earlier ships mentioned in the above cases and are, perhaps, less liable to obstruction or poor fittings of sidelights. Nevertheless, it is as vital as ever to check that sidelights do show over the correct arcs.

The positioning and spacing of sidelights are also defined in the revised rules. In the past the inland rules somewhat loosely stated that the lights were to be on the port and starboard side, which is to say, apparently, that moving the sidelights inboard would not make a non-seagoing vessel liable for a collision as long as such lights were visible over the prescribed arcs.[18]

Annex I to the 1972 International Regulations, which forms the basis for Annex I of the Inland Rules, is more precise:

2. Vertical positioning and spacing of lights

(g) The sidelights of a power-driven vessel shall be placed at a height above the hull not greater than three quarters of that of the forward

---

[14] The *Vesper* (N.Y. 1881) 9 F.569; the *Johanne Auguste* (N.Y. 1884) 21 F.134; *Carleton* v. U.S. (1874) 10 Ct. Cl. 485.

[15] The *North Star* (1882) 27 L. Ed. 91.

[16] Clendinin v. the *Alhambra* (N.Y. 1880) 4 F.86.

[17] The *Santiago de Cuba* 10 Blatch. U.S. 444.

[18] But see *Samuel H. Crawford* (N.Y. 1881) 6 F.906, which although not faulting the vessel in this instance as the port light did show ahead without obstruction, nevertheless intimated that the fitting of sidelights on a deckhouse of a sailing schooner rather than on the rigging "is not to be approved."

masthead light. They shall not be so low as to be interfered with by deck lights.

(h) The sidelights, if in a combined lantern and carried on a power-driven vessel of less than 20 metres in length, shall be placed no less than 1 metre below the masthead light.

3. Horizontal positioning and spacing of lights

(b) On a vessel of 20 metres or more in length the sidelights shall not be placed in front of the forward masthead lights. They shall be placed at or near the side of the vessel.

The placing of sidelights abaft the forward masthead light should aid other vessels in the visual assessment of a vessel's course. Their position "at or near the side of the vessel" bears out the prophecy of footnote 18. However, for vessels of special construction, particularly smaller warships, the placing of lights abaft the usually single masthead light will not always be practicable. Mariners will constantly have to bear in mind the possibility that a combination of sidelights ahead of a single masthead light could well indicate the presence of a vessel much larger than 20 meters in length.

The precise positioning and spacing of lights can cause a problem for very large ships. On certain common types of VLCCs in ballast condition and normal trim, which represents some 50 percent of their working life at sea, it is physically impossible to see their sidelights from dead ahead if the observer is in a small vessel up to two miles away. The specifications of paragraph 2(g) of Section 84.03(g) of Annex I result in the inability to carry the sidelights on the bridge wings because they would then be higher than the forward masthead light. They are placed lower, and because of the normal trim of the vessel in ballast, they are cut off between one-half and three-quarters of the length of these very long ships, leaving a blind-zone some 2 miles dead ahead. A small ship that did not have the height of eye to see "above" the VLCC's bow would, when in the blind-zone, be denied any information from the VLCC's sidelights and might disastrously consider her farther away because only the masthead lights would be visible. Fishing vessels, sail boats, and other small craft engaged in coastal passages would do well to bear this limitation in mind.

## Masthead Lights; Sternlights

In addition to describing the sidelights for power-driven vessels and sailing vessels, the rules also describe in considerable detail the masthead lights to be carried by an independent power-driven vessel. Essentially there are few significant differences between the masthead and sternlights prescribed by both the international regulations and the inland rules. Both seagoing and non-seagoing vessels carry a 20-point masthead light forward and may, if less than 50 meters, and must, if 50 meters or more in length, carry a second 20-point masthead light higher than and abaft the forward one. Minor deviations are permitted for the positioning of a single masthead light for vessels less than 20 meters in length. All such vessels carry a 12-point sternlight, though a power-driven vessel of less than 12 meters in length is allowed to carry an all-round white light in lieu of the masthead and sternlights.

A major difference from the international regulations is that on the Great Lakes, a power-driven vessel of any length may carry an all-round white light in lieu of the second masthead light and sternlight. This light is carried in the position of the second masthead light and is visible at the same minimum range. Such a departure from the otherwise uniformity of rules governing United States waters was granted in recognition that the all-round light, being higher on the vessel than a sternlight, provided a greater degree of safety during the frequent low-hanging fogs prevalent on the Great Lakes. This permissive use of an all-round light to power-driven vessels under way is limited to the Great Lakes and is not extended to any other classification of vessels or to any other area.

The international regulations make equally specific requirements for the positioning of masthead lights, as they do for sidelights:

2. *Vertical Positioning and Spacing of Lights*
   (a) On a power-driven vessel of 20 metres or more in length the masthead lights shall be placed as follows:
      (i) the forward masthead light, or if only one masthead light is carried, then that light, at a height above the hull of not less than 6 metres, and, if the breadth of the vessel exceeds 6 metres, then at a height above the hull not less than such breadth, so however that the light need not be placed at a greater height above the hull than 12 metres;
      (ii) when two masthead lights are carried the after one shall be at least 4.5 metres vertically higher than the forward one.
   (b) The vertical separation of masthead lights of power-driven vessels shall be such that in all normal conditions of trim the after light will be seen over and separate from the forward light at a distance of 1000 metres from the stem when viewed from sea level.

Slightly reduced dimensions are spelled out in the inland rules equivalent of the above, probably reflecting the more compact nature of non-seagoing vessels. All vessels are granted permanent exemption of any repositioning of lights as a result of conversion from imperial to metric units.

## Importance of Second Masthead Light

While the combination of masthead, stern, and sidelights are generally adequate to convey a satisfactory indication of one vessel's movements to another, there is at least one situation peculiarly fraught with the danger of misunderstanding, where the arrangement of two white lights in range is invaluable. This is where two power-driven vessels are crossing at a very fine angle on courses differing by as much as 170 degrees, and the give-way vessel, seeing both sidelights of the other a little on the starboard bow, mistakenly assumes that a starboard-to-starboard meeting is proper. The stand-on vessel, seeing only the green light of the other slightly to port and expecting her to give way, maintains course and speed, which may result in a stalemate until the two vessels are in dangerous proximity, particularly if the approaching vessel veers somewhat to port.

The obvious advantage of the second masthead light here is that, with vessels as nearly end-on as indicated, the slightest change of course by either is instantly revealed to the other. For this reason, notwithstanding its partly optional nature under both the international regulations and the inland rules, the after masthead light should be carried whenever practical.

Apart from the meeting situation, the presence of the second masthead light can provide valuable visual confirmation of the course of the other ship, as well as give an indication of approximate length. The international regulations require:

*3. Horizontal Positioning and Spacing of Lights*
   (a) When two masthead lights are prescribed for a power-driven vessel, the horizontal distance between them shall not be less than one half of the length of the vessel but need not be more than 100 metres. The forward light shall be placed not more than one quarter of the length of the vessel from the stem.

The inland rules make similar provision, though again with reduced dimensions to cater to the non-seagoing vessel. Under both rules permanent exemption from repositioning of masthead lights was given to vessels of less than 150 meters in length.

Both the 1972 International Regulations and the 1980 Inland Rules increased the visibility range requirements of lights for larger vessels.

Rule 22. Visibility of Lights
   The lights prescribed in these rules shall have an intensity as specified in Section 8 of Annex I to these regulations so as to be visible at the following minimum ranges:
   (a) In vessels of 50 metres or more in length:
   —a masthead light, 6 miles;
   —a sidelight, 3 miles;
   —a sternlight, 3 miles;
   —a towing light, 3 miles;
   —a white, red, green or yellow all-round light, 3 miles.
   (b) In vessels of 12 metres or more in length but less than 50 metres in length:
   —a masthead light, 5 miles; except that where the length of the vessel is less than 20 metres, 3 miles;
   —a sidelight, 2 miles;
   —a sternlight, 2 miles;
   —a towing light, 2 miles;

—a white, red, green or yellow all-round light, 2 miles.
(c) In vessels of less than 12 metres in length:
—a masthead light, 2 miles;
—a sidelight, 1 mile;
—a sternlight, 2 miles;
—a towing light, 2 miles;
—a white, red, green or yellow all-round light, 2 miles.
(d) In inconspicuous, partly submerged vessels or objects being towed:
—a white light, 3 miles.

The equivalent Rule 22 of the Inland Rules is the same as the above, except for the addition of a special flashing light with a visibility of 2 miles for use in certain categories of tows. This is the same color (yellow) as the light prescribed for air-cushion vehicles but flashing at about half the rate of the latter.

## Towing Lights

Perhaps next in importance to proper running lights for independent vessels are the lights of vessels towing and being towed. Generally speaking, such vessels move slowly, but tugs are hampered by their tows and relatively unable to maneuver in close situations, while vessels and rafts in tow are, of course, almost completely helpless. The lights for a vessel towing or pushing as set forth in Rule 24, International Rules, consist of the usual sidelights, a fixed sternlight, and in place of the masthead light a pair of similar lights in a vertical line at least 2 meters apart (for a vessel 20 meters or more in length); or if towing *and* the tow extends more than 200 meters astern of the tug, then a third similar white light in line with the others, the three at such a height that the lowest is at least 4 meters above the hull. An after masthead light is mandatory if the towing vessel is 50 meters or more in length; the light is optional in the case of smaller vessels. When towing astern, a yellow towing light is required above the sternlight.

Referring to the inland rules, we find that the lights for vessels towing and pushing are essentially the same as required by the international regulations, but with the usual modifications to accommodate the different dimensions of non-seagoing vessels. International Regulation 24(a) has been changed to make it clear that the corresponding Inland Rule 24(a) applies to a vessel towing astern. An example of U.S. practice influencing international regulations can be seen, now, in that both sets of rules permit the carriage of these lights on either the forward or after mast. If they are carried forward, then a masthead light higher than and abaft the forward white lights must be carried. If they are carried aft then a forward 20-point masthead light must be carried. Behind this option lies the fact that, in many cases, the requirement to carry two or three white masthead lights on the foremast of small tugs would cause glare problems on the bridge.

A power-driven vessel pushing ahead or towing alongside in inland waters carries the same two masthead lights as a vessel on the high seas but adds two yellow towing lights in a vertical line. The international regulations do not require such distinctive stern lighting, and the provision for them in the inland rules is to eliminate the problem of an overtaking vessel, seeing only a white light and not appreciating the task in which the overtaken vessel is engaged.

On the Western Rivers, and on any other waters specified by the secretary, vessels towing alongside or pushing ahead are exempt from the requirement to display any white masthead lights. This continuation of previous practice makes allowance for the limiting vertical clearances of bridges under which the tug will pass. If white lights were fitted, they would be close to the pilothouse and create excessive reflection and backscatter, impairing night vision. Also, little additional warning would be afforded by using white lights because of the frequent bends on the Western Rivers.

Finally, both sets of rules provide for the case where in distress situations, mariners who normally do not engage in towing operations cannot comply with the rules for towing lights when they are attempting to render assistance to another vessel.

## Lights for Tows

The international rules make a distinction between vessels towed and vessels being pushed ahead. The latter-type vessels are lighted by a single pair of sidelights at the forward end, whether being pushed singly or in a group. However, there is a modern development in which tugs and barges are capable of being mechanically locked so rigidly that they can operate in the pushing mode as one unit even on the high seas. Between them they show only the lights for a single power-driven vessel.

The lights for a vessel being towed astern or alongside are the same as for sailing vessels under way, consisting of the usual sidelights and the fixed 12-point sternlight. Several vessels being towed alongside as a group are lighted as one vessel. Inconspicuous tows, such as partly submerged objects, do not show such lights but instead must exhibit one or, more likely, several all-round white lights. Finally to cover all eventualities Rule 24(h) states:

> Where from any sufficient cause it is impractical for a vessel or object being towed to exhibit the lights prescribed . . . all possible measures shall be taken to light the vessel or object towed or at least indicate the presence of the unlighted vessel or object.

One difference between the international regulations and the inland rules is that the latter prescribe a special flashing light for certain towing operations. This light is additional to the normal sidelights for a vessel, or a group of vessels lighted as one vessel, being pushed ahead. It is a

16- to 20-point yellow light placed as far forward as practicable on the centerline of the tow. The frequency of flashes of this light should clearly distinguish it from the flashing light used by non-displacement craft.

### Tug and Tow Jointly Responsible for Proper Lights on Tow

A tug is not only liable for showing improper lights herself that contribute to a collision, but is jointly responsible with the vessel in tow for proper lights on the tow. An interesting case involving in liability both tug and tow occurred some years ago in Norfolk harbor, when a tug with a covered barge on each side brought one of the barges into collision with a ferry crossing from starboard and therefore having the right-of-way. On the showing that there were no lights on the barges, which were high enough to blanket the tug's sidelights, and that towing lights of the tug, instead of being in a vertical line, were suspended from either end of a horizontal spar across the flagstaff at distances below the spar supposed to differ by three feet, the tug and the tow were found fully liable for the damage to the ferry.[19] Another case confirming the doctrine of the towing vessel's responsibility for the absence of proper lights on her tow was decided in a collision in New York harbor between a ferryboat which should have kept out of the way and a barge in tow having no light on her bow. In a unique decision, the three vessels involved—ferry, tug, and barge, the last two belonging to the same owner—were found equally liable, with the result that the ferry recovered from the other two an amount equal to two-thirds of her damage.[20]

It should be noted that all of the above cases refer to the towing of barges, presumably with no motive power available, i.e., "dumb" barges. In a situation where the tug is the servant of the tow—i.e., the tug is assisting and responding to the orders from a manned ship, perhaps when maneuvering in confined waters—then it is more probable that it is the tow's responsibility for exhibiting proper lights.[21] In England, the Court of Appeal, in 1953, found the uncompleted aircraft carrier *Albion*, although under tow on the high seas, at fault after a collision in which a merchant vessel was sunk. The carrier, and not the tugs, was held liable for her defective port sidelight and also for her failure to show not-under-command lights.[22]

### Anchor Lights

Reference has already been made to a case proving that the same strictness in regard to lights is applied to vessels at anchor as when under way.[23]

---

[19] Foster v. Merchants and Miners Transportation Co. (Va. 1905) 134 F.964.
[20] The *Socony No. 123* (N.Y. 1935) 10 F. Supp 341.
[21] The *Mary Hounsell* (1879) 4 PD 204.
[22] The *Albion;* Thomas Stone (Shipping) Ltd. v. Admiralty [1953] Lloyd's Rep. 239.
[23] The *Chester O. Swain* (CCA N.Y. 1935) 76 F.2d 890.

The *Scantic* shared the damages in that case because of her inability to satisfy the court that her irregular lights *could not have contributed to the collision*. It was the same relentless test that is put on every infraction of the rules that precedes a collision.

Similarly, the Monrovian ship *Coral I* was at anchor in light conditions in the Suez Bay on a dark, clear night when she was struck by the Greek ship *Neil Armstrong* in ballast. Evidence revealed that the Monrovian ship had run out of fuel for the ship's generator, that the ship was lit internally by oil lamps, and the court concluded that she was not exhibiting anchor lights in accordance with the regulations.[24] Although the Greek ship was faulted for failing to keep a proper lookout and proceeding at an excessive speed, the *Coral I* was found to bear the greater part of the blame and apportioned 60 percent of the damages.

More recently, however, even though a moored vessel's failure to display an all-round white light may have violated inland Rule 30, this omission in restricted visibility in the Gulf Intracoastal Waterway neither caused collision nor would have prevented her from being struck by an imprudently navigated tug.[25]

The lights for a vessel at anchor are described in Rule 30 of both international and inland rules. (Subsection (d) applies only to vessels aground, and so has been omitted from this discussion.) The international regulation is as follows:

Rule 30 Anchored vessels
    (a) A vessel at anchor shall exhibit where it can best be seen:
        (i) in the fore part, an all-round white light or one ball;
        (ii) at or near the stern and at a lower level than the light prescribed in subparagraph (i), an all-round white light.
    (b) A vessel of less than 50 metres in length may exhibit an all-round white light where it can best be seen instead of the lights prescribed in paragraph (a) of this rule.
    (c) A vessel at anchor may, and a vessel of 100 metres and more in length shall, also use the available working or equivalent lights to illuminate her decks.
    (e) A vessel of less than 7 metres in length, when at anchor, not in or near a narrow channel fairway or anchorage, or where other vessels normally navigate, shall not be required to exhibit the lights or shapes prescribed in paragraphs (a) or (b) of this rule.

The inland rule is the same as that of the international regulations with but one addition. The addition provides that vessels less than 20 meters in length need not show anchor lights when in a specially designated anchorage area.

Especially noteworthy is the fact that anchor lights are visible all around the horizon, and that where the length of the vessel requires two lights,

---

[24] The *Coral I* [1982] 1 Lloyd's Rep. 441.
[25] Self-Towing v. Brown Marine, 1987 AMC 1068.

or a small vessel elects to be lighted as a large vessel, it is the forward light that is the higher, reversing the relative heights of the underway range lights. One practical import of this is that in maneuvering to avoid a large vessel at anchor forward, it should be remembered that any effect of wind or current would be in the direction indicated by a line from the higher (bow) light toward the lower. While the courts failed to find a steamship at fault for having her forward anchor light 10 feet higher than her after light instead of the then-required 15 feet higher, in a case where the testimony showed the lights were seen by other pilots 5½ miles away and the collision was due to improper lookout on the colliding steamer,[26] nevertheless, the distinction in the requirements due to a vessel's length is likely to be strictly enforced, particularly when the vessel involved is 50 meters in length or longer. Thus, in the case of a 271-foot barge anchored in Chesapeake Bay that was struck by a pilot boat five minutes after her after light had blown out in a puff of wind and while a seaman was overhauling the light, the barge (which was sunk) was held solely at fault for the collision. As said by the court in referring to Article 11 of the then relevant inland rules:

> The provisions of this article, which requires a vessel of 150 feet or upwards in length when at anchor to carry two lights, one at the forward part and the other at or near the stern at a lower height, to indicate the length of the vessel and the direction in which she is pointing, is of great importance and must be strictly observed, and, if violated, a loss caused by a collision resulting must be borne by the vessel so violating it.[27]

There is also a requirement for vessels at anchor to illuminate their decks with such working lights as they may have. It is possible that such lights could be confusing, particularly against background lighting, and that illumination of the stack could be a more effective measure.

Subject to any local rules, a vessel secured to a buoy may be regarded as a vessel at anchor. She is made fast to moorings that are themselves attached to the ground by an anchor or the equivalent of an anchor.[28]

### Vessel Made Fast to Another Must Have Own Lights

Of particular interest to the naval service, with the frequent nesting of vessels at anchor, is the requirement of the courts that a vessel made fast to another at anchor must maintain her own proper anchor lights. It was so held in a collision between one of two barges attached to each other and a car float in Norfolk harbor.[29] It has long been held by the courts that every vessel in an anchor nest in fog must make proper sound signals

---

[26] The *John G. McCullough* (CCA Va. 1916) 239 F.111.
[27] The *Santiago* (Pa. 1908) 160 F.742.
[28] The *Dunhelm* (1884) 9 P.D. 164, 171.
[29] The *Prudence* (Va. 1912) 197 F.479.

for a vessel at anchor whether her own anchor is down or not.[30] On the other hand, in a case with the impressive title Emperor of All the Russias v. the *Heipershausen,* the district court of New York held that a steam launch made fast to a boom projecting 60 feet from the side of a man-of-war at anchor in New York harbor need not exhibit any light. It seems that the Russian cruiser *Dimitri Donskoi* was visiting the East Coast during the Columbian Naval Exposition of 1893, and while she was lying in the North River at anchor with proper lights burning, two tugs with a tow of barges passed between her and the piers, so close that one of the barges struck and sank the steam launch, at the same time knocking the boom around against the captain's gig, which was also damaged. It was argued that the steam launch was not lighted, but the court held that inasmuch as the boom did not project over 60 feet, the minimum passing distance at that time prescribed by statute in New York harbor, no light was necessary on the launch, and the tugs were fully liable for the damage.[31]

### Lights for a Vessel Alongside Wharf

Strictly speaking, a vessel moored at a wharf is not at anchor, as implied by the distinction in the rules: A vessel is "underway" when she is not at anchor, or made fast to the shore, or aground. From the standpoint of her ability to maneuver to avoid collision, of course, there is little to distinguish the three not-underway situations. The practical necessity of lights to give notice to approaching vessels varies according to circumstances. In several old cases the courts have decided that a vessel moored in the usual way alongside a wharf and not in the way of other boats need not exhibit lights.[32] But a vessel lying moored at the end of a wharf on a dark night in the navigable part of a narrow stream, constantly traversed by different kinds of craft, is required by the special circumstances, in the exercise of common prudence, to carry a light, whether or not it is expressly required by the rules.[33] And, of course, the rule may be further modified by a local harbor regulation, disregard of which is legally as serious as disregard of the inland or international rules. The following extract from the Seattle harbor ordinance is typical of the rule that prevails in many organized ports:

> Every vessel or obstruction . . . while lying at any pier or other structure in Seattle Harbor between the hours of sunset and sunrise shall display at least one (1) white light at the outer end of the vessel or obstruction, which

[30] The *Cohocton* (CCA N.Y. 1924) 299 F.319; the *Southway* (N.Y. 1924) 2 F.2d 1009.
[31] The *Dimitri Donskoi* (N.Y. 1894) 60 F.111.
[32] Denty v. the *Martin Dallman* (Va. 1895) 70 F.797; City of New York v. the *Express* (N.Y. 1891) 61 F.513.
[33] The *Millville* (N.J. 1905) 137 F.974.

white light or lights shall show clearly from seaward and be so constructed and of such character as to be visible at least one (1) mile in clear weather.[34]

Lights for barges moored to a bank or a dock are included in the Pilot Rules of Annex V of the Inland Navigational Rules Act of 1980.

### Lights for a Vessel Aground

Rule 30, international regulations, also contains the following provision:

Rule 30. Anchored vessel and vessel aground
(d) A vessel aground shall exhibit the lights prescribed in paragraph (a) or (b) of this rule and in addition, where they can best be seen:
(i) two all-round red lights in a vertical line;
(ii) three balls in a vertical line.
(f) A vessel of less than 12 metres in length, when aground, shall not be required to exhibit the lights or shapes prescribed in sub-paragraphs (d) (i) and (ii) of this Rule.

The significance of this rule is, of course, that it provides statutory sanction to the fact that a vessel aground is in the same helpless category as a vessel at anchor, though additional lights must be carried not only to indicate her predicament, but also to warn other vessels.

### Fishing Vessel Lights

Previously, the lights for vessels engaged in fishing in inland waters were slightly different from those pertaining to the high seas. Under the Inland Navigational Rules Act of 1980 both are now the same, eliminating the variance in requirements and extending the application of the lights to all waters of the United States.

### Vessels Not Under Command or Restricted in Their Ability to Maneuver

Other than for the Great Lakes, there were no previous rules for vessels of the above category in our internal waters. Now Inland Rule 27 provides for the lighting of vessels not under command or restricted in their ability to maneuver. The rule is essentially the same as International Regulation 27.

A vessel not under command is one which through some *exceptional* circumstance is unable to maneuver as required by the rules. She then, by night, displays two all-round red lights in a vertical line, which gives her right-of-way over all other categories of vessels under way that are in sight of her. This important privilege must not be assumed for mere convenience but must be justified by genuine defects that prevent compliance with the rules. A collision occurred in the Dover Straits on 10 November 1969 in good visibility, but with a force-eight wind blowing.

---

[34] Seattle Harbor Ordinance (1921).

One of the ships, the *Djerba*, had been subjected to four days of heavy weather and was carrying not-under-command lights, although she had full use of her engines and steering. It was held in the admiralty court that the *Djerba* was not justified in carrying not-under-command lights and that she was in breach of the collision regulations. Moreover, as a ship that would otherwise be a give-way vessel under the crossing rule, she was not relieved of her duty to give way, although she carried such lights. Furthermore, under the 1960 Rules then in force, she should not have carried a white masthead light as well as the two red not-under-command lights. On apportioning 60 percent of the blame for the collision to the *Djerba*, Mr. Justice Brandon said:

> It is important that ships which are genuinely disabled from manoeuvring adequately should have both the right and the duty to advertise the fact by exhibiting appropriate signals and so to make it clear to other ships that they must take steps to keep clear of them. It is equally important that ships which are not genuinely disabled, although they may be under certain difficulties, should not claim this special right and privilege . . . without proper justification.[35]

This judgment was upheld on appeal, when it was clearly stated that it was not right to say that the *Djerba* was not under command and that:

> even if only the red lights had been shown instead of the white masthead light and red lights, *Djerba* was not excused from complying with rule 19 (duties of a give-way vessel in the crossing situation) unless she was actually not under command.[36]

A vessel restricted in her ability to maneuver is covered in those cases where the nature of her work imposes restriction on the movement of the vessel to such an extent that she cannot readily keep out of the way of another vessel. Rule 3(g) of each set of rules lists identical operations that justify displaying these lights, though the preamble makes it clear that the list is not exhaustive. It can be expected that the courts are unlikely to find favor with a vessel that claimed the privilege that these lights bring without proper justification. It is not intended that vessels engaged in routine towing operations should declare that they are restricted in their ability to deviate from their course.

Within the category of vessels restricted in their ability to maneuver there are four different kinds of lighting prescribed:
- mine-clearance vessels show three all-round green lights in addition to the normal lights for a power-driven vessel under way;
- dredgers and similar vessels show three all-round lights (red-white-red) in a vertical line in addition to the normal lights for a power-driven

---

[35] The *Djerba*, Q.B. (Adm. Ct.) [1976] 1 Lloyd's Rep. 50.
[36] The *Djerba*, C.A. [1976] 2 Lloyd's Rep. 41.

vessel under way and, where an obstruction exists, two red lights on the obstructed side and two green lights on the clear side;

- tugs towing astern with a difficult tow show the same red-white-red configuration in addition to normal towing lights;
- other vessels show the red-white-red configuration in addition to normal lights.

Another collision in the Suez Bay illustrates the importance of showing the correct combination of these lights. The hopper dredger *Maria Luisa Prima,* on charter to an Italian company, was struck by the Chinese motor vessel *Jin Ping.* The court found that the collision was solely caused by the fault of the dredger in not exhibiting the correct lights for a dredger making way in that *Jin Ping* could only see the hopper's accommodation lights and the red-white-and-red lights in a vertical line. In a confusing situation it would appear that an inexperienced officer of the watch failed to display side and sternlights when changing from a stationary to moving mode.[37]

### Vessels Constrained by Their Draft

Unique to the international regulations is the three all-round red lights in a vertical line for a vessel whose draft in the available depth of water severely restricts her ability to change course. Not only the depth of water, but also the available navigable water width should be used as a factor to determine whether a vessel may consider herself as constrained by her draft. A vessel navigating in an area with a small underkeel clearance but with adequate space to take avoiding action in good time should not be regarded as a vessel constrained by her draft.

This category originated from the very real problems experienced by deep-draft ships on passage through shallow seas, where shallow-water effect should impinge on normal maneuverability. The signal does not give right-of-way to the constrained vessel, but International Regulation 18(d) directs other vessels to avoid impeding her. There have been complaints voiced that large ships are displaying these lights in areas where there are no constraints caused by depth of water or sea room, obviously hoping that other vessels will keep clear of them. In the event of a collision it is certain that the courts would look closely at the reasons why the three red lights were displayed.

Although the lights are optional on the high seas, they are mandatory in some ports of the world. On 11 October 1972, a collision occurred in the Thames Estuary in darkness and in clear weather, between the West German coaster *Rustringen* and the Dutch tanker *Kylix.* Both ships were

---

[37] The *Jin Ping* [1983] 1 Lloyd's Rep. 641.

inward bound, and while overtaking the coaster, the *Kylix* struck and sunk the *Rustringen*. Among many other faults that emerged, the *Kylix* was in breach of a local rule, Bylaw 27, for failing to show three red all-round lights.[38]

The Inland Navigational Rules Act of 1980 avoids the subjective nature of the international regulations, pointing out in the accompanying House of Representatives report that it could lead to abuses and result in situations wherein a vessel might claim a right-of-way to which she was not entitled, thereby creating a dangerous situation. Accordingly, there is no provision in U.S. inland waters for lights of a vessel constrained by her draft. Nonetheless, mariners should be aware of the international signal, which could be met on the high seas outside of the demarcation line for inland waters.

### Requirements Regarding Lights Should Be Strictly Observed

In conclusion, it may be said that the courts are strict in enforcing the requirements for proper lights—and rightly—but not unreasonably so. In a collision between two sailing vessels approaching so that one of them had her red light toward the other, it was held to be immaterial that her green light was out, since its presence could not have averted, nor its absence contributed to, the collision.[39] It should be remembered that neglect by a vessel to show regulation lights does not relieve another vessel from observing the rules of navigation and using every precaution to avoid collision with her,[40] and that a steamer failing to see lights on a sailing vessel, which were clearly visible from the steamer's position, was not absolved from responsibility merely because the lights were somewhat faultily placed. This case, like many others, became one of mutual fault.[41] In any doubtful situation the courts are very likely to have the attitude that:

> The rule requiring lights may as well be disregarded altogether as to be only partially complied with, and in a way which fails to be of any real service in indicating to other vessels the position and course of the one carrying them.[42]

After all, the only safe rule to follow is to be sure that one's running or riding lights during darkness or restricted visibility conform as closely as possible to the lights specified by the rules *in force where the vessel may happen to be,* remembering that any departure from the rules that is

---

[38] The *Kylix*, Q.B. (Adm. Ct.) [1979] 1 Lloyd's Rep. 133.
[39] The *Robert Graham Dun* (CCA N.H. 1895) 70 F.270.
[40] Swift v. Brownell (CC Mass. 1875) Fed. Case No. 13,695.
[41] The *Samuel H. Crawford* (N.Y. 1881) 6 F.906.
[42] The *Titan* (CC N.Y. 1885) 23 F.413.

followed by a collision will be subject to the test so often annunciated by the Supreme Court:

> But when a ship at the time of collision is in actual violation of a statutory rule intended to prevent collision, it is no more than a reasonable presumption that the fault, if not the sole cause, was at least a contributory cause of the disaster. In such a case the burden rests upon the ship of showing, not merely that her fault might not have been one of the causes, or that it probably was not, but that it could not have been.[43]

If lights are lost or extinguished, then this must be detected by the watch and repair or replacement carried out as soon as possible. Emergency lights, whether oil or battery, should comply with the regulations as strictly as normal lights and should be properly maintained and kept ready for use. If severe weather prevents immediate attention, because of danger to personnel, a delay may be justified, but should be recorded in the official deck log.

## SUMMARY

The importance of proper running and riding lights is emphasized by the fact that so many of the international and inland rules relate to them, and that in collision cases the courts construe strongly against vessels that disregard their requirements.

The international regulations and the inland rules are now largely in agreement, with clear requirements for the placing of lights. Important differences between the rules are now confined to the range light on the Great Lakes and the special flashing light on the Western Rivers.

With virtually no major recent court cases concerning the incorrect siting of lights, the lessons for mariners today must be:

• display the correct lights for the situation they are in;
• scrupulously avoid a misleading mixture of lights when the situation changes;
• do not falsely claim privilege through the display of improper lights; and
• be alert for those vessels that cannot comply with the letter of the law and may give an inadvertent impression of their course, size, and proximity.

---

[43] The *Pennsylvania* 86 U.S. (19 Wall) 125 (1873).

# 4

# Sound Signals

---

### Difference in Meaning of Signals
The most important differences to be found in the rules of the road on the high seas and in the inland waters of the United States have to do with the sound signal requirements for vessels approaching one another in clear weather. The purpose of this chapter is to analyze the differences in whistle signals prescribed by the respective rules for vessels meeting, overtaking, or crossing in good visibility.

As a preliminary consideration, it may be pointed out that there is a fundamental difference in the meaning of the conventional one- and two-short-blast signals in the two jurisdictions. Under international rules the signals are purely rudder signals, to be given when, and only when, a change of course is executed. It is therefore unnecessary to specify the use of a signal in a particular situation, a general rule being stated that provides for a signal in every situation when the course is changed. Under the inland rules, on the other hand, the one- and two-short-blast signals are not for the purpose of announcing a change in course, but to indicate the side on which an approaching vessel will pass.

### Signals Compulsory Since 1890
It is interesting to note that it was not until the adoption of the 1889 International Rules in 1890—made effective in the United States by presidential proclamation 1 July 1897—that the use of sound signals by power-driven vessels at sea, except in fog, became compulsory. The first international rules, adopted by England and France in 1863, and the revised rules, adopted in 1885 by those countries and the United States, Germany, Belgium, Japan, Norway, and Denmark, authorized certain whistle signals but made their use discretionary with the navigator. At

the International Convention of 1889, however, the delegates, after some debate on the subject, decided that they would no longer leave to the discretion of the mariner the question of whether, in a particular case, there was less risk of using the whistle and being misunderstood or in not using it at all. Accordingly, the former Article 28, International Rules, was passed to read:

> Art. 28. The words "short blast" used in this article shall mean a blast of about one second's duration.
> When vessels are in sight of one another, a steam vessel underway, in taking any course authorized or required by these rules, shall indicate that course by the following signals on her whistle or siren, namely:
> One short blast to mean, "I am directing my course to starboard."
> Two short blasts to mean, "I am directing my course to port."
> Three short blasts to mean, "My engines are going at full speed astern."

When the 1889 rules were revised in 1948, the International Conference reiterated the substance of the former Article 28, modifying the three-blast signal's meaning to correspond to the interpretation of the courts, namely, that the backing signal is proper when the engines are going astern at any speed. A limited in-doubt signal was provided and additional special whistle signals were authorized. In 1960 when further revision of the rules occurred at the International Conference on Safety of Life at Sea, 1960, a new optional whistle signal was authorized. The International Conference in 1972 added a new set of signals to be given and answered by vessels in an overtaking situation in a narrow channel or fairway, and removed the restriction that the optional in-doubt signal be used only by the stand-on vessel, making its use mandatory for all vessels in doubt. The present rule now reads:

> Rule 34. Manœuvring and warning signals
> (a) When vessels are in sight of one another, a power-driven vessel underway, when manœuvring as authorized or required by these rules, shall indicate that manœuvre by the following signals on her whistle:
> —one short blast to mean "I am altering my course to starboard";
> —two short blasts to mean "I am altering my course to port";
> —three short blasts to mean "I am operating astern propulsion."
> (b) Any vessel may supplement the whistle signals prescribed in paragraph (a) of this rule by light signals, repeated as appropriate, whilst the manœuvre is being carried out.
> (i) these light signals shall have the following significance:
> —one flash to mean "I am altering my course to starboard";
> —two flashes to mean "I am altering my course to port";
> —three flashes to mean "I am operating astern propulsion";
> (ii) the duration of each flash shall be about one second, the interval between flashes shall be about one second, and the interval between successive signals shall be not less than ten seconds;
> (iii) the light used for this signal shall, if fitted, be an all-round white light, visible at a minimum range of 5 miles, and shall comply with the provisions of Annex I to these Regulations.
> (c) When in sight of one another in a narrow channel or fairway:

(i) a vessel intending to overtake another shall in compliance with Rule 9(e)(i) indicate her intention by the following signals on her whistle:

—two prolonged blasts followed by one short blast to mean "I intend to overtake you on your starboard side";

—two prolonged blasts followed by two short blasts to mean "I intend to overtake you on your port side".

(ii) the vessel about to be overtaken when acting in accordance with Rule 9(e)(i) shall indicate her agreement by the following signal on her whistle:

—one prolonged, one short, one prolonged and one short blast, in that order.

(d) When vessels in sight of one another and approaching each other and from any cause either vessel fails to understand the intentions or actions of the other, or is in doubt whether sufficient action is being taken by the other to avoid collision, the vessel in doubt shall immediately indicate such doubt by giving at least five short and rapid blasts on the whistle. Such signal may be supplemented by a light signal of at least five short and rapid flashes.

(e) A vessel nearing a bend or an area of a channel or fairway where other vessels may be obscured by an intervening obstruction shall sound one prolonged blast. Such signal shall be answered with a prolonged blast by any approaching vessel that may be within hearing around the bend or behind the intervening obstruction.

(f) If whistles are fitted on a vessel at a distance apart of more than 100 metres, one whistle only shall be used for giving manœuvring and warning signals.

If we scrutinize the present rule with a little more than ordinary care, five important provisions will become apparent:

• The mandatory use of the signals mentioned in Rule 34(a) is evident in the words "shall indicate." Even if it is thought that the signals may not be heard,[1] or the officer on watch considers they would disturb his or her own ship, especially the master,[2] does not matter—they still must be given.

• The one-blast signal indicates a lawful change of course to the right and the two-blast signal indicates a lawful change of course to the left. That is, both the one- and the two-blast signals are rudder signals and therefore should never be used, either for an original signal or a reply, except when the course is changed. Thus, these signals are not required if the rudder is used to counteract the effect of the wind and tidal current,[3] or if using the rudder to check the swing of the ship when backing,[4] and even, apparently, if a vessel rounds the bend of a river with her rudder amidships.[5]

---

[1] The *Haugland* (1921), 15 Aspinall M.C. 318.

[2] The *Fremona* (1907) Deane J.

[3] The *Gulf of Suez* (1921) 7 Ll. L. Rep. 159.

[4] The *Aberdonian* (1910) 11 Aspinall MC 393.

[5] The *Heranger* (1937) 58 Ll. L. Rep. 377.

- If a change of course is made or the engines are reversed in accordance with the rules, the one-, two-, or three-blast signal must be given by a power-driven vessel whenever another vessel is in sight. The obligation of signaling is plain, whether the other vessel is ahead, abeam, or astern, and whether she is a power-driven vessel with a whistle or a sailing vessel without one.[6] Thus, a tug in collision with a sailing vessel was found at fault for failure to signify by two short blasts her alteration of course to port.[7] And conversely, the use of any of these signals under conditions of visibility so low that neither the other vessel nor her lights can be seen is prohibited.[8] However, a vessel is unlikely to be exonerated for not sounding signals through failure to sight another vessel because of a poor lookout[9] or because the other vessel was momentarily out of sight.[10]
- The signal of five or more short blasts is required of any vessel in doubt and, like the blind bend and overtaking signals, is not restricted to power-driven vessels. It can, however, be used only by vessels in sight of one another.
- The one-, two-, three- and five-blast signals may be supplemented by light signals. The latter need not be synchronized with the sound signals and may be repeated at intervals, without the sound signal, while the immediate maneuver is in progress. If a further alteration is made shortly after the initial maneuver is completed, it is still necessary to make a sound signal for the second maneuver even if it is identical to the first. The light signal alone will not suffice. As the reception of sound signals in other vessels can never be certain, especially in diesel and gas-turbine ships with high noise levels, the visual light signals are an important additional indication of action taken or for the reinforcement of the in-doubt or wake-up signal of five short blasts.

### Signals Under International Rules

Let us consider the application of the sound signals in Rule 34 when two vessels encounter each other outside the inland waters of the United States.

(1) Vessels meeting under international rules. Rule 14(a), governing the head-on or meeting situation, states: "when two power-driven vessels are meeting on reciprocal or nearly reciprocal courses so as to involve risk of collision each shall alter her course to starboard so that each will

---

[6] The *Comus* (CCA N.Y. 1927) 19 F.2d 774.

[7] The *Kathy K* (Can. Ct.) [1972] 2 Lloyd's Rep. 36.

[8] The *Parthian* (CCA 1893) 55 F.426.

[9] The *Lucille Bloomfield* [1966] 2 Lloyd's Rep. 245.

[10] The *Heire* (1935) 51 Ll. L. Rep. 325.

pass on the port side of the other." It is clear that when risk of collision exists in this situation, each vessel must turn to the right, at least enough to render safe a port-to-port passing, and when the necessary change in course is made, Rule 34 requires the one-blast signal. It is equally clear, in the language of the rule, that the mandate to change course does not apply if the present course of the two vessels will carry them well clear of each other. If the course is not changed, no whistle signal is authorized or permitted, the one-blast signal being a mandatory rudder signal. Should one vessel be in doubt as to whether holding on will give sufficient clearance and accordingly execute right rudder and give the one-blast signal, the other vessel then finding the clearance even more ample without change of course on her part, may lawfully hold her course. But if she does, she cannot use her whistle, since to do so would indicate an action that she is not taking. The practical risk of this apparent ignoring of the other vessel's signal is obvious, and may be avoided by the very simple expedient of keeping within the law by changing course to the right and blowing one blast. The point to remember here is that there is legal fault if you use your whistle without at least a slight change in course.

Conversely, you cannot, in the meeting situation under international rules, lawfully change course at any time without using the one-blast signal. In the collision of the *Anselm* and the *Cyril,* the two vessels met end on in the estuary of the Amazon River, and when they were about 2 miles apart the *Anselm* changed course slightly to the right. A moment later, seeing that the *Cyril* was apparently changing to port, she again executed right rudder, and this time gave the required one-blast signal. In the collision that followed the *Anselm* was held at fault by the British court of appeals for failure to blow one blast the first time she altered her course.[11] Under very similar circumstances the *Malin Head* met the *Corinthian* in the St. Lawrence River. The *Malin Head* changed course to the right and blew one blast, but did not repeat the signal when the failure of the *Corinthian* to go to starboard compelled her again to change course, after steadying for about two minutes, this time with hardover helm. As in the other case, the court of appeals held the offending vessel accountable for the omission, notwithstanding that the lower court exonerated her on the grounds that testimony showed the failure did not contribute to the collision.[12]

In a harbor collision at Harwich, England, the coaster *Thuroklint* was held mainly to blame when, among other things, she failed to indicate a series of alterations of course to starboard by sounding signals of one

---

[11] The *Anselm,* 10 Aspinall M.C. (N.S.) 438.
[12] The *Corinthian,* 11 Aspinall M.C. (N.S.) 264 (Admiralty).

short blast. An inward-bound vessel, she had changed her pilots on the port side of the approach channel and then crossed ahead of the outcoming ferry *Koningin Juliana* in an attempt to gain her correct side. The *Koningin Juliana* was also castigated for using an incorrect whistle signal, namely two short blasts, when she stopped her alteration to starboard, having turned nearly 30 degrees, and attempted to pass ahead of the *Thuroklint* on a steady course across the channel. The signal was unlawful because she "was not directing her course to port at the time when she sounded them."[13]

In another meeting case in a narrow channel, the *Joaquin Ponte Naya* was proceeding up the River Parana on the wrong side of the channel when she met the *Martin Fierro* coming downriver. In attempting to cross to her starboard side the *Joaquin Ponte Naya* failed to sound one short blast on altering course, a fault that contributed to her receiving 85 percent of the blame for the subsequent collision.[14]

An interesting interpretation of the use of the one-short-blast signal arose from the court findings of a collision on the River Maas. The *City of Capetown* was inbound and collided with the outward-bound *Adolf Leonhardt*. The latter vessel failed to get to her own starboard side of the channel promptly enough after leaving her dock and was found to be two-thirds to blame. However, she was found not to be at fault for failing to sound one short blast when first altering to starboard some five minutes before the collision, because she was not then taking action to avoid a collision situation. Although this finding was based on the local collision regulations, which supplemented the international regulations, it was further said that even if the latter had required her to sound such a signal, the failure to do so was not causative to the collision.[15] This, perhaps, highlights the point that maneuvering and warning signals under the international regulations are required only when "manoeuvring as authorized by these Rules," which in this meeting case did not apply until the second alteration of course to starboard. However, it is unlikely that a vessel would be faulted for sounding the *correct* whistle signals when *maneuvering* on the high seas in sight of another vessel, even if risk of collision did not exist at that moment.

As indicated in the wording of the rule, vessels meeting end on or nearly end on are bound to pass port to port. It is only when the vessels are so far to starboard of each other as not to be considered as meeting head-on, that they escape the requirements to change course to starboard; and in that case no change of course, and therefore no whistle signal, is required. It is difficult to picture a meeting situation at sea where the

---

[13] The *Koningin Juliana* Q.B. (Adm. Ct.) [1973] 2 Lloyd's Rep. 308.

[14] The *Martin Fierro* Q.B. (Adm. Ct.) [1974] 2 Lloyd's Rep. 203.

[15] The *Adolf Leonhardt* Q.B. (Adm. Ct.) [1973] 2 Lloyd's Rep. 324.

two-blast signal would be valid, for in any borderline case where there is doubt as to whether the two vessels are meeting end on or are already heading clear for a starboard-to-starboard passing, then the vessel(s) in doubt must assume it is a head-on situation in accordance with Rule 14(c).

(2) Overtaking and overtaken vessels under international rules. When any vessel is overtaking another vessel at sea, her action is governed primarily by Rule 13, International Rules. This rule, which applies not only when the overtaking vessel is coming from well aft but when she is so near the dividing bearing between an overtaking and a crossing vessel as to be in doubt as to her status, provides in part:

> Notwithstanding anything contained in the Rules of this Section any vessel overtaking any other shall keep out of the way of the vessel being overtaken.

The overtaken vessel, thus having the right-of-way, is governed by Rule 17, International Rules, which provides in part:

> Where one of two vessels is to keep out of the way the other shall keep her course and speed.

Applying Rule 34 to this situation, it is evident that the overtaking vessel, unless she slows down, must change her course to one side or the other if necessary to clear, announcing any change in course with an appropriate whistle signal. The overtaken vessel, on the other hand, being under compulsion to maintain her course and speed, cannot answer the whistle of the other, though she may, if in doubt as to whether the overtaking vessel is taking sufficient action to avert collision, sound the signal of five or more short and rapid blasts to call the attention of the overtaking vessel to its duty to keep clear. Because of the provisions of Rule 34, the use of a rudder or reversing whistle signal here, too, is unlawful when there is no change in course or speed. When the overtaking vessel has passed well clear of the overtaken vessel and changes course a second time in order to return to her original heading, she must again use the proper signal, which will, of course, if the first signal was one blast, be two blasts. This signal, likewise, must remain unanswered.

Not only the overtaken vessel should consider the use of the danger signal. In 1972 off the Diamond Shore the Colombian freighter *Republican de Colombia* had overtaken the American container ship *Transhawaii* when she suffered a steering gear breakdown and swung across to port impaling herself on the bows of the latter. Among other failures the *Republican de Colombia* was at fault for not sounding a warning signal as soon as the situation began to develop, the officer of the watch having spent some three minutes attempting to rectify the malfunction.[16]

---

[16] R. A. Cahill, *Collisions and Their Causes* (London: Fairplay Publications, 1983), 94; also the *Fogo* [1967] 2 Lloyd's Rep. 208.

In narrow channels or fairways, the overtaken vessel is often required to assist in the manœuver, and the international rules provide for an *exchange* of whistle signals "when overtaking can take place only if the vessel to be overtaken has to take action to permit safe passing." The vessel intending to overtake shall indicate her intention by sounding one of the following signals on her whistle:

—two prolonged blasts followed by one short blast to mean "I intend to overtake you on your starboard side";
—two prolonged blasts followed by two short blasts to mean "I intend to overtake you on your port side."

The vessel to be overtaken shall, if in agreement, sound the following signal on her whistle: one prolonged, one short, one prolonged, and one short, in that order (International Code group "Charlie" meaning "affirmative"). The overtaken vessel shall then take steps to permit safe passing. If the overtaken vessel is not in agreement, she may sound instead the doubt signal of five or more short blasts. The overtaking vessel should not attempt passing until an agreement is reached, nor does agreement relieve her of her obligation to keep out of the way until well past and clear.

The tanker *Kylix*, which was mentioned earlier in Chapter 3 for not showing three red lights, was found to be at fault for failure to indicate that she was about to overtake the coaster *Rustringen* in the Thames Estuary. Local Bylaw 42 then made similar provision to the international regulation described above and the court found:

if such a signal had been sounded at a proper time, it would have alerted the master of *Rustringen* to what *Kylix* was doing appreciably earlier . . .which might well have prevented, or at any rate mitigated, the collision.[17]

The *Rustringen* compounded matters by altering course to starboard in front of the overtaking vessel, without making a signal of one short blast. The collision occurred one and one-half minutes later, with the *Rustringen*'s unsignaled alteration being held contrary to the international regulations and one of several causative factors.

(3) Crossing vessels under international rules. When two power-driven vessels are crossing so as to involve risk of collision, Rule 15 requires the vessel that has the other on her own starboard side to keep out of the way of the other. The stand-on vessel in the crossing situation, like the overtaken vessel, must hold her course and speed and consequently is forbidden to use the one-, two-, or three-blast signals of Rule 34. The give-way vessel, on the other hand, is required to keep out of the way, to take positive early action toward this end, to avoid, if the circumstances admit, crossing ahead of the other, and on approaching her, if necessary,

---

[17] The *Kylix* Q.B. (Adm. Ct.) [1979] 1 Lloyd's Rep. 141–142.

to slacken her speed or stop or reverse. If she turns to starboard to go under the stand-on vessel's stern, Rule 34 requires her to sound one blast; if she avoids crossing by sheering to port, a questionable maneuver, two blasts; and if she reverses her engines, three blasts; and all of these signals, so far as the stand-on vessel is concerned, must remain unanswered for the reason already given, that the latter can change neither course nor speed.

In a crossing case off Cape St. Vincent, a tanker, the *Statue of Liberty*, was the give-way vessel but took tardy and indecisive action to pass astern of the motor-vessel *Andulo*, which was the stand-on vessel. When about 1,600 yards apart, the *Andulo* first made a small alteration to port (mainly to get her on course for Casablanca), during which time the *Statue of Liberty* altered farther to starboard. Both ships increased their turn but a collision occurred. With regard to sound signals, neither ship signaled their first alteration nor did the *Statue of Liberty* indicate her second. Both were found at fault for these omissions, but only that of the *Statue of Liberty* was considered causative to the collision, which, compounded with other faults, resulted in her receiving 85 percent of the blame.[18] When two vessels on a fine crossing situation turned into each other and collided, both were held at fault for not signaling alterations of course.[19]

A vessel doubting the intentions or actions of the other vessel, whether stand-on or give-way, is required to give the signal prescribed in Rule 34(d). However, the sounding of this signal was judged as no excuse for a give-way vessel's failure to take appropriate action in a crossing situation in the Dover Straits. The Liberian ship *Genimar* was navigating contrary to the flow of a traffic separation scheme and approached the Greek bulk carrier *Larry L* on the latter's starboard bow. *Larry L* was navigating correctly in accordance with the traffic separation scheme, and her master's attitude appears to have been that since *Genimar* was proceeding in the wrong direction, it was for her to keep out of the way of *Larry L*.

> This attitude is exemplified by his two peremptory signals of five short blasts and his failure to take any action of any kind . . . In adopting this attitude the master of *Larry L* was plainly wrong.[20]

The *Larry L* was found two-thirds responsible for the subsequent collision.

In the *Ek/Debalzevo* collision (see Chapter 7) the former vessel, who was the stand-on vessel in a crossing situation, was found at fault for not sounding five short blasts when the other vessel failed to give way.[21]

In addition, 1972 Rule 17(a)(ii), subject to the qualification in Rule 17(c), now permits the stand-on vessel to "take action to avoid collision

---

[18] The *Statue of Liberty* (H.L.) [1971] 2 Lloyd's Rep. 277.
[19] The *Toni* [1973] 1 Lloyd's Rep. 79.
[20] The *Genimar*, Q.B. (Adm. Ct.) [1977] 2 Lloyd's Rep. 25.
[21] The *Ek* [1966] 1 Lloyd's Rep. 440.

by her manoeuvre alone, as soon as it becomes apparent to her that the vessel required to keep out of the way is not taking appropriate action in compliance with these Rules." When taking action under this rule, which applies equally to any stand-on vessel, not just the one in the crossing situation, the appropriate whistle signal in Rule 34(a) must be given. When, from any cause, the stand-on vessel "finds herself so close that collision cannot be avoided by the action of the give-way vessel alone, she *shall* take such action as will best aid to avoid collision." Even in extremis, she may not be excused for failure to indicate such action by the proper whistle if at that point she sheers to starboard or to port, or reverses her engines.[22]

(4) Nearing a bend in a channel under the international rules. Rule 34(e) prescribes a signal for a vessel approaching a bend or similar obstruction:

> A vessel nearing a bend or an area of a channel or fairway where other vessels may be obscured by an intervening obstruction shall sound one prolonged blast. Such signal shall be answered with a prolonged blast by any approaching vessel that may be within hearing around the bend or behind the intervening obstruction.

A prolonged blast is defined in Rule 32(c) to be a blast of four to six seconds' duration. A vessel around the bend hearing the signal must answer with a like signal. Henceforth, no other signals are given by either vessel until and unless one of the vessels changes course or backs down.

### Signals Under Inland Rules

We will next consider the action required of two power-driven vessels approaching each other so as to involve risk of collision in the inland waters of the United States, with particular reference to sound signals when meeting, crossing, or overtaking. Except that a somewhat larger angle on the bow is included by the courts to take care of vessels proceeding in opposite directions through winding channels, the three situations in the inland rules are similarly defined. In addition, the secretary of the department in which the Coast Guard is operating is authorized to develop local pilot rules as necessary to implement and interpret the inland rules.

The first important difference to note in the rules for inland waters is that the one- and two-short blasts are signals of intent and not of action. This will be discussed in the meeting and crossing situations sections. The three-short-blast signal remains, however, as in the international regulations, a signal of action meaning "I am operating astern propul-

---

[22] The *Comus* (CCA N.Y. 1927) 19 F.2d 774.

sion." Finally, there are different signals used in inland waters for the overtaking situation, also to be discussed later in this chapter.

**The In-Doubt or Danger Signal**

The definition and use of the in-doubt signal of at least five short and rapid blasts are the same for both sets of rules, although the inland rules also refer to it as the danger signal. It should be noted that this signal is in no sense optional but must be used whenever any vessel is in doubt as to the intentions or actions of another, whether the vessels are meeting, crossing, overtaking, or being overtaken. A vessel was found at fault for failure to use it in clear weather when in doubt as to the course or intention of another vessel whose lights were obscured by a deck load of lumber but whose whistle signal was heard somewhere ahead.[23] More recently, following a collision on the Mississippi River in 1974 when a tanker crossed from her starboard to her port side of the river ahead of a tug and tow on a reciprocal course, the tug was found partially at fault for not "immediately sounding what is commonly called a danger signal" when uncertainty as to the tanker's intentions arose. Although heard under Canadian jurisdiction, a similar opinion was voiced following an incident on the St. Lawrence Seaway where a motor vessel, forced into collision with a dock because another motor vessel failed to give sufficient room to pass, was to a minor extent at fault "for not giving the danger signal."[24]

An interesting test of the applicability of Inland Rule 34(d) concerning the danger signal arose in 1981. It was argued that the rule only applied when vessels saw each other and either had, or should have been, exchanging whistle signals to effect a safe passing in a head-on or crossing situation. It was submitted the rule did not apply in the case under consideration because the vessels had not been "approaching each other" since one vessel was overtaking another, rather than meeting or crossing its path. It was held that the language of the rule did not limit the danger signal to the situation where vessels are or ought to be exchanging maneuvering signals. The rule required a danger signal regardless of whether a threatening vessel was meeting, crossing, or overtaking another vessel. It was also held that the rule applied whenever danger of collision was, or should have been, recognized. The test was objective, and it was irrelevant that the officer of the watch had been quite certain in his own mind that no danger existed if that conviction had been unreasonable.[25]

[23] The *Virginia* (CCA 1916) 238 F.156.
[24] Gulf Coast Transit Co. v. M.T. *Anco Princess* et al. E.D. La. (1977) [1978] 1 Lloyd's Rep. 299.
[25] Hosei Kaiun Shoji Co. Ltd. v. The Canadian Tug *Seaspan Monarch*, U.S. District Court, Oregon, 1981.

The in-doubt signal is clearly intended by Inland Rule 34(d) to be used by vessels in sight of one another. If the vessels are not in sight of one another due to restricted visibility, only the signals prescribed in Rule 35 are required.[26]

## Signal for Blind Bend and Power-Driven Vessel Leaving Her Berth

The signal of one prolonged blast to be used by *all* vessels nearing a blind bend is the same under both sets of rules. Unlike the international regulations, this same signal is required in inland waters for a power-driven vessel leaving a dock or berth in clear weather. If she should back out of the berth, then the prolonged blast must be followed by three short blasts as soon as she comes in sight of another vessel.

## Bridge-to-Bridge Radiotelephone and Whistle Signals

A feature unique to the inland rules is that vessels reaching agreement on how to pass each other by use of bridge-to-bridge radiotelephone need not sound whistle signals. Mariners should not allow this practice to affect their use of whistle signals on waters not covered by the inland rules. For example, although no collision occurred, an ore carrier, the *Ore Chief,* was found totally to blame for forcing the tanker *Olympic Torch* aground when overtaking her in the River Schelde. Apart from condemning the unseamanlike behavior of the *Ore Chief,* it was held that

> the misunderstanding between the pilots as to the intentions of *Ore Chief* illustrated the undesirability of substituting imprecise signals on VHF for precise exchanges by whistle signals. . . . The provisions . . . were mandatory and it was not open to navigators to disregard them by agreement, whether overt or tacit. . . .[27]

Clearly, this last does not apply to waters governed by the inland rules. Moreover, mariners on inland waters should not neglect to use the bridge-to-bridge radiotelephone. In the case mentioned in the earlier discussion of danger signals, the tanker *Anco Princess*'s

> failure to attempt to contact the *Libby Black* via bridge-to-bridge radio was contrary to the purpose, if not the terms, of Vessel Bridge-to-Bridge Communications Act, 33 U.S.C. ss 1201 etc. . . . The mere presence of a radio on the bridge of a vessel obviously is meaningless if it is not put to use.[28]

Thus, on the inland waters of the United States, the radiotelephone should be used—at a minimum—to communicate intentions and thus

---

[26] *Liquilassie* Shipping Ltd. v. M.V. *Nipigon Bay* (Canada Fed. Ct. 1975) [1975] 2 Lloyd's Rep. 286.

[27] The *Ore Chief,* Q.B. (Adm. Ct.) [1974] 2 Lloyd's Rep. 433.

[28] Gulf Coast Transit Co. v. M.T. *Anco Princess* et al. E.D. La. (1977) [1978] 1 Lloyd's Rep. 299.

supplement whistle signals. Experience has shown that it is often possible to arrange a passing agreement on the radiotelephone prior to exchanging whistle signals, in which case the latter may be dispensed with. However, a timely exchange of whistle signals is required if for any reason a positive agreement cannot be reached.

## One- and Two-Short-Blast Signals, Inland Waters

As mentioned earlier, there is a major difference between the international regulations and the inland rules over the use of one- and two-short-blast signals by power-driven vessels in sight of each other. Inland Rule 34 retains the "signals of intent and reply" that are imbedded in the maritime custom of the United States. They were considered to be safer for use in confined inland waters than the international regulations' "signals of action" that are used on the high seas. Disregarding for the time being the overtaking situation, the one- and two-short-blast signals have identical meaning in both meeting and crossing situations. One short blast means "I intend to leave you on my port side" and two short blasts means "I intend to leave you on my starboard side." The signals may be supplemented by one-second flashes on an all-round white or yellow light, synchronized with the whistle.

Inland Rule 34(a) uses the expression "when maneuvering as authorized or required by these Rules." This is not interpreted as meaning the short blasts should be used only when a course alteration is anticipated, for the preamble to Rule 34(a) also contains the qualification when "meeting or crossing at a distance within half a mile of each other." This is a retention of a former pilot rule, often referred to as the half-mile rule. Effectively it means that signals of intention and agreement by power-driven vessels should be exchanged if the closest point of approach will be within half a mile, whether or not a course change is required. Previously, the half-mile rule only applied to meeting vessels but it is now extended to cover crossing vessels. Clearly vessels should not wait until within or reaching half a mile of each other before exchanging signals, but should initiate the proper signals in a timely manner, taking full advantage of the bridge-to-bridge radiotelephone.

> If signals are to be of any value, they must be given with an allowance of a sufficient time to exchange signals and agree on a passing, taking into consideration the speed, power and apparent agility of the vessels.[29]

In the crossing and meeting situations one- or two-short-blast signals may be initiated by either vessel and must, if in agreement, be acknowledged by the other vessel repeating the same signal. If, however, the other vessel is in any doubt whatsoever as to the safety of the proposal,

---

[29] River Terminals Corp. v. U.S., DC La. 1954, 121 F. Supp 98.

she must sound the danger signal of at least five short and rapid blasts on her whistle. She should not respond to the signal that worried her by sounding an alternative proposal, e.g., to respond to a two-short-blast signal with a one-short-blast signal. Despite an earlier history of acceptance, such "cross signals" have been invalid since 1940. In a crossing situation between the steamships *Eastern Glade* and *El Isleo* in a channel approaching Baltimore harbor, in which the privileged *El Isleo* answered the two-blast proposal of the *Eastern Glade* to yield her right-of-way with the danger signal *followed by one blast*, she was exonerated by both the lower courts, but the Supreme Court reversed the decree and remanded the case to the circuit court of appeals.[30] Upon rehearing of this case, the circuit court of appeals duly reversed its original decision and held both vessels at fault. It seems highly probable, therefore, that in future cases in inland waters, vessels will be held at fault for using cross signals. Having sounded the danger signal, each vessel takes "appropriate precautionary action" *before* concluding a safe-passing agreement.

### Meeting Vessels, Inland Waters

Inland Rule 14, describing action to be taken in the head-on or meeting situation, is virtually identical to that of the international regulations. It is clearly the intent of the inland rules to have vessels meeting head-on in inland waters pass in the same way as required by the corresponding international regulations. If there is any doubt that vessels are meeting on reciprocal or nearly reciprocal courses, then the vessel(s) must assume the situation is a head-on one and act accordingly.

While the actions required to maneuver to avoid each other are the same, namely both power-driven vessels alter course to starboard and pass port-to-port, the signals differ in meaning. In inland waters one short blast is initiated by either vessel stating her intention to leave the other on her port side, which must then be similarly answered by the other vessel, if in agreement. Both vessels are committed to take the steps necessary to effect a safe port-to-port passage, though the alteration of course, and perhaps speed, may take place after the exchange of signals.

If no alteration of course is necessary to achieve a safe passing, signals are still required if the vessels will pass within half a mile of each other. Should the vessels be passing port-to-port, they exchange the one-short-blast signal. If the vessels anticipate passing starboard-to-starboard then two short blasts are required. It is not considered that the latter case would be a frequent occurrence on most waters: a vessel proceeding along a channel is bound by Inland Rule 9(a)(i) to keep over to her

---

[30] Postal S.S. Corp. v. *El Isleo* (1940) 308 U.S. 378, 84 L. Ed. 335, reversing (CCA N.Y. 1939) 101 F.2d 4: rehearing (CCA N.Y. 1940) 112 F.2d 297.

starboard side, thus facilitating a port-to-port passage. However, Inland Rule 9(a)(ii) provides priority for a downward-bound vessel, with a following current, in narrow channels or fairways of the Great Lakes, Western Rivers, or other waters specified by the secretary. This right-of-way supersedes the normal meeting rules of Inland Rule 14 and could well lead to exchanges of two short blasts, initiated by the downbound vessel.

In summary, vessels in a meeting situation have a compulsory duty to signal their intentions by means of a whistle signal,[31] unless agreement has been reached by bridge-to-bridge radiotelephone. In the meeting case twice mentioned earlier in this chapter, the tanker *Anco Princess*'s faults were compounded by her failure to signal intentions to the *Libby Black* either by whistle signal or by radio communication.[32]

### Crossing Vessels, Inland Waters

Inland Rule 15(a) describes the crossing situation and is the same as in the international regulations. The whistle signals to be made are identical to those required for meeting vessels, being contained in the same Inland Rule, 34(a), though, again, these are signals of intent and assent rather than action signals. It is the intent of the rules that the give-way vessel should avoid crossing ahead of the stand-on vessel, if the circumstances of the case permit. Thus, the normal situation will be for the two vessels to leave each other on their port sides, requiring an exchange of signals of one short blast. Having achieved agreement, the stand-on vessel maintains her course and speed, while the give-way vessel can either alter course to starboard, slow, stop, or reverse her engines. Only the last action requires a further signal—one of three short blasts.

If the circumstances do not permit a port-to-port passing, then an agreement for the give-way vessel to cross ahead of the stand-on vessel will have to be negotiated by an exchange of two short blasts. This should be an unusual occurrence and one best avoided whenever possible. However, Inland Rule 9(d) prescribes that a vessel should not cross a narrow channel or fairway if she will impede the passage of a vessel that is confined to the channel, and in some circumstances, this could lead to the use of two-short-blast signals. If the vessel navigating along the channel is uncertain of the crossing vessel's intention, then she is required to sound the danger signal.

Different from the international regulations is Inland Rule 15(b), which requires a vessel crossing a river to keep out of the way of a power-driven

---

[31] Chotin, Inc. v. S.S. *Gulfknight*, E.D. La. (1966) 266 F. Supp. 859, *aff'd*, 5 Cir. (1968) 402 F.2d 293.

[32] Gulf Coast Transit Co. v. M.T. *Anco Princess* et al. E.D. La. (1977) [1978] 1 Lloyd's Rep. 299.

vessel ascending or descending on the Western Rivers and the Great Lakes and can be extended by the secretary to include other waters. Unlike Rule 9(d), this rule is not limited to narrow channels, nor does it depend on the maneuverability of the ascending or descending vessel. Thus, if the crossing vessel should be a power-driven one, an exchange of two short blasts on these waters could be as common as that of one short blast.

### Overtaking and Overtaken Vessels, Inland Waters

In the overtaking situation signals of one or two short blasts have a different meaning from those used in the meeting or crossing situations. They are still signals of proposal and require consent before overtaking can commence and are applicable only to power-driven vessels. If the overtaking vessel desires to overtake on the starboard side of the vessel ahead, she sounds one short blast, and two short blasts if she desires to pass on the port side. The overtaken vessel answers with the same signal if in agreement or she must answer promptly with the danger signal if in disagreement.

The Inland Navigational Rules Act of 1980 retained the previous signals for overtaking in inland waters, as they were considered superior to the corresponding international regulations: they reduce the risk of collision by applying to *all* overtaking situations of power-driven vessels, are firmly implanted in U.S. maritime practice, and have worked well. One might add that the simpler inland rules avoid the cacophony of noise possible under the international regulations.

### Meaning of Maneuvering Signals a Major Difference Between Rules

Probably the most significant difference between the international regulations and the inland rules can be found in Rule 34 concerning maneuvering and warning signals for power-driven vessels in sight of each other. The arguments over the relative merits of the international system, which restricts the use of one- and two-short-blast signals to indicate change of course, and the inland system of proposal and agreement are finely balanced. Certainly the hodge-podge of previous inland signals has been clarified, and the signals brought closer to the international ones by the passing of the Inland Navigational Rules Act of 1980. The retention in this act of "signals of intent" seems appropriate for the more restrictive waters inside the demarcation lines. Regrettably, however, cases continue to occur, outside of U.S. inland waters where there are no local rules to authorize such use, of vessels improperly using whistle signals to express intentions rather than rudder action.[33] Thus mariners must continue to

---

[33] The *Shell Spirit* [1962] 2 Lloyd's Rep. 252; *see also* the *Friston* [1963] 1 Lloyd's Rep. 74; the *Century* [1963] 1 Lloyd's Rep. 99; the *Koningin Juliana* [1973] 2 Lloyd's Rep. 308.

use sound signals with the most careful regard to the geographical location of their vessels in any particular situation, and to fall back on the exercise of good seamanship when they get into a collision approach where two vessels are on opposite sides of the demarcation line and neither set of rules governs both vessels.

## SUMMARY

Under international regulations, one- and two-short-blast signals, as provided in Rule 34, are rudder signals that must be given whenever, and only when, a vessel in sight of another changes course, irrespective of the kind of approach. Under inland rules, one- and two-short-blast signals are prescribed to indicate the manner of passing and to be given *and answered* regardless of change in course. At least five short and rapid blasts is the in-doubt signal for vessels in sight of each other in both sets of rules, although the inland rules additionally refer to it as the danger signal. The mariner must be aware of the important differences in the signal requirements for all situations on the high seas and in inland waters.

In the meeting situation, vessels under international regulations sound one short blast concurrent with a change of course to the right; under inland rules both vessels sound one short blast for a port-to-port passage within half a mile, whether or not either changes course.

In the crossing situation under inland rules, both vessels again exchange one short blast to express their intentions to leave each other to port. Under international regulations the stand-on vessel may not announce her intention of maintaining course and speed with one short blast. She can only question the actions of the give-way vessel, when in doubt that that vessel will keep clear, by sounding the in-doubt signal.

In the overtaking situation on the high seas, the overtaking vessel sounds one or two short blasts as she makes course changes to avoid the overtaken vessel. In a narrow channel or fairway subject to the international regulations, or in inland waters, the overtaking vessel must first give a signal indicating the side on which she intends to pass, and receive an answer before carrying out the maneuver. To propose passing on the starboard side, the signal is two prolonged blasts followed by one short blast under the international regulations, or one short blast in inland waters. To propose passing on the port side, the signal is two prolonged blasts followed by two short blasts under the international regulations, or two short blasts in inland waters. In inland waters agreement is signaled by the overtaken vessel's answering with the same signal, while under the international regulations agreement is signaled by one prolonged, one short, one prolonged, one short. Under both sets of rules, disagreement with the proposal is indicated by use of the in-doubt or danger signal.

Unique to the inland rules is that whistle signals may be dispensed with if agreement for passing is reached by use of the bridge-to-bridge radiotelephone. This is not permitted on the high seas.

The bend signal of one prolonged blast is identical under both sets of rules, but is also used in inland waters for a power-driven vessel leaving her moorings.

# 5

# Head-On Encounters in Open Waters

## Open v. Restricted Waters

Although sometimes difficult to separate the open-water situation from the same one in restricted waters, there is no doubt that the latter circumstance brings with it many more considerations to effect a safe passage. Aside from the acknowledged impact of the likes of shallow water, narrow channels, and traffic congestion, the rules themselves elaborate detailed conduct for vessels operating in narrow channels. Rule 9, in both regimes, provides for keeping to the right of the channel, special rules for specific areas, unimpeded use of a channel, special sound signals, and a prohibition against anchoring in a channel. Even so, it will come as a surprise to no one that the greater peril for collision exists in inshore waters. For these reasons, this edition brings with it a separate chapter on encounters in restricted waters, and a more detailed treatment of the head-on situation in such waters can be found in Chapter 8. It is only the open spaces of the high seas, with the mutual sighting of ships at relatively long ranges and the ample room to maneuver, that lend themselves to the bold, simple action necessary to turn an uncertain meeting situation into a safe and timely passing.

## The Meeting Situation

Rules 14 of the inland rules and the international regulations are virtually identical. They describe an approach situation by two power-driven vessels in sight of each other meeting in a head-on situation, the conditions being that (1) they are approaching on reciprocal or nearly reciprocal courses ahead or nearly ahead of each other so as to involve risk of collision, (2) by night one vessel sees the masthead lights of the other in line, or nearly in line, and/or both sidelights, and (3) by day one vessel observes the corresponding aspect of the other vessel.

Both sets of rules require both vessels to alter course to starboard and pass port-to-port, although the inland rules do make provision for an agreed departure from this norm. If there is any doubt as to whether a vessel is in a meeting or crossing situation, she must assume it is the former and act accordingly.

Clearly the description contained in the rules only applies to the initial sighting and assessment of the situation. Two vessels on exactly opposite courses at night, following tracks that will take them clear of each other, port-to-port by, say 500 yards, will, in the earlier stage of their approach, each see both sidelights of the other, almost, although not exactly ahead. It is obvious that sooner or later the green light of each vessel will be shut out to the other, leaving vessels "red-to-red," but this certainly does not remove the application of the head-on rule. For the words "so as to involve risk of collision" oft repeated in the regulations, are held not necessarily to refer to an existing state of affairs but also to the earlier time when there was a risk of collision if nothing had been done to avert it.

Again, if two vessels are approaching end on, as soon as one of them, in obedience to the rules, makes a marked change of course to starboard, she will at night exhibit one sidelight ahead as seen by the other vessel, and by day will be seen ahead crossing the course of the other. This does not absolve the ship who has yet to alter course from her obligation under the head-on rule.

Still another discrepancy between the literal phraseology and its practical application may be expected because of the physical imperfections of sidelights, which have a certain amount of leakage outside the designated arcs they cover. The specifications in the technical annexes to both sets of rules provides for sidelights to be screened so as to show between 1 and 3 degrees across the bow, thus avoiding a theoretical dark lane immediately ahead of the ship. This overlap, plus the effect of any yawing, may make appreciation of whether a situation is a head-on or a crossing one somewhat uncertain. In such circumstances Rule 14(c) applies, both on the high seas and on inland waters, and requires the vessel in doubt to assume a meeting situation. The earlier she does this the better and, although the expression "act accordingly" allows room for discussion, conformance to the principle of altering course to starboard can be inferred and, indeed, firmly commended.

Furthermore, in a marginal case, if a vessel considers herself privileged in a crossing situation, the latitude granted in Rule 17(a)(ii) of both sets of rules allows her to take action early rather than having to stand on until in extremis. Such action should be in accordance with Rule 17(c), applicable in both jurisdictions, by avoiding an alteration to port. Thus, there is less need to draw a fine distinction between the boundary line dividing the two situations.

Having altered to starboard, it is necessary to achieve a passing at "a safe distance" (Rule 8(d) ) as well as to "avoid a close-quarters situation" (Rule 8(c) ). Neither phrase is defined in the regulations or by the courts, but the two are undoubtedly linked in meaning. Since passing at a safe distance ideally should remove *all* risk of collision, then to trespass inside that distance is surely to get into a close-quarters situation. The risk to be eliminated is not solely that arising from the steady bearing of a closing vessel but also the possibility of some emergency in either vessel while in close company. Thus, the passing distance must be sufficient to allow time to recover from a casualty or detect and react to aberrations. Neither will it be a straightforward linear distance but more an area of water, perhaps a variable circle or something oval shaped determined by the size, speed, and maneuverability of the ships involved. Many mathematical models have been devised for these ship domains, though the practicing mariner needs a simpler guide, one developed from *his* or *her* knowledge of the ship's capabilities. In the clear-weather meeting situation, this essentially boils down to altering course sufficiently to achieve a closest point of approach that allows for the unexpected. For many ships this is a distance measurable in miles rather than yards. Of course, this is not achievable in confined waters (which will be discussed in Chapter 8) but in any waters a prudent mariner might ask "why put myself in a close-quarters situation unnecessarily?" This theme will be picked up time and time again in succeeding chapters.

From the wording of Rule 14(b) it is clear that the course referred to in Rule 14(a) is the direction of the ship's head and not the course being made good over the ground. This could be significant where strong cross winds or tidal currents are experienced, transferring what would be, in still waters, a head-on situation into more of a crossing one. The temptation to alter course to port in such circumstances must be resisted, as witnessed by a collision in a channel swept in a mine field in 1945. A strong tidal current was sweeping across, and two approaching ships were necessarily compensating for it, with the result that their headings were different from their tracks along the channel. The *British Engineer* was found at fault for altering course to port to avoid a green light seen almost dead ahead.[1] *Karanan*, the other ship, altered to starboard as was her duty as give-way vessel.

In a case of a collision in the open sea, where two vessels approached each other so that their courses were within ³/₄ point (about 8 degrees) of opposite, the court held them to be under the crossing rule because of the lights that could be seen:

These vessels were on crossing courses: as respects the *Knight* because she saw only the other's green light; as respect the *Gulf Stream* because the two colored lights were seen not ahead but from a half a point to a point and

[1] The *British Engineer* (1945) 78 Ll. L. Rep. 31.

a half on her own starboard bow for a considerable time before any risk of collision commenced, so that she showed to the *Knight* only her green light.[2]

In an even earlier case in the open waters of Lake Erie, when a schooner and a bark collided after approaching each other within half a point (about 5½ degrees) on opposite courses, the Supreme Court held that:

> the variation, in any view of the evidence, did not exceed half a point by the compass, which is clearly insufficient to take the case out of the operation of that (end-on) article.[3]

It would therefore seem that while the head-on rule must always be construed in the strictest accordance with the explanatory words of the rule, construction was a matter for the court.[4] In other words, every case should be tested against the explanatory words of the rule itself, rather than solely against previous cases or an arbitrary cut-off point based on the differences between the courses of the vessels involved. Nevertheless, the tendency of decisions appears to have been for a difference between courses (±180 degrees) of one point or more to be treated as crossing situations, and a difference of half a point or a little more to be treated as head-on situations.[5] We shall see in Chapter 8 how this construction has varied for that hazardous passing encounter between two ships meeting in a narrow channel.

It is clearly the intent of Inland Rule 14 that vessels meeting head-on in inland waters, which, remember, do encompass some open waters, should each alter to starboard to achieve the same port-to-port passage that is required under the international regulations. Nonetheless, the rule does contain the proviso *unless otherwise agreed*. Should such agreement be forthcoming, then the whistle signals of Inland Rule 34(a), which were discussed in Chapter 4, equally clearly provide the means for agreeing to a starboard-to-starboard passage. The retention of the half-mile rule in the preamble to Inland Rule 34(a) effectively means that an exchange of signals will be made when two vessels expect to close to within that distance when passing on opposite courses. If the vessels were sufficiently apart that they could pass starboard to starboard *without altering course* to avoid meeting head-on, then such a passing is probably acceptable. Apart from special circumstances in some rivers, such occasions should be rare. A starboard-to-starboard passage within half a mile of another vessel, under any rules, can give one an uncomfortable feeling and is best avoided.

---

[2] The *Gulf Stream* (N.Y. 1890) 43 F.895.
[3] The *Nichols* (1869) 19 L. Ed. 157.
[4] The *Kaituna* (1933) 46 Ll. L. Rep. 200; also the *Gitano* (1940) 67 Ll. L. Rep. 339.
[5] Marsden, *Collisions at Sea*, 551.

## Port-to-Port Required

It will be seen from the rules that when two vessels meet head-on or nearly so in open waters, they are not merely permitted, but are *required*, to pass port to port, and to alter course to starboard *as may be necessary to make such a passage safe*. In this connection it should be noted that the change in course should be both timely and substantial and that *a change of 20 degrees or more is far more effective than one of only 2 degrees*. A sound rule, where circumstances permit, is that the amount of alteration should be more than sufficient to clear the other ship, even if she fails to alter course to starboard. If the vessels are exactly end on, so that both have to change course to the right, then both the maneuver and the whistle signal of each vessel will be the same under international rules as under inland rules, always bearing in mind that the whistle is blown by each vessel in the first case *because* she is changing course, and in the second case *because* she is proposing or accepting a port-to-port passage. In a case with both vessels so far to port of each other as to pass port to port without a change in course by either, the one-blast signal required in inland waters would be omitted at sea. Similarly, with both vessels so far to starboard of each other as to pass starboard to starboard without a change in course by either, the two-blast signal required in inland waters would be omitted at sea.

The first point to be emphasized here is that the obligations to alter course and to signal are mutual in their application, and therefore neither vessel, after a head-on collision, can ever sustain the plea that she was waiting for the other vessel to change course or to signal *first*. The second point is that the injunction to turn to the right or to pass port to port given in all these sets of rules is meant to be obeyed, and should be disregarded for only one purpose—to avoid immediate danger.

Sometimes mariners act on the assumption that since neither vessel in the meeting situation has the right-of-way or its attendant obligation to hold course and speed, the vessel getting out her signal first properly determines whether the passage shall be port to port or starboard to starboard. Certainly any disregard of the port-to-port requirement is not due to any ambiguity in the rules. The international rules contain no reference whatever to a starboard-to-starboard passage. In the inland rules, the two-short-blast signal is available to propose a starboard-to-starboard passage but, apart from special circumstances, this should not be the norm in open waters. The rules are therefore unanimous in requiring a port-to-port passage in every genuine head-on situation. Moreover, it is interesting to note that numerous court decisions have agreed in upholding this basic provision of the rules. A two-blast signal has been held to be merely a proposal to depart from the rules, not binding upon the other vessel unless and until she assents by a similar signal,[6] and a vessel initiating the two-blast agreement assumes all risks of the attempt, including a misunderstanding of signals.[7] In the light of these decisions it would seem to be the part of common sense to adhere scrupulously to the rules, and at least never to *propose* a departure unless special circumstances necessitate.

## Keynote Is Caution

Referring again to the fact that in the head-on situation neither vessel has the right-of-way over the other, in the broader sense even a proper port-to-port signal in inland waters may well be regarded by the vessel giving it as merely a proposal until it is accepted by the whistle of the other. It is true that the other vessel is legally bound to accept it. But the proper keynote of the meeting situation is caution, and the degree of caution required goes much further than a perfunctory observance of the rule. Indeed it is just about the time of giving the first signal that the real necessity for caution may be said to begin. The other vessel may misunderstand or fail to hear the signal, she may ignore it, she may deliberately disregard it, or she may make a simultaneous counterproposal. Unfortunately the first vessel is far from being in a position to say, "We have changed course to starboard and blown one blast. The rest is up to you." The moment the signaling vessel discovers definite evidence of the other's failure to obey the rules, however flagrant the fault, she must take immediate steps to avert collision. The first and most important step, in the eyes of the courts, is to reduce headway to a point where she is under perfect control; if she fails to do this she is practically certain, in the event of collision, to be held guilty of contributory fault. Vessels have been so held for failure to stop or reverse as soon as there was any uncertainty of the other vessel's course,[8] or an apparent misunderstanding of signals,[9] or where the other vessel was seen to be using left rudder in the face of a proper one-blast proposal.[10]

It must be remembered that the signal requirements of both the international regulations and inland rules include the obligation to use the in-doubt signal, five or more short blasts, whenever there is doubt as to the course or intention of another vessel. In a head-on approach in inland waters, such doubt should be deemed to exist and the danger signal used whenever a signal is ignored, after one repetition, or disputed; whenever the vessel is slowed or stopped as a precautionary measure; and whenever

[6] Southern Pacific Co. v. U.S. (N.Y. 1929) 7 F. Supp 473.

[7] The *St. Johns* (1872) 20 L. Ed. 645.

[8] The *Munaires* (CCA N.Y. 1924) 1 F.2d 13.

[9] The *Transfer No. 9* (CCA N.Y. 1909) 170 F.944; the *Teutonia* (La. 1874) 23 L. Ed. 44.

[10] The *Albert Dumois* (La. 1900) 44 L. Ed. 751.

the other vessel proposes, or is seen attempting to execute, a dangerous maneuver.[11] If the engines are reversed, the three-blast signal in accordance with Rule 34(a) must be given. In a collision below Owl's Head Buoy in New York harbor between two steamships that sighted each other exactly end on when about a mile apart, it was held that the inbound vessel that blew one whistle, righted her rudder, reversed her engines when the other swung to port, gave a second signal of one whistle, and then blew three whistles, had done all that could be expected of her in efficient endeavor to avoid collision, and the outbound vessel was held solely liable.[12]

If the situation is under international rules, the one- and two-blast signals denote change in course rather than proposal-agreement on the method of passing. However, if either vessel fails to understand the intentions or actions of the other, she is required to sound the international in-doubt signal of five or more short blasts. In addition she should immediately consider revising her safe speed (Rule 6), which would possibly, in a head-on situation, mean reducing or stopping her way in accordance with Rule 8(e).

### When Starboard-to-Starboard Passage Is Proper

The reader should not infer from earlier discussion that a starboard-to-starboard passage is never legitimate. If such were the case, there would be nothing for meeting vessels to do when approaching each other starboard to starboard within two points but follow the old merchant marine precept (meaning right rudder) of, "port your helm and show your red." Indeed, on the high seas under international rules, with the vessels visible to each other through several miles of approach, there is much to justify such a procedure, at least in cases where it is doubtful if the vessels can pass a safe distance off without some change in course. A critical study of the statutory language raises a doubt whether a two-blast signal is ever strictly proper on the high seas with the vessels on approximately opposite courses. That is to say, if they are so far to starboard of each other as to be able to clear, and actually do clear, without a change of course, no whistle signal is permissible; and if they are somewhat to starboard of each other, but not enough for safe clearance, then they are within the purview of the head-on rule and bound to pass port to port. Several collisions have been caused by one vessel altering to port to increase the passing distance and the other vessel turning to starboard. If it is thought necessary to increase the distance of passing starboard to starboard, then the implication is that risk of collision exists and the situation should, in

---

[11] The *Commercial Mariner* (2 CCA) 1933 AMC 489.
[12] The *Bilbster* (CCA 1925) 6 F.2d 954.

a timely manner, be treated as a head-on one. In such a case, the first vessel to alter course to starboard must cross the course of the other, and hence it is increasingly important that both the visible action and the audible notice of it be timely.

However, occasions do occur when a green-to-green passing can be sensibly and safely achieved, providing clear agreement has been reached beforehand. Under the inland rules this requires the two-blast proposal and under international regulations, it is strongly suggested, should only be undertaken by prior VHF radio concurrence. The latter occurrence should be rare, but not totally extinct. Any sound signal in inland waters defining a proposed maneuver, particularly such an unexpected one as suggested by two blasts, or any radio communication on international waters proposing a starboard-to-starboard passage, should be given whenever possible in ample time to allow for disagreement before the vessels are in extremis. As a federal judge aptly expressed it, such a proposal should be made in time to maneuver out of a misunderstanding.

Prior to the Inland Navigational Rules Act of 1980 there had been specific recognition, albeit in cumbersome language, of the starboard-to-starboard passage. Consequently, when conditions were appropriate, the courts were inclined to enforce that part of the former rules almost as strictly as the port-to-port provision. An examination of these past decisions discloses that at least in inland waters a vessel in a proper position for a starboard-to-starboard passage was at fault for a collision that occurred because she insisted on meeting port to port.

There have been precious few comparable decisions under international regulations, and it may be that the courts accepted the absence of any reference in the rules to a starboard-to-starboard passage as an indication that it is not an enforceable procedure. There was, however, one case following a disastrous collision where the possibility of a safe starboard-to-starboard passing on the open seas was implicitly recognized. Due to the deaths of so many involved and the lack of a lookout, it was difficult to reconstruct what happened or why in this attempted conversion of a starboard-to-starboard passage to a port-to-port passage.

The Brazilian motor tanker *Horta Barbosa,* of 62,619 tons gross, was on voyage from Rio de Janeiro in ballast and met the South Korean motor tanker *Sea Star,* of 63,988 tons gross, which was outward bound in the Gulf of Oman for Rio de Janeiro fully laden with crude oil (see Figure 7). The visibility was good and the night clear. Both ships detected each other on radar at about 14 to 16 miles and could see each other's masthead lights at 8 miles. Their courses were nearly reciprocal, and both were proceeding at 16 knots. For some six minutes or so the bridge of the *Horta Barbosa* was unmanned while the lookout and cadet called their reliefs and the officer on watch was in the charthouse obtaining a radar fix. According to this officer, the *Sea Star* was about 3 to 4 miles

**Fig. 7.**

away bearing 30 degrees on the starboard bow when he had left the bridge. Just before 0400 the lookout returned to the bridge, saw the *Sea Star* on a crossing course and called the officer. The engines were ordered full astern, but collision took place almost at once and was followed by an explosion. The *Sea Star* was destroyed by fire and sank; eleven of her crew lost their lives, including four of the five who were then on the bridge—the cadet, who was in the charthouse, alone surviving. The *Horta Barbosa* had to be abandoned, though she was later towed, gutted by fire, to harbor.

It was claimed in court for the *Horta Barbosa* that both ships would have safely passed starboard to starboard at a distance of 1 mile if the *Sea Star* had not altered course. In defense it was alleged by *Sea Star* that the two ships were end on or nearly so and that both ships should have altered to starboard. The judge was not impressed by the evidence presented by either side, finding the witnesses from the *Horta Barbosa* "lacking in a proper sense of responsibility" and the cadet survivor from *Sea Star* too young and inexperienced to appreciate all the implications of what had happened. Fortunately, there was a third ship some distance off, the *Amoco Baltimore*, whose evidence was crucial in the court's acceptance of the *Horta Barbosa*'s broad case that the two ships were green to green, with each on the starboard bow of each other before:

> . . . the *Sea Star* made an apparently inexplicable alteration to starboard which changed a relatively safe situation into one of acute danger. There must have been reasons why such an alteration was made, even though they were bad reasons. Because the officer or officers responsible are dead, however, it is not possible to ascertain what those reasons were.[13]

---

[13] The *Sea Star*, Q.B. (Adm. Ct.) [1976] 2 Lloyd's Rep. 123.

The blame for the collision was divided; the *Sea Star* 75 percent because the situation of danger was created by her fault, and the *Horta Barbosa* 25 percent because of her failure to react properly to the situation so created.

Another recent example of what should have been a safe passing, this time port to port, was the multiple collisions in the international waters of the Malacca Strait between two tankers and a dry cargo ship (see Figure 8).[14] The two tankers were proceeding southeasterly down the strait: the Liberian *Brazilian Faith* was being towed by three tugs at 5 knots and was being overhauled on her port side at a distance of about half a mile by the *Diego Silang* of Manila with a speed of about 13 knots. The night was fine and clear with good visibility.

The *Diego Silang* first spotted an oncoming vessel at a range of about 10 miles fine on her starboard bow. Not having much room to starboard because of the larger tanker under tow close aboard, she first altered 3 degrees to starboard, changed her mind, altered back 8 degrees to port to bring about a starboard-to-starboard passage, realized that this was an error of judgment and resumed her original course, by which time the oncoming vessel was still 7 miles off. This apparent dithering was not noticed by the approaching ship, the Russian cargo ship *Vysotsk*. She maintained her northwesterly course, her projected track set for a port-to-port passage with the Philippine tanker, albeit with a smallish CPA (closest point of approach) of about half a mile. However, when the ships were about 4 miles apart, the *Vysotsk* inexplicably altered course to port, subsequently colliding with the *Diego Silang*. The reasons for this alter-

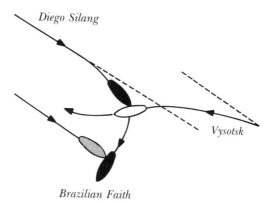

*Diego Silang*

*Vysotsk*

*Brazilian Faith*

**Fig. 8.**

[14] The *Vysotsk* [1981] 1 Lloyd's Rep. 439.

ation in defiance of good sense, truly an aberration, never emerged in court as the master of the *Vysotsk* deliberately tried to pull the wool over the eyes of anyone investigating the collision. He was unsuccessful, with the *Vysotsk* found 80 percent to blame for the collision, though the *Diego Silang* attracted 20 percent for not being sufficiently prompt in responding to the new and dangerous situation. After the collision, the *Diego Silang* lost way and fell off to starboard into the path of the *Brazilian Faith* when the second collision occurred. The chain of events between this collision and the causes of the first was found not to be broken by any intervening negligence, so liability for damage caused by the second collision was in the same proportions as for the first collision.

Fortunately, no one died in these collisions, but the point here is that it should have been a safe, but close, port-to-port passage; it was an irrational act that converted it into a collision. The case graphically illustrates yet again that unexpected and unsound maneuvers do occur at sea and demonstrates what can go wrong at a late stage in any passing situation. It supports the argument to avoid a close-quarters situation if you can, and if you can't, be extra vigilant. Additionally, it serves as another horrible example of the disastrous results that can be achieved when one of the vessels in the head-on situation elects to turn to port, for whatever reason.

Considerably more legal precedent exists for inland waters. In a collision in New York harbor where two steamers approached each other with ample clearance for meeting starboard to starboard, the one that proposed a port-to-port passage and then made a wide sheer to starboard was held at fault by the circuit court of appeals.[15] In another case a passenger vessel was held negligent for leaving her course and turning to starboard into the path of an oncoming steam lighter without getting an answer to her one-blast signal.[16] In another case, a steamship and a ferry exchanged two-blast signals and then the steamship, confused by the ferry's whistle to another vessel, suddenly changed course in an attempt to pass port to port, for which she was held solely liable for the collision.[17]

Similarly, in an old case in Long Island Sound at night between the side-wheeler *Rhode Island* and the steam propeller *Alhambra*, the court found after an analysis of unusually conflicting testimony that the vessels were in a proper position to pass starboard to starboard, and that the

[15] The North and East River Steamboat Co. v. Jay Street Terminal (CCA N.Y. 1931) 47 F.2d 474.
[16] The *Kookaburra* (N.Y. 1932) 60 F.2d 174.
[17] The *General Putnam* (CCA N.Y. 1914) 213 F.613. *See also* Kiernan v. Stafford (CC N.J. 1890) 43 F.542.

*Rhode Island*'s red light had already shut in and her green light was widening on the *Alhambra*'s bow, when she suddenly blew one blast and swung to starboard. The *Alhambra* reversed, but a collision followed for which the *Rhode Island* was solely liable.[18] When two tugs with tows met in the Delaware River in a starboard-to-starboard approach, one of them made a one-blast proposal when they were only 700 feet apart and the other accepted it. Both were at fault. As said by the court:

> The *Crawford*'s fault was in giving the wrong signal, offering to pass on the wrong side, and in attempting to carry out a dangerous maneuver. The *American* was at fault in accepting an obviously improper proposal and in taking part in the effort to carry it out.[19]

In a more recent case, two steamships met above the Delaware River Bridge, and the *Manchester Merchant,* bound down the river, had just overtaken a tug and houseboat close aboard to starboard, when in answer to a two-blast signal of the *Margaret,* bound upward, she sounded one blast and went to starboard. Again both were held at fault for the collision, the *Manchester Merchant* for attempting to force a port-to-port passing, and the *Margaret* for not sounding the danger signal and for not stopping when the *Manchester Merchant* refused to accept her starboard-to-starboard signals.[20] From these decisions it may be reasonably inferred that the rule is as pointed out many years ago by the circuit court of appeals:

> When two meeting vessels by keeping their courses would pass to the left of each other in safety, one of them, which insists on the naked right of passing to the right, and changes the course when it is attended with danger, is in fault for a collision which results.[21]

No doubt this finding will continue to be applicable to open stretches of water where ships in their normal course of business happen to meet broad on each other's starboard bow while on opposite, or nearly opposite, courses and can safely pass starboard to starboard. However, in narrow channels, to be discussed in Chapter 8, the injunction for vessels to keep to their starboard side will place an onus on a vessel provoking a starboard-to-starboard passage to justify her presence on her port side of the channel.

### The Usual Cause of Head-On Collisions

In conformity with the foregoing discussion it may be said that a striking similarity appears in the causes of most head-on collisions. It is preeminently a situation where the surest way to produce a collision is for one

---

[18] The *Alhambra* (CC N.Y. 1887) 33 F.73.
[19] The *American* (Pa. 1912) 194 F.899.
[20] The *Margaret* (Pa. 1927) 22 F.2d 709.
[21] The *City of Macon* (CCA Pa. 1899) 92 F.207.

vessel to obey, and the other to disobey, the rule. The end-on rule, when obeyed by both, is so nearly collision proof that it will be no surprise to the reader to be told that the very large majority of collisions of this kind occur simply because *one of the two vessels turns to the left.* While various reasons may be assigned for this disregard of the rule—a misunderstanding of signals, a mistaken notion that the other vessel is intending to turn left, a misapprehension of the requirement to pass port to port, a deliberate usurpation of what is considered the favorable side of a channel—they all point to the same result, and the vessel wrongfully swinging left collides with the vessel properly swinging right. If this obvious cause of disaster could be impressed on the consciousness of every navigator, cases of head-on collision at sea would become extremely rare, being confined largely to those borderline cases at night where there is doubt as to whether the situation is meeting or crossing, and to the even less frequent case where a vessel makes a mistaken attempt to convert a normal starboard-to-starboard passage into one that is port to port.

## Physical Characteristics of Head-On Situation

The head-on situation has certain definite characteristics that it would be well to bear in mind. Vessels approach each other in this situation at a rate equal to the sum of their speeds, whereas in the overtaking situation the rate of approach is, of course, the difference of the two speeds, and a varying, but intermediate, rate of approach marks the crossing collision. When vessels strike full on, even at slow speed, the result, in accordance with the well-known mathematical rule expressing the respective kinetic energies, is extremely destructive. The rule is $E = W \times V^2 \div 2g$; that is, the energy of each vessel (in foot tons) equals the weight (in tons) times the velocity squared (in feet per second) divided by 64.4. There was such a collision at night between two large, full-powered ocean ships, the steamship *Edward Luckenbach* and the Italian motorship, *Feltre,* in which the latter was said to have been sunk with three distinct gashes in her hull, two of which must have been inflicted after a double recoil by the crumpled bow of the *Edward Luckenbach.* In this situation the least time is allowed for proper action to avoid collision—hence the primary importance of taking such action in a timely manner. To offset the superior hazard of this situation having the most rapid approach, it is true that the target is the smallest; that any change of course by one vessel—through changed alignment of mast by day or of masthead lights by night—should be instantly apparent to the other; and that the smallest change of course will be much more effective than in either the crossing or the overtaking situation, with a strong possibility of a glancing blow if the collision cannot be avoided altogether. It is also true, however, that many so-called head-on collisions become physically, though not legally, crossing collisions, as one vessel makes a last desperate attempt to swing clear of the other and succeeds only in attacking or being attacked at a more vulnerable angle.

### Legal Characteristics

Legally, the head-on situation resembles the crossing, and differs from the overtaking, situation in that the manner of passing is not optional but prescribed; and it is unlike both of these in that neither vessel has the right-of-way, and both must therefore take definite and positive action to avoid collision. Under international and inland rules alike, vessels meeting head-on *must* pass port to port, and each *must* alter her course to starboard enough to make that maneuver safe, with the concomitant obligation of a proper whistle signal.

### Signal Differences

At this point attention is again called to the fundamental difference in the meaning of one- and two-short-blast whistle signals under international and inland rules, discussed in the preceding chapter. Under international regulations, these signals are described in Rule 34(a) and apply alike to all situations in clear weather. Under Inland Rule 34(a), the one- and two-short-blast whistle signals are provided to indicate the manner of passing without reference to changes in course. The signals shall be given and answered by pilots in compliance with these rules, not only when meeting head-on or nearly so, but at all times when the power-driven vessels are in sight of each other, when passing or meeting within half a mile of each other, and whether passing to the starboard or port. As explained in Chapter 4, in the head-on situation the practical import of these differences is that:

- *Outside the inland waters of the United States,* the one-blast signal is a rudder signal indicating a change of course to the right, and two blasts are a similar signal indicating a change of course to the left. Hence, the one-, two-, or three-blast signal *must* be given by a power-driven vessel in sight of another vessel whenever she changes course, or reverses her engines, the obligation being plain whether the other vessel is ahead, abeam, or astern, and whether she is a power-driven vessel with a whistle or a sailing vessel without one. Additional changes in course require another signal. Conversely, the one- or two-blast signal can never be used, either for an original signal or a reply, except when the course is changed, nor can either be used under conditions of visibility so low that neither the other vessel nor her lights can be seen.
- *In the inland waters of the United States,* the one-blast signal is required of either vessel as an announcement to the other of a port-to-port

passing, whether a change in course is made or not. The two-blast signal is required of either vessel as an announcement to the other of a starboard-to-starboard passing, whether a change in course is made or not. It will be noted that the rule requires a prompt reply in each case. An exchange of signals is required when the predicted distance of passing each other in clear weather is within half a mile.

Sound signals are mandatory and although courts are tending to treat the lack of them, in certain circumstances, as sins of omission and perhaps give them less weight in fault appropriation, they are nonetheless an important unambiguous international means of communication. Far from unambiguous can be the ubiquitous talk on Very High Frequency (VHF) radio! Nonetheless this most important facility can do much to declare intentions, resolve uncertainties and thereby avoid collisions. A common tongue is required and here the IMO's Standard Marine Navigational Vocabulary, which standardizes the words used in communications for navigation at sea, is an invaluable tool in overcoming the language/accent barrier. For meeting ships in open waters, having shifted to a common VHF working channel, the mutual agreement to pass "red-to-red" should, earlier than sound signals, determine the method of passing. Successful exchanges on VHF do not release ships from the need to sound mandatory signals on the high seas, especially if other vessels are about. Equally, unsuccessful attempts of VHF communication should not lead to dilatory alteration of heading.

## SUMMARY

A head-on approach is where two vessels approach on substantially opposite courses. The manner of passing is prescribed as port to port in both international and inland waters. The international regulations make no mention of a starboard-to-starboard passage, but the inland rules provide a two-short-blast signal for the meeting situation that assumes the possibility of a starboard-to-starboard passage for ships passing within half a mile. However, apart from the special cases in designated waters, such a passing should be uncommon, particularly as both sets of rules require vessels to keep to the right in a channel or fairway.

The meeting situation is also characterized by maximum speed of approach, maximum effect of a small change in course by either vessel in avoiding collision, and maximum damage in case of actual collision. Inasmuch as neither vessel has the right-of-way, neither is under obligation to hold course and speed. On the contrary, both are charged with a positive duty to avoid collision, and hence the keynote of this situation should be extreme caution from the moment the approach becomes evident until collision between the two vessels is no longer possible. By the rules each vessel is bound to sound the in-doubt signal and otherwise bring herself under control whenever it is apparent that the other vessel's maneuver/proposal is a cause for concern. It is important to remember that when making a proposal for a green-to-green passage, agreement must be obtained in plenty of time. Nearly all head-on collisions occur where there has been a misinterpretation of the situation and one vessel turns to the left in violation of the rules.

# 6

# The Overtaking Situation in Open Waters

**Open v. Restricted Waters**

As will be seen, the overtaking rule applies in all waters, whether restricted or open. However, the overtaking situation, as with head-on encounters, becomes vastly more complex when surrounded by the mitigating circumstances inherent in narrow channels and shallow water. In fact, the international regulations provide for a different set of signals for vessels overtaking in a narrow channel. As in the case of the head-on situation, a more detailed approach to overtaking in restricted waters can be found in Chapter 8.

**Definition and Characteristics**

Rule 13(b) of both the international regulations and the inland rules describes the overtaking situation in the following clear-cut terms:

> (b) A vessel shall be deemed to be overtaking when coming up with another vessel from a direction more than 22.5 degrees abaft her beam, that is, in such a position with reference to the vessel she is overtaking, that at night she would be able to see only the sternlight of that vessel but neither of her sidelights.

It will be noted that the rule attempts to define the overtaking approach at night in terms of the visibility of sidelights, and the tolerances allowed for the arcs of these lights will, of course, cause some fluctuation in the actual limits of the overtaking approach in terms of arc of the compass, even if the overtaken vessel is proceeding on a perfectly steady course. Moreover, the exact angle of approach cannot always be determined even in daylight, as frankly conceded by the rules in the admonition to regard all doubtful cases as subject to the overtaking rules:

> (c) When a vessel is in any doubt as to whether she is overtaking another, she shall assume that this is the case and act accordingly.

Although the ColRegs maneuvering rules do not specify precisely when the initial characterization of one vessel as overtaking or crossing another is to be made, the logical time is when the former is (or should be) maneuvering vis-à-vis the latter.[1]

Rule 13 of both sets of rules differs from the rules describing the meeting and crossing situations in that the words "so as to involve risk of collision" are not included—the stricture being that "any vessel over-taking any other shall keep out of the way of the vessel being overtaken." Therefore, apart from being applicable to all kinds of vessels, not just power-driven ones, it is open to interpretation as to whether risk of collision is a necessary condition for the overtaking rule to be in force, a point we shall return to shortly. Before then, however, it is necessary to point out that Rule 13(a) of the international regulations and Inland Rule 13(a) cover not only vessels in sight of each other but also vessels in any condition of visibility, although stopping short of including conduct of vessels in restricted visibility in their embrace. This is undoubtedly right, for the overtaking situation, as well as the crossing and meeting situations, cannot be properly determined in restricted visibility. Never-theless, the implication is that the overtaking vessel should have less of a problem in keeping clear and avoiding collision than the vessel being overtaken, regardless of visibility.

Taking only the case where vessels are in sight of each other, and risk of collision does exist, there are really two characteristics necessary to any overtaking situation: first, the overtaking vessel must be proceeding in the same general direction as the other, that is, within six points of the same course; and second, her speed must be greater. It has been held that the overtaking rule applies only when the vessel ahead is on a definite course. A freighter was ruled not to be overtaking a shrimp boat that had crossed a mile ahead of the freighter's course and then made a series of erratic port and starboard turns prior to collision.[2] Also vessels in a naval convoy are neither overtaking nor overtaken in the legal sense, as long as their speed remains uniform, though, of course, a vessel joining such a column is an overtaking vessel until she takes up her position. From the nature of the case, it will be seen that the speed of approach in this situation tends toward the difference in speed of the two vessels, and will be exactly that difference when the vessels approach on identi-cal courses. This fact gives more time for decisive action to avoid col-lision and usually lessens the force of the blow if a collision finally oc-curs. An ocean vessel has been sunk, however, by being overtaken and struck on the quarter by another vessel making only 3 or 4 knots more speed.

---

[1] Hosei Kaiun v. *Seaspan Monarch*, 1981 AMC 2162.
[2] McDonald v. *Archangelos* G., 1980 AMC 88.

Every vessel overtaking any other is obliged by Rule 13(a) to keep clear of the vessel to be overtaken, even if the usual test for risk of collision—the bearing of the other vessel—is changing appreciably. If a vessel comes up relatively close to another vessel from any direction more than 22.5 degrees abaft the latter's starboard beam, draws ahead, and subsequently turns to port to come onto a crossing course, she is not relieved of her duty to keep clear. Both sets of rules lay down in Rule 13(d):

> (d) Any subsequent alteration of the bearing between the two vessels shall not make the overtaking vessel a crossing vessel within the meaning of these rules or relieve her of the duty of keeping clear of the overtaken vessel until she is finally past and clear.

If she had passed at a considerable distance away from the slower vessel, however, the overtaking rule would not have applied, and the other vessel could be obliged to keep clear if a subsequent crossing situation brought risk of collision between the same two vessels. This eventuality was first formulated in the judgment on the collision between the *Baine Hawkins* and the *Molière*, where, although the latter was found guilty of improperly overtaking, it was said;

> . . . It may, on the other hand, be that, when there is no risk of collision at the time (of overhauling)—if, for example the vessel comes within sight of a sidelight at a considerable distance—the crossing rule comes into force; . . .[3]

If the faster vessel is in any doubt, she should assume the obligation to keep out of the way (Rule 13(c)) if it becomes necessary to turn onto a crossing course that brings about risk of collision. In such a case, she should bear in mind the admonition in Rule 16 to take early action to keep well clear and, even if she should consider herself the stand-on vessel in a crossing situation, she should avoid an alteration of course to port (Rule 17(c)).

The actual separation between vessels when such a judgment comes into force probably depends not only on whether risk of collision originally existed, but also on the relative speed of approach once the crossing situation comes into being. For vessels proceeding on similar courses with hardly any difference in their speeds it might be as little as a mile. In one case, two vessels proceeding in approximately the same direction collided after the leading ship, which was 2 points on the port bow of the second ship, altered course to starboard, flying the correct international flag hoist for adjusting compasses. The ships were between 2 to 3 miles apart, and it was held that, up to the time of the alteration, the regulations did not apply as there had been no risk of collision and therefore no overtaking situation. After the alteration the vessels were considered to be in a crossing situation before colliding.[4]

---

[3] The *Molière* (1893) 7 Aspinall MC 364.
[4] The *Manchester Regiment* (1938) 60 Ll. L. Rep. 279.

*Pacific Glory*

*Allegro*

**Fig. 9.**

A more gradual drawing together of two tankers upbound in the English Channel occurred in 1970 (see Figure 9). The Liberian *Pacific Glory* was on an easterly heading passing the Isle of Wight. Both the officer of the watch and the deep-sea pilot noticed another vessel abaft the starboard beam showing a red sidelight and open masthead lights: both believed the vessel to be an overtaking ship. She was the fellow flag state *Allegro* heading approximately 060 degrees, awaiting entrance to Fawley. For some forty minutes, spanning the change of watch from the last dog to the first, the two vessels closed with watch keepers not noticing the other ship, until they were about a cable and a half apart. Emergency action could not prevent a disastrous collision. Apart from an abysmal lookout in the *Allegro*, serious fault lay with *Pacific Glory* for not taking bearings to determine whether risk of collision existed in what was an uncertain situation.[5]

*Pacific Glory* firmly upheld at the inquiry that she was being overtaken by *Allegro,* but agreed in cross-examination that the latter vessel might see her starboard sidelight and masthead light occasionally. This meant that the ships were on the boundary line between a crossing and an overtaking situation. The case serves to illustrate the uncertainties that can arise when ships slowly converge, sometimes for several hours, while heading in the same general direction. Only the most accurate of observations can resolve whether it is an overtaking or crossing situation and no automatic assumption should ever be made that any vessel overhauling is always an overtaking one.

A further case hinging on whether the crossing rules or overtaking rules were applicable arose from a collision between the Cypriot ship *Olympian* and the Polish ship *Nowy Sacz* off Cape St. Vincent (see Figure 10). Both ships were proceeding on about parallel courses in a northerly direction, the *Olympian* at 14¹/₂ knots and the *Nowy Sacz* at 12¹/₂ knots. The night was clear and the visibility good. At about 0245 the *Olympian* bore about 25 to 30 degrees abaft the starboard beam of the *Nowy Sacz*

---

[5] Report of the Liberian Board of Investigation.

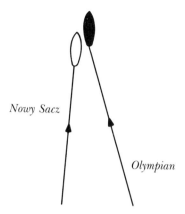

**Fig. 10.**

at a distance of some 3 miles. By 0300 the *Olympian* no longer was more than 2 points abaft the beam of *Nowy Sacz* and could see the masthead lights and green sidelight of the latter. At 0330 the *Olympian* was on the *Nowy Sacz's* starboard beam and it appeared to her that the *Nowy Sacz* was closing on a crossing course from port to starboard at an angle of 25 to 30 degrees. At 0350 the *Nowy Sacz* made five short flashes on the signaling lamp and, receiving no response, slowed and stopped her engines. The *Olympian,* then 300 to 400 yards away, sounded one short blast and altered hard to starboard. The *Nowy Sacz* put her engines full astern, sounding three short blasts and also altered hard to starboard. Shortly afterwards, at 0357, a collision occurred between the stem of the *Nowy Sacz* and the port quarter of the *Olympian* at an angle of about 10 degrees.

The Admiralty Court held that the overtaking rules were only applicable if, before 0300 when the *Olympian* was still more than 2 points abaft the beam of the *Nowy Sacz,* two conditions were fulfilled—first, that the two ships were in sight of each other, and second, the risk of collision between them had by then already arisen. The court found the first condition fulfilled, but not the second:

> . . . such risk did not arise until much later when the distance between the ships had decreased to something like a mile. That was about 0330 by which time . . . the *Olympian* was bearing about abeam.[6]

Accordingly, the situation was deemed a crossing and not an overtaking one and the *Nowy Sacz* was found three-quarters to blame with the *Olympian* one-quarter for taking tardy emergency action.

[6] The *Nowy Sacz,* Q.B. (Adm. Ct.) [1976] 2 Lloyd's Rep. 695.

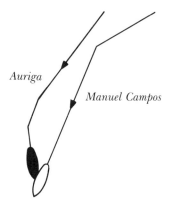

**Fig. 11.**

This decision was overturned by the court of appeals, who pointed out that the overtaking rule does not contain the qualification "so as to involve risk of collision" but does contain the words "coming up with another vessel." Furthermore, the latter part of the rule contemplated that there may be alterations of bearing after the rule had begun to apply:

> Since a constant bearing between two ships points to a risk of collision and an alteration of bearing against such a risk, this part of the rule suggests that the rule applies before there is a risk of collision.[7]

The *Olympian* was found to be a vessel "coming up with another vessel." Although risk of collision had not yet arisen, the words "coming up with another vessel" were deemed to incorporate the concept of proximity in space, which the *Olympian,* passing *Nowy Sacz* at about 400 yards, clearly met. Accordingly the *Nowy Sacz* was the stand-on ship and the *Olympian* the give-way vessel. The lower court's apportionment of blame was reversed: three-quarters to the *Olympian* and one-quarter to the *Nowy Sacz.*

In considering the above case, it should be borne in mind that neither vessel altered course or speed as the close quarters situation developed until a very late stage. Where a faster ship comes upon a slower vessel heading in the same general direction and, while some distance from her, alters course, an overtaking situation may not exist. A collision occurred off the west coast of Spain between two vessels, the Spanish ship *Manuel Campos* and the Italian ship *Auriga,* both proceeding in a southerly direction at speeds, respectively, of about 12 and 14 knots (see Figure 11). The *Manuel Campos* saw, in good visibility, the two white masthead lights and red sidelight of the *Auriga* bearing about 10 degrees

[7] The *Nowy Sacz* (C.A.) [1977] 2 Lloyd's Rep. 95.

off the starboard quarter, distant about 3 miles, and assumed the *Auriga* was overtaking. The *Auriga* was proceeding at full speed, and the courses of the two vessels were diverging at an angle of 7 degrees. Later, the *Auriga*, when almost abeam of *Manuel Campos* at a range of 2¼ miles, altered course to port. The two vessels were then converging at an angle of 24 degrees, with a risk of collision if the courses were maintained. They were—and some twenty minutes later the collision occurred, causing substantial damage to both vessels. Apart from castigating the very bad lookout kept by both vessels, the admiralty court again reiterated its *Nowy Sacz* finding that the overtaking rules only applied when risk of collision existed. An overtaking situation did not exist during the period when the *Auriga* was bearing more than two points abaft the beam of the *Manuel Campos*, because there never was at any time a risk of collision between them since the courses of the two vessels were diverging and the distance between them too great for risk of collision to exist. Accordingly, the crossing rules applied when the two vessels were subsequently on convergent courses.[8] However, the *Manuel Campos*, although therefore the give-way vessel, was only apportioned 40 percent of the blame since the risk of collision coming into being was entirely the fault of the *Auriga* for altering her course at an improper time.

It will be seen from the rules that an overtaking vessel has the option of passing on either side of the overtaken vessel, subject only to the modification that in a narrow channel the overtaken vessel should be on the right-hand side of the channel and it would ordinarily be better seamanship in such waters for the overtaking vessel to pass on the left. The overtaking situation thus becomes the only one of the three approaches where any discretion is given as to the lawful manner of passing. Meeting vessels must pass port to port, and in the crossing situation the vessel having the other to starboard must keep out of the way. But while the rule does not prescribe any specific maneuver, this situation is, to a greater degree than any other, one of privilege and burden, and the obligation is put upon the overtaking vessel to keep well clear not only throughout the approach and during the actual passing, but long enough afterward so that she is in the most literal sense "finally past and clear."

It should be noted that International Rule 13, the overtaking rule, takes precedence over all other rules in both Sections I and II of Part B, namely conduct of vessels in any condition of visibility as well as in sight of one another and that Inland Rule 13 takes precedence over Inland Rules 4 through 18. Therefore, sailing vessels and all other vessels given priority in Rule 18, even those hampered in some way by their

---

[8] The *Auriga*, Q.B. (Adm. Ct.) [1977] 1 Lloyd's Rep. 386.

activity, size, or casualty, must consider themselves bound by Rule 13 and keep out of the way of a vessel they are overtaking. Normally this should be possible by alteration of course or speed; however, some activities do not readily permit an alteration, such as an aircraft carrier recovering aircraft or a minesweeper with gear fully streamed. The special circumstances of the case may then deem it prudent for a vessel being overtaken by the like to get out of the way.

Although International and Inland Rule 13 does override other rules, it would still be good sense for small vessels, sailing vessels, or vessels engaged in fishing, to avoid impeding the passage of any vessel overtaking them in a narrow channel or following a traffic separation scheme. Such vessels should conduct themselves so as to keep clear of the deeper part of channels to allow passage for those vessels restricted to the channel. It should be borne in mind by small vessels that many large ships can only transit a channel at certain states of the tide and that they have a limited time to achieve the passage safely. Nevertheless, in the event of coming upon smaller vessels in a channel, the burden of keeping clear still rests with the overtaking vessel, in accordance with Rule 9(e)(ii).

## Signals

As pointed out in Chapter 4, one must bear in mind the fundamental difference in the meaning of clear-weather sound signals in the overtaking situation as in the meeting and crossing approaches. On the high seas, A, if a power-driven vessel, overtaking B and desiring to pass her, does not signal unless the approach will be sufficiently close to make advisable a change of course to clear her. Then A blows one blast if changing to the right and two blasts if changing to the left, in accordance with Rule 34(a). B is required by Rule 17(a)(i) to hold course and speed, and cannot properly give any whistle signal except the in-doubt signal. When A has reached a position well ahead of B, so as to be past and clear within the meaning of the rule, she may return to her course, using the proper signal to indicate the direction she now turns and once again receiving no answering signal from B. In a fairway under the jurisdiction of the international regulations, where the overtaken vessel must take action to permit a safe passage, the overtaking vessel, whether a power-driven one or not, sounds two prolonged blasts followed by one short blast or two short blasts, indicating a desire to pass on the starboard or port side, respectively. The overtaken vessel signals agreement by sounding a prolonged-short-prolonged-short signal. The overtaken vessel may answer with the in-doubt signal if not in agreement.

In inland waters the overtaking vessel, if a power-driven one, must initiate an exchange of signals with another power-driven vessel she intends to overtake, regardless of the need to maneuver. The requirement to exchange signals is not restricted to use in narrow channels and fairways but is for use in *all* inland waters, and unlike the signals for the crossing and meeting situations, there is no reference to the half-mile rule. Under Inland Rule 34(c), *A* signifies a desire to pass to starboard with one blast, or to port with two blasts, and *B* is required to answer promptly, returning *A*'s original signal as assent to the proposed maneuver or blowing the danger signal as dissent to it. In the latter case, *A* should not press her attempt to pass, though she could propose subsequently to overtake on the other side. When *A* is finally past and clear she may come back to her original course, but no whistle signal, such as is required by the international regulations, is provided for announcing the maneuver in inland waters. Perhaps the most important difference to remember in the signal requirements of this situation on the high seas and in inland waters is that under international regulations *B* cannot properly use her whistle except to warn *A* of her duty to keep clear, while under inland rules she must whistle, and has repeatedly been held at fault for failure to answer *A*'s proposal by signaling one way or the other.[9]

### Rule Applies in All Waters

The overtaking rule has long been recognized by the courts as applying not only in restricted waters but wherever an attempt to pass might mean risk of collision. An early case in point was a collision on a winter night in the wide open waters of Narragansett Bay in which the tug *M. E. Luckenbach*, with a tow 2,500 feet long consisting of two coal-laden barges, overtook and passed the tug *Cora L. Staples* with a similar tow of three barges. The *Staples*, with the heavier tow, was making about 4 knots, and the *Luckenbach*, at 6 or 7 knots, overtook and passed the other on the starboard hand without any signal and then crowded to port in such a manner that the hawser to her barge fouled the wheelhouse of the *Staples*. Despite frantic danger signals from the latter, the *Luckenbach* held on while her heavy hawser ripped off the wheelhouse roof, smokestack, and mast of the *Staples*, seriously injured the master, and knocked the mate overboard. The mate was picked up by a passing vessel after clinging to the wreckage of the wheelhouse for an hour and a half. Both he and the master libeled the *Luckenbach* and the first barge in her tow. The vessels had been on nearly parallel courses, and in holding the *Luckenbach* at fault for close-shaving, for changing course toward the other when passing, for not signaling as required by the inland rules, and for attempting to pass without the consent of the *Staples,* and the barge for contributory fault in sheering to port as she was passing and thereby causing the hawser

[9] The *Mesaba* (N.Y. 1901) 111 F.215; Ocean SS. Co. v. U.S. (CCA N.Y. 1930) 39 F.2d 553.

to foul the *Staples*, the court answered the plea of the *Luckenbach* that the overtaking rule was meant for narrow channels by saying:

> I do not think that the rule was designed for narrow waters only but for any waters where an attempt to pass would involve danger of collision.[10]

Similarly, the overtaking rule was invoked against a steamer that overtook a sailing schooner on the open ocean 60 miles northeast of Cape Hatteras on a dark, overcast night, and collided with her after she failed to show a torch, as at that time was required. While the schooner was unquestionably at fault for this omission, the steamer was held equally at fault when it developed that the mate sighted the schooner less than half a point on the bow, knew from the invisibility of sidelights that she was on the port tack, and could easily have cleared her by executing left rudder. The court said:

> Though the overtaken sailing vessel failed to exhibit a torch, as required, the burden is still upon the overtaking vessel to show that she used all reasonable diligence to avoid the other.[11]

**Important Significance of Exchanging Signals**

There is an important legal significance in this requirement as interpreted by the courts. In one sense it is doubtful whether *B*'s dissenting signal really adds anything to the obligation of *A*. It must be remembered that if *B* maintains her course and speed as required under the rule, all the burden of avoiding collision by keeping sufficiently clear is put upon *A*—whether she has *B*'s permission to pass or not—and that in the event of collision under such circumstances, *A* would ordinarily be solely liable anyway. To be sure, she would violate good seamanship by passing in the face of *B*'s danger signal, but if guilty already on the charge of passing too close, this could not, under American admiralty law, add to *A*'s liability. In another sense, however, in inland waters and in fairways under jurisdiction of the international regulations the requirement that *A* obtain permission by signal to pass the overtaken *B* has a most important bearing on the duty of each vessel to the other. It means that while on the high seas, an overtaken vessel incurs the obligation of a stand-on vessel to keep her course and speed from the moment the overtaking vessel approaches until the latter is finally past and clear, while within the jurisdiction of inland rules, or international regulations in a fairway, the overtaken vessel is under no obligation unless and until she assents to the overtaking vessel's proposal to pass. If the overtaking vessel neglects her duty to signal, the overtaken vessel is free to reduce speed or alter course, however abruptly, provided, of course, she does not delay such

[10] The *M. E. Luckenbach* (N.Y. 1908) 163 F.755.
[11] The *City of Merida* (N.Y. 1885) 24 F.229.

action until the other vessel is so close that it would make collision inevitable, which would be a violation of good seamanship. But as held by the Supreme Court in a very early case on the Mississippi above New Orleans, so long as the overtaking vessel can avoid collision by reversing or sheering out, she must pay for her silent approach with full liability for a collision resulting from an unexpected change in course or speed by the vessel ahead.[12]

On the high seas, where no exchange of signals is necessary, similar judgments have been made that the stand-on vessel need not rigidly adhere to its original course and speed. The requirement under international regulations, now Rule 17(a)(i), for the stand-on vessel to maintain course and speed has been interpreted as follows: "Course and speed"—in Rule 17(a)(i)—"mean course and speed in following the nautical manoeuvre in which, to the knowledge of the other vessel, the vessel is at that time engaged."[13] This judgment was given in a case where two steamships were each making to pick up a pilot, and it was held that the burdened vessel was justified in slowing down, as the other vessel should have been aware of her intention to pick up a pilot. This principle has been consistently applied in all situations, whether they be overtaking or crossing.[14]

Equally, in numerous decisions applied to collisions in inland waters, a similar doctrine has been followed. In several cases where the overtaking vessel was held solely at fault, the circuit court of appeals has gone so far as to excuse the overtaken vessel from not discovering the presence of the other vessel before the collision. Thus, in a case off Pier 4 in New York harbor, in which a rapidly overhauling steamer that had not announced her approach rammed and sank a small tug that was deflected from her course somewhat by the action of the tide, the appellate court held that:

> An overtaken vessel receiving no signal from an overtaking vessel is not required to look behind before she changes course however abruptly. . . .
> If the overtaking vessel without signal comes so close to the overtaken vessel that a sudden change of course by the latter may bring about a collision, the fault is that of the overtaking vessel.[15]

However, this approval of what under some circumstances would be an improper lookout aft should not be accepted too literally. It really amounts to little more than a refusal to inculpate a vessel that *is* flagrantly

---

[12] Thompson v. the *Great Republic* (1874) 23 L. Ed. 55.

[13] The *Roanoke* (1908) 11 Aspinall MC 253.

[14] The *Echo* (1917) 86 L.J.P. 121; the *Taunton* (1929) 31 Ll. L. Rep. 119; the *Manchester Regiment* (1938) 60 Ll. L. Rep. 279; the *Statue of Liberty* [1971] 2 Lloyd's Rep. 277.

[15] The *M. J. Rudolph* (CCA N.Y. 1923) 292 F.740; *see also* the *Holly Park* (CCA N.Y. 1930) 39 F.2d 572.

run down by another vessel that has no right to overtake her without a signal and is still able by smart maneuvering to avoid the collision. It merely says that with respect to a particular offending vessel approaching from more than 2 points abaft the beam, there is no obligation to sight her before hearing her required whistle. It should not be construed as a blanket provision removing the obligation of a proper lookout astern with eyes as well as ears. On the contrary, it is distinctly poor seamanship to change course or reduce speed materially without first checking the situation all around the compass. There may be an overtaking vessel under sail, which is not under the signal requirement of Inland Rule 34(c) and has no means provided of requesting passage. (Similarly, the rule does not apply to a power-driven vessel overtaking a sailing vessel in inland waters because the sailing vessel has no way of assenting or dissenting.) As already pointed out, one power-driven vessel overtaking another, whose whistle has not been blown, or whose signal has not been heard, may be so close to the stern of the other that a sudden change in the action of the vessel ahead may make collision inevitable, in which case the latter will be liable for at least part of the damages and may not be able to recover from the other vessel at all.[16] An overtaking vessel following another and for the time being having no intention to pass is ordinarily under no obligation to signal.[17] The point is that inasmuch as we are bound to observe a vessel astern under some circumstances, the only safe procedure is to look astern under all circumstances where a change in maneuver can be followed by an overtaking collision. As long ago held by the Supreme Court in a case where a steamer was overtaking a schooner in Delaware Bay and sank her when she tacked unexpectedly across the steamer's bow:

> While a man stationed at the stern as a lookout is not at all times necessary no vessel should change her course materially without having first made such an observation in all directions as will enable her to know how what she is about to do will affect others in her immediate vicinity.[18]

The schooner was solely liable for the collision. As was the Great Lakes fishing boat, whose crew were guilty of willful negligence in putting the boat on automatic pilot in a shipping lane and going below to clean fish without leaving a lookout. A cargo vessel overtook on the starboard side of the fishing vessel when the latter took an unexpected starboard turn into the larger vessel resulting in collision and deaths.[19]

---

[16] Long Id. R.R. Co. v. Killien (CCA N.Y. 1895) 67 F.365; the *Pleiades* (CCA N.Y. 1926) 9 F.2d 804.

[17] The *Pleiades*, supra.

[18] The *Illinois* (1881) 26 L. Ed. 562; *see also* the *Philadelphian* (CCA N..Y 1894) 61 F.862.

[19] Slobodna Plovidba, Lim. Procs., 1988 AMC 2307.

If the overtaking vessel in inland waters signals one or two blasts and the vessel ahead does not answer, it is her duty to repeat the signal. In a very early case it was held that this was necessary, and that even when the signal is repeated and unanswered, the overtaken vessel's silence may not be regarded as acquiescence.[20] If the overtaking vessel persists in passing without receiving the necessary response, both vessels are breaking the rule and will divide the damage.[21] There is, thus, a requirement so rigid with respect to the overtaking vessel in inland waters that unless she signals and receives permission to pass, the only question usually left the courts to decide after a resulting collision is whether she shall pay all the damages or only some proportionate share.

## Initial Signal by Overtaken Vessel

An overtaken vessel is under no obligation to make an initial signal to a vessel coming up astern if there appears to be ample room for her to pass in safety. It was so held when two tugs with tows in Baltimore harbor on slightly converging courses, but with one a little in the lead, gradually drew together in broad daylight and finally collided. It developed that the master of the overtaking tug was partially blind in one eye and did not see the other vessel until too late to prevent collision; his tug was, of course, fully liable for the damage.[22] But it is clearly the duty of the overtaken vessel, both in inland waters and on the high seas, to sound the proper danger/in-doubt signal if she actually sees that collision is possible. In a somewhat unusual case the steamship *Howard*, on her regular run from Baltimore to Providence, overtook the seagoing tug *Charles F. Mayer* with two laden coal barges under tow on a clear night near Point Judith and sank one of the barges, drowning three of the crew. The watch of the *Howard* had just been changed, and the relieving watch officer had his attention suddenly attracted to port by sighting the red light of a steamer, on opposite course altogether too close for comfort. He immediately changed course sharply to the right, which cleared the other steamer, but brought him into dangerous proximity to the barges of the *Mayer*, which he had not noticed. The barges were in tandem on a very long towline, with about a thousand feet between them, and the mate of the *Mayer*, seeing by the *Howard*'s lights that she was heading for the barges, called the captain instead of taking preventive action himself. The captain rushed to the bridge and, instead of blowing the danger signal to warn the *Howard*, immediately slowed his engines in the hope that the towline between the barges would sag and that the *Howard*

---

[20] Erwin v. Neversink Steamboat Co. (1882) 88 N.Y. 184.
[21] The *Mesaba;* the *Pleiades* (CCA N.Y. 1926) 9 F.2d 804.
[22] The *Albemarle* (Md. 1927) 22 F.2d 840.

would pass clear above it. Of course, this was a violation of his duty, knowing the other vessel's presence, to keep course and speed; and on the showing that the mate had deferred proper action until the captain had taken charge, this could not be excused as an error in extremis. The *Howard*'s fault was obvious, but the *Mayer* was also held in fault, not only for her untimely reduction in speed but for her failure to sound the inland danger signal as soon as the danger became apparent, and for failure to have an officer on watch who was qualified instantly to take the decisive action required.[23]

## Legal Effects of Assent to Passing

The international regulation requiring an exchange of signals in a fairway assumes that the overtaken vessel must assist in the maneuver. The legal effect of her assent, therefore, is an agreement to maneuver in such a way as to give the overtaking vessel more room, if necessary. While the overtaken vessel is required to help, the overtaking vessel is still responsible for the safety of the maneuver.

When an overtaken vessel in inland waters assents to the proposal of an overtaking vessel to pass, she neither yields her right-of-way in the slightest degree nor assumes responsibility for the safety of the maneuver, and the fear that either of these results will follow is not an excuse for failure to answer. As already pointed out, in inland waters she *must* answer, and promptly. She must examine the situation ahead as thoroughly as conditions permit, and immediately express the assent or dissent provided by law. As said by the circuit court of appeals:

> The passing signal from an overtaking vessel is not solely a request for permission to pass. It also asks for information which the overtaking vessel is entitled to have. When the overtaken vessel knows of conditions which may make the passing unsafe it has no right to refuse to inform the overtaking vessel of such conditions, and if it does refuse it cannot throw the entire blame for an accident upon the other vessel.[24]

This should not be taken to mean that the mere act of assenting to the proposal ensures a safe passage, however, and inculpates the overtaken vessel in an action following collision. The general rule is that it does not inculpate her at all. However, she can be charged with fault for her assent only when it is given in the face of conditions that ought to make it apparent that a passing is fraught with serious peril and is almost certain to cause a collision. In other words, she cannot deliberately lead the following vessel into a trap and escape liability. But if, in her judgment, the overtaking vessel can, with the exercise of a high degree of skill, successfully make her way past, then she is legally justified in giving

[23] The *Howard* (CCA Md. 1919) 256 F.987.
[24] The *M. P. Howlett* (CCA Pa. 1932) 58 F.2d 923.

her signaled consent to the attempt. The burden of clearing her is left almost entirely to the overtaking vessel. As said in a very old case:

> The approaching vessel, when she has command of her movement, takes upon herself the peril of determining whether a safe passage remains for her beside the one preceding her, and must bear the consequences of misjudgment in that respect.[25]

Nonetheless, the overtaken vessel must not forget, on waters covered by the international rules, to make appropriate sound signals should she maneuver. An overtaken vessel has been held 15 percent at fault for altering course without signaling this change prior to collision.[26] Generally, however, an overtaking vessel that fails to keep out of the way of the ship being overtaken is presumed to be at fault and must sustain the *Pennsylvania* rule burden of proving that the other's statutory violation could not have contributed to the collision.[27]

## Duty of Overtaking Vessel to Keep Clear

The courts have not been more specific than the rule itself in regard to the duration of the overtaking vessel's duty to keep clear. The rule lays that obligation upon her until "she is finally past and clear." Many years ago the point was settled that the rule applies not merely until the overtaken vessel is abeam, but until she has completely passed the other.[28] In a later case, when an overtaking steamship, just after passing a tug with barges, lost headway in order to come to anchor and was struck by one of the barges, the steamship was held not to have fulfilled her duty to keep clear.[29] Perhaps the best policy in deciding this point in practice is to fall back on the literal provision of the overtaking rule, and consider that the overtaking vessel must keep clear until far enough ahead so that her maneuver cannot embarrass the vessel she has overtaken, as long as the latter holds course and speed. Of course, if she has to stop in the path of the vessel she has left astern there is an added reason for the prompt use of the danger signal.

Under both sets of rules, the action by a give-way vessel is covered by Rule 16 and enjoins her to pass "well clear," an injunction that does not prevent her from passing ahead of the stand-on vessel. Thus, an overtaking vessel may cross ahead, but the stricture of Rule 8(d) makes it imperative that it shall be at a "safe distance," with the maneuver not

---

[25] The *Rhode Island* (N.Y. 1847) Fed. Case No. 11,745.

[26] MISR v. *Har Sinai*, 1979 AMC 2367.

[27] Sea hand v. *Nelly Maersk* 1983 AMC 472; *also* Alter Barge v. TPC Transp., 1987 AMC 1788.

[28] Kennedy v. American Steamboat Co. (1878) 12 R.I. 23.

[29] Brady v. the *Bendo* and the *Sampson* (Va. 1890) 44 F.439.

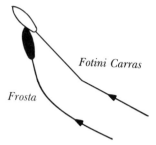

*Fotini Carras*

*Frosta*

**Fig. 12.**

cut so fine as to result in danger. Where vessels have a large advantage in speed, such as a surface effect ship overtaking a more pedestrian vessel, then such a maneuver is probably safe. However, the constant risk of mechanical breakdown should always be borne in mind in assessing what is a "safe distance" ahead. For more conventional vessels the more prudent action would be to alter course or reduce speed to pass under the stern of the vessel being overtaken. Such action must be taken in good time, for there is a risk that a vessel being overtaken may become sufficiently concerned to take action that might be conflicting under Rule 17(a)(ii). Early action is particularly important in a marginal case, where a vessel to starboard of another may assume herself the give-way vessel in an overtaking situation and turn to port to duck under the stern, whereas the vessel to port thinks she is the give-way vessel in a crossing case and alters to starboard. Perhaps the best solution is for the vessel to starboard, if she is relatively close to the other, to turn to a parallel course and pass ahead, or slow and wait for enough room to pass safely under the other vessel's stern, keeping a sharp lookout for any maneuver by the other.

### The Usual Cause of Overtaking Collisions
In concluding this discussion, it may be said that the duties of the respective vessels in the overtaking situation are clear, and it is only by disregarding them that collision is likely to occur. The burden of keeping a safe distance away is placed on the overtaking vessel. The overtaken vessel has the simple obligation of maintaining course and speed as far as practicable, and in inland waters, or in a fairway under international rules, the additional duty of answering the other vessel's signals. In many overtaking collisions, the cause is the impatience or negligence of the faster vessel, which in an ill-advised effort to save minutes or seconds, crowds the slower vessel too closely, or attempts to pass her when the time and place are not safe. The *Frosta*, already discussed in Chapter 3,

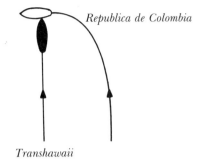

*Republica de Colombia*

*Transhawaii*

**Fig. 13.**

was an example of the former when she chose to overtake the *Fotini Carras* at a distance apart of only 500 yards, despite having the open expanse of the Indian Ocean available (see Figure 12). The sudden failure of the *Frosta*'s steering gear resulted in that narrow gap between the two vessels being closed in less than three minutes. The *Frosta* was found totally liable for the collision, in part for overtaking too close when:

> both sides accepted that a proper overtaking distance for ships of this size in the open seas was not less than half a mile.[30]

When the Colombian cargo vessel *Republica de Colombia* was overtaking the American container ship *Transhawaii* off the Diamond Shoal, she did choose to pass at about half a mile (see Figure 13). But this proved totally inadequate when, at the moment of passing, the automatic steering gear seized with 10 to 15 degrees of port wheel on. Frantic efforts to rectify the defect were made, but to no avail and some four minutes later the *Transhawaii* plunged into *Republica de Colombia*'s port side.[31] The passing distance might have been sufficient if greater alertness existed in both ships, with watch officers ready to spring into immediate action while the potentially dangerous period of close-quarters existed.

Yet again, an example of passing at unnecessary close quarters such that a mechanical failure could not be corrected in time to avoid a collision was the case of the Portuguese tanker *Fogo* and the British freighter *Trentback* (see Figure 14). The two vessels had cleared the Suez Canal together and were heading westwards on a clear day in the open Mediterranean Sea. The *Trentback* passed the *Fogo* at about two cables' range. The British mate on watch turned his attention to the deck log and did not detect that *Trentback*'s automatic steering had malfunctioned. A deck

---

[30] The *Frosta*, Q.B. (Adm. Ct.) [1973] 2 Lloyd's Rep. 355.
[31] Flota Mar. Gr. Lim Procs., 1979 AMC 156.

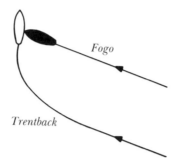

**Fig. 14.**

hand, working other than on the bridge, alerted him, but it was too late to stop the freighter falling off across the tanker's path. The *Trentback* subsequently sank and her owners bore full responsiblity for damage.

> Automatic steering is a most valuable invention if properly used. It can lead to disaster when it is left to look after itself while vigilance is relaxed.[32]

Vigilance is indeed necessary and so is prudence in determining passing distances.

There are many cases in the books where vessels have ignored the well-known danger of suction and disaster has resulted. A collision due to suction is nearly always chargeable to the overtaking vessel, because it is prima facie evidence that she tried to pass too close. While the effect of suction is undoubtedly strongest, and therefore most properly to be anticipated, in shallow channels,[33] it has been alleged to have caused a collision in the deep waters of the Hudson River with vessels more than 200 feet apart.[34]

Suction, or more properly interaction, between two vessels is present whenever they are relatively close aboard each other (a more detailed discussion of this effect in restricted waters is found in Chapter 8). When the vessels are moving in the same direction with little difference in speed between them, and especially if they are of dissimilar size, the risk from interaction is greatest. Even in deep water interaction effects may be experienced by fast-moving vessels overtaking at close distances. The collision between the *Queen Mary*, overtaking at 28½ knots, and the cruiser HMS *Curacao*, proceeding at 25 knots, was considered partly due to interaction even though the charted depth was approximately 120 meters. Hence, it is not prudent to attempt to pass close in open waters

---

[32] The *Fogo* [1967] 2 Lloyd's Rep. 208.

[33] The *Sif* (Pa. 1910) 181 F.412; the *Aureole* (CCA Pa. 1902) 113 F.224.

[34] The *Cedarhurst* (CCA N.Y. 1930) 42 F.2d 139; certiorari denied (1930) 75 L. Ed. 767.

when there is plenty of sea room available. As was said in the *Queen Mary–Curacao* case:

> . . . the vessels should never have been allowed to approach so closely as to bring the forces of interaction into existence.[35]

In all cases under the rule the keynote is caution, bearing in mind that as the stand-on vessel the one ahead has a very strong presumption in her favor. In the eyes of the courts she has an indisputable right to use the public navigable waters in which she is navigating, and so far as that particular stage of the voyage is concerned, she was there first and no one passes but by her leave. Perhaps the whole matter has not been more succinctly stated than by the Supreme Court as to a collision at night more than one hundred years ago, when one sailing schooner overtook and sank another in the open waters of Chesapeake Bay:

> The vessel astern, as a general rule, is bound to give way, or to adopt the necessary precautions to avoid a collision. That rule rests upon the principle that the vessel ahead, on that state of facts, has the seaway before her, and is entitled to hold her position; and consequently the vessel coming up must keep out of the way.[36]

## SUMMARY

An overtaking vessel is one that approaches another from a direction more than 22.5 degrees abaft her beam. The overtaking rule, which requires the overtaking vessel to keep out of the way and thus binds the overtaken vessel to hold course and speed, applies in open waters as well as in narrow channels. In the overtaking situation, the vessels are proceeding in the same general direction and the vessel astern is faster than the vessel ahead. The overtaking vessel may pass on either side, subject to the modification in narrow channels that if the leading vessel is keeping to the right in accordance with Rule 9(a), it may be better seamanship to pass her on her port side.

Under international regulations in open water, the overtaking vessel signals course changes during passing with one or two short blasts. In a fairway under international regulations, where the overtaken vessel has to take action to permit safe passing, a proposal to pass to starboard is signaled by two prolonged and one short blasts, and two prolonged and two short blasts for passage to port. The same proposals in inland waters are made without the prolonged blasts, one short to starboard and two short blasts for passage to port. Agreement is signified by answering with the same signal in inland waters, or by a prolonged-short-prolonged-short signal in international waters. Under both sets of rules, disagreement with a proposal must be made known with the in-doubt/danger signal. In

---

[35] The *Queen Mary* (1949) 82 Ll. L. Rep. 303.
[36] Whitridge v. Dill (1860) 16 L. Ed. 581.

international waters only, agreement signifies that the overtaken vessel will assist in the maneuver.

In inland waters, an overtaken vessel has been found equally at fault with the overtaking vessel when she failed to answer the latter's signal and her silence was mistaken for acquiescence. When the overtaken vessel in inland waters assents, she does not assume responsibility for the safety of the maneuver but merely agrees not to thwart the attempt of the other vessel to pass; however, in the face of apparent danger, it is her duty to prohibit the passage by sounding the prescribed danger signal, and if she assents instead, she will also be held at fault. Even after a proper assent, the overtaking vessel is bound to pass a safe distance off, and will be liable for a collision brought about by passing too closely, provided the other vessel maintains course and speed. Most overtaking collisions are due to this cause, and particular care must be given to pass far enough off to avoid the effect of suction, especially in shallow water. The obligation of the overtaking vessel to keep clear holds until her maneuvers can no longer embarrass the overtaken vessel, or until she is "finally past and clear."

# 7

# The Crossing Situation
# in Open Waters

**Open v. Restricted Waters**
The considerations already addressed that come into play concerning
the head-on and overtaking situations in restricted waters also lend themselves to placing the primary discussion of crossing situations in such
waters within the framework of a separate chapter. Hence the crossing
situation in confined waters, with the special situation relating to a narrow
channel, is further dealt with in Chapter 8.

**Crossing Situation Very Hazardous**
Few approaches of vessels at sea or in inland waters can be so trying to
the souls of seamen as that of two vessels on a near-collision course in a
crossing situation. What navigator of a stand-on vessel, about to cross
another, has not experienced certain tense moments when it appeared
doubtful if the give-way vessel was going to do her duty and give way?
Moments when the impulse to reverse or sheer out and yield the right-
of-way were barely balanced by a realization of the risk, legal and physical,
of changing course or speed? Or what navigators of a give-way vessel in
the same situation have not at some time convinced themselves by a
pair of bearings that they had plenty of time to cross ahead, and then
experienced a harrowing interval wondering whether they were going
to make it, conscious that if the race ended in a tie, they would be hanged
higher than a kite? When we consider the nervous psychology nearly
always present on one or both vessels in these cases, one is almost inclined
to the belief that the crossing situation should have a law against it. It
was to reduce, perhaps, this tenseness that the 1972 conference introduced the most revolutionary change in recent years to the crossing
situation: namely, the stand-on vessel may now maneuver before reaching

in extremis. This change is now also reflected in the rules for preventing collisions on the inland waters of the United States.

In the past it was unfortunate that under American law an approach often in confined waters that is naturally fraught with a certain degree of mental hazard should have been made legally so complex that some of its intricacies were puzzling even to admiralty lawyers and were completely baffling to the average mariner, whose duty is not to argue fine distinctions of law but to avoid collision. The Inland Navigational Rules Act of 1980 was a bold attempt to clarify the ad hoc collection of rules that governed the crossing situation as well as attempting to achieve unity, not only within inland waters, but with the international regulations. Some differences, however, remain, and these will be discussed later in this chapter, as well as differences in the rules for restricted waters in greater detail in Chapter 8. Of more importance is what will happen to the wealth of legal precedents concerning the crossing situation that has been built up in United States courts. Some former judgments will undoubtedly be cast aside by the new inland rules, but there is much that was founded upon common sense that will undoubtedly remain relevant.

### The Same Maneuvers Are Required by Both Sets of Rules

Despite the differences that remain between the separate jurisdictions, it must be stressed that both sets of rules employ, in open water, the same principle for maneuvering to avoid collision. International Rule 15, which is identical to Inland Rule 15(a), clearly spells out the status of ships in a crossing situation:

> When two power-driven vessels are crossing so as to involve risk of collision, the vessel which has the other on her own starboard side shall keep out of the way and shall, if the circumstances of the case admit, avoid crossing ahead of the other vessel.

Therefore, any power-driven vessel that is involved in risk of collision with another in sight on her starboard side—that is, the arc from dead ahead up to 22.5 degrees abaft the starboard beam—and the situation being neither a meeting nor an overtaking one, is a give-way vessel. She is enjoined not to cross ahead of the other by Rule 15, bound to take early and substantial action in accordance with Rule 16, as well as being required by Rule 8 to see that the action is positive, made in ample time, and acceptable to the practice of good seamanship. Thus, the timely options available to the give-way vessel are to keep out of the way by altering course to starboard, to slacken speed or stop or reverse, or to alter to port sufficiently to avoid passing ahead. Whatever action is taken it must be bold enough to be clearly understood by the other vessel. The most common maneuver is for the give-way vessel to alter sufficiently to starboard to place the stand-on vessel well on the port bow. Nibbling alterations to starboard do not constitute bold action to keep clear, as was illustrated in the case mentioned in Chapter 4, when the *Statue of Liberty*'s two belated and minimal alterations were adjudged inadequate in the circumstances.[1]

The action to be taken by the stand-on vessel, in any situation, is governed by Rule 17(a)(i) of both sets of rules:

> Where one of two vessels is to keep out of the way the other shall keep her course and speed.

This is a clear enough injunction that satisfactorily covers the majority of crossing situations in open waters. However, the stand-on vessel is not required to maintain her course and speed blindly until collision occurs. If the other vessel fails to give way and approaches so close that any avoiding measure by her alone cannot avoid collision, then the stand-on vessel must take whatever action, under Rule 17(b), she thinks best will avert collision. This traditional maintenance of course and speed by the stand-on vessel until reaching in extremis is now further modified by Rule 17(a)(ii) where she

> . . . may, however, take action to avoid collision by her maneuver alone, as soon as it becomes apparent to her that the vessel required to keep out of the way is not taking appropriate action in compliance with these Rules.

Further, and unique to the crossing situation, Rule 17(c) goes on to stipulate that, in taking the permissive avoiding action, the stand-on vessel

> . . . shall, if the circumstances of the case permit, not alter course to port for a vessel on her own port side.

The theory, long enshrined in the rules and upheld by courts, that collision is less likely to occur if one vessel is directed to keep clear of another vessel that is required to stand on, is not invalidated in the face of Rule 17(a)(ii). Only when it has become apparent that the give-way vessel has failed to assume her obligation to keep clear is the stand-on vessel permitted to deviate from faithful adherence to course and speed. The danger of the theory breaking down lies in the occurrence of the delayed compliance of the give-way vessel to maneuver to avoid collision, coincident with the decision of the stand-on vessel that the time had come to exercise her prerogative to take avoiding action. Now awakened to danger, the give-way vessel can no longer be sure that the stand-on vessel is in fact standing-on. In order to avoid this situation, it becomes even more important for the give-way vessel in a crossing situation to adhere strictly to the requirement of Rule 16—that is, to take early action to keep well clear.

---

[1] The *Statue of Liberty* (H.L.) [1971] 2 Lloyd's Rep. 277.

And the stand-on vessel? When is she advised to proceed under Rule 17(a)(ii)? Certainly not until risk of collision has been established. Probably not until she has sounded the signal of doubt/danger as a wake-up signal (supplemented by flashes of a light if possible), possibly after failure to achieve VHF contact, but definitely prior to in extremis. This point was made in a case discussed in more detail in the pages following, where the court held:[2]

> The second mate knew that, as the give-way vessel, the *Globe* was required to take action to avoid a collision. As he watched the *Globe*, it became apparent that the *Globe* was not going to take action. At that time he was required to sound the *Sanko*'s whistle signal in accordance with Rule 34(d). Had he done so, the *Globe*'s watch might have been alerted and taken evasive action. Therefore, the court finds that Rule 34 was violated and the violation contributed to the collision.

The distance at which to take action under Rule 17(a)(ii) will vary considerably. It will be much greater for high-speed vessels involved in a fine crossing situation than for low-speed vessels in an abaft-the-beam crossing situation, which is not to say that the latter is the least risky situation! For a crossing case in open waters it is suggested that the maximum range for most ships to take permissive action would be in the order of about 2 to 3 miles. However, this figure will clearly vary with the capabilities and characteristics of individual ships, with a very large ship having a "domain" in excess.

Four years after the 72 ColRegs became effective for the United States, the courts indicated that this relatively new aspect of the rules is to be taken seriously. In a collision between a fishing vessel and a tow in 1981, the court[3] was of the opinion that Rule 17 does not require the stand-on vessel to hold on until collision is practically inevitable. In fact, the stand-on vessel was found partially at fault for failing to take action to avoid a collision once it became apparent that the give-way vessel was not meeting its obligation to keep clear.

The collision took place on the high seas off the Oregon coast, in a moderate sea with a visibility of 10 miles (see Figure 15). The *Mary Catherine* and her tow, the barge *Bandon*, were proceeding in a southerly direction. The watch officer observed the fishing vessel *Shaun* approaching from the south about a half hour before the collision. The *Shaun* subsequently passed *Mary Catherine* abeam to starboard, crossed over the tow cable, collided with the forward port corner of *Bandon*, and rolled over with the loss of three lives. Although there was some discussion to the contrary, the court held that as the *Mary Catherine* had the *Shaun* on her starboard hand, she was the burdened or give-way vessel under

---

[2] Rich Ocean Carriers v. *Sanko Diamond*, 1989 AMC 220.
[3] Shaun Fisheries, Lim. Procs., 1984 AMC 2650.

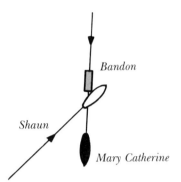

**Fig. 15.**

Rule 15. However, the court held each vessel liable for 50 percent of the damages resulting from the collision because of violations of the rules including failure to keep a proper lookout and failing to sound appropriate and timely danger signals, and found:

> Even though *Shaun* did have the right of way, she had the duty to avoid collision when it became apparent that *Mary Catherine* was not obeying the rules of the road. *Shaun* had ample warning of the fact in *Mary Catherine*'s steady course and speed throughout the time the vessels were in sight of each other. As collision became more and more probable, *Shaun* could have radioed *Mary Catherine* and asked her intentions, or, as the vessels came still closer, have sounded a warning signal to alert the other ship. Even after *Shaun* passed abeam of the tug, she could have turned to port and avoided the collision. . . . I find that both ships were at fault in failure to give way. *Mary Catherine* was obliged to give way under the rules of the road. *Shaun* was obliged to avoid collision when *Mary Catherine* failed to give way.

In a more recent case,[4] the need for the stand-on vessel to take timely action in a crossing situation to avoid collision was reaffirmed. The 75-foot fishing vessel *McKinley* and the 649-foot car carrier *Tosca* collided at night, in perfect visibility, on the open ocean (see Figure 16). The two vessels were approaching each other on roughly opposite courses, with their tracks varying approximately 20 degrees from each other. Well before the collision the *McKinley* was visually sighted 20 degrees on the starboard bow of *Tosca*. The watch keeper on the *McKinley* was judged to be totally incompetent because of a fundamental lack of knowledge of rules of the road and the constant bearing rule. The *McKinley* was the give-way vessel in a crossing situation, and in addition to a failure to keep a proper lookout, she was judged at fault for taking no early and substantial action to avoid the other vessel. The *Tosca*, meanwhile, as the

[4] Ocean Foods Lim. Procs., 1989 AMC 579.

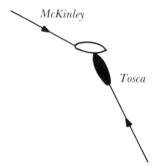

**Fig. 16.**

stand-on vessel, failed to make proper use of her radar, failed to observe the lights of the fishing vessel approaching on a collision course on her port side, and failed to take timely action to avoid collision as the stand-on vessel. She steamed on at 20 knots, and cut the *McKinley* in two, resulting in the death of one of her crew.

In apportioning the liability of 65 percent to *McKinley* and 35 percent to *Tosca* because each violated numerous rules of the road, the court held:

> Rule 17 allowed the *Tosca* to take unilateral action to avoid the collision once it became apparent that the *McKinley* was not following the rules and that the *Tosca's* maneuver was necessary to avoid collision. The *Tosca* failed to take such action. She must accept some responsibility for the collision.

In yet another recent case,[5] where the motor vessel *Sanko Diamond* collided with the motor vessel *Globe R. World,* the court held that the stand-on vessel was 15 percent at fault because the watch officer, among other things, failed to take timely evasive action. The court noted that the established courses of the two ships placed them in a crossing situation, and neither ship changed its course prior to the collision. In addressing the *Sanko's* statutory violations, the court noted that her watch officer spotted the *Globe* at a distance of 10 miles, determined that the ships were on a collision course, and tracked the ships as they approached each other. Some fifteen minutes before the collision he took another bearing, estimated the *Globe* to be 5 miles away, became alarmed because the two ships were in a crossing situation with the *Globe* burdened, and decided she was not going to give way. Only just a few minutes before the collision did *Sanko* steer hard starboard. The court found the delay in maneuvering violated ColReg Rule 8, which requires timely action, and Rule 17(d), which requires action by the stand-on vessel that finds

[5] Rich Ocean Carriers v. *Sanko Diamond,* 1989 AMC 220.

herself so close (in extremis) that collision cannot be avoided by the action of the give-way vessel alone. In the opinion of the author, the court should have noted violation of Rule 17(a)(ii) as well because of the overwhelming weight of the testimony that points to an early obligation to maneuver because the *Sanko* was well aware and concerned that the *Globe* was not meeting her obligations as the give-way vessel long before the point of in extremis was reached. Regardless of the rule applied by the court, the message is clear when it is apparent to the stand-on vessel that the give-way vessel in a crossing situation is not tending to business. Take action to avoid collision in compliance with the rules.

These instructive cases make it seem likely that the courts would never establish a norm for the observance of Rule 17(a)(ii), but always consider each case on its merits: the ships involved, the proximity of other dangers, the diligence of those on watch, etc., etc. The ordinary practice of good seamanship should serve to guide mariners in their decision to take permissive action. An important point here is to realize that although these cases properly affirm the intent of rule 17(a)(ii), that is, to avoid collision when the other vessel fails to give way, the stand-on vessel in a crossing situation has not been granted license to maneuver at will. She is not permitted to alter course or change speed under Rule 17(a)(ii) solely because she thinks it might help the situation or once she observes the other vessel maneuvering to meet her obligations as the give-way vessel. It would seem, however, that for one vessel to stand on and watch another vessel reduce the distance between them to the point of collision, steadfastly maintaining the point of privilege as the *Shaun* appeared to have done, is far removed from the dictates of good seamanship.

In considering permissive action, it is well for the stand-on vessel to bear in mind that the give-way vessel may belatedly wake up to her responsibilities, probably by altering course to starboard, and to adhere to the provision of Rule 17(c)—that is, not to alter course to port for a vessel on her own port side. Additionally, a reduction of speed might make it more difficult for the give-way vessel to pass astern. A major alteration to starboard may well be the best course of action, not forgetting to sound the proper sound signal so that the other vessel might speedily understand the intent of the maneuver.

Action to avoid collision becomes compulsory for the stand-on vessel when she finds herself so close that collision cannot be avoided by the give-way vessel alone, i.e., in extremis. The distance between the two vessels when this moment arrives will vary with the direction and speed of approach of the other vessel, an estimate of her maneuvering characteristics, and a thorough knowledge of one's own vessel's capabilities and limitations. The precise point at which to cease maintaining course and speed is difficult to determine, and some latitude has been allowed in court cases. When it is shown that the other vessel had been carefully watched and that the stand-on vessel had endeavored to do her best to act at the correct moment, she will not be held to blame, though subsequent analysis shows she waited too long or acted too soon.

Tᵥₑ conduct of a prudent seaman in such circumstances is not to be tried by mathematical calculations subsequently made.[6]

An alteration to starboard to avoid a vessel close on the port bow could be most dangerous, as it will take the stand-on vessel across the other ship's bow. Left too late and she might be struck amidships, the most vulnerable spot. Rule 17(c) therefore does not apply when in extremis is reached, as a vessel is permitted to take any action that might best avert collision. Turning towards the other vessel may well be the best action to take at such close quarters, particularly if she is likely to strike abaft the stand-on vessel's beam.

When collision, despite all efforts, appears to be inevitable, the aim should be to reduce the effect to a minimum. A glancing blow is normally better than a direct impact, though with tankers and the like it is unlikely to reduce the risk of fire. If a glancing blow is impossible, it is probably best to take the impact on the bow, forward of the collision bulkhead. An alteration away that exposes the vulnerable ship's side might well be the most damaging course of action to take.

To make totally clear to a give-way vessel that the permissive action open to a stand-on vessel in no way excuses the former from her responsibilities, Rule 17, under both jurisdictions, concludes:

(d) This Rule does not relieve the give-way vessel of her obligation to keep out of the way.

Thus, the give-way vessel must not hang on in the hope that the stand-on vessel will opt out of the situation early, nor is she released from her duty to ensure that a safe passing distance is achieved even if the stand-on vessel does maneuver.

An example of dilatory action in giving way, and then in the wrong direction, was the *Konakry* (see Figure 17). Originally a point on the port bow of an approaching vessel, she did not alter to starboard until she was dead ahead of the *Orduna* at about a quarter of a mile. The latter as stand-on vessel had maintained course and speed until the same moment before altering course to port. Collision followed. Both vessels were held to blame: *Konakry* for not altering in due time and *Orduna* for altering to port when she did. The latter contended that, as she had the green light of *Konakry* dead ahead of her when she altered, the crossing

---

[6] Compagnie des Forges d'Homecourt (1920) S.C. 247; 2 Ll. L. Rep. 186.

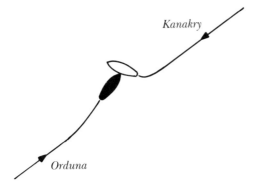

*Kanakry*

*Orduna*

**Fig. 17.**

rules had ceased to apply. It was held by the highest court in the land that,

> The conditions which render the regulations for crossing ships applicable begin as soon as the two ships are approaching each other on courses which, if continued, may cause a collision. These conditions continue to subsist until the vessels have definitely passed out of the phase of crossing ships.[7]

The fact that the green light of *Konakry* got ahead of *Orduna* did not mean the operation of passing was completed. Once a situation exists in the high seas, it cannot be unilaterally converted or subsequently claimed to be another.

**Confusion of Crossing Situation with Starboard-to-Starboard Passage**
From time to time approaching vessels sometimes fail to appreciate that they are in a crossing situation and seek to alter course to port to clear a ship fine on their starboard bow. Two such examples of ships so altering to port follow.

One such approach from ahead that ended in disaster was the intersection of the Italian passenger/cargo vessel *Verdi*'s track with that of the Panamanian tanker *Pentelikon* in the Strait of Gibraltar (see Figure 18). Again it was good visibility. The *Verdi* originally assessed that the *Pentelikon*'s bearing was drawing right, i.e., they would pass starboard to starboard. However, the *Verdi* had to alter course to starboard to pass under the stern of a closer vessel, after which she altered back to port to her previous course. This placed her on a collision course with the *Pentelikon*, but still thinking she was going to achieve a starboard-to-starboard passing

[7] The *Orduna* v. The Shipping Controller (1921) 1 A.C. 250.

*Pentelikon*                    *Verdi*

**Fig. 18.**

she did nothing until in extremis, when she altered to port. Meanwhile, the tanker was expecting the Italian to give way in a crossing situation, but the latter failed to do so despite warning and in-doubt signals from the Panamanian. Belatedly, the tanker altered course to starboard, canceling out the *Verdi*'s alteration to port. There were serious faults of lookout, plus surprising indecision in both vessels, who nonetheless knew the risk of collision existed and, in one, the tanker, that in extremis had not only been reached but passed. So the *Pentelikon* collected some blame, though the overwhelming fault lay with the *Verdi*'s failure to recognize the changed circumstances and to give way to another vessel nearly 30 degrees on her starboard bow.[8]

The Norwegian tanker *Cardo* was placed in a similar setting when the Somalian motor vessel *Toni* approached from about 10 degrees on her port bow off the southeast coast of Africa (see Figure 19). Both ships, in good visibility at night, were aware of each other's presence at about 14 miles' range. The *Toni* was remiss in watch-keeping practices, including altering course to port during the approach. This was probably about the same time that the *Cardo,* unbelievably misinterpretating the situation as a meeting one, altered for the first time to starboard. As the gap closed, belated awareness of the hazard led to further alterations to starboard placing the *Cardo* in the path of the dilatory *Toni*. Both vessels were found to blame for the subsequent collision: 50 percent to the *Toni* for not taking, among other things, early positive action to keep out of the way; and 50 percent to the *Cardo* for not keeping her course and speed in a crossing situation.[9]

**Confusion of Crossing Situation with the Overtaking Situation**
As illustrated in Chapter 6 on the overtaking situation by the *Pacific Glory/Allegro* disaster, ships on slowly converging courses when approaching from the same general direction can fail to recognize the true

[8] The *Verdi* (1970) AMC 1140; *see also* the *Vysotsk* [1981] 1 Lloyd's Rep. 439.
[9] The *Toni* [1973] 1 Lloyd's Rep. 79.

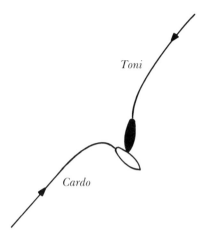

**Fig. 19.**

situation. The Russian motor vessel *Debalzevo* and the Norwegian tanker *Ek* were about a mile apart from each other, both proceeding in a general southerly direction (see Figure 20). In fact, both vessels believed they were on parallel courses until four minutes before collision when the faster Russian thought the Norwegian had altered to port. But this was an illusion, and it was held that *Debalzevo* should have avoided collision by altering to starboard under *Ek*'s stern as give-way vessel in a crossing situation. As she did not, she still, at a later stage, i.e., in extremis, could have altered to port. She did neither and attracted three-quarters of the blame, with the *Ek* collecting the remainder for not altering course to starboard on reaching in extremis.[10]

### Special Circumstances Not a Substitute at Will for Crossing Rule

An examination of past cases disclosed among navigators a common misconception of the law in regard to the crossing situation. This was that the application of the crossing rule was modified by special circumstances to such an extent that whenever the stand-on vessel recognized any risk of collision whatever, she immediately had complete discretion as to whether or not she would attempt to pass ahead. This is not so, for any departure from the rules is only permitted by Rule 2(b) when there are special circumstances *and* there is immediate danger. Both conditions must apply.

---

[10] The *Ek* [1966] 1 Lloyd's Rep. 440. *See also* the *Auriga* [1977] 1 Lloyd's Rep. 384; the *Nowy Sacz* [1977] 2 Lloyd's Rep. 91.

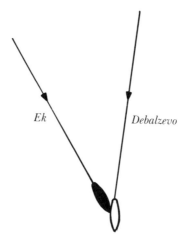

*Ek*            *Debalzevo*

**Fig. 20.**

There are many navigators who openly express the belief that, even when they have the right-of-way, in a close situation the safest plan is to yield it at once upon the slightest evidence of dispute. The trouble with this in practice is that oftentimes it may lead us into the very collision we are seeking to avoid, with the stigma of legal liability added to physical injury. The road hog is a notorious bluffer, and there is always the danger that his intention to usurp the right-of-way may weaken, and he may sheer suddenly to starboard in conformity with the requirement just at the time the stand-on vessel slows down or sheers to port to avoid him, with incriminating consequences to the latter if collision ensues. The moral culpability of the stand-on vessel in such a case may be slight, but legally she will be held as guilty as the other, and may even be found solely at fault.

With the law on this point as specific as it is the courts could hardly decide otherwise. The crossing rule represents the second of two distinct methods of procedure prescribed in the rules when two vessels approach each other so as to involve risk of collision. The first requires each vessel to take some positive action that has the effect of changing her *status quo*. It is illustrated by the rules that govern when vessels meet end on. Both must alter course to starboard, both are equally bound to signal, and neither can claim that the other should have whistled first. The second method is based on the assumption that one vessel shall maintain her *status quo*, and that any positive action to avoid collision shall be taken by the other. It is illustrated by the rules when one vessel is overtaking another, or a power-driven vessel meets a sailing vessel, or a sailing vessel with the wind on the port side meets another with the wind on the starboard side, or two power-driven vessels meet on crossing courses. The whole theory of such rules is that collision is less likely to occur if one vessel is directed to avoid the other and the other is then required to continue exactly what she is doing. As discussed earlier, the theory breaks down the moment that the give-way vessel cannot rely with certainty on the correct action by the stand-on vessel.

Thus, the permissive action now available to the stand-on vessel makes it imperative that the give-way vessel takes her avoiding action well before the former gets sufficiently concerned to depart from her course and speed. Neither should the stand-on vessel be precipitate.

Action should not be taken by the stand-on vessel without first determining that risk of collision does in fact exist. Compass bearings should be observed accurately, and the radar should be used to measure the range of the approaching vessel. The earliest moment for permitted action will obviously be related to the range and rate of change of range. Without such measurement the stand-on vessel might have difficulty in later justifying her action:

> Mere apprehension of danger of collision will not justify change of course in a vessel whose duty under the rules is to keep her course. A change should only be made where there is actual danger.[11]

### Meaning and Use of Signals Differ on High Seas and Inland Waters

Despite the uniformity between the two sets of rules on the maneuvers to be taken in the crossing situation, there is a major difference between them on the use of sound signals. The meaning and use of three short blasts is, however, identical in both rules: namely that the vessel making the signal is operating astern propulsion.

As discussed in Chapter 4, whistle signals under the international regulations are signals of action. Thus, in the crossing situation the give-way vessel sounds one short blast if she alters to starboard, two short blasts if she alters to port and three short blasts if reversing. She sounds no signal if she slows or stops.

The stand-on vessel on the high seas does not answer these signals if she maintains her course and speed. Only if she takes permissive action under Rules 17(a)(ii) and 17(c) would she sound a whistle signal. This is likely to be one short blast for the preferred alteration to starboard. If she stood on until in extremis she must also sound the requisite one, two, or three short blasts when taking the action that best avoids collision. Should she at any time stop or slow, there is no signal to signify the reduction in speed.

---

[11] The *General U. S. Grant* (N.Y. 1873) Fed. Case No. 5,320.

Long before reaching in extremis, and preferably before taking permissive action, the stand-on vessel should have been so concerned by the action or non-action of the give-way vessel to have sounded the in-doubt signal of five or more short blasts, ideally supplementing it with five short flashes of a light. Hopefully, hearing or seeing this signal, the give-way vessel will be reminded of her responsibility. Equally the give-way vessel can use the in-doubt signal if she should fail to understand the intentions or actions of the stand-on vessel. Such a situation might arise if the stand-on vessel should, inadvisably, take permissive action by altering to port.

In inland waters a totally different principle is employed. Here, one and two short blasts are signals of intent that demand a reply from the other vessel. Such signals are required when two power-driven vessels in sight will cross within a predicted distance of half a mile of each other. Either vessel may initiate the exchange, which common sense decrees should not be delayed until the vessels close to half a mile.

One short blast means "I intend to leave you on my port side." This should be the normal signal in most crossing situations. If initiated by the give-way vessel it indicates an intention that can be, if necessary, subsequently executed by altering course to starboard when no further signal is made, or by reduction of speed. On hearing the signal the other vessel, in this example the stand-on vessel, must, if in agreement, immediately respond with one short blast even though she will be making no change to her course and speed.

The provisions of Inland Rule 34(a) also allow for a signal of two short blasts, meaning "I intend to pass you on my starboard side." Such a signal, apart from the special case of narrow channels yet to be discussed, should not be normal in the crossing situation. Nevertheless, the rule provides for such an eventuality. Given the stricture of the half-mile clause and the constraints of confined waters, it is feasible to recognize that occasions can occur when a two-short-blast signal is appropriate within the dictates of good seamanship. If the proposal is made by one ship and the other agrees, she must reply immediately with two short blasts herself. Thus, the give-way vessel is granted acquiescence to pass ahead of the stand-on vessel, a situation about which any mariner should feel distinctly uneasy.

It must be clearly stated that "cross" signals are not provided for—that is, the answering of one short blast with two, or two short blasts with one. Until 1940 the lower courts were agreed that it was always proper to "cross" an improper signal and that the stand-on vessel, unless agreeing to a two-short-blast signal, was bound to hold course and speed until literally in the jaws of collision. The proper procedure had been to respond with the danger signal and then a single short blast until in extremis was reached.

Such was the decision of both the district court and circuit court of appeals in New York in 1939 in the case of the Baltimore harbor collision of the steamships *Eastern Glade* and *El Isleo*. In this case the two vessels sighted each other at night over a mile apart in converging channels, and the *Eastern Glade,* which was the give-way vessel, blew two blasts. The *El Isleo* interpreted this as an announcement of intention to cross her bow and immediately responded with the danger signal, followed by one blast, and continued to hold course and speed until the two vessels were in extremis, when she sheered out to starboard in a futile effort to avoid collision and was rammed nearly amidships at a point about 200 yards outside the buoyed channel. The fault of the *Eastern Glade* was glaring, and in accordance with the long line of its own previous decisions, the circuit court of appeals upheld the district court in exonerating the *El Isleo* and then finding the *Eastern Glade* solely liable for the collision. The court took the opportunity to express dissatisfaction with the line of reasoning underlying these decisions but felt powerless to change what had become established procedure without an opinion from the Supreme Court. The case was appealed, and the highest tribunal reversed the lower court and held that:

> . . . when two steamships are on crossing courses, the privileged vessel has no absolute right to keep her course and speed, regardless of danger involved; her right to maintain her privilege ends when there is danger of collision; and in the presence of that danger both vessels must be stopped and backed, if necessary, until signals for passing with safety have been made and understood. . . .[12]

The case was remanded to the circuit court of appeals, second circuit, which reconsidered its former verdict and held both vessels at fault. In its new decision 3 June 1940, the circuit court said:

> There can be no doubt that the Supreme Court meant to hold in a crossing case, when the holding-on vessel gets two blasts from the giving way vessel, which are unacceptable to her, she must neither cross the signal, nor keep her speed, but must at least stop her engines, and if necessary back "until signals for passing with safety are made and understood."

Effectively, Inland Rule 34(a)(ii) now places this historic interpretation of the Supreme Court into the body of the rules. In effect it means that the stand-on vessel is deprived of her right and relieved of her duty to hold course and speed the moment there is an unacceptable or disputed signal that must be challenged by the use of the in-doubt signal. In practice, the right referred to has so often proved unenforceable and the duty so difficult that the mariner is, on the whole, much better off under the new requirement.

---

[12] Postal SS. Corp. v. *El Isleo* (1940) 84 L. Ed. 335, reversing (CCA N.Y. 1939) 101 F.2d 4.

In summary, although one and two short blasts have different constructions between international regulations and inland rules, the basic intent is the same: the give-way vessel should avoid passing ahead of the stand-on vessel. When doubt exists as to the sufficiency of action/intention, both sets of rules provide for a signal of five short blasts. Both rules allow the stand-on vessel to take early permissive action to resolve the issue, though only the inland rules clearly specify that the sounding or receipt of the danger signal requires precautionary action by both ships. It should be noted, however, that International Regulation 8(e), as indeed does Inland Rule 8(e), requires *any* vessel to "slacken her speed or take all way off" if necessary to avoid collision or to give more time to size up the situation.

### Two Blasts by Give-Way Vessel Do Not Give Her Right-of-Way

In inland waters in the past there was a belief that an initial two-short-blast signal by the give-way vessel conferred upon her the right-of-way. Apart from those waters specified in Inland Rule 15(b), where there might be some justification, such a belief is a misconception of the rules, despite its frequent use in the past. Whatever may be the local custom, it is never safe to assume that it can displace a positive statutory provision. Moreover, notwithstanding local custom, the practice is at least questionable, and every navigator who makes use of it should fully understand its legal and judicial significance. It is true that there was at one time a pilot rule that permitted the vessel having the other on her starboard hand to proceed if it could be done without risk of collision, and provided a two-blast signal therefor; but even this was regarded as contrary to the spirit of the crossing rule, and was repealed after being invalidated by the federal court stating that the rule

> . . . which permits the vessel having the other on her starboard hand to cross the bows of the other if it can be done without risk of collision, is invalid, as repugnant to the starboard hand rule.[13]

In the second place, if the give-way vessel, assuming that she has ample time to cross ahead, initiates the two-blast signal, which in the absence of any statutory provision can have no sanction but that of local custom, she thereby expresses an admission that risk of collision exists, and lays herself open to the charge of proposing a violation of the law. Recognizing this, the lower courts have repeatedly ruled that such action is at best no more than a proposal that the other vessel is under no obligation to accept; that unless and until the proposal is agreed to by the other, as indicated by a reply of two blasts, the stand-on vessel must hold on; and that even after such agreement the give-way vessel assumes any risk of carrying out the maneuver.

---

[13] The *Pawnee* (N.Y. 1909) 168 F.371.

The following decisions, although antedating the present rules for inland waters, are ample evidence of the attitude of the courts on this question:

> If a burdened steamer, by her signals, invites a departure from the ordinary rules of navigation she takes the risk both of her own whistles being heard, and, in turn, of hearing the response, if a response is made, and of the success of the maneuver.[14]

> Two whistles given in reply to a signal of two whistles from a steamer bound to keep out of the way mean only assent to the latter's course at her own risk, and an agreement to do nothing to thwart her. It does not relieve the latter of her statutory duty to keep out of the way; but when collision becomes imminent, both are bound to do all they can to avoid it whether the previous signals were of two whistles or one. If imminent risk of collision is involved in the maneuver assented to, and the maneuver was unnecessary, both are responsible for agreeing on a hazardous attempt.[15]

> When the boat having the right-of-way fails to respond to the signal of the boat whose duty it is to keep out of the way, the latter has no right to assume, because of such silence, that the former abandons her right-of-way.[16]

> The failure of the privileged vessel to assent to a signal contrary to the rule is equivalent to a dissent which holds the burdened vessel bound to observe the starboard rule.[17]
> The privileged vessel is entitled to assure that, although the burdened vessel may at first propose to exchange rights-of-way, it will, if such a proposal be rejected, conform to the rules of navigation.[18]

In the light of these decisions the risk in the use of an initial two-blast signal by the give-way vessel is apparent, and should generally be avoided. Certainly it can never be legally justified when the vessels are approaching each other so as to involve risk of collision; and when it is possible for the vessel having the other to starboard to pass so far ahead of the other that risk of collision may be deemed not to exist, whistle signals are not only unnecessary, because of the half-mile clause, but are better omitted. But there is no harm in announcing such an intention on VHF.

## Departure from Rules by Agreement

If, as sometimes happens, the stand-on vessel offers to yield the right-of-way by blowing two blasts first, the situation with regard to the give-way vessel is somewhat different. Once the give-way vessel assents to the arrangement by answering with two whistles and the desired agreement

---

[14] Hamilton v. the *John King* (1891) 49 F.469; the *Admiral*, 39 F.574.
[15] The *Nereus* (N.Y. 1885) 23 F.448.
[16] The *Pavonia* (N.Y. 1885) 26 F.106.
[17] The *Eldorado* (N.Y. 1896) 32 CCA 464, 89 F.1015.
[18] L. Boyers' Sons Co. v. U.S. (N.Y. 1912) 195 F.490.

is thus established by the interchange of signals, she becomes, in a limited sense, a privileged vessel, though not under the same legal obligation as a stand-on vessel to hold her course and speed.

An interesting sidelight on the legal complexities that are introduced when the stand-on vessel initiates the two-blast signal, the signal is accepted, and a collision follows, is revealed in the deliberations of the circuit judges in a crossing collision:

> It is good law that when the burdened vessel decides to keep out of the way by crossing the bows of the privileged vessel, though she gets an assent to such a proposal, she assumes the risks involved in choosing that method. The duty of the privileged vessel in such cases is to cooperate and she need not keep her course. The situation, at least in this circuit, after the agreement, is one of special circumstances. But such an agreement initiated by the privileged and assented to by the burdened vessel, might be regarded as creating other duties. It could be considered as a proposal that the duties of the vessels should be reversed, and that the burdened (now the privileged) vessel hold her course and speed, so that the privileged (now the burdened) vessel might be able to forecast her positions at future moments precisely as the rule requires when no agreement has been made.
>
> We have been unable to find much in the books that touches on this precise point. In the *Susquehanna*, 35 F 320, the burdened vessel was exonerated because she did not "thwart" the proposal, having apparently kept her course. On the other hand, in the *Columbia*, 29 F 716, Judge Brown thought it a matter of indifference which vessel proposed the change; the burden always remaining upon the vessel originally burdened. In Stetson v. the *Gladiator*, 41 F 927, Judge Nelson said that the exchange justified the burdened vessel in keeping her course.
>
> In none of these cases was the originally burdened vessel held to any duty to keep her course. On the whole we are disposed to think that any agreement to change the usual rules should be treated as creating thereafter a position of special circumstances. If so, we think that, although the proposal emanates from the privileged vessel, and should be taken as meaning that she will undertake actively to keep out of the way, it need not absolve the burdened vessel from her similar and original duty also to keep out of the way, nor will it impose on her a rigid duty to hold her course and speed. It is true that that duty is imposed by the rule generally as a correlative to the duty to keep out of the way, but only in cases where no agreement has been reached. Some convention is essential when neither knows the other's purposes, but where both have agreed upon a maneuver by an exchange of signals their accord should be left for execution by movements adapted to the circumstances. For example, if the angle of crossing is wide, it will usually be best for the originally burdened vessel to hold her course and speed; but if it be narrow, it is safest for both to starboard and pass at a greater distance. No doubt the proposal involves the proposer in a duty to give a wide enough margin for safety, even though the assenting vessel does not starboard.[19]

[19] The *Newburgh* (N.Y. 1921) 273 F.436.

The foregoing discussion shows that even the seasoned admiralty judges of the circuit court of appeals are sometimes compelled to struggle with the intricacies of the law of crossing. If a single useful fact emerges from the involved discussion in this decision, it is that changing the lawful signal by both vessels has the important effect of destroying the right-of-way of one of them, and making her share with the vessel contemplated by the rules the burden of avoiding collision. This in itself is an excellent argument, in the crossing situation, for sticking to the procedure in practice provided by law.

**Two Blasts by Stand-On Vessel**

From the viewpoint of the stand-on vessel, for her to initiate the two-short-blast signal must appear as a very foolish act. For she is either suggesting that in her opinion the vessel to port already has ample clearance, a questionable opinion as the other vessel must be passing ahead within half a mile for the need to signal to arise, or else she is giving notice to the give-way vessel that she (the stand-on vessel) proposes to waive her privilege and act contrary to the law, in which case, if the other assents by answering with two short blasts, she is bound to do her part in carrying out the maneuver.

Except in certain narrow channels and rivers, not only should the stand-on vessel scrupulously avoid proposing a two-short-blast signal but she should be somewhat chary about assenting when it is proposed by the give-way vessel. It would be unwise to lay down an arbitrary rule here, and the individual case must be decided on its merits, remembering that avoidance of collision is always the prime desideratum. The navigator must determine, in the particular instance, which action involves the least risk: agreeing to the proposal with two answering blasts or dissenting by sounding five short blasts, taking way off and proceeding only after passing signals are satisfactorily exchanged. This is the procedure approved by the Supreme Court.[20] However, when adopting the first action it should be borne in mind that while a stand-on vessel is not in fault, according to the circuit court of appeals, for holding her course even though she fails to receive a response to her first signal of one whistle,[21] if she assents to the crossing of her bows by the other vessel she waives her privilege absolutely.[22] When she assents to this by repeating the two whistles, it is her duty at once to assist the maneuver, a point which the

[20] The *Transfer No. 15* (CCA N.Y. 1906) 145 F.503; Yamashita Kisen Kabushiki (CCA Cal. 1927) 20 F.2d 25; the *Norfolk* (Md. 1924) 297 F.251; Postal SS. Corp. v. *El Isleo* (1940) 84 L. Ed. 335.

[21] The *E. H. Coffin*, Fed. Case No. 4,310.

[22] The *Sammie* (N.Y. 1889) 37 F.907; the *Albatross* (1910) 184 F.363.

United States Supreme Court, on appeal, declined to review.[23] However, this point is now incorporated in Inland Rule 34(a)(ii), whereby a vessel if in agreement with any proposal in the crossing, and indeed meeting, situation "shall . . . take the steps necessary to effect a safe passing."

Finally, a vessel that assents by signal that another shall cross her bows cannot urge the attempted maneuver as a fault, though it results in a collision.[24] These decisions make it evident that even an undisputed acceptance of an irregular proposal carries with it certain risks and that the second procedure, compelling both vessels to stop, often has decided merit.

## When Crossing Rule Begins to Apply

The navigator is sometimes puzzled to know just how close a vessel approaching from starboard must be to make the law of crossing apply. It will be noted that the same crossing rule is applicable to both inland and outside waters *when vessels are crossing so as to involve risk of collision.* In another part of the rules we are told that risk of collision can, when circumstances permit, be ascertained by carefully watching the compass bearing of an approaching vessel, and that if the bearing does not appreciably change, such risk should be deemed to exist. This should not be taken to imply that obtaining a series of bearings of an approaching vessel is an absolute test of risk of collision. It is undoubtedly a valid test to the extent that if the bearings observed are constant, collision will occur if neither vessel changes course or speed, and consequently, vessels have been held at fault for failure to take such precautionary bearings.[25] But it does not follow that in all cases where the bearing is changing, no risk of collision is involved. As said by the circuit court of appeals:

> This section is not a rule of navigation, but merely a suggestion of one circumstance which denotes that there is danger of collision; and a steamer is not justified in assuming that there is no risk because there is an appreciable change in the compass bearing of the lights of a sailing vessel seen at night, which would manifestly be an unwarranted assumption under some circumstances.[26]

Thus, in the crossing situation, the bearings of a vessel on the starboard bow may be constant, indicating that the two vessels will reach the point of intersection at the same time; they may be drawing ahead, indicating the stand-on vessel will reach the point of intersection first; or they may be drawing aft, indicating the give-way vessel will reach that point first. The rapidity of change in bearing depends on the distance apart and

[23] The *Boston* (N.Y. 1922) 258 U.S. 622, 66 L. Ed. 796.
[24] The *Arthur M. Palmer* (N.Y. 1902) 115 F.417.
[25] The *President Lincoln* (1911) 12 Aspinall MC 41.
[26] Wilders SS. Co. v. Low (Hawaii 1911) 112 F.161.

the relative speeds of the two vessels. It would be a mistake to assume that only in the first case is there risk of collision. It is true that if the bearings of the stand-on vessel draw ahead with a certain degree of rapidity, there is a presumption that she will have clearance across the bow of the burdened vessel; but this does not relieve the latter of her obligation to watch the stand-on vessel closely, and to slow down or stop or reverse, if necessary, before coming into dangerous proximity. Conversely, if the bearings of the stand-on vessel draw aft with sufficient rapidity, there is a presumption that the burdened vessel might cross with safety; but wide indeed must be the margin in that case before she is legally justified in making the attempt. As a matter of law, it must be wide enough so that no risk of collision is involved; as a matter of practice and of common prudence, it should be wide enough so that no collision can occur no matter what the other vessel does.

This is a sweeping statement, but its validity is established by court decisions in both the United States and in England. As early as 1869 the Supreme Court held:

> Rules of navigation such as have been mentioned (as to the duties of two vessels approaching each other) are obligatory upon such vessels when approaching each other from the time the necessity for precaution begins; and they continue to be applicable as the vessels advance so long as the means and opportunity to avoid the danger remain. They do not apply to a vessel required to keep her course after the approach is so near that collision is inevitable, and are equally inapplicable to vessels of every description while they are yet so distant from each other that measures of precaution have not become necessary to avoid collision.[27]

This decision was referred to by the district court of Michigan in a Great Lakes case a short time later, and amplified in the following unmistakable language:

> Risk of collision begins the very moment when the two vessels have approached so near each other and upon such courses that by departure from the rules of navigation, whether from want of good seamanship, accident, mistake, misapprehension of signals, or otherwise, a collision might be brought about. It is true that prima facie each man has a right to assume that the other will obey the law. But this does not justify either in shutting his eyes to what the other may actually do or in omitting to do what he can to avoid an accident made imminent by the acts of the other. I say the right above spoken of is prima facie merely, because it is well known that departure from the law not only may, but does, take place, and often. Risk of collision may be said to begin the moment the two vessels have approached each other so near that a collision might be brought about by any such departure and continues up to the moment when they have so far progressed that no such result can ensue. But independently of this, the idea that there was no risk of collision is fully exploded by the fact that there was a collision.[28]

[27] The *Winona* (19 Wall) 41 (1873).
[28] The *Milwaukee* (1871) Fed. Case No. 9,626.

Similarly, in the case of the *Philadelphia,* the district court said:

> The term "risk of collision" has a different meaning from the phrase "immediate danger" and means "chance," "peril," "hazard," or "danger of collision"; and there is risk of collision whenever it is not clearly safe to go on.[29]

Two statements from decisions of Dr. Lushington, famous admiralty jurist of the mid-nineteenth century, will suffice to show the English parallel of this doctrine. In a case of 1851 he said:

> This chance of collision is not to be scanned by a point or two. We have held over and over again that if there be a reasonable chance of collision it is quite sufficient.

In another case, he said:

> The whole evidence shows that it was the duty of the *Colonia* . . . to have made certain of avoiding the *Susan.* She did not do so, but kept her course till she was at so short a distance of a cable and a half's length [1,000 feet] in the hope the vessels might pass each other. Now it can never be allowed to a vessel to enter into nice calculations of this kind, which must be attended with some risk, whilst it has the power to adopt, long before the collision, measures which would render it impossible.[30]

These observations on the meaning of *risk of collision* and the action to avoid such risk are crystal clear. In the crossing situation the give-way vessel should maneuver early to pass at a sufficient distance to allow for any contingency that could turn risk into actual collision. In open waters there is no excuse in passing so close to another vessel that risk arises. Not so in confined waters, which is discussed in the next chapter.

No special rights accrue to a vessel lying stopped on the high seas, unless she is in one of the categories of Rule 27. She must keep out of the way of a vessel, with whom risk of collision exists, which approaches from her starboard bow. However, a recent decision of the Scottish Court of Session caused a flurry of alarm about this principle.[31] Contrary to an earlier decision by the English Admiralty Court (The *Broomfield* 1905) and of courts in the United States, the Scottish court held that a power-driven vessel that was under way but lying stopped, was not a give-way vessel in relation to another power-driven vessel approaching from her starboard side. The collision arose between two fishing vessels—neither at the time actually engaged in fishing—one of whom, the *Mayflower,* was sunk. The case was, regrettably, not the subject of appeal. However, international representations were made to IMO who provided clarification in 1982 stating that the word "underway" in Rule 3(i) also applied to a vessel that was lying stopped in the water. It is to be hoped that this will take care of the aberration of the Scottish court decision.

---

[29] The *Philadelphia* (Pa. 1912) 199 F.299.
[30] Marsden, *Collisions at Sea,* 462.
[31] The *Devotion II,* Sc. Ct. [1979] 1 Lloyd's Rep. 509.

Rule 15, the crossing situation on the high seas, is abrogated if one of the two vessels is not under command, restricted in her ability to maneuver, or engaged in fishing. Rule 18(a) applies in such circumstances, and a vessel that normally would be stand-on in a crossing situation is required to keep out of the way. Passing ahead is not ruled out, though an alteration to starboard might prove most prudent. A tug towing is not automatically conferred any rights, unless she shows the shapes or lights authorized by Rule 27(b), but it behooves a stand-on vessel to take into account the hampered movements of a tug and tow when contemplating action under Rules 17(a)(ii) or 17(b).

Under International Rule 18(d), all vessels are enjoined to avoid impeding the safe passage of a vessel constrained by her draft. The expression to "avoid impeding" is different from "to keep out of the way," being far less imperative. If a power-driven vessel is unable to avoid impeding the passage of a vessel constrained by her draft, then the rules for the crossing situation, or indeed the meeting or overtaking situations, apply.

There is no equivalent rule in inland waters, not least because the inland rules do not provide for the category of vessels constrained by their draft. This was a deliberate exclusion for inland waters, as it was felt that such a subjective rule might lead to abuses and result in situations where a vessel constrained by her draft might claim a right-of-way to which she was not entitled, thereby creating a dangerous situation. There are indications that some ships on the high seas do indeed display the appropriate lights or shapes for a vessel constrained by her draft when the circumstances do not justify such use.

### Crossing Rules Equally Binding on Both Vessels

Perhaps in the very nature of the case common sense would permit no other interpretation. For in the final analysis, it is as logical to place an absolute obligation upon one vessel not to cross ahead as upon the other vessel to maintain course and speed. And when a collision occurs because a give-way vessel that thought she had time to get across is hit by a stand-on vessel that sheered to the right in an ill-timed attempt to clear her, the courts cannot consistently find that one was under compulsion to hold course and speed if they do not find that the other was equally under compulsion to avoid crossing her bow.

If we exclude all those cases that frequently arise in crowded harbors where the presence of a third, or even other additional vessels, creates special circumstances that modify the rules, then we may draw a very practical lesson from the foregoing decisions—namely, the manifest danger of crossing a vessel to starboard unless she is so far away that it would be impossible for her to bring about a collision. If she is that far away, the navigator need not worry, for there is no risk of collision.

## SUMMARY

In accordance with the theory of stand-on and give-way the crossing situation requires, both in inland waters and on the high seas, that the vessel having the other to port maintain course and speed, and that the vessel having the other to starboard keep out of the way, avoid crossing ahead, and if necessary slacken speed or stop or reverse. This arrangement creates a serious hazard when, as frequently happens, either vessel fails to do her duty.

On the high seas and in inland waters, the stand-on vessel is required to maneuver when in extremis. Under both jurisdictions, the stand-on vessel *may* maneuver earlier when it becomes apparent to her that the give-way vessel is not taking appropriate action.

The give-way vessel under international regulations must signal if she alters course or reverses engines, and the same applies in extremis and in the exercise of Rule 17(a)(ii) to the stand-on vessel. In inland waters the use of one or two short blasts is a declaration of intent that requires an immediate response from the other vessel. If doubt or disagreement arises, the in-doubt signal must be sounded and both vessels must take appropriate precautionary measures until agreement is reached. Should engines be reversed, then the signal is the same as the international one of three short blasts. The signal of two short blasts, except in specified waters where the vessel in the river has right-of-way over a crossing vessel, should never be proposed by the stand-on vessel, and should be accepted when proposed by the give-way vessel only when the maneuver indicated can be done with a high degree of safety. The effect of such assent is to take the right-of-way from the stand-on vessel without conferring it on the give-way vessel, and thus to put vessels under special circumstances, with the mutual duty of taking any positive action to avoid collision.

# 8

# Encounters in Restricted Waters

The three previous chapters have discussed encounters in open waters, where ships in sight of each other had the sea room to take early bold action and avoid a close-quarters situation. This chapter looks mainly at all three types of encounters but in circumstances where geography, water flow, water depth, and traffic density reduce room for maneuver and require ships to enter into the domain of others. This is most keenly felt on leaving or entering harbor but can be as applicable in straits, bays, anchorages, canals, estuaries, and rivers and is so complicated that often, even in excellent visibility, ships may only see each other at a late stage. In crowded waters the number of encounters increases, frequently requiring ships to pass at close quarters. It is a period of heightened risk, not only from collision but from grounding. One national study into the causes of collisions and groundings over an eight-year period[1] found that just over 50 percent of 3,599 casualties occurred in coastal waters, 25 percent in harbor areas, and about 10 percent in rivers or canals. Even making due allowance for the extensive nature of Norway's restricted channels, these figures emphasize the obvious fact that greater risk of incidents to ships exists inshore rather than in deep sea. In a well-run vessel this has long been recognized by taking precautions such as increased bridge and engine-room manning, perhaps the employment of a deep-sea pilot, and finally a harbor pilot. The advent of deep-draft ships, which, for example, can only safely transit the English Channel inbound on a rising tide, has pushed the boundaries of inshore waters farther seaward: restricted waters no longer just exist close to the land but can be extensive over much of a continental shelf.

[1] Cause relationships of collisions and groundings, conclusion and statistical analysis, Norwegian Maritime Research Institute No. 3/1981.

## Special Rules

For ports and rivers local rules have long existed, but few have been as extensive as those governing the waterways of the United States, now known as the inland rules. While all such special rules have to conform to the international regulations as closely as possible, there are differences brought about by the conditions prevailing in different localities. Some of these differences have been mentioned earlier in the book, and more will be brought out in this chapter. Equal emphasis will be given to international regulations that particularly affect restricted waters.

## Growth of Traffic Management

For many years special rules have attempted to influence the actions of ships in coastal and confined waters. But, as mentioned above, such waters now extend farther afield than hitherto. And the modern cargoes that many of these deeper-draft ships carry can be highly dangerous. Today's ship casualty can lead to great damage to the ecology, as well as to the people and their livelihood on the adjacent, but not necessarily close, shore. Modern media swiftly relay news and pictures of any marine disaster and arouse the consciousness, indeed fears, of a wide audience. The latter's concern leads to demands to reduce the risk to them and their environment. The consequential growth of national and international regulation has been remarkable, affecting training, equipment, seaworthiness and what may be loosely termed "traffic management." There are several components to the latter, mostly developed *ad hoc* but slowly becoming more integrated and rapidly receiving acceptance. Water space management, long practiced by our submariners, is the basic tool to reducing risk of collision in busy waters. Scientific analysis is also being brought to bear. In a four-year period COST 301[2] determined that, of the 4,000 odd vessels at sea in European waters at any one time, the average number of collisions each year over the period 1978–82 was:
- meeting situation: 119;
- crossing situation: 66;
- overtaking situation: 26.

The annual number of collisions expected has been calculated for various COST 301 sea areas. An extract of those around the United Kingdom is illustrated in Figure 21. Overall, the mean collision rate for Europe (determined by the number of collisions per 1 million ship-miles) was 0.495, with large ships, i.e., 10,000 gross tons and above, having higher rates. Since this size of ship includes many oil and chemical tankers,

[2] The European Economic Community (1987), "Committee on Science and Technology, Project 301 (*COST 301*)." Annex to main report, volume 2.

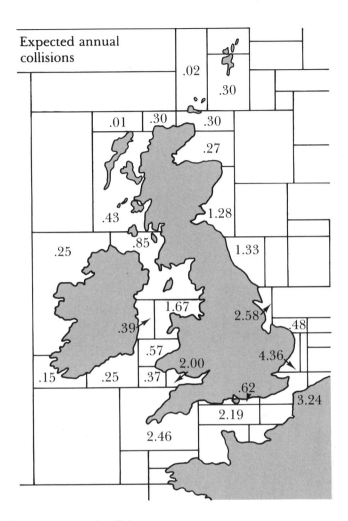

**Fig. 21.** Expected annual collisions.

the theoretical prospect of a collision every second year or so lends strength to the cause of traffic control. As stated earlier, this can be achieved mainly by keeping vessels apart, i.e., water space management, and can be done by either time or physical separation.

**Traffic Separation Schemes**

Rule 10 of the international regulations provides for separation of traffic proceeding in opposite directions. Official adoption by IMO of such schemes is given where the details meet the laid-down guidelines of that body. The rule basically requires vessels using the schemes to keep to lanes flowing in the same direction. Provisions are made for local crossing traffic and its relation to the scheme, as well as for emergencies and fishing vessels. The use, by through traffic, of inshore traffic zones is discouraged.

The advent of separation schemes, especially where monitored by shore radar, has led to a marked reduction in the number of collisions. To take but one example, in the busy Dover Strait, where the TSS was introduced in 1967 and monitored from 1972, the figures over five-year periods for all conditions of visibility are presented in Figure 22.[3]

The bringing of order to what was once almost a free-for-all has undoubtedly been successful, particularly with respect to meeting encounters. Prolonged debate over vessels crossing the TSS has led to one of the latest amendments to International Rule 10(c), which makes it clear that vessels shall cross *on a heading* as near possible at right angles to the direction of traffic flow. Although this might cause some extra work for enforcement authorities who measure course over the ground on their shore-based radar, the revised rule clarifies matters for mariners.

Concern, too, had been raised over the interpretation of the term *through traffic* used in International Rule 10(d). Taken to mean that the term was applicable to any vessel *not* calling at a location within the inshore traffic zone (ITZ), it was argued that much, previously coastal, traffic was forced offshore into the TSS, increasing the number of vessels proceeding in the same direction and/or crossing a lane. This is countered by the fact that, since the decline of the number of collisions in TSSs, a large number of subsequent collisions have been in ITZs. Nonetheless, an underlying motive in closing ITZs to through traffic is to keep potential pollution casualties away from the coast. Thus, the latest change (effective 1990) to Rule 10(d) effectively upholds that "keep-out" principle unless a vessel is either in the exempt category or has business in the ITZ.

|  | 1957–61 | 1962–66 | 1967–71 | 1972–76 | 1977–81 |
|---|---|---|---|---|---|
| Opposite Directions | 45 | 47 | 27 | 7 | 3 |
| Broadly Crossing | 0 | 0 | 0 | 0 | 2 |
| Same Direction | 6 | 7 | 8 | 6 | 7 |
| Unknown | 1 | 2 | 1 | 1 | 0 |
| Total | 52 | 56 | 36 | 14 | 12 |

**Fig. 22.** Number of collisions in Dover Strait before and after introduction of traffic separation.

[3] A. N. Cockcroft, "The Effectiveness of Ship Routing off NW Europe," *Journal of Navigation* 36 (1983), 362.

Most TSSs are not supervised, though where they are, enforcement has brought about a high level of compliance with International Rule 10. Cases have been successfully brought against mariners who have not crossed lanes at right angles,[4] taken passage through an ITZ,[5] passed too close ahead of a through ship in a lane,[6] and proceeded against the flow of traffic in a lane.[7] The latter case emphasized the point, now contained in International Rule 10(a), that being in a TSS does not relieve any vessel of her obligation under any other rule. Even though the *Larry L* was navigating in accordance with the traffic separation scheme, and the other vessel, the *Genimar*, was not, both vessels were found at fault for not taking appropriate action in a crossing situation, with the *Larry L* attracting two-thirds of the blame for failing to give way.

Another case, involving crossing a separation zone, was the collision between the Swedish general cargo vessel *Cinderella* and the Cypriot motor vessel *Achilleus* in the Baltic Sea (see Figure 23). The latter had left the Kiel Canal and was on the correct side of the separation zone. She turned to port to create a lee for the pilot cutter but failed to check her headway and crossed the zone into the path of the canal-bound Swede. Although faulted for transgressing the separation zone, the *Achil-*

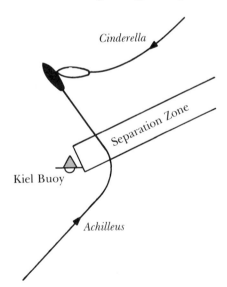

**Fig. 23.**

[4] The *NF Tiger* [1982] 2 Lloyd's Rep. 564.
[5] The *Nordic Clansman* [1984] 1 Lloyd's Rep. 31.
[6] The *Saint Anselm* [1988] Lloyd's List 8 February 1988, 3.
[7] The *Genimar* [1977] 2 Lloyd's Rep. 25: *see also* the *Estrella* [1977] 1 Lloyd's Rep. 534.

*leus* was also to blame for not giving way in the crossing situation she had created. She attracted 70 percent of liability with *Cinderella* 30 percent for failing to take way off in time.[8]

The establishment and enforcement of mandatory TSS regulations have undoubtedly led to a reduction in incidents. Most *total* losses, sometimes over half the world total, used to occur off Northwest Europe. Based on casualty returns published for 1987, NW Europe and North America in that year each accounted for 12.5 percent of total losses caused by collision, with some 41 percent happening off East Asia.[9]

**Vessel Traffic Systems**

Although traffic separation schemes grew up more or less independently, they are now recognized to be but one part of a wider concept known by the generic term vessel traffic services (VTS). Even before TSSs many ad hoc forms of port control became established around the world and gradually extended seaward. The factors mentioned at the beginning of this chapter led to the establishment of a more active, comprehensive system of control of ships, spurred on by disasters such as: the grounding off Europe and Cape Cod, respectively, of the *Torrey Canyon* and the *Argo Merchant;* the 1971 collisions in San Francisco (the *Oregon Standard* and the *Arizona Standard*); and in the Dover Strait (the *Paracas* and *Texaco Caribbean* into the wrecks of which plowed the *Brandenbery* and the *Nikki*). In the United States the Ports and Waterways Safety Act (PWSA) of 1972 and the Port and Tanker Safety Act of 1978 authorized the Coast Guard to operate VTSs in waters with congested vessel traffic. The Coast Guard exhaustively examined the problem[10] and progressively established VTSs at San Francisco, Puget Sound, Houston/Galveston, New Orleans, and New York. Separately, one was founded in Prince William Sound.[11] Inland waters' VTSs also are in force at Berwick Bay, Louisiana, on the St. Mary's River (established in 1952) and at Louisville, Kentucky (seasonally only during high water on the Ohio River). These VTSs now monitor 51 percent of the total tonnage moved on U.S. waters, including 68 percent of the petroleum and 84 percent of the chemical waterborne tonnage and over 70 million passengers.[12] In Canada a program of establishing fifteen various forms of VTSs commenced in 1967 and now effectively covers most major Canadian waterways. Similar progress is being made in Eu-

---

[8] The *Achilleus* [1985], 2 Lloyd's Rep. 338.

[9] Lloyd's Register, *Casualty Return for 1987.*

[10] U.S. Coast Guard, *Analysis of Port Needs* (Washington, D.C., 1973).

[11] While navigating this scheme, the *Exxon Valdez* went aground in Prince William Sound leading to the worst-ever U.S. oil spill (Good Friday, March 1989).

[12] Paper presented at Sixth International Symposium on Vessel Traffic Services, Gothenburg, Sweden, 17 May 1988.

rope, Japan, and to a lesser extent in Russia. Around the world VTSs
are coming of age.

VTSs are tailored to meet local and regional needs. They vary in size
and structure but essentially consist of:
- surveillance systems;
- traffic separation schemes;
- communication systems;
- vessel traffic centers (VTCs).

They provide the strategic means of space management, information,
and a tactical ability for collision avoidance. Ships are required to report
in and out of the system. They receive guidance and advice from the
VTC. Although the onus on collision avoidance properly remains with
ships, directions, as opposed to helm orders, can be given by VTCs. As
VTSs grow, so does the need for common procedures and language,
both matters under active consideration. Guidelines on the establishment
of VTSs have been produced by IMO.[13]

One inestimable advantage conferred by a VTS is the provision of
advance warning of approaching ships still out of sight, thereby providing
greater time to consider where to pass, not least avoiding the surprise
factor of meeting a vessel unexpectedly on a bend. Equally, the information that flows over the radio within a VTS should serve to give timely
warning of any maneuvers expected to be carried out by ships. Consider
the case of the *American Jurist* proceeding downriver at night, more or
less in the center of the channel (see Figure 24). She saw the *Claycarrier*

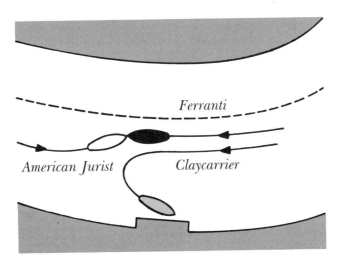

**Fig. 24.**

[13] *Guidelines for Vessel Traffic Services.* London: IMO, November 1985.

approaching her, having just overtaken the *Ferranti.* No doubt expecting a normal port-to-port passage, the *American Jurist* was surprised when the *Claycarrier,* at a distance of 2 cables, turned right around to port to shape up for a berth on the southern bank of the river. The *American Jurist* instinctively altered to port, perhaps too much, and met the *Ferranti.* While recognizing that the *Claycarrier* started her maneuver at an improper time, 50 percent of the blame fell on the *American Jurist* for not slowing and for altering to port for too long.[14] Knowledge of the *Claycarrier*'s intended movement would have alerted both of the other ships and no doubt prevented a collision. This knowledge the VTC can provide.

A 1986 collision in the Black Sea was used by the Soviet delegation to an international symposium to illustrate the necessity of further development of the Novorossiysk VTS (see Figure 25).[15] The passenger ship *Admiral Nakhimov* was outbound from Novorossiysk when she agreed with the inbound bulk cargo ship *Petr Vasev,* on her starboard bow, that the latter vessel should give way. This did not happen and 423 people lost their lives in the subsequent collision. The Soviet paper at the symposium stated that "the proper and timely information of the VTS operator could have prevented the above mentioned." There then followed a call for standard procedures for VTS to be applied outside territorial waters on a mandatory basis under the aegis of IMO.

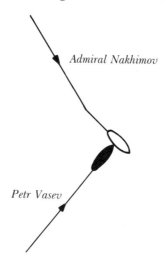

*Admiral Nakhimov*

*Petr Vasev*

**Fig. 25.**

[14] The *American Jurist* [1958] 1 Lloyd's Rep. 423.

[15] Paper presented at Sixth International Symposium on Vessel Traffic Services, Gothenburg, Sweden, 17 May 1988.

While the VTSs of North America have settled down to a steady working state, some of those in Europe and Japan are experiencing problems
associated with a rapid growth phase, not the least of which is achieving
regional coordination. There is little doubt that VTS, particularly the
TSS and early warning functions, can reduce the risk of collisions. But,
like the appearance of radar a few decades ago and, later, its descendant
automated radar plotting aids (ARPA), VTS is no panacea. It is the
human factor that remains paramount, as the *Exxon Valdez* has shown,
with constant vigilance required by operators afloat and ashore. VTC
personnel are now, where a VTS exists, firmly part of the anticollision
team in confined waters.

Whether or not a VTS exists, the behavior of ships passing each other
in confined waters remains governed by the Collision Regulations, modified as appropriate by local rules. Encounters in restricted visibility are
dealt with in the next chapter; those in clear weather in restricted waters
are presented below.

### Head-On Encounters in Confined Waters

As discussed in Chapter 5, head-on encounters in both international and
inland waters are covered by an identical Rule 14, namely that ships
should pass port to port. The fact that the encounter is a head-on one
is, simply put, determined by observing that a vessel dead ahead, or
nearly so, is on a reciprocal or near reciprocal course. Where sufficient
open water exists for this simple test to be applied the rule is crystal
clear; less so when ships are confined to rivers, channels, and routes that
require alterations of course to stay within prescribed waters. Indeed,
the majority of clear-weather head-on collisions occur in restricted channels, such as rivers and fairways. In restricted waters there is greater
navigational risk, not just from collision but from grounding, shipwreck,
interaction, tides, reduced warning time, and an often confusing back-
drop of lights, that adds to the dangers of a meeting situation. In addition,
the existence of local rules and the ubiquitous presence of a pilot can
sometimes produce uncertainty in what, on the high seas, was an efficient
bridge oganization.

The requirement to conform to the channel has been long recognized
by the courts, which have oft found that, what in some circumstances
might have the first appearance of crossing at a considerable angle, was
encompassed by the old head-to-head rules. Indeed, as pointed out in
the case of the *Milwaukee:*

> In determining how vessels are approaching each other, in narrow tortuous
> channels like the one here in question, their general course in the channel
> must alone be considered, and not the course they may be on by the

compass at any particular time while pursuing the windings and turnings of the channel.[16]

From this it may be seen that vessels approaching a sharp bend in a river from opposite directions might even be moving at right angles when first mutually sighted, yet still be under the head-on rule. One might logically raise the question as to whether vessels are ever crossing in the legal sense, when they approach in the ship channel of a river. The best discussion found on this point, together with a definite answer to the question in the affirmative, was in a case of collision between two steamships on the Whangpoo River, which the learned justice of the Supreme (admiralty) Court of China and Japan thus commented on the rules:

> The cases of the *Velocity*, the *Ranger*, and the *Oceano* have explained and illustrated the distinction which exists in the effect of the crossing rule as regards vessels navigating the open sea and those passing along the winding channels or rivers. The crossing referred to is "crossing so as to involve a risk of collision" and it is obvious that while two vessels in certain positions and at certain distances in regard to each other in the open sea may be crossing so as to involve risk of collision it would be completely mistaken to take the same view of two vessels in the same positions and distances in the reaches of a winding river. The reason, of course, is that the vessels must follow, and must be known to intend to follow the curves of the river bank. But vessels may, no doubt, be crossing vessels in a river. It depends on their presumable courses. If at any time, two vessels, not end on, are seen keeping the courses to be expected with regard to them respectively, to be likely to arrive at the same point at or nearly at the same moment, they are vessels crossing so as to involve risk of collision; but they are not so crossing if the course which is reasonably to be attributed to either vessel would keep her clear of the other. The question therefore always turns on the reasonable inference to be drawn as to a vessel's future course from her position at a particular moment, and this greatly depends on the nature of the locality where she is at the moment.[17]

It was in the fairly wide Irako channel connecting the Japanese port of Nagoya to the open sea, that a British ship, the *Glenfalloch* was held 20 percent liable for a collision that occurred after she maintained course and speed until in extremis having assessed she was in a crossing situation (see Figure 26). The Pakistani vessel *Moenjodaro* was outbound down the channel and strayed over towards her port side, thus presenting a green sidelight to the inbound *Glenfalloch* and "although *Moenjodaro* was steering a course of about 10 degrees to port of a direct course along the channel she was a ship proceeding along the channel in a contrary direction to that of *Glenfalloch*, rather than a ship crossing more or less directly from one side of the channel to the other . . . the Collision Regulations did not apply so as to oblige *Glenfalloch* to keep her course and speed until

---

[16] The *Milwaukee* (1871) Fed. Case No. 9,626.

[17] The *Pekin* (1897) AC 532, Supreme Court for China and Japan.

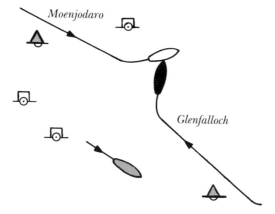

**Fig. 26.**

the two ships were so close to each other that a collision could not be avoided by the action of *Moenjodaro* alone; on the contrary *Glenfalloch* was free to alter either her course or her speed . . ."[18]

### Meeting in Narrow Channels

Aside from the doctrine discussed above, it may be pointed out that vessels proceeding up or down a river are usually under Rule 9(a) and Rule 9(a)(i), international regulations and inland rules, respectively, with an obligation to keep to the side of the channel that would naturally produce a port-to-port passing. It should be noted that Rule 9, unlike Rule 14 for the head-on situation, is contained, in both sets of rules, in the section concerning action under any condition of visibility and applies to all vessels, not just power-driven ones. This rule places a burden on any vessel that is on the port side of a channel to have a need for being there or to establish agreement for a starboard-to-starboard passage.

However, under the inland rules, in narrow channels or fairways on the Great Lakes, Western Rivers, or any other water specified by the secretary, a power-driven vessel proceeding *downbound with a following current* has right-of-way over an upbound vessel and the responsibility for proposing the manner and place of passage. Inland Rule 9(a)(ii) makes it crystal clear that this right-of-way supersedes the normal requirement to keep to the starboard side of the channel (Rule 9(a)(i)) and the normal head-on situation of having to pass port-to-port (Rule 14(a)). Found in similar waters throughout the world, this rule recognizes the limited

---

[18] The *Glenfalloch* Q.B. (Adm. Ct.) [1979] 1 Lloyd's Rep. 247.

maneuverability of a downbound vessel and the *occasional* need to deviate from the standard port-to-port passing as a result of river current patterns when rounding a bend in twisting, narrow channels and fairways. Giving the right-of-way and choice in method of passing to such vessels in these designated waters is essential for safety of navigation. It is clearly incumbent on the downbound vessel to initiate in good time an exchange of one- or two-short-blast signals so that the upbound vessel may adjust course and/or speed as necessary. The latter vessel may often have to slow or hold her position against the current in order to allow the downbound vessel to negotiate a bend.

Apart from the unequivocal right-of-way for downbound vessels in certain waters, it is necessary for all vessels less than 20 meters in length, all sailing vessels, and all fishing vessels engaged in fishing, in any channel governed by either the international regulations or the inland rules, to navigate in such a manner so as not to impede the passage of a vessel that can safely navigate only within the narrow channel or fairway. The use of the word "impede" in Rules 9(b) and (c) of both sets of rules does not fully confer right-of-way status on the vessel confined to the channel. Nonetheless, new Rule 8(f)(i) spells out that a vessel who shall not impede must take early action to give room to another who has priority under the international regulations. These rules advise all mariners, operating large as well as small craft, that vessels navigating a narrow channel or fairway can be at a disadvantage and that the navigational situation between them and less restricted vessels should be considered so as not to impede their safe transit within the channel. In some channels the small craft or fishermen might be able to clear the channel, or hold up at a convenient passing place, but if this should not be possible, then the normal strictures of keeping to starboard and of the head-on situation apply, except, of course, in those waters covered by Inland Rule 9(a)(ii).

Collisions have sometimes led to later dispute in court over the meaning of the term "narrow channel," and it might be worthwhile considering some past interpretations. In the *Stelling* and the *Ferranti* case,[19] it was held that the word "fairway" meant the whole area of navigable water between lines joining the buoys on either side and that "mid-channel" meant the centerline of that area. In the *Crackshot*,[20] it was held that "narrow channel" meant the dredged channel marked by the pecked lines on the chart and that mid-channel meant the centerline of that dredged channel. In the *American Jurist* and the *Claycarrier* case,[21] the potential contradiction between the two previous decisions was noted,

---

[19] The *Stelling* and the *Ferranti* (1942) 72 Ll. L. Rep. 177.
[20] The *Crackshot* (1949) 82 Ll. L. Rep. 594.
[21] The *American Jurist* and the *Claycarrier* (1958) 1 Lloyd's Rep. 423.

but no further ruling emerged until the *Koningin Juliana* case, already mentioned in Chapter 4. Then, the judge:

> did not think that it would be right to hold that, in relation to these waters, the expression "narrow channel" means the dredged channel and no more. A great many vessels using the harbour can and do navigate outside the dredged channel; and so to hold would mean that such vessels were not subject to rule 25(a) at all[22]. . . .
>
> It does not follow, however, because the expression "narrow channel" means the whole of the navigable water, that the word "mid-channel" means the centreline of that area without regard to the existence and position within that area of the dredged channel . . . as a matter of common sense . . . the centre of the dredged channel must be regarded as mid-channel, not only in relation to the dredged channel itself but also in relation to the wider navigable area as a whole.[23]

In amplification of his phrase "as a matter of common sense," the judge stated that he used it because it was essential that the keep-to-starboard rule should be applied uniformly to all ships navigating up and down the river, irrespective of their draft and whatever the state of the tide might be. Common sense indeed; and, apart from the special circumstances of some tricky rivers, it would seem equally pertinent to most narrow channels.

Yet nearly eleven years later the approaches to Harwich were again the scene of a collision arising from misunderstanding caused by a failure to keep to the starboard side of the approach channel (see Figure 27). The ferry *European Gateway* was outward bound intending to cross ahead of the inbound ferry *Speedlink Vanguard* before the latter reached the Cork Spit and then to alter course to starboard to proceed on an easterly

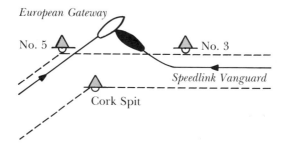

**Fig. 27.**

[22] 1960 International Regulations, Rule 25(a) provided that: In a narrow channel every power-driven vessel when proceeding along the course of the channel shall, when it is safe and practicable, keep to that side of the fairway or mid-channel which lies on the starboard side of such vessel.

[23] The *Koningin Juliana*, Q.B. (Adm. Ct.) [1973] 2 Lloyd's Rep. 308; (C.A.) [1974] 2 Lloyd's Rep. 353; (H.L.) [1975] 2 Lloyd's Rep. 111.

course outside the dredged channel. The *Speedlink Vanguard* was proceeding westerly close to the northern edge of the dredged channel, expecting the outbound ship to round to starboard at Cork Spit and pass port to port. As the ships closed, *Speedlink Vanguard* altered course to starboard to give the other ship more room for her turn. However, confident that the *Speedlink Vanguard* would remain in the channel, the *European Gateway* maintained her course and speed. Despite right full rudder by the *Speedlink Vanguard* her bow visor tore open the *European Gateway*'s shell plating at main and upper deck level, while her bulbous bow smashed into the generator room. Ten minutes later the *European Gateway* lay on her starboard side, aground: six lives were lost.

The formal investigation, while acknowledging mitigation, considered that the *European Gateway* had failed to keep a good lookout, displayed bad seamanship in crossing ahead of the other ferry and, earlier, had not kept to the starboard side of the deep-water channel.[24] Subsequently, the local VTS has required inward vessels to keep to the north of the center of the deep-water channel and seabound ships to keep to the south.

In the United States, the question of whether the narrow channel rule applies to the Algiers Point area on the Mississippi River was not decided in an appeal case concerning allocation of navigational fault after a collision. In upholding the trial judge's allocation of one-third fault to a downbound tug and two-thirds to the upbound vessel meeting at high water, it was noted that the "point-bend" custom is not a rule of law that frees approaching vessels to make their own arrangements for passing.[25] More positively, the 2-mile-wide safety fairway in the Gulf of Mexico's international waters running between offshore structures for some 6 miles south of South West Pass sea buoy, did not constitute a narrow channel, and vessels using this voluntary shipping lane did not acquire any special rights.[26]

**Failure to Keep in Own Water**
The tendency of ships not to keep to the starboard side of a channel is remarkable. Possibly the reason is a natural propensity to stick to the middle, equidistant from dangers at the edges, a tendency no doubt accentuated by ranges that do run down the center of channels. Equally at bends or junctions some mariners seem to have difficulties keeping on the right-hand side, often literally "cutting the corner." This is not necessarily deliberate but probably brought about by the lack of an aiming

[24] "*European Gateway/Speedlink Vanguard* Collision: Results of the Formal Investigation," *Seaways*, October 1984.
[25] Canal Barge v. China Ocean, 1986 AMC 2042.
[26] Zim Israel v. Special Carriers, 1986 AMC 2016.

mark at the bend, such as a mid-channel buoy, which it is known has to be left to port.

This tendency to stray from the starboard side of the channel was very evident as *Durmitor* sped downriver, assisted by a strong current and comfortably to the right of the centerline, when she met *The Marchioness*, upbound, rounding a bend in her wrong water (see Figure 28). The latter was blamed for being on the wrong side of the river and for failing to take sufficiently energetic steps by starboard helm action to get to her proper side. *Durmitor* was blamed for avoiding to port and for not taking way off. She received 50 percent of the blame for the collision that sank *The Marchioness*.[27]

Paradoxically, the steam hopper *Mersey No 30* was held alone to blame for altering to port for steamship *Senville*, which had not kept on her own starboard side of mid-channel.[28] More appropriately, the tanker *Shelbit 2* was apportioned only one-quarter of the responsibility when she collided with the steamship *Clara Monks*, which was in her wrong water.[29] Similarly the *Edison Mariner* was mainly to blame for navigating on her wrong side of the fairway of the River Scheldt after colliding with the outward-bound *Kittiwake*.[30] On appeal in another case, the tanker *British Patrol* had her apportionment of blame, resulting from a collision in the Thames Estuary, reduced because the lower court had not directed its mind to the vital fact that the other ship, the *Finwood*, was at all material times proceeding down on her wrong side of the channel. Commenting

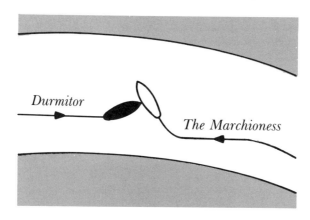

**Fig. 28.**

[27] The *Durmitor* [1951] 1 Lloyd's Rep. 22.
[28] The *Mersey No. 30* [1952] 2 Lloyd's Rep. 183.
[29] The *Clara Monks* [1954] 1 Lloyd's Rep. 359.
[30] The *Edison Mariner* [1955] 1 Lloyd's Rep. 235.

on the rule that a vessel proceeding along the course of the channel shall keep to that side of the fairway or mid-channel that lies to her starboard side, one of the appeal judges said

> I have always held the view, and I express it once again, that this is a most important rule which calls for strict observance on the part of vessels navigating in narrow waters.[31]

Yet infractions continue to occur. A vessel proceeding downstream in the River Maas failed to get over to her correct side and struck the upbound motor vessel *City of Capetown* (see Figure 29). It was a fine, clear night with the tidal stream ebbing at 2 knots. The *City of Capetown* was proceeding on her starboard side of the channel with engines at dead slow ahead. Her pilot attempted to contact the downbound vessel, *Adolf Leonhardt*, on the VHF radio, without success. The *Adolf Leonhardt*, which was by then distant about half a mile, 5 degrees on the *City of Capetown*'s starboard bow, opened her red sidelight and closed her green sidelight. The *City of Capetown* then stopped her engines, later putting them to full speed astern. On board the *Adolf Leonhardt*, due to the bend of the river, only the green sidelight and masthead lights of the *City of Capetown* could be seen, and it was thought that the latter was attempting to cross the channel. The *Adolf Leonhardt* attempted a port-to-port passage, but with her engines first at slow ahead then at emergency full astern, she drifted downstream into the other vessel.

The admiralty court held that the *Adolf Leonhardt* was navigating on the wrong side of the channel. She had found herself there initially

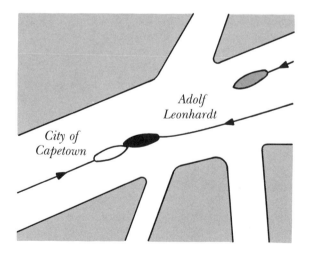

**Fig. 29.**

[31] The *British Patrol* [1968] 1 Lloyd's Rep. 118.

because of an earlier passing situation, but had failed to cross back to her correct side as quickly as she reasonably could and to remain there. Sufficient time and space existed for the *Adolf Leonhardt* to do this but

> . . . the burden of the case against her is that because those on board did not appreciate how far to the south she was, they did not take such action in time.[32]

Not knowing where she was laterally in the channel, the *Adolf Leonhardt* misconstrued the meaning of the other vessel's green sidelight. She received two-thirds of the blame, with the *City of Capetown* one-third for failure to reduce speed earlier and, even though on her correct side of the channel, for not edging farther to starboard where sufficient sea room existed.

A case in inland waters where two vessels, one a tug with a tow, meeting end on in the Mississippi River, collided after the upbound ship, a tanker, abandoned her position on her starboard side of the river (see Figure 30). Severe damage was caused to the tanker, the *Anco Princess* and to the barge, the *Barbara Vaught,* which was under tow by the tug *Libby Black.* The *Anco Princess* entered the river, took a pilot aboard, and proceeded upriver under the direction of the pilot at full speed and at about 400 feet from the right-hand bank. The *Libby Black* and her tow were making their way downriver. It was afternoon and visibility was excellent. The pilot on the tanker first sighted the tug when the two vessels were

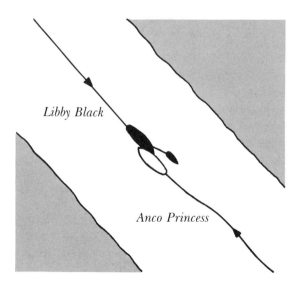

**Fig. 30.**

[32] The *Adolf Leonhardt,* Q.B. (Adm. Ct.) [1973] 2 Lloyd's Rep. 318.

some 5 miles apart. He made no attempt to contact her by radio or by signal. The pilot, in the belief that the *Libby Black* was too close to the east bank to permit a port-to-port passage, ordered the *Anco Princess* to change course so that the vessels would pass starboard to starboard. In doing so, the *Anco Princess* cut across the course of the *Libby Black*, which rammed her broadside on.

The Eastern District Court of Louisiana concluded that the tug was navigating approximately along the mid-channel and that she was on the tanker's port bow just prior to the *Anco Princess*'s change of course to port. This alteration, made while the master was absent from the bridge making a radiotelephone call to the ship's agents, "amounted to gross fault and was the major cause of the collision." This fault was compounded by the failure of the pilot to signal his intentions to the *Libby Black*, either by whistle signal or by radio communication or by sounding the in-doubt signal, as was mentioned in Chapter 4. In court, the operators of the tanker pleaded that, after the *Anco Princess*'s course alteration, the courses of the vessels were "so far apart on the starboard of each other as not to be considered meeting head to head," and therefore a starboard-to-starboard passing was required. This plea received short shrift from the judge, who said that a meeting situation existed before the alteration of course, and that being so, "a vessel cannot change what is an end-on situation to one which requires a starboard-to-starboard passage." The *Anco Princess* was held 85 percent at fault, with the *Libby Black* attracting 15 percent for her failure to signal in time her doubt as to the intentions of the *Anco Princess* when the latter did not reply to either her one-short-blast whistle signal or to calls on the radiotelephone.[33]

Sometimes a ship allows the elements to carry her to the wrong side of the channel. The *City of Leeds* was inward bound along a dredged channel on the River Mersey. She passed one ship successfully port to port, and knowing that another outward-bound ship, the *Anco Duchess*, was due to leave her dock, she slowed and eventually stopped to allow passing at a suitable place in the channel. The weather was fine and clear, and it was still substantially dark although dawn was beginning to break. The wind was west-southwest force 4 and pushed the *City of Leeds* over to the port side of the channel. To clear a buoy close on the port side the engines were put ahead for two minutes and once again stopped, with the ship still well over to the port side of the channel. To prevent further leeway the engines were later put to slow ahead, and the ship crept slowly up the port side of the channel with her head angled about 20 degrees to starboard of an up-channel course so as to counteract the

---

[33] Gulf Coast Transit Co. v. M. T. *Anco Princess* et al., E.D. La. (1977) [1978] 1 Lloyd's Rep. 293. *See also* the *Argo Hope* [1982] 2 Lloyd's Rep. 559.

very considerable effect of the wind on her starboard side. Thus, her red sidelight was presented to the *Anco Duchess,* who had just cleared her dock and entered the channel. Because of the bend, the *Anco Duchess* was showing the *City of Leeds* her green sidelight only. The latter decided it was time to get over to her correct side of the channel, and she sounded one short blast, but she had left it too late. As she crossed the channel, the *Anco Duchess* sounded two short blasts and altered to port. Collision took place one and one-half minutes later.

The *City of Leeds* was found more culpable and apportioned 70 percent of the blame. The *Anco Duchess* was also criticized for not appreciating that the upbound vessel would attempt to pass port to port, for not proceeding at a much slower speed, and for not hearing the *City of Leeds'*s whistle signal—thus receiving the remaining 30 percent apportionment of fault.[34]

**Interaction**

But keeping to starboard is not always sufficient to avoid collision in a close port-to-port passage. Careful consideration must be given to the width of the channel and the proximity of the channel's edge. When two vessels close each other in relatively shallow and confined channels, interaction can be expected not only between the ships but also between the banks of the channel. Fortunately, the complicated interactions that are set up are of less magnitude in the more common meeting situation than they are in the less frequent overtaking situation. Nevertheless, they do exist, with the magnitude of pressures around a ship varying approximately with the square of the speed of the ship. There is a critical speed when the combination of circumstances produces a sheer that will take the ship away from the near bank and that will be rapid and uncontrollable. Such was the experience of the East German ship *Schwarzburg* when she attempted to pass port to port with the Liberian steamship *Sagittarius* in a dredged channel in the River Plate (see Figure 31). Both ships had sighted each other at some 10 miles distance and, when about 1/2 to 1 mile apart, had each sounded the one-short-blast signal as they adjusted their course along the channel. Shortly after this the *Sagittarius* heard three short blasts from the *Schwarzburg* and put her wheel to starboard and stopped engines. Simultaneously, the *Schwarzburg* appeared to swing rapidly to port. Later it transpired that this was due to an involuntary sheer. Her engines were put full astern, but some two or three minutes later she had crossed the channel, struck the *Sagittarius* at an angle of about 60 degrees, killed four people, and caused severe

[34] The *City of Leeds,* Q.B. (Adm. Ct.) [1978] 2 Lloyd's Rep. 346.

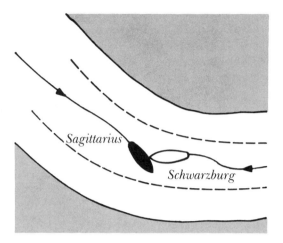

**Fig. 31.**

damage. In apportioning two-thirds of the blame to the *Schwarzburg*, the court held that she

> would not have got into the difficulty, and would accordingly not have sheered uncontrollably to port across the channel, if she had not been going so fast; the dangers of interaction between a ship and the bottom and sides of a channel . . . at anything but carefully controlled speeds should have been well known. . . . the speed of *Schwarzburg* was excessive while approaching a passing with *Sagittarius*.[35]

The *Schwarzburg*'s speed initially had been 15¹/₂ knots, with a reduction to about 12 knots shortly before the sheer began—with the result that, despite putting her engines full astern, she struck the *Sagittarius*, whose own headway was down to 4 knots, at about 8 to 9 knots. Expert testimony was that a speed of 8 to 9 knots was required for a safe passing, provided that the *Schwarzburg* had got down to that speed well before meeting the other ship.

Although not criticized for placing her engines full astern, there is little doubt that such action reduced the effectiveness of the *Schwarzburg*'s rudder, increased the suction of the stern towards the near bank, and aggravated the sheer of the bow across the channel. When proceeding in narrow channels, it is a sound practice to do so at a speed well below the maximum available, thus maintaining a ready reserve of revolutions to improve rudder effect by going full ahead for a short time. A brief burst of high revolutions improves water flow past the rudder without appreciable gain in speed and is far more effective in correcting a sheer

---

[35] The *Schwarzburg*, Q.B. (Adm. Ct.) [1976] 1 Lloyd's Rep. 39.

than going astern. Also, the use of an anchor can be of great assistance, and this valuable brake should always be immediately available when in confined water.

One of the greatest loss of lives brought about by a collision caused by interaction also occurred in the River Plate (see Figure 32). The British steamship *Royston Grange* was outbound when she passed the inbound Liberian tanker *Tien Chee*. The latter was a deep-draft vessel, fully laden, attempting the passage at low water. She was proceeding at maneuvering speed (about 12 knots) and probably had a squat of nearly 3 feet. Both ships had sighted each other when well apart and both had nudged to starboard to pass port to port, perhaps at under 100 meters apart. As the bows passed, *Royston Grange* sheered violently to port, struck the *Tien Chee,* and the two became locked together. The vapor released by the oil pouring from *Tien Chee*'s ruptured tanks ignited and a fireball swept the *Royston Grange,* engulfing her sixty-three crew and ten passengers. Both ships were burnt out and a further eight lives subsequently lost.

The consequent investigation concluded that the tanker was almost certainly "ploughing through the mud on the bottom of the channel." Although shallower, the British ship had probably been skimming over the top of a bank. Finally, not only was it low water, but the passing place was one of the shallowest in the Plate.[36] Today, the strategic planning capability of VTS should prevent imprudent selection of passing places, but the other lesson, loud and clear for mariners, is to proceed at a safe speed on meeting another vessel.

Failure to proceed at a slow speed was the root cause of a collision in the Kiel Canal. The westbound steamship *Isaac Carter* overtook the smaller *Ligovo* and approached a bend at 11 knots (see Figure 33). The eastbound steamship *Karen Toft* safely passed the *Isaac Carter* port to port at 7½ knots and at about 10 meters apart. On clearing the stern of the west-bound ship the *Karen Toft* took on abnormal sheer to port straight into the *Ligovo* who was proceeding at about 6 knots. The court found

*Tien Chee*

*Royston Grange*

**Fig. 32.**

[36] "Report of the Marine Board of Investigation and Decision of the Commissioner of Maritime Affairs," 1973, Monrovia, Liberia. *See also* Cahill, *Collisions and Their Causes,* 119–21.

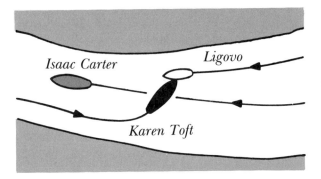

**Fig. 33.**

that both *Isaac Carter* and *Karen Toft* were at fault in passing at excessive speed, which contributed to the interaction between them that caused the sheer. No fault was attributed to *Ligovo*, and the other two ships were declared equally to blame.[37]

Another involuntary sheer, this time caused by a crosscurrent, led to a collision and a grounding in the Schelde Estuary (see Figure 34). The Panamanian tanker *Miraflores* was inbound when she was forced to reduce speed because a small coaster ahead of her, caught by the crosscurrent, oscillated to starboard then to port and then described a full turn to starboard before being able to resume her passage. On seeing the coaster recover, the *Miraflores* put her engines ahead again. Then, off No. 71 buoy she too experienced the crosscurrent and was set to starboard. She corrected with port wheel, and as the vessel came back, starboard wheel was applied. This was unable to overcome the sheer that developed to port and she swung into the path of the outward-bound British motor vessel *Abadesa*. The oil spilled from the tanker ignited. Meanwhile, astern of the *Miraflores* was a second Panamanian tanker, the *George Livanos*. Observing the collision ahead, the *Livanos* reduced speed, went astern, dropped anchors, and altered to starboard only to go hard aground.

Judgment was that the *Abadesa* was proceeding at a speed that did not allow her to slow in time to hold back, as required by the local rules, and permit the inbound ship unrestricted passage through the difficult area. She was found two-fifths to blame, with *Miraflores* attracting one-fifth for not backing down and not using an anchor. As for *Livanos* she was originally declared "author of her own subsequent misfortune," but at the end of the appeal process was also found two-fifths responsible for

[37] The *Karen Toft* [1955] 2 Lloyd's Rep. 120.

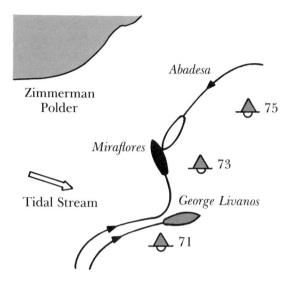

Abadesa

Zimmerman
Polder

75

Miraflores

73

Tidal Stream

George Livanos

71

**Fig. 34.**

her damages and thus able to recover the remainder from the other
ships.[38]

Finally, there is the case in clear weather in the St. Lawrence Seaway,
where vessels did not fully consider the effects of interaction (see Figure
35). The motor vessel *Liquilassie* proceeded upriver from the lock and,
1¹/₂ miles farther, she had to pass the motor vessel *Nipigon Bay*. The
latter had been coming downriver but was now stationary. There was
little room to pass, and creeping along at about 2 knots, the *Liquilassie*

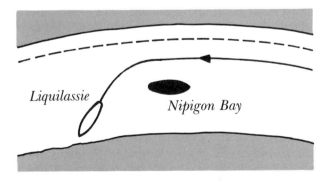

*Liquilassie*

*Nipigon Bay*

**Fig. 35.**

[38] The *Miraflores* (1967) 1 Lloyd's Rep. 191.

attempted a port-to-port passage, as the greatest water existed on that side. During the course of this maneuver she came near the stern of the *Nipigon Bay*. The latter then gave a kick to her engines to straighten herself out, the force from which was sufficient to cause the *Liquilassie* to take a sheer and collide with the dock, despite taking bold and drastic actions with her engines and dropping an anchor. The Federal Court of Canada held that the bank suction that forced the *Liquilassie*'s critical sheer resulted not so much from any errors of judgment on her master's part in going too close to the bank or too fast, as from the fault of the *Nipigon Bay* in not allowing the *Liquilassie* the full half of the navigable space to which she was entitled. The *Nipigon Bay* was, if not actually on the wrong side of the channel, at least in the dead center of it. The collision was caused by the kick delivered to *Nipigon Bay*'s engines when the *Liquilassie* was so close to her stern and to the bank.

> The *Nipigon Bay* should have known that a kick of this magnitude and this duration delivered when the *Liquilassie* was so close to the stern of the *Nipigon Bay,* and was so much lighter, would have had the effect which it did on her.[39]

The *Nipigon Bay* received 80 percent of the blame, and the *Liquilassie* attracted 20 percent for her failure to sound a danger signal and for not coming to a stop while waiting for the stationary ship to move (as discussed in Chapter 4).

### Starboard-to-Starboard Passage

Mention was made in both Chapter 5 and earlier in this section of the provision for a starboard-to-starboard passage in a head-on encounter. In many rivers or channels around the world a vessel, especially one towing, negotiating a bend with a following current must, as a seamanlike measure, be accorded priority against a vessel stemming the flow. The latter can often wait or occasionally accede to a green-to-green passing. In inland waters the two-short-blast signal is sanctioned for use in a head-on encounter and thus can be used in the above, as well as in other situations.

### The Two-Blast Proposal

Whether to assent when a vessel approaching from ahead proposes a two-blast agreement is a question that must be answered very often in practice. The decision of the prudent navigator will be on the basis of what he or she considers the lesser risk under the circumstances. Many mariners are of the opinion that to dispute a proposal that can safely be accepted is bad practice regardless of the technical invalidity of the

---

[39] *Liquilassie* Shipping Ltd. v. MV *Nipigon Bay* [1975] 2 Lloyd's Rep. 279.

proposal. On the other hand, the view is also widely held that the Rules of the Road are so nearly collision-proof that it is always safer to obey them and to refuse to become a part of their nonobservance. When we remember that more than 99 percent of all collisions follow infractions of these rules by one or both vessels, there is some force to this argument. Our first consideration in all cases should be to avoid collision and our second to avoid liability when the wrongful act of another vessel threatens to force collision upon us. The immediate effect of assenting to a two-blast proposal in the meeting situation is to put both vessels under the rule of special circumstances.[40] As said by the circuit court of appeals:

> A two-whistle agreement varying what would otherwise be the normal method of navigation creates a situation of special circumstances. If the proposal is made when there is reasonable chance of success the other vessel is justified in assenting.[41]

This places an equal burden on both vessels to navigate with caution and to take necessary steps to avoid collision, as agreed, by altering course to port. In effect, the assenting vessel puts the stamp of approval on meeting contrary to law, and thereby assumes an equal responsibility with the proposing vessel to carry out the maneuver in safety. Such assent should therefore never be given when, because of current conditions, bends in the channel, speed, proximity of the land, low visibility, or other unfavorable circumstances, a starboard-to-starboard passage seems to be hazardous. It will then be much the better procedure to reply promptly to the two-blast signal with the in-doubt signal and take appropriate precautionary action, such as a marked reduction in speed, until a safe passing agreement has been reached.

**Keynote Is Caution Regardless of Side of Passing**

Referring again to the fact that in the head-on situation neither vessel has the right-of-way over the other, in the broader sense even a proper port-to-port signal may well be regarded by the vessel giving it as merely a proposal until it is accepted by the whistle of the other. It is true that the other vessel is legally bound to accept it. But the proper keynote of the meeting situation is caution, and the degree of caution required goes much further than a perfunctory observance of the rule. Indeed it is just about the time of giving the first signal that the real necessity for caution may be said to begin. The other vessel may misunderstand or fail to hear the signal, she may ignore it, she may deliberately disregard it, or she may make a simultaneous counterproposal of two blasts. Unfortunately, the first vessel is far from being in a position to say, "We have changed

[40] The *Newburgh* (CCA N.Y. 1921) 273 F.436.
[41] The *Transfer No. 15—Lexington* (2 CCA) 1935 AMC 1163.

course to starboard and blown one blast. The rest is up to you." The moment the signaling vessel discovers definite evidence of the other's failure to obey the rules, however flagrant the fault, she must take immediate steps to avert collision. The first and most important step, in the eyes of the courts, is to reduce headway to a point where she is under perfect control; if she fails to do this she is practically certain, in the event of collision, to be held guilty of contributory fault. Vessels have been so held for failure to stop or reverse as soon as there was any uncertainty of the other vessel's course,[42] or an apparent misunderstanding of signals,[43] or where the other vessel was seen to be using left rudder in the face of a proper one-blast proposal.[44]

Finally it must be remembered that the signal requirements of both the international regulations and inland rules include the obligation to use the in-doubt signal, five or more short blasts, whenever there is doubt as to the course or intention of another vessel.

## Overtaking in Confined Waters

Unlike open waters, where sea room is available, overtaking in restricted waters usually requires vessels to pass fairly close to each other. The concerns of a quite often necessarily close passage are made more severe when the overtaking maneuver takes place in a shallow channel. This aspect of the overtaking situation is discussed in more detail later in this section, but above all, ships should bear in mind that they are less maneuverable in shallow waters, particularly when overtaking or when passing from "deep" to "shallow" water.

The circumstances that make up an overtaking situation have already been described in Chapter 6. Both the international and the inland rules use the same description to cover the case of a faster vessel coming up on another slower one more than 2 points abaft the latter's beam and wishing to overtake. In international open waters the overtaking vessel acts on her own initiative, passing either side of the vessel being overtaken and making the appropriate signals to indicate any change of course.

In inland waters and in narrow channels governed by the international regulations, however, the procedure is one of proposal and agreement. If the latter is not forthcoming from the ship to be overtaken, then the faster ship should hold back. If agreement is forthcoming, then the option

---

[42] The *Munaires* (CCA N.Y. 1924) 1 F.2d 13.

[43] The *Transfer No. 9* (CCA N.Y. 1909) 170 F.944; the *Teutonia* (La. 1874) 23 L. Ed. 44.

[44] The *Albert Dumois* (La. 1900) 44 L. Ed. 751.

still exists of passing on either side of the overtaken vessel, though in a narrow channel the latter vessel should already be on the right-hand side of the channel thus facilitating the overtaking vessel to pass on the left. Nonetheless, the overtaking situation is the only one of the three approaches where any discretion is given as to the lawful manner of passing. Also it is one of those circumstances where a sail, or any other vessel given priority in Rule 18, does not enjoy right-of-way over steam. However, special circumstances might modify even that!

## Signals

As pointed out in Chapter 6, the major difference between International and Inland Rules 9(e)(i) lies in the signals to be made when wishing to overtake in a narrow channel. Under the international regulations, where the overtaken vessel must take action to permit a safe passage, the overtaking vessel sounds two prolonged blasts followed by one or two short blasts, indicating a desire to pass on the starboard or port side, respectively. The vessel to be overtaken signals agreement by sounding a prolonged-short-prolonged-short signal. She may answer with the in-doubt signal if not in agreement.

In inland waters the overtaking vessel, if a power-driven one, must initiate an exchange of signals with another power-driven vessel she wishes to overtake, regardless of the need to maneuver. The requirement to exchange signals is not restricted to use in narrow channels and fairways but is for use in all inland waters, and unlike the signals for the crossing and meeting situations, there is no reference to the half-mile rule. The vessel astern signifies a desire to pass to starboard with one blast, or to port with two blasts, and the vessel ahead is required to answer promptly, returning the original signal as assent to the proposed maneuver or sounding the in-doubt signal as dissent to it. In the latter case, the first ship should not press her attempt to pass, though she could propose subsequently to overtake on the other side. When the overtaking ship is finally past and clear, she may come back to her original course without a signal.

A vessel being overtaken has been held at fault for failure to answer a proposal from a ship wishing to overtake.[45] A plea that the need for signals applied only to narrow channels in inland waters has not been upheld.[46] If an overtaking vessel fails to signal, the overtaken ship is free to alter course, provided, of course, she does not delay such action until the other vessel is so close that it would make collision inevitable,

[45] The *Mesaba* Ocean SS Co. v. U.S. (CCA N.Y. 1930) 39 F.2d 553.
[46] The *Luckenbach* (N.Y. 1908) 163 F.775.

which would be a violation of good seamanship.[47] The overtaking vessel should be

> obliged to hold herself in check against unexpected changes of course, and be prepared to meet them, until by the consent of the vessel ahead, she gets assurance that it is convenient for her to hold on.[48]

Where the international regulations are in force, similar judgments have been made that the stand-on vessel need not rigidly adhere to her original course and speed. Interpretation has been that "course and speed mean course and speed in following the nautical maneuver in which, to the knowledge of the other vessel, the vessel is at that time engaged."[49] In the overtaking situation this could apply, for example, to the need of the overtaken ship to adjust course to conform to the channel. Nonetheless, it is prudent for the overtaken ship to look over her shoulder before making such alterations. The duty of keeping a good lookout by eye and ear applies as much to the stern sector as to any other.

### Legal Effects of Assenting to Passing

The international regulations requiring an exchange of signals in a narrow channel or fairway assume that the overtaken vessel must assist in the maneuver. The legal effect of her assent, therefore, is an agreement to do so in such a way as to give the overtaking vessel more room, if necessary. While the overtaken vessel is required to help, the overtaking vessel is still responsible for the safety of the maneuver.

When an overtaken vessel in inland waters assents to the proposal of an overtaking vessel to pass, she neither yields her right-of-way in the slightest degree nor assumes responsibility for the safety of the maneuver, and the fear that either of these results will follow is not an excuse for failure to answer. As already pointed out, in inland waters she must answer, and promptly. She must examine the situation ahead as thoroughly as conditions permit, and immediately express the assent or dissent provided by law. As said by the circuit court of appeals:

> The passing signal from an overtaking vessel is not solely a request for permission to pass. It also asks for information which the overtaking vessel is entitled to have. When the overtaken vessel knows of conditions which may make the passing unsafe it has no right to refuse to inform the overtaking vessel of such conditions, and if it does refuse it cannot throw the entire blame for an accident upon the other vessel.[50]

This should not be taken to mean that the mere act of assenting to the proposal ensures a safe passage, however, and inculpates the over-

---

[47] Thompson v. the *Great Republic* (1874) 23 L.Ed.55.

[48] The *Industry* (CCA N.Y. 1928) 29 F.2d 29; certiorari denied (1929) 73 L. Ed. 985.

[49] The *Roanoke* (1908) 11 Aspinall MC 253.

[50] The *M P Howlett* (CCA Pa. 1932) 58 F.2d 923.

taken vessel in an action following collision. In narrow channels, where these collisions usually take place, she can be charged with fault for her assent only when it is given in face of conditions that ought to make it apparent that passing is fraught with serious peril and is almost certain to cause a collision. In other words, she cannot deliberately lead the following vessel into a trap and escape liability. But if, in her judgment, the overtaking vessel can, with the exercise of a high degree of skill, successfully make her way past, then she is legally justified in giving her signaled consent to the attempt. The burden of clearing her is left almost entirely to the overtaking vessel.[51] Thus, while in inland waters an over-taken vessel can be held to account for imprudently consenting to a proposed passage, she will never be held to account for holding up a following vessel with the prescribed danger signal, and this option should always be used in any situation where a reasonable doubt exists as to the safety of a proposed passage.

Even with assent given, the overtaking vessel has a bounden duty to keep out of the way of the vessel being overtaken until "she is finally past and clear." Rule 13(d) makes it crystal clear that any subsequent alteration of the bearing between the two vessels cannot turn an overtaking situation into a crossing one. Thus, the overtaking vessel must keep clear until far enough ahead so that any further maneuvers by her cannot embarrass the vessel she has overtaken, as long as the latter holds course and speed.

### The Usual Cause of Overtaking Collisions in Confined Waters

As discussed in Chapter 6, the usual cause of overtaking collisions in open waters is not passing at a safe distance, making no allowance for interaction, or for the unexpected casualty to either ship. In confined waters ships of necessity pass close aboard each other and it behooves them to choose with care the place of passing and the speed at which they both proceed.

In shallow waters, where the flow of water beneath the keel is restricted, the effects of interaction between ships are enhanced. In addition, even without another ship in close proximity, proceeding at a speed too great for the amount of water depth available will cause the rudder to become "sloppy" and, in extreme cases, result in a loss of directional stability; i.e., the ship can take an uncontrollable sheer. When the shallow water is confined to a channel, there is also interaction between a vessel and the channel bank—sometimes called "canal effect"—that can also lead to a sheer to the far bank. For very large vessels with small keel clearance,

---

[51] The *Rhode Island* (N.Y. 1847) Fed. Case No. 11,745. *Also,* Charles Warner Co. v. Independent Pier Co. (1928) 73 L. Ed. 195.

there is also the prospect of "squat" or bodily sinkage that might result in touching the bottom and producing an appreciable trim by the bow, with consequent impairment to shiphandling abilities. The sum effects of all types of interaction are much exaggerated when vessels are overtaking in shallow channels, as the process takes longer than with meeting vessels. Before overtaking another vessel in such waters, full consideration should be given to the risk of collision with other marine traffic; to the effects of interaction between vessels; to canal effect causing a possible sheer towards the far bank; to sinkage effect for large vessels and, for all vessels, to the possible loss of control due to proceeding at too high a speed for the water depth available. These risks should be carefully weighed against the benefits of getting past the other vessel, especially if she is moving at a relatively high speed, albeit slower than yours, and is of a dissimilar size.

An example of the effects of interaction on ships of dissimilar size occurred in the Thames Estuary at night and in clear weather. The *Kylix*, ladened with oil products, was inbound at 13 knots and had ahead of her the much smaller coaster *Rustringen* also inbound proceeding at about 10 knots (see Figure 36). The latter rounded the West Oaze Buoy first, about 3 cables ahead of the tanker and settled on her course. The *Kylix* very shortly after rounded the buoy, much closer than the coaster, and settled on her course broad on the latter's starboard quarter. The two ships' courses converged by 13 degrees and the *Kylix* continued to overhaul. However, she failed to sound the signals for overtaking laid down by the local rules, which required a reply from the coaster; she incorrectly assessed the course of the other ship and attempted to pass too close at too great a speed. When about 100 meters apart on the port bow of the tanker, the *Rustringen* was spun by interaction across the bow of the *Kylix*. She sank almost immediately. While faults lay with *Rustringen*, the main burden of effecting an overtaking lay on the overtaking ship, and the *Kylix* was found 80 percent to blame.[52]

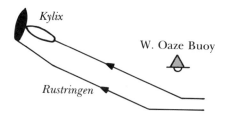

**Fig. 36.**

[52] The *Kylix* [1979] 1 Lloyd's Rep. 133.

In another international river, the *Irish Coast* sought to overtake the similarly outbound *Amenity* (see Figure 37). The latter was only slightly to right of the centerline and remained unaware of the proximity of the other ship until a late moment. As a result, she altered to port, though not by much, at an inopportune moment, reducing the passing distance to about 100 feet. Apart from bad lookout she was faulted for not sounding two short blasts. However, the preponderance of blame attached to the *Irish Coast* for passing too close. This time interaction was experienced after the larger ship's bow had passed the smaller ship. The *Amenity* took a sheer to port and hit the *Irish Coast*'s starboard quarter.[53]

Illustrating the point that a vessel's duty to maintain course on being overtaken can accommodate alterations of course was the collision in a non-U.S. river between the tanker *Firle* and the motor vessel *Cadans* (see Figure 38). The *Firle* was well over to starboard of the centerline of the channel when she was overtaken on her port side by the *Cadans*. As the two vessels drew abreast, they approached a bend. The *Firle* commenced porting and sounded two short blasts. *Cadans*, seeing what she thought was *Firle* shaping to cross her bows, put the wheel hard over to port and ordered full astern. The latter maneuver overcame the former, and *Cadans*'s bow canted to starboard, resulting in the collision. It was held that although *Firle* could have altered less to port, her alteration was not negligent. *Cadans* was held solely to blame as she was slow to anticipate or observe the other vessel's alteration and could have matched the turn or dropped back.[54]

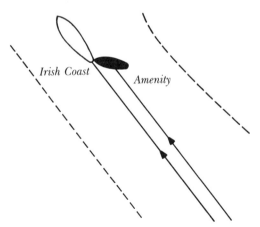

**Fig. 37.**

[53] The *Irish Coast* [1956] 1 Lloyd's Rep. 165.
[54] The *Cadans* [1967] 2 Lloyd's Rep. 147.

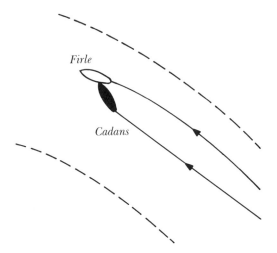

*Firle*

*Cadans*

**Fig. 38.**

Although less frequent than the more numerous head-on encounters, overtaking in confined waters is fraught with danger. Planning on where to overtake, rather than chancing it whenever one comes up on another vessel, is as vital as passing at a sensible distance at a safe speed.

### The Crossing Situation in Confined Waters

The principles of the crossing situation in the high seas, discussed in Chapter 7, remain valid in less open waters. Essentially, where risk of collisions exists, a vessel that has another on her own starboard side keeps out of the way and avoids passing ahead of the other vessel. We have seen earlier in this chapter that vessels approaching each other along and within the run of a channel or fairway, despite initial relative bearings, are not crossing but meeting in a head-on encounter. For there to be a true crossing situation in such a channel, then at least one of the vessels must be moving from outside the nearest channel limit to a destination beyond the farthest limit, i.e., such vessel is not taking passage along the channel but traversing it at a broad angle. While the essentials of a crossing situation are still present in such a circumstance, certain rules for narrow channels do draw, at least initially, a distinction from crossing in open waters. Remember, too, the meaning and use of signals differ between the high seas and inland waters, as highlighted in Chapter 4.

### Crossing Narrow Channels

As for the overtaking and meeting situations, the crossing situation can be modified by the rules for narrow channels and fairways. Both international regulations and inland rules have common Rules 9(b) and (c).

(b) A vessel of less than 20 meters in length or a sailing vessel shall not impede the passage of a vessel that can safely navigate only within a narrow channel or fairway.

(c) A vessel engaged in fishing shall not impede the passage of any other vessel navigating within a narrow channel or fairway.

Thus, a power-driven vessel navigating in such channels can reasonably expect vessels engaged in fishing, under sail, or less than 20 meters in length to avoid creating a situation that places her in a give-way role. Specifically, for a vessel that wishes to cross a narrow channel or fairway, Rule 9(d) of both jurisdictions goes on to forbid any such attempt if it will impede the passage of vessels, confined for navigational reasons, to such channels and fairways. This rule has wide application in harbor channels and river areas. It recognizes the problems experienced by mariners in narrow channels—currents, congestion, restricted maneuverability, squat, interaction, as well as time and tidal constraints. However, the words "avoid impeding" do not have the same unequivocal meaning as do those of "give-way." A new international regulation, Rule 8(f) addresses this subject, which while not restricted in authority to the crossing situation, spells out more clearly what "not to impede" means.

Firstly, sticking to the narrow channel scenario, any vessel to which Rule 9(d) applies must give sea room to a vessel confined to the channel or fairway in accordance with Rule 8:

(f) (i) A vessel which, by any of these rules, is required not to impede the passage or safe passage of another vessel shall, when required by the circumstances of the case, take early action to allow sufficient sea room for the safe passage of the other vessel.

Secondly, if the early action above has not been taken, and risk of collision arises, the "shall not impede" vessel is not relieved of her responsibility, though the nature of her not impeding action may change. That is, instead of having got out of the way in good time, she will now have to take action in accordance with the rules of Part B. In a crossing situation, say, this could mean exercising her option under Rule 17(a)(ii) and 17(c) to alter her course and speed:

(f) (ii) A vessel required not to impede the passage or safe passage of another vessel is not relieved of this obligation if approaching the other vessel so as to involve risk of collision and shall, when taking action, have full regard to the action which may be required by the rules of this part.

And, finally, the obligation of the vessel who should not be impeded is covered, that is, she too complies with the rules of Part B—the steering and sailing rules:

(f) (iii) A vessel the passage of which is not to be impeded remains fully obliged to comply with the rules of this part when the two vessels are approaching one another so as to involve risk of collision.

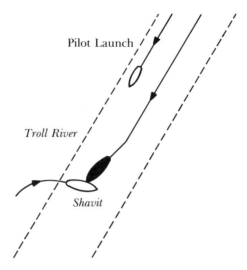

Pilot Launch

Troll River

Shavit

**Fig. 39.**

Thus, in a crossing scenario this means that, depending on location, International Regulation 15 or Inland Rule 15(a) comes into play. Whether stand-on or give-way vessel in this situation, there is not overmuch a vessel confined to a narrow channel can do. Apart from possible minor adjustments of course to starboard, the only option to her is to slow, stop, or reverse engines, maneuvers not always navigationally prudent in narrow channels. If these are likely to be inadequate, or if there is earlier doubt as to the movements of a crossing vessel, then the vessel proceeding along the channel *may,* under the international regime, sound the in-doubt signal, or in inland waters *must* sound it. This signal should help to clarify the crossing vessel's intentions and alert her to the anxiety of the other. It is important for the crossing vessel, who is well able to navigate outside the channel, to understand the concern on the bridge of the vessel confined to the channel. Early exchange of signals and/or unambiguous alterations of course and speed are essential in order to avoid forcing risky give-way action on the part of the vessel in the channel.

In many ports of the world local bylaws, but not the international regulations, clearly give right-of-way to vessels in the channel and relegate crossing vessels, such as ferries, to a permanent give-way status to through traffic. Similarly, in some inland waters, the normal crossing situations of Inland Rule 15(a) are abrogated, and the quasi-precautionary nature of Inland Rule 9(d) made mandatory, by Inland Rule 15(b):

Notwithstanding paragraph (a), on the Great Lakes, Western Rivers, or

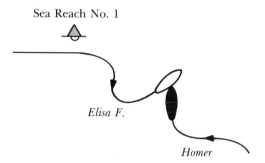

Sea Reach No. 1

*Elisa F.*

*Homer*

**Fig. 40.**

water specified by the Secretary, a vessel crossing a river shall keep out of the way of a power-driven vessel ascending or descending the river.

The meaning of the rule is unambiguous. Unlike Rule 9(d) it is not limited to narrow channels or fairways, nor does it depend on the maneuverability of the ascending or descending vessel.

However, clear delineation of when a river ceases to be a river is essential to avoid uncertainty of application. Not only must the delineation of rivers, as well as narrow channels and fairways anywhere in the world, be unambiguous, they must also be known by ships. In a collision off Nagoya, Japan, the British motorship *Troll River*, outbound for New Orleans, was struck by the inbound Israeli motor vessel *Shavit* (see Figure 39). It transpired that the *Shavit* was misled about the extent of the fairway by having an out-of-date chart and formed an erroneous view of what the other ship was likely to do, thinking the *Troll River* was a give-way vessel in a crossing situation who failed to alter course to starboard sufficiently early. The *Shavit* alone was found to blame.[55]

Assumptions about another vessel's intentions are equally no cause for departing from the crossing rules. Two vessels were approaching a junction of three channels in the Thames Estuary (see Figure 40). The inward-bound *Homer*, in one channel, mistakenly formed the impression that the outward-bound *Elisa F*, in another channel then on her port bow, was navigating to pass into the third channel. However, on reaching the junction, the *Elisa F* turned to starboard to enter the *Homer*'s channel, sounding one short blast as she did so. The *Homer* never heard the blast and altered course early to port, without signal, to enter the *Elisa F*'s former channel. Belatedly, VHF messages were exchanged, mutually conflicting orders were passed to helmsmen, and the two vessels swung

---

[55] The *Troll River* [1974] 2 Lloyd's Rep. 181.

together with resultant collision. Apart from bad aural and visual lookout and failure to sound two short blasts, the *Homer* was at fault because:

> the situation was one of crossing vessels and *Homer* should have kept her course and speed.[56]

The *Elisa F* was not at fault and the *Homer* was alone to blame. An appeal by the *Homer* that *Elisa F,* in view of the lower court's finding, should have altered earlier to starboard was dismissed.

In confined waters apparent crossing situations can arise fairly swiftly, especially in busy anchorages and off pilot stations. In one such case, the *Sestriere,* however, the crossing situation was found not to exist because the other ship, the *Alonso,* never settled on a clearly defined course.[57] Clearly then, whether a ship is on a sufficiently settled course is a factor in determining the existence of a crossing situation. Thus, it was so in the case arising from the collision between the Dutch tanker *Forest Hill* and the Greek tanker *Savina* in the roadstead of Ras Tanura (see Figure 41). The *Forest Hill* was proceeding from an anchorage in the southern part of the roadstead on a northerly course. The *Savina* was proceeding to an anchorage in the northern part of the roadstead on an easterly course. The stem of the *Savina* struck the port side aft on the *Forest Hill.*

The *Forest Hill* had altered course to starboard as she got under way, eventually some eight minutes before the collision, steadying on a course of 350 degrees. From this time, the court held that a crossing situation existed but not at any earlier time:

> because, until C minus 8, *Forest Hill* was not on a definite course at all.

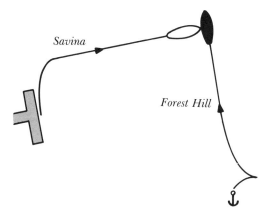

**Fig. 41.**

---

[56] The *Homer* Q.B. (Adm. Ct.) [1972] 1 Lloyd's Rep. 429 C.A. [1973] 1 Lloyd's Rep. 501.

[57] The *Sestriere,* Q.B. (Adm. Ct.) [1976] 1 Lloyd's Rep. 125.

Both ships were castigated for keeping a poor lookout—the *Savina* for failing to stop as give-way vessel, and the *Forest Hill* for increasing speed when the stand-on vessel. Blame was apportioned 40 percent to *Savina* and 60 percent to *Forest Hill,* the latter attracting major blame because her increase of speed was calculated to force drastic avoiding action by the *Savina.* This interpretation of the *Forest Hill's* increase of speed was not accepted by the court of appeal, which reversed the apportionment of blame, as the *Savina*

> having failed to take the necessary avoiding action was the more to blame of the two.

However, on further appeal, the House of Lords decided that there was evidence that entitled the admiralty court to hold that the *Forest Hill* did intend to force her way across the head of the *Savina* and that therefore the original apportionment would be respected.[58] Among these vicissitudes of apportionment, the salient point for the mariner to hoist in is that all three courts upheld that the crossing situation came into effect when the *Forest Hill* steadied on her course of 350 degrees at collision minus eight minutes (C − 8).

The cause of collisions in crossing encounters in confined waters seems mainly to be one of misjudgment in appreciating the situation. This is hardly surprising considering the difficult circumstances that can prevail, particularly the short period of time usually available for observation and assessment. If ever there was a need for heightened alertness backed up by sound preparation and intelligent foresight, it is the crossing situation in restricted areas.

### SUMMARY

A majority of collisions occur in coastal, river, and harbor areas, which for the purpose of this chapter comprise restricted waters. The latter have gradually extended seaward as larger ships and hazardous cargoes have proliferated. Spawned by local rules and spurred on by ecological disasters brought about by ship casualties, a rapid growth in marine traffic organization has commenced. Traffic separation schemes have reduced collisions especially where enforcement is present. Various forms of vessel traffic systems have sprung up, mainly covering restricted waters, and form a useful strategic tool in collision avoidance. The collision regulations and local rules provide the tactical means.

Head-on encounters in restricted waters are the most numerous types of meeting. Essentially a port-to-port passing is required, though the inland rules have provision for starboard-to-starboard passage. Many meeting collisions in channels occur because of a failure to keep to star-

[58] The *Savina* [1976] 2 Lloyd's Rep. 132.

board in one's own water. The effects of interaction are sometimes not sufficiently allowed for, particularly in proceeding at an unsafe speed.

Overtaking encounters in restricted waters also suffer from interaction and, although the manner of passing is similar under both international regulations and inland rules, there are differences in sound signals between the regimes. Passing too close, at an unsafe speed and at an inopportune place or time, is the usual cause of overtaking collisions.

The crossing situation in wider restricted waters is much the same as for the open waters of the high seas, though the inland rules again have a difference in meaning of sound signals, as well as a provision to pass ahead. Narrow channels' rules enjoin a crossing vessel not to impede a vessel confined to a channel. New International Rule 8(f) expands on the meaning of not to impede. Local rules and Inland Rule 15(b), in certain waters, give right-of-way to vessels proceeding up or down channels and rivers.

Passage in restricted waters is a time of increased risk, when close-quarters situations cannot always be avoided. Heightened awareness of the circumstances to be encountered and sharp alertness in all manner of "routine" passings are required. The dictates of good seamanship may well alter the circumstances of some such encounters, a matter to be examined in Chapter 10.

# 9

# The Law in Fog

### Restricted Visibility

Despite the concentration of law relating directly to the navigation of vessels in restricted visibility in both the inland rules and international regulations, and the remarkable technological advances in the ability to detect and track vessels by radar, fog remains a major factor in many marine collisions and a prolific source of litigation arising out of those collisions. Some 40 percent of the cases considered for this edition occurred in conditions of restricted visibility. Of these, 88 percent involved vessels on opposing courses where the other vessel was ahead of the beam.

Prior to the advent of radar, the regulations depended entirely upon the fog signal: vessels in fog sounded fog signals and when other vessels heard them, they stopped. The widespread use of radar has meant that this approach has had to be supplemented, for the means of navigation in fog has improved substantially. First, in 1960, a radar annex was appended to the international regulations and, in 1972, incorporated into the body of the rules—a move followed by equivalent action for U.S. inland waters in 1980. Second, indicative of the changes were the discarding of the word "fog" in official phraseology and its replacement by the term "restricted visibility." Fog, while never defined in either the rules or the courts, has a meteorological association with visibility of less than half a mile. With today's high-speed shipping this is too short a range to invoke "fog rules," whereas restricted visibility is a sufficiently elastic phrase to encompass varying states of visibility and varying circumstances that require action at greater ranges.

In the meantime, considerable legal comment has been passed on those collision cases reaching the courts, particularly on the use of radar as an anticollision device. Despite this focus by the courts, it must be emphasized that radar is but one element in the solution to the problem of avoiding collision when visibility is impaired. It does not, for example, supplant the need for fog signals.

## Uniformity of Fog Signals

With the entry into force of the Inland Navigational Rules Act of 1980, the differences between sound signals to be used in restricted visibility on the high seas and those for use in inland waters have been largely eradicated. The international reference to a sound signal for "vessels constrained by their draught," however, has been deleted from the inland rules in keeping with the U.S. decision not to legislate for this category of vessel. Also, the inland rules allow a waiver for small vessels anchored in designated special anchorage areas.

## When Fog Signals Are Required

Exactly when the weather is thick enough to require fog signals to be sounded can be difficult to determine. In the absence of positive court authority, previous editions of this book have cited the very practical suggestion of La Boyteaux that the prescribed minimum visibility of sidelights (then 2 miles) indicated that notice of approach should be given at least at that distance and that therefore when proper lights cannot be seen by vessels 2 miles apart, fog signals were in order.[1] Now that the required visibility of sidelights for the larger vessels is 3 miles, this guideline is perhaps less relevant, particularly as the audibility range of the whistle on even the largest of ships is, theoretically, only 2 miles,[2] but the underlying rationale remains valid. In particular, the implication that signals should be sounded not only when actually in fog, but when steaming toward, away from, or near, a fog bank is important.

Both inland rules and international regulations specifically cover this point by requiring fog signals when navigating not only in but near an area of restricted visibility. How close one has to be is undefined, but there would seem little merit in sounding signals if the visibility is greater than the audibility range of the appliance concerned. However, care must be taken against using the audibility ranges quoted in the annexes to the rules as an infallible yardstick, for the equipment might be heard at greater distances. Moreover, if there is uncertainty as to the true extent of visibility, prudent mariners should err on the side of caution and make the appropriate signal at a visibility limit greater than the distance their particular appliance can be heard. In the *Elwick*, failure to sound fog

---

[1] La Boyteaux, *Rules of the Road at Sea*, 67.
[2] International Regulations, Annex III, 1(c).

signals in visibility between ¹/₂ to ³/₄ of a mile was held to be a fault.[3] However, it would be misleading to try and set any precise limit, for each case will undoubtedly be judged on the circumstances prevailing at the time.

The exigencies of war are no excuse in the eyes of the law for failure to sound fog signals, even when dispensation has been given by duly authorized naval orders.[4] While these decisions do not mean that in time of hostilities vessels have to go about giving legal due notice of their presence to an enemy, it does mean that damage that results from any errors of omission or commission must be paid for out of the public treasury. However, the facts of modern naval warfare make it unlikely that there is anything to be gained by not sounding fog signals.

In recent cases, where ships have had the ability to detect each other by radar, failure to sound fog signals, while condemned, has not always been held to be causative step towards collision. Thus, a ship at anchor was not held liable when she did not ring her bell or sound the permissive short-prolonged-short whistle signal because it would have made no difference to the other vessel's navigation[5]; similarly, the alleged lack of a signal on weighing anchor in a crowded anchorage would not have added to the knowledge of an approaching ship whose emergency full astern action to avoid collision had already been taken prior to the first ship's anchor being aweigh[6]. When two approaching ships met in a narrow channel, the failure of both to sound signals was not causative of the collision since fog signals would not have indicated that one ship was crossing into her wrong water[7]. Nonetheless, the sounding of appropriate signals is considered a precaution to be taken in any well-run ship when navigating in reduced visibility[8].

Do recent court findings stress sound signals less because of the greater ranges afforded by radar and VHF? Such a tendency would not be inconsistent with the fact that modern electronic equipment permits, and in the case of radar requires (Rule 19(d)), action at ranges outside the maximum range of audibility at which a sound signal could be expected to be heard. However, it would not be consistent with the practice of good seamanship to assume these recent court cases grant tacit approval to refrain from sounding fog signals as required by the rules. In fact, such an assumption would be contrary to the rules. It would be more prudent to assume that the greater emphasis by the careful navigator

---

[3] The *Elwick* (1923), Shipping Law, 131.
[4] Watts v. U.S. (N.Y. 1903) 123 F.105; Thurlow v. U.S. (1924) 295 F.905.
[5] The *St Louis* [1986] 2 Lloyd's Rep. 128.
[6] The *Filiatra Legacy* [1986] 2 Lloyd's Rep. 264.
[7] The *Maritime Harmony* [1982] 2 Lloyd's Rep. 406.
[8] The *Roseline* [1981] 2 Lloyd's Rep. 411.

proceeding in reduced visibility would be directed toward all the dictates of good seamanship—especially safe speed, proper lookout, and the efficient use of radar as also required by the rules, but not to the exclusion of whistle signals. Moreover, few need be reminded that reliance on an electronic device such as radar, with its susceptibility to inconvenient and sometimes unnoticed error, can be a sure way to precipitate an unwanted close-quarters situation. In fact, a malfunctioning radar was a significant contributory cause in a collision that occurred on the high seas off the eastern coast of the United States in 1981.

The *Lash Atlantico,* proceeding in a southeasterly direction with visibility reduced to about a cable, detected the *Hellenic Carrier* on radar about 5 miles on what she thought was her port bow. Acting on that information, the *Lash Atlantico* commenced a series of small alterations to starboard that ultimately brought her bow into the side of the *Hellenic Carrier.* The two vessels had been on approximately opposite courses proceeding at an unsafe speed (18 knots and 14 knots, respectively), and the courts later found that the *Hellenic Carrier* when initially detected was actually on the *Lash Atlantico's* starboard bow. The faulty radar alone was not to blame for the collision, however. Indeed, this collision amply demonstrates how disregard for the precepts of cautious navigation in reduced visibility will lead to what is often the only inescapable, unpleasant result. The district court, after an appeal, found each vessel to be 50 percent at fault.[9] Neither vessel reduced to safe speed in violation of Rules 6 and 19(b). Initially establishing radar contact with the *Lash Atlantico* at a range of 12 miles, the *Hellenic Carrier* sighted her on her own starboard side for the first time just one minute before the collision, at which time she went to full left rudder, counter to the provisions of Rule 19(d)(i). Neither vessel maintained a systematic radar plot in violation of Rule 7(b). Although not considered to have contributed to the collision, only one vessel sounded fog signals and then only belatedly. And finally, though not specifically required by the rules, neither vessel availed herself of VHF. As this case illustrates, our primary concern should not be one of trying to anticipate what the courts might decide as a contributing factor towards a collision but rather one of doing all within our power and in accordance with the rules to prevent one.

### Time Interval Between Signals

Under both sets of rules, vessels under way make the appropriate sound signal on their whistle at intervals not exceeding two minutes, whereas bell and gong signals of vessels not under way have an interval of not more than one minute.

[9] Hellenic Lines, Limited v. Prudential Lines, Inc., E.D. Va. (1984) 730 F.2d 159, 164 (4th Cir. 1984).

The two-minute maximum interval for whistles was standardized because temporary deafness can be caused by too frequent a sounding, and there must be sufficient listening time between one's own signals to be able to hear those of an approaching vessel. This does not mean that signals should not be made at lesser intervals than those specified, particularly when other vessels are close and bearing in mind they may not have operational radar. Indeed, there are occasions where good seamanship requires signals to be given much oftener. Vessels at anchor have been found at fault for not striking their bells more frequently than the specified interval,[10] while a vessel turning into an occupied anchorage was equally at fault for not increasing the frequency of her whistle to warn vessels already at anchor.[11] And so when vessels are feeling their way past each other in dense fog, there can be little doubt that legal obligation, as well as good seamanship, may require signals to be at greatly reduced intervals until both vessels are past and clear. However, it should be borne in mind that in a crowded harbor area the continuous sounding of fog signals could tend to confuse rather than add to safety.

### Two Prolonged Blasts

This signal, applicable both on the high seas and in inland waters, conveys valuable information to a vessel encountering another in fog. It signifies the presence of a power-driven vessel under way but who is stopped in the water, and its use is only lawful when those conditions are met. Great care must be exercised, particularly at night, to ascertain that the vessel is dead in the water before changing from one blast to two. The courts have been quick to find a vessel guilty when wrongfully using this signal:

> You are not to blow this signal until you are stopped and you must be quite certain that you really are.[12]

Other vessels are entitled to assume that the two-blast signal will only be given when the signaling vessel is stopped.[13] However, that is all they may assume, for:

> The signal of two long [sic] blasts . . . advertised only the fact that the other vessel was at that moment stopped in the water. It contained no guarantee that the other vessel would remain stopped in the water. . . .[14]

When a vessel starts making way again after having stopped, she should

---

[10] The *Chancellor* (1870) Fed. Case No. 2,589; Brush v. the *Plainfield* (1879) Fed. Case No. 2,058.

[11] The *Quevilly* (1918) 253 F.415.

[12] The *Lifland* (1934) 49 Ll. L. Rep. 285; *see also* the *Ansaldo Savoia* (1921) 276 F.719; the *Haliotis* (1932) 44 Ll. L. Rep. 288; the *British Confidence* [1951] 1 Lloyd's Rep. 447; the *Almizar* [1971] 2 Lloyd's Rep. 290.

[13] The *Matiana* (1908) 25 T.L.R. 51; the *Kaiser Wilhelm II* (1915) 85 L.J.P. 26; the *Marcel* (1920) 2 Ll. L. Rep. 52.

[14] The *Cornelis B* [1956] 2 Lloyd's Rep. 540.

change her signal to one prolonged blast "immediately she begins to gather headway."[15] However, this is not necessarily applicable when a vessel uses her rudder and engines merely to prevent her bow from falling off.[16]

## Hampered Vessels

Vessels that are in some way constrained in their activities are provided with special sound signals in Rule 35(c) and (d). The minor differences between international regulations and inland rules for these vessels have already been mentioned. While the rules for vessels in sight of each other give a pecking order for give-way status among hampered vessels, there is no such explicit status in restricted visibility. Despite the provision of unique signals for hampered vessels, Rule 19—the conduct of vessels in restricted visibility—affords them no specific rights. Strictly, they must behave themselves the same as any other vessel, but clearly the distinctive signals for them have the obvious purpose of causing ordinary vessels to approach them with greater caution and to give them as wide a berth as circumstances permit.

Sailing vessels under way now give the same signal as hampered vessels. With the revised requirement for sound signal appliances it was considered that the previous one-, two-, or three-short-blast signals might be confused with maneuvering signals and were, anyway, of limited value to other vessels.

## In-Doubt/Danger Signal in Restricted Visibility

The international in-doubt signal of five or more short blasts is restricted to use when vessels are in sight of each other. The inland danger signal, now Inland Rule 34(d), is equally confined to occasions when vessels are in sight. This used not to be the case, for the danger signal was held to be required when vessels did not understand the course or intention of an approaching vessel in fog,[17] or when a vessel was aground in fog.[18] It has been mooted that the danger signal, while in no way a substitute for fog signals, could be used in restricted visibility by a vessel detecting an immediate situation on radar or by other means that could result in a collision. In such a case, it is argued, the responsibility requirement of Rule 2 would permit the vessel to sound the danger signal if it thought such a signal would help to avoid immediate danger. However, this suggested, permissive use of the danger signal is very different from the positive requirement just cited in the cases above.

[15] The *Dimitrios Chardris* (1944) 77 Ll. L. Rep. 489.
[16] The *Canada* (1939) 63 Ll. L. Rep. 112.
[17] The *Virginia* (1916) 238 F.156; the *Celtic Monarch* (1910) 175 F.1006.
[18] The *Leviathan* (1922) 286 F.745.

Hopefully, this sort of aberration is now obsolescent in the newfound near-uniformity between international and inland fog signals. Certainly it should prevent repetition of the unfortunate circumstances where, in a collision in Juan de Fuca Strait, both navigators acted under the conviction that they were in inland waters and therefore subject to a different regime, whereas the court concluded that they were 100 yards into the international regime.[19]

### Some Rules Are Applicable to Any Condition of Visibility

The general requirements of both the inland rules and the international regulations as to lookout (Rule 5), safe speed (Rule 6), risk of collision (Rule 7), action to avoid collision (Rule 8), narrow channels (Rule 9), and vessel traffic services/traffic separation schemes (Rule 10) apply equally to vessels in restricted visibility. These rules, common to whether a vessel is in sight or not, are important in understanding what is required of mariners should they find themselves approaching a close-quarters situation with another ship regardless of the extent of visibility. The great increase in maritime traffic density and in the size and speed of ships, with a consequent decrease in the time available to determine how the rules should be applied as vessels approach each other, has led, as previously mentioned, to the need to take action at greater ranges than hitherto. The rules of Part I of both jurisdictions therefore require careful considertaion, for they form the bedrock of precautions to take in all kinds of visibility and, with reference to this chapter, the necessary preliminary actions to be taken before nearing restricted visibility. A ship who conscientiously applies the rules of Part I is unlikely to be caught short by the sudden advent of poorer visibility. As in all well-run ships, the time to take precautions, whether they be for seamanship, navigation, or rules of the road reasons, is when there is still time to complete those precautions before the danger arises. Failure to do so, with particular reference to the latest rules of the road, are:

> regarded as serious faults because they are breaches of the regulations committed at a time when there was or should have been plenty of time to consider carefully the correct course of action to be taken.[20]

It has been suggested that a difficult situation arises for the mariner when some vessels are in sight while others, including the "another vessel" quoted in Rule 19(d) and (e), are not.[21] Clearly much depends on the particular circumstances prevailing at the time, but in open waters, no ship should allow herself to be so boxed in by others that she cannot

---

[19] Border Line Transportation Co. v. Canadian Pacific Ry. Co. (Wash. 1919) 262 F.989.
[20] The *Roseline*, [1981] 2 Lloyd's Rep. 714.
[21] S. Mankabady, *Collision at Sea: A Guide to the Legal Consequences* (Amsterdam: North-Holland Publishing Co., 1978), 207.

avoid a close-quarters situation; whereas, in confined waters, VTS/TSS and narrow channel rules should provide a useful background against which to exercise judgment. Only one case,[22] and that before the advent of TSSs, has been found illustrating this difficulty, which probably says much for the forehandedness and sound seamanship of those mariners who have encountered such a dilemma. Not so in the relatively more simple case where only two vessels were involved, initially out of sight but later becoming visible to each other. Clearly both should have taken early avoiding action in accordance with Rule 19(d), but this has not stopped appeals in court that the crossing rules applied when ships became visible at, say, 3 or 4 miles apart. In the *Genimar/Larry L* collision (see Chapter 4), the crossing rules were held to apply; but in the *Ercole/Embiricos* collision, those applying to restricted visibility were applicable.[23]

No doubt detailed circumstances varied in each case, but the moral does seem to be that, when having exercised good lookout and determined that a ship detected by radar is heading towards a close-quarters situation with you, you should not delay taking early avoiding action.

The subject of maintaining a lookout will be discussed in Chapter 11, though many relevant facets of the use of radar as a lookout will be covered later in this chapter, as well as their impact on safe speed. Suffice it to say for now that restricted visibility imposes a greater responsibility on mariners to use all means available in maintaining a proper lookout, not least so that a continuous appraisal can be made of what is a safe speed for the circumstances and conditions prevailing.

### Safe Speed Not the Same as Moderate Speed

Previous international and inland rules required a vessel to "go at a moderate speed" in restricted visibility, but there were no strictures on speed in clearer weather. With the advent of very large vessels that carry their way for some considerable time after engines are stopped, thus traveling well over a mile before coming to rest, there is a need to relate speed to all conditions and circumstances prevailing and not just when fog per se was present. Thus "safe speed" replaced "moderate speed," with an extended applicability to all conditions of visibility. It is, of course, in restricted visibility that the need for a safe speed particularly applies. Hence, the state of visibility is first in the list of factors that Rule 6 states shall be taken into account in determining safe speed.

Clearly the very term *safe speed* does not preclude the setting of a high speed in appropriate circumstances. Furthermore, even if a collision

[22] The *Nassau* [1964] 2 Lloyd's Rep. 509.
[23] The *Ercole* [1977] 1 Lloyd's Rep. 516.

should occur, it does not necessarily follow that a ship was proceeding at an unsafe speed. Poor lookout or incorrect avoiding action might well be to blame, rather than a high initial speed. However, for a high speed to be accepted as safe, it must be shown that circumstances and conditions were continuously monitored and speed was adjusted when fresh information came to hand.

> . . . such a speed can only be justified so long as it is safe to proceed and provided that timely action is taken to reduce it or take off all the way in the light of the information supplied. . . .[24]

Too high a speed might render a ship unable to take such "timely action" because of insufficient time to do so after sighting or detecting a vessel at relatively short range. This has often been the case in collisions occurring in fog. More rarely, on the other hand, too low a speed might be unsafe if the ship loses steerageway.

> . . . it was the duty of those on the bridge of the *Ring* to appreciate that they had lost steerage-way and were going off course and it was their duty to correct it by appropriate engine and helm movement.[25]

Excepting this unusual case of stopping engines in the path of a ship following close astern, a prime requirement of safe speed is that a ship can "be stopped within a distance appropriate to the prevailing circumstances and conditions." This might seem to be a mere rewording of the former rules for restricted visibility specifying "a moderate speed, having careful regard to the existing circumstances and conditions." But it is not: in part because safe speed applies to all conditions of visibility, but more crucially because the concept of safe speed is different from the more restrictive term moderate speed. What constituted moderate speed has had a wide variety of construction by the courts, all of which may be characterized as much less liberal than the interpretation put on the term in practice by the most careful of navigators. The original rules' reference to existing circumstances may have intended to leave some discretion on this point to the mariner, but certainly very little discretion has been left by decades of court decisions. Perhaps the arrival of safe speed will restore some of that discretion.

Early United States Supreme Court decisions established what may perhaps be termed the general rules of what was moderate speed. Firstly, moderate speed was defined as bare steerageway,[26] followed a few years later by a second definition that implied the right to navigate a vessel only at such speed as would enable her to stop in half the distance of visibility then existing.[27] It is apparent that the two definitions were at

---

[24] The *Kurt Alt* [1972] 1 Lloyd's Rep. 31.
[25] The *Ring* [1964] 2 Lloyd's Rep. 177.
[26] The *Martello* (1894) 153 U.S. 64.
[27] The *Umbria* (1897) 166 U.S. 404.

times contradictory; that is, there could be conditions when to maintain even steerageway, a speed would be necessary that would make it impossible to stop in time after first sighting an approaching vessel, or even an anchored vessel. In inland waters in such cases, in order to obey the law, it was therefore necessary sometimes to come to anchor[28] or to delay leaving a dock.[29] These are sensible measures when they can be taken, but are of no value to a ship in deep water who cannot anchor and who would have to drift until visibility improved, an arguably greater danger in crowded or close waters, particularly for large ships with hazardous cargoes capable of causing widespread pollution.

The acceptance of the moderate speed rule into the half-distance rule spread worldwide[30] but received its first check in British courts where it was held that it was not a rule of law[31] and that each case must be judged in the context of the original wording of "existing circumstances and conditions." Several United States courts have espoused a similar approach,[32] with the Supreme Court ruling in one case that

> Implicit in that portion . . . of the Inland Rules of Navigation that directs a moderate speed for vessels proceeding in foggy weather, and in the concomitant half-distance rule, is the assumption that vessels can reasonably be expected to be travelling on intersecting courses. On the facts of this case, it was totally unrealistic to anticipate the possibility that the vessels were on intersecting courses and the rule was not applicable.[33]

The Supreme Court decision did not do away with the half-distance rule, merely modifying its applicability to vessels in the vicinity of a fog bank.

The moderate speed requirement and its associated half-distance rule ignored the realities of today's shipping industry. Ships must often of necessity navigate in reduced visibility and by so doing they undoubtedly proceed at times at "immoderate speeds." This is not necessarily reckless driving on the part of masters, but is caused by financial realities, which dictate a need to *reasonably* maintain schedules. Rigid application of the half-distance rule took no account of this or of the greatly increased capability of ships to navigate safely in restricted visibility. The rule was developed in an earlier day when speeding blindly through fog was sheer folly. Today, the rule might be appropriate for a vessel without radar, but a ship that is making proper use of radar in, say, the open ocean cannot be realistically expected to take all way off when the fog becomes

---

[28] The *Southway* (1924) 2 F.2d 1009; the *Lambs* (1926) 17 F.2d 1010, affirming 14 F.2d 444.

[29] The *Georgia* (1913) 208 F.635.

[30] HMS *Glorious* (1933) 44 Ll. L. Rep. 321; Silver Line Ltd. v. U.S. (1937) 94 F.2d 754.

[31] Morris v. Luton Corporation (1946) K.B. 114 (C.A.).

[32] Hess Shipping Corp. v. the SS *Charles Lykes* (1969) 417 F.2d 346; Polarus S.S. Co. v. T/S *Sandefjord* (1956) 236 F.2d 270, 272.

[33] Union Oil Co. v. the *San Jacinto* (1972) 401 U.S. 145.

so dense that it is not possible to see beyond her bows. Further, too strict a compliance with the half-distance rule might lead a ship, although well capable of pulling up in half the visibility, to proceed at an unsafe speed when other factors should have been taken into account. This is, of course, what Rule 6 and Rule 19(b) now demand of mariners by providing a list of factors, not necessarily exhaustive, for their guidance. It would seem appropriate that the actions of those unfortunate enough to be involved in collisions should be considered in the light of those factors rather than on too strict an interpretation of the half-distance rule. Of course, the handling of the vessel under the circumstances must also be taken into account and should be in accord with the dictates of good seamanship and recognized practices of navigation.

### Factors to Be Taken into Account

Safe speed is a relative term. It cannot be defined so as to apply to all cases; it depends on the circumstances of each case. The factors in Rule 6 provide a valuable check-off list of points the courts have considered over the years. Visibility tops the list. Earlier in this chapter there was discussion on when visibility was sufficiently restricted to require sound signals to be made. A similar process must be gone through when deciding visibility is such as to affect safe speed. This is without doubt likely to be at a greater limit than that used to determine when to start fog signals. Visibility of less than 5 miles should cause sufficient concern about safe speed to, at least, place the engine spaces on alert, even though it would not warrant the sounding of signals. Prudent mariners, however, would do well to consider themselves in or near an area of restricted visibility for the purpose of Rule 19 when they cannot visually distinguish the type and aspect of a closing vessel within the distance they would normally expect to do so, a distance for many ships that should be measured in miles rather than in a few hundred yards.

When the visibility is so restricted, other important factors will obviously include the size and maneuverability of a ship, particularly her stopping power. The ability to take way off is relevant in considering a ship's speed in fog:

> It would be absurd, to take an extreme case, to suggest that a speed of ten knots in a destroyer would be as excessive as ten knots in an old collier.[34]

However, not too much weight should be given to this factor, for

> . . . it is not enough to say that because a vessel has remarkable pulling-up power she is therefore justified in proceeding at high speed in fog. Regard must be had to the chance other ships have of receiving her fog signals. If two vessels are approaching each other at very high speed, it

[34] The *Munster* (1939) 63 Ll. L. Rep. 165.

must be quite obvious that their chance of hearing each other's fog signals are very much reduced.[35]

Neither will high speed give much opportunity for assessing what action should be taken when a vessel is sighted or first detected at short range.

Traffic in the vicinity will also be an important factor. In the open sea, with little or no traffic around, a relatively high speed may be appropriate provided a proper radar watch is being kept and the engines are ready for immediate maneuver. However, even a vessel with good stopping power using an advanced collision avoidance system would not be justified in proceeding at high speed in dense fog through congested waters or areas where fishing vessels or other small craft are likely to be encountered.

When visibility is restricted, Rule 19(b) requires a vessel to have her engines ready for immediate maneuver as well as to proceed at a safe speed. This applies in open as well as restricted waters. Because it can take some time to round up the necessary personnel and prepare the engines for instant use, forehandedness should be shown in giving the engineers as much warning as possible. For ships with bridge control of engines, there is, of course, less need for advance notice of a speed change. Such a change is envisaged by Rule 19(e), which lays down occasions when speed is to be reduced to steerageway and, if necessary, for all way to be taken off. Clearly, under the circumstances of Rule 19(e), the term "safe speed" has much in common with the old "moderate speed" (but not necessarily with the half-distance rule), and many previous court interpretations of "moderate" will still be relevant in those circumstances.

In restricted visibility a vessel making proper use of radar may often be justified in going at a higher speed than that which would be acceptable for a vessel not so equipped, but not usually at the speed that would have been considered safe for clear weather. A recent example of what one court considered these speeds should be, in the circumstances it was examining, were: 6 to 7 knots for a non-radar-fitted ship in a busy area at night with 1-mile visibility; and 8 to 9 knots for a radar-fitted ship in the same vicinity at the same time but with her visibility about 1,400 yards and a caveat that further reduction was necessary on seeing a close-quarters situation developing.[36] Clear-weather speeds for both ships were 17 and 13½ knots, respectively. While not too much importance should be attached to the specific speeds quoted, it is instructive to note that the speed accorded the radar-fitted ship was, in those circumstances, not

---

[35] The *Arnold Bratt* [1955] 1 Lloyd's Rep. 16, 24.

[36] The *Hagen* [1973] 1 Lloyd's Rep. 257; *see also* the *Zaglebie Dabrowskie* [1978] 1 Lloyd's Rep. 570, where a proper speed in ¾- to 1½-mile visibility would have been no more than 8 to 9 knots.

much higher than that for the other vessel. Of course, radar is only one factor to be considered, and the existence of an operational set on board requires several further factors to be taken into account when determining safe speed. These will be covered in the discussion on radar later in this chapter.

**Excessive Speed**

Any speed that is not safe within the judicial construction of the word is excessive, and an examination of reported cases reveals the fact that vessels colliding in fog have, in an extremely wide range of existing circumstances, been convicted of excessive speed from barely making way to 22 knots, the first named being a case of giving a brief kick ahead on the engine to maintain course.[37] On the other hand, also in a wide variety of visibility and traffic conditions, speeds ranging from 3.5 knots to a half speed of 8 to 9 knots have been specifically approved as moderate, the last named being an instance concerning a rogue vessel in the approaches of a traffic separation scheme in visibility between 50 to 200 meters.[38] There would appear to be a slight upward trend, but not by more than a knot or two, in the more recent cases of what is a safe speed where a proper radar watch was kept. However, it must be stressed yet again that such a safe speed was only applicable for the circumstances prevailing and is invariably accompanied by the qualification that further reductions were necessary should visibility further decrease, or if there was detection of a potential close-quarters situation. It is obvious that the use of radar does enable vessels to travel safely at a somewhat higher speed than would be safe without radar—if the circumstances are right—for the installation of radar is not a license to speed if the conditions are not right. Thus, while the courts may approve a slightly higher safe speed for radar-fitted ships than hitherto in less severely restricted visibility, they are likely to continue to be as strict in their former judgments of moderate speed as they are of safe speed in dense fog when other shipping has been detected. As was said in the *Kurt Alt* case, previously cited

> radar . . . while, if properly used and can be relied upon to indicate all potential dangers in ample time to safely avoid them, it may give some justification for a speed in restricted visibility, which would otherwise be immoderate, such a speed can only be justified so long as it is safe so to proceed and provided that timely action is taken to reduce it or take off all the way in the light of the information supplied or to be inferred from radar.[39]

[37] Afran Transport Co. v. the *Bergechief* (1960) 170 F. Supp. 893 (SD N.Y.), *aff'd* 274 F.2d 469.

[38] The *Zaglebie Dabrowskie* [1978] 1 Lloyd's Rep. 570.

[39] The *Kurt Alt* [1972] 1 Lloyd's Rep. 31.

Court rulings in cases brought under the 1972 ColRegs have consistently condemned vessels of excessive speed in restricted visibility, especially where full and systematic use of radar has not been implemented to justify their speeds. Off Korea, two vessels initially proceeding at 13½ and 15 knots, respectively, in thick fog were guilty of proceeding at excessive speed since safe speed for both was judged to be 7½ knots.[40] In the North Sea, another two ships, one at 14 knots and the other at 13 knots, in visibility of 2 cables, should have been at a safe speed of 8 and 6 knots, respectively.[41] In a busy river, a downbound ship's speed of 8½ knots was deemed unsafe because she was not keeping a proper or efficient radar watch and could not justify a speed greater than 5 knots.[42] As a result of a three-ship encounter in dense fog in the Dover Strait, two of the vessels involved were judged to be proceeding at excessive speeds of 12 knots and 16 knots when their safe speeds were considered to be 8 knots and 10 knots, respectively.[43] Also in dense fog, this time in the Mediterranean, two ships, one at a good 10 knots and the other at 15 knots, were found to be in excess of their respective safe speeds of 8 knots and 10 knots.[44] When visibility in the Baltic was about 2 cables, two vessels, who had been initially traveling at 13 knots, should have been at a safe speed of no more than 8 knots.[45] As said earlier the trend of recent court findings is to allow a slightly higher figure for safe speed than used to be the case for moderate speed. But that higher figure is only a guide, and lesser speeds may well be necessary as circumstances unfold.

Many have been the excuses offered by mariners for excessive speed in collision cases, and scant indeed has been their judicial consideration. Some of the arguments tried and found wanting were: (1) that full speed was the safest speed, as it enabled the vessel to get through the fog sooner; (2) that the speed was customary for liners; (3) that the vessel was a passenger steamer and obliged to maintain schedule; (4) that the vessel was carrying passengers to whom it was important to get into port; (5) that the vessel was under contract to carry United States mail; (6) that in the opinion of her officers the vessel could not be properly controlled at a lower speed; (7) that the slowest speed of the engines would not drive the vessel at the moderate speed demanded; (8) that the other vessel was more seriously at fault; (9) that the vessel was a ferry; (10) that the regular speed, or at least a speed faster than that allowed, was necessary to keep

---

[40] The *Sanshin Victory* [1980] 2 Lloyd's Rep. 359.
[41] The *Roseline* [1981] 1 Lloyd's Rep. 416.
[42] The *Maritime Harmony* [1982] 2 Lloyd's Rep. 406.
[43] The *Credo* [1989] 1 Lloyd's Rep. 593.
[44] The *Tenes* [1989] 2 Lloyd's Rep. 367.
[45] The *Oden* [1989] 1 Lloyd's Rep. 280.

track of the vessel's position; (11) that a vessel in convoy had to maintain the speed of her naval escort; (12) that an aircraft carrier in peacetime had planes in the air and that to go more slowly meant danger to the lives of those in them. The judges have listened to these excuses and many more, and have then decided the cases on the coldly practical and unanswerable basis as stated by the circuit court of appeals:

> Speed in a fog is always excessive in a vessel that cannot reverse her engines and come to a standstill before she collides with a vessel that she ought to have seen, having regard to fog density.[46]

Pressure to "catch the tide" or otherwise maintain their schedule sometimes makes masters reluctant to come to a safe speed in poor visibility. The owners and operating authorities have a responsibility in ensuring they exert no such pressure on the master. In a recent case, where a ship under way struck another at anchor and the owners sought to limit their liability, it was held that the owners were guilty of actual fault because their ship had proceeded at excessive speed in fog. It came out in evidence that the master had habitually navigated his vessel in fog at excessive speed over several voyages, and that the marine superintendent, to whom the ship's logs were regularly submitted, failed to check the records, which would have revealed this fact, and thus failed to bring it to the master's attention. Consequently, the owners were unable to limit their liability and the master's certificate was suspended. "Excessive speed in fog is a grave breach of duty, and shipowners should use all their influence to prevent it."[47]

### Radar—A Statutory Requirement

The vast majority of ships these days are equipped with at least some of the wide range of modern navigational devices that can remove much of the uncertainty as to a vessel's position. Of these aids to navigation, as was said earlier, radar has received the greatest attention of the courts, primarily in its use as an anticollision device. While acknowledging this supremacy of radar it should not be forgotten that the other equipment can also be of value in the anticollision role—either as an important input to radar systems, e.g., gyrocompass and log; as means of information, e.g., VHF radio; or as an accurate positional device when approaching traffic separation schemes, e.g., hyperbolic fixing systems, inertial navigational systems, and, of course, radar itself. Neglect of these ancillary equipments, and indeed the lack of relevant publications, may not cause collision by themselves, but have sometimes been contributory factors to the scenario that led up to collision.

[46] The *John F. Bresnahan* (1933) 62 F.2d 1077.
[47] The *Lady Gwendolen* [1965] 1 Lloyd's Rep. 335.

Until recently there was no statutory requirement for vessels to carry radar. In the United States, the Ports and Waterways Safety Act of 1972 provided the first basis for vessels to carry "electronic devices necessary for the use of" a vessel traffic service, with an amendment in 1977 requiring every self-propelled vessel of 1,600 or more gross registered tonnage (grt) operating in U.S. waters to have on board a marine radar system. In the United Kingdom from 1976, vessels of more than 1,600 grt had to carry specified radar equipment, though without any obligation to use such equipment. Long before that, however, the courts had consistently faulted those who failed:

> to take full advantage of any equipment with which a vessel is equipped . . . this equipment [*radar*] is supplied to be used and used intelligently. . . .[48]

Spurred on by pollution disasters, the cause for mandatory carriage of radar was taken to the international forum. Under the auspices of IMO, the International Convention of Safety of Life at Sea 1974 (SOLAS), requires all ships between 1,600 grt and 10,000 grt to be fitted with at least one radar. All ships of 10,000 grt and above must be fitted with at least two radars, each capable of operating independently of the other.

## Malfunction of Radar

If the required radar should fail, then in U.S. waters the local USCG authority must be informed, and there are some similar requirements in other parts of the world. Courts have held that in the face of serious defects the master of a vessel is not, except in extenuating circumstances, at liberty to postpone attempts to make corrective action. He or she is obliged to ensure that an effort is made, employing the resources available, to correct faulty equipment that has a potential influence upon safe vessel operation. A decision not to attempt repairs to such equipment could lead to a presumption of negligence and consequent liability upon a vessel involved in a collision in which the faulty equipment was or should have been an ingredient. The majority of U.S. owners of U.S. flag merchant ships have agreed "repairs shall not be delayed until reaching port if the necessary spare parts are available and the Radio Officer or Radio Electronics Officer has a Radar Endorsement, if such equipment is involved."

It is, of course, a function of a vessel's owner to exercise due diligence to make a vessel seaworthy, which increasingly includes radar:

> It is the owner's duty to see to it that a vessel's equipment is in safe working order.[49]

[48] The *Chusan* [1955] 2 Lloyd's Rep. 685.
[49] Greater New Orleans Expressway Commission v. tug *Claribel* (1963) E.D. La. 222 F. Supp. 521, 382 U.S. 974 (1965).

Even if the radar is only partially defective, and the master attempts to exercise good judgment in relying upon it, the owner may not escape liability, for

. . . the navigation of a ship defectively equipped by a crew aware of her condition does not relieve the owner of his responsibility or transform unseaworthiness into bad seamanship. . . .[50]

However, since then IMO has provided an escape clause that states that

. . . malfunction of the radar equipment . . . shall not be considered as making the ship unseaworthy or as a reason for delaying the ship in ports where repair facilities are not readily available.[51]

Moreover, if the radar had failed after departure from port, provided the master had exercised due diligence in clearly providing for routine repairs and maintenance, the owner probably would escape liability on that score. Of course, if radar does fail, safe speed in restricted visibility must be kept low. The *John C Pappas*, whose radar was out of order, was found 70 percent to blame for, *inter alia*, failing

to reduce speed substantially on entering the fog (i.e., she should have stopped her engines).[52]

### Additional Safe Speed Factors for Vessels with Operational Radar

To be operational in the context of the rules, a radar must not only be technically functioning correctly, but must also be operated by personnel who understand the *characteristics, efficiency, and limitations* of the equipment. A large variety of equipment is available at varying degrees of cost and sophistication, each with its own peculiarities. Watch keepers must be familiar with the one on their ship before standing their first watch, apart from being well educated in general radar theory. They must know of any blind arcs, and therefore be aware of the need to vary course from time to time to clear those arcs, of how to adjust controls to obtain optimum performance, and of how to monitor that performance. Judging from the inquiry into the collision between the tankers *Atlantic Empress* and *Aegean Captain* off Tobago in 1979, the certificated watch keeper in the latter ship apparently did not successfully manipulate the rain-clutter control and gain control when a rain squall created a white area on the radar screen. Initially, the other ship, the *Atlantic Empress*, was beyond the clutter, which was obscuring part of the *Aegean Captain*'s radar coverage, but was not detected, probably due to a large reduction in gain. In the *Atlantic Empress*, the watch keeper, using a 3-centimeter radar, did not pick out the *Aegean Captain* from the rain squall that enveloped her.

[50] The *Maria* (1937) 91 F.2d 819.
[51] Regulation 12(e), Chapter V of the 1974 International Conference on Safety of Life at Sea.
[52] The *Almizar* [1971] 2 Lloyd's Rep. 290.

However, the use of the 10-centimeter radar set, with which she was also fitted, almost certainly stood a better chance of penetrating the rain area and detecting such a large contact.[53] In addition, the watch keeper in the *Aegean Captain* had left the bridge two or three times before the collision.

Interrupted observation of a radar screen is not proper use that can justify a high speed in, or near, restricted visibility, for

> . . . when reliance is placed on the radar, it cannot be too strongly empha-
> sized that a continuous watch should be kept by one person experienced
> in its use. . . .[54]

Furthermore, that experienced person must know how long it will take him or her to extract further information about the other vessel's track and closest point of approach (CPA), apart from the warning of another vessel's presence that a radar supplies. With manual plotting this is likely to be a minimum of six minutes, a factor that must bear heavily on the decision of what is a safe speed.[55]

Any *constraints imposed by the radar scale* in use will vary, as each scale has its disadvantages. The longer the range the less discrimination is possible, the greater the effect of bearing error, and the less likely it is that a small contact at close range will be spotted. Conversely, with short radar range scales no early warning is achieved and no overall traffic pattern can be discerned. The ideal is to have two radar displays each on a different scale, one to give the close-in picture and the other for longer-range warning. This avoids changing scales and temporarily disrupting the picture, especially when in a close-quarters situation. If only one display is available, it must not be kept continuously on one scale:

> If the master of the *Nassau* was relying upon radar to justify his speed
> in reduced visibility it was not good seamanship to have kept his radar
> permanently on the short range. . . . They should have extended the
> range periodically at intervals appropriate to the circumstances to inform
> themselves of the general situation and, in particular, of the probable effect
> of the approach of otherwise invisible vessels upon the action of the vessel
> known to be, and seen to be, ahead of them . . .[56]

The effect on radar detection of the *sea state, weather, and other sources of interference* can sometimes be so severe that, as was seen in the earlier-mentioned collision between two tankers off Tobago, even large ship contacts may be obscured by precipitation. Wave clutter relatively close in to the center of the radar display can seriously degrade the picture,

---

[53] "Report on Inquiry, Liberian Bureau of Maritime Affairs in London," *Seaways*, November 1980; *also* A. N. Cockcroft, "The S- and X-Band Debate," *Seaways*, April 1981.

[54] The *Fina Canada* [1962] 2 Lloyd's Rep. 113.

[55] Afran Transport Co. v. The *Bergechief* (1960) 70 F. Supp 893. (SD N.Y.).

[56] The *Nassau* [1964] 2 Lloyd's Rep. 514; *see also* the *Bovenkerk* [1973] 1 Lloyd's Rep. 62; the *Roseline* [1981] 2 Lloyd's Rep. 410.

and although adjustment of the controls may enable sizable contacts to be held, there is likely to be suppression of small echoes. Indeed, small craft may only give a radar response when they are on the crest of a wave, leading to an intermittent echo that could be taken for yet another part of the wave clutter. Closer inshore, side echoes from land can confuse the picture and contribute toward collision.[57]

The possibility that *small vessels may not be detected* by radar at an adequate range is ever present, despite the increased use of radar reflectors. The loss of the *Jane*, in the Straits of Juan de Fuca, and the *Powhatan* off the eastern seaboard—both wooden-hulled fishing vessels and neither detected on radar—illustrate the dangers of proceeding too fast in restricted visibility in areas where small craft may be expected. Both of the fishing vessels were visually sighted, but neither merchant ship was able to pull up or avoid.[58]

The number, location, and movement of *vessels detected by radar* clearly have impact on what is a safe speed. The denser the traffic the longer it takes to assess risk of collision and the more complex is the effect of evasive maneuvers. Compared to raw radar displays, automated radar plotting aids (ARPA) will speed this process up, but it is still necessary for the mariner to absorb the wealth of information that ARPA provides, which must be allowed for in the chosen speed. Where the presence of other shipping may hinder early avoiding action, a drop in speed is essential. The *Larry L,* cited in Chapter 4, detected the *Genimar* on radar some 7 miles distant. Visibility was variable from 3 to 4 miles. Because of the presence of another vessel to starboard, the *Larry L* made a succession of small alterations of course to port before she sighted the *Genimar.* The court commented that *Larry L:*

> should have made a substantial alteration of course to starboard at an early stage, or, if she was inhibited from doing so by the presence of the *Pearl Creek* on her starboard side she should have made a substantial reduction of speed.[59]

As the courts have been consistent in faulting ships for not slowing down more in restricted visibility when they detect but one ship with a CPA that would result in a close-quarters situation, it can be expected that they will insist on low safe speeds when more than one ship is detected.[60]

Of course, it is radar that makes possible the *more exact assessment of the visibility* by observing the ranges at which other ships or navigational marks either first become visible or are lost from sight. A deterioration

---

[57] The *Bovenkerk* [1973] 1 Lloyd's Rep. 62.

[58] SS *Mormacpine (Jane)* 1959 USCGI; the *South African Pioneer (Powhatan)* 1961 USCGI.

[59] The *Genimar* [1977] 2 Lloyd's Rep. 25; *see also* the *Nassau* [1964] 2 Lloyd's Rep. 509; the *Sanshin Victory* [1980] 2 Lloyd's Rep. 359.

[60] The *Bovenkerk* [1973] 1 Lloyd's Rep. 62.

in visibility is not always possible to detect with certainty, especially at night, and watch standers should use the radar to aid the lookout's eye. Particularly they should be alert to the presence of restricted visibility when they fail to sight a vessel detected on radar, or a navigational mark that should have been within the expected visual range.

> . . . the *Gunnar Knudsen* failed to appreciate the presence of this fog bank as soon as they ought to. She was provided with radar . . . and . . . it ought . . . to have been brought into operation . . . when buoy No. 9 was not seen.[61]

**Automatic Radar Plotting Aids Also a Statutory Requirement**

It can be seen from earlier discussion that radar cannot be used casually to justify a high speed in restricted visibility. To draw the maximum benefit from it requires constant, knowledgeable appraisal by at least one person dedicated to the task and not distracted by other duties. Some mariners, lulled by a radar-induced sense of security, felt that they could rationalize increased speeds without extra vigilance. Added to this over-confidence was sometimes a reluctance to undertake the tedious nature of manual plotting. The result was that those ships did not make proper use of radar.

Partly because of this, since 1974 the United States has been urging that large ships of over 10,000 grt, carrying bulk cargoes of oil and hazardous materials, be fitted with an electronic relative motion analyzer (ERMA), sometimes also called collision avoidance aid or collision avoid-ance system (CAS). Although IMO examined this proposal, other nations were unwilling to proceed apace with an equipment considered to be still under development. The IMO solution was to schedule a gradual introduction of what is now internationally known as an automated radar plotting aid (ARPA), into *all* ships of over 10,000 grt, commencing in 1984 and completing in 1989.[62] This was insufficient to satisfy U.S. domestic concerns, however, particularly after the "winter of the *Argo Merchant*," and an impatient Congress passed the Port and Tanker Safety Act of 1978. This act required bulk carriers of oil and hazardous materials of over 10,000 grt to be equipped with an ERMA by 1 July 1982. Thus, all such ships calling at U.S. ports must have an electronic system that analyzes their radar picture, providing auto-tracking and vector resolu-tion of up to twenty contacts (depending on whether contact acquisition is automatic or manual) that would otherwise require manual plotting.

This use of modern technology is laudable, for as a general rule ARPA, with multiple echoes, should perform as well as or better than a trained

---

[61] The *Gunnar Knudsen* [1961] 2 Lloyd's Rep. 440; *see also* the *Fina Canada* [1962] 2 Lloyd's Rep. 117; the *Almizar* [1971] 2 Lloyd's Rep. 290.
[62] IMO Resolution A.422(XI) November 1979: Performance standards for ARPA.

radar observer using a radar display with a single echo. There is also provision for an alarm system to alert the bridge watch keeper, but while the United States requires both audible and visual alarms, IMO allows the option of either.

ARPA's primary function is to reduce the workload for the bridge personnel, and it can provide fuller information with greater accuracy and less delay than can be obtained by manual methods. The rapid increase in the installation of ARPAs on ships in the 1980s is comparable to the rate of fitting early radars to ships in the 1940s. Radar was expected to result in an early and vast improvement in navigational safety, but the anticipated reduction in the incidence of collisions was not achieved. Indeed, there arose an era of "radar-assisted collisions," which only gave signs of improvement when thorough radar training was established and the limitations of this new aid were better understood. The benefits of ARPA are considerable, but more sophisticated equipment by itself does not bring about an instant improvement in navigational safety unless it is operated by trained personnel who fully appreciate its capabilities and limitations and who are not lulled into a false sense of security by expecting too much from it. While there are few examples to date of "ARPA-assisted collisions," similar to the radar ones of the 1950s, there is considerable unease among mariners about declining skills afloat.

> It is on men that safety at sea depends and they cannot make a greater mistake than to suppose that machines can do all their work for them.[63]

The Soviet investigation into the collision between the passenger ship *Admiral Nakhimov* and the cargo ship *Petr Vasev* in the Black Sea in 1986 indicated that "radar hypnotism" in the latter vessel, brought about by continuously looking at the ARPA screen, was a major factor. It would appear that ARPA limitations were not allowed for, placing excessive reliance on the equipment to the detriment of visual observation.[64] However, this charge can only be truly leveled at the *Petr Vasev*, the one vessel so fitted, and even then, it is overshadowed by the incomprehensible bad seamanship shown in both ships.

### The Use of Radar in Determining Risk of Collision

Rule 7(b) strengthens the many court findings that radar, if fitted and operational, must be properly used to obtain early warning of risk of collision, an admonition reinforced by Rule 19(d) when restricted visibility exists. The first U.S. court case involving a collision of a radar-equipped vessel found the failure of the *Barry* to use her radar a most serious fault

---

[63] The *Fogo* [1967] 2 Lloyd's Rep. 208.

[64] R. Chernyaev, "Impact of ARPA Limitations on Collision Avoidance" (extract), *Seaways*, February 1982. *See also Seaways*, April 1989.

when visibility was restricted.[65] The earlier discussion on what factors to take into account when determining safe speed provides an intimation of what the courts will consider constitutes the proper use of radar. An efficient radar watch, with controls at optimum settings, must be maintained with long-range scanning at regular intervals.

In waters where safe navigation of the ship requires accurate fixing of her position and frequent alterations of course, there should be a bridge team of at least two competent officers, one to concentrate on plotting the position of the ship while the other keeps the radar watch.[66] This watch must be continuous and cannot be casual. The choice of display can be important, one that is gyro-stabilized to be preferred where possible. True-motion displays can be of value in congested waters, though they can be subject to errors from log input. Again, the ideal would be two radar displays, one for true motion and the second for relative motion, but where only one is available the choice, in pilotage waters, should be made by the master and not solely by the pilot.[67] Notwithstanding what preference of mode of display is made, the requirement is for early warning of risk of collision, and this can only be obtained by systematic plotting of contacts, either manually or with ARPA.

A radar presentation will show only the bearing and range of an echo. Only plotting will ascertain closest points of approach (CPA), a major determinant of risk of collision, as well as course and speed—all of which are needed to make proper use of radar. Systematic plotting in a busy situation is a labor-intensive and time-consuming procedure, and many vessels have failed to make the effort, but the courts "have been uniform in their condemnation of such failures."[68] No doubt the advent of ARPA will ease the burden of plotting, provided proper use is made of it. However, not all ships will be fitted with ARPA—indeed, it could malfunction—and the plotting of bearings will be essential if reliable inferences are to be drawn.[69] The well-known use of the cursor and grease pencil marks on the screen will not suffice in restricted visibility,[70] though it must be accepted that in heavy traffic it is often impractical to make and evaluate a comprehensive manual plot. In such circumstances, provided the radar is being carefully and continuously observed, it should be possible to carry out some form of "threat reduction" and discard

[65] *Barry-Medford* (1946) 65 F. Supp 622; *see also Burgan-Bergechief* (1960) 274 F.2d 469.

[66] The *Roseline* [1981] 2 Lloyd's Rep. 411.

[67] The *Atys*—The *Siena* (1963) Netherlands Inquiry.

[68] Orient Steam Navigation Co. v. United States (1964) 231 F. Supp. 474 (SD Calif.); *Australia Star-Hindoo* (1947) AMC 1630.

[69] The *Prins Alexander* [1955] 2 Lloyd's Rep. 8.

[70] Skibs A/S Siljestad v. SS *Matthew Luckenbach* (1963) 215 F. Supp. 680 (SD N.Y.), *aff'd* 324 F.2d 563.

contacts that are clearly passing well clear, concentrating only on those that are not.

Unless some form of systematic plotting is undertaken, there is a grave risk that action may be taken on insufficient evidence. Rule 7(c) is crystal clear on this aspect that assumptions shall not be made on the basis of scanty radar information. Plotting errors will occur whether computerized or manual methods are used, particularly at longer ranges where inherent bearing inaccuracies of radar may well give an incorrect impression of CPA in the early stage of an encounter. Observation must therefore be based on several successive readings taken over a realistic period of time. Far too often, ships approaching each other in fog, sometimes even in excellent visibility, have misassessed the radar CPA and taken inadequate or conflicting action with disastrous results.[71]

### Detection by Radar Alone Requires Early Action

If proper use of radar has shown that risk of collision exists and/or that continuing on the present course and speed will lead to a close-quarters situation, then in restricted visibility ships must take action in accordance with Rule 19(d). This first level of action in restricted visibility applies when the determination of risk has been made by radar alone, without sighting the other vessel or hearing her fog signal. Ships must not delay in taking the action couched in the somewhat awkward terms of Rule 19(d)(i) or (ii) to avoid the impending close-quarters situation. Rule 8(a), equally applicable in any condition of visibility, also requires action to be taken in ample time. The purpose of the requirement to avoid turning to port for a vessel forward of the beam is to reduce the possibility of conflicting action being taken by vessels on opposite courses. Hanging on in the expectation of sighting the other vessel and changing the situation from a restricted visibility to a visual one is to court disaster. Ships have often detected each other on radar at considerable ranges but for various reasons have failed to take bold action until far too late.[72] A predicted CPA of several hundred yards is too small in fog on the open seas, and vessels should endeavor to achieve a more substantial distance apart, one measurable, as has been said before, in miles rather than in yards.[73] Two to 3 miles would seem a seamanlike distance, as

[71] The *Evje* (1950) 84 Ll. L. Rep. 20; the *Andrea Doria—Stockholm, Journal of Navigation* 30 no. 2 (1956), 238; the *Santa Rosa—the Valchem* (1959) USCGI; the *Niceto de Larrinaga* [1963] 1 Lloyd's Rep. 205; the *British Aviator* [1965] 1 Lloyd's Rep. 271; the *Toni* [1973] 1 Lloyd's Rep. 79; the *Ercole* [1977] 1 Lloyd's Rep. 516; the *Sanshin Victory* [1980] 2 Lloyd's Rep. 359; the *Roseline* [1981] 2 Lloyd's Rep. 417.

[72] The *Sanshin Victory* [1980] 2 Lloyd's Rep. 359; *see also* the *Tenes* [1989] 2 Lloyd's Rep. 367.

[73] The *Verena* [1961] 2 Lloyd's Rep. 133.

maneuvering to achieve this safe distance should be detectable on the other ship's radar, should make due allowance for any radar plotting errors especially at long range, should ensure that the echo is not lost at a later stage in any sea clutter near the center of the display, and should reduce the risk of a conflicting maneuver by the other ship. However, in congested waters when safe speed should be lower, lesser distances may be sufficient. A major reduction of speed, particularly effective for a vessel closing from abeam, is, of course, an option available—as well as, and perhaps in conjunction with—an alteration of course. A change of speed, however, for a vessel closing on a near-reciprocal course will little affect the CPA, but it will give more time for assessment and, should it be necessary, more time to hear her fog signals. Above all, the aim is to avoid getting into a close-quarters situation, and radar, properly used, can help.

Following a collision in the North Sea in visibility of not more than 2 cables, it was held that the ships should have attempted to pass each other at 3 miles to avoid a close-quarters situation at the unsafe speed at which they had been proceeding. At safe speed this could have been reduced to a distance of 1 1/2 miles.[74] The easterly bound ship with plenty of sea room should have altered about 60 degrees to starboard, while the westerly bound ship with sea room to starboard confined, should have substantially reduced speed together with a bold alteration to starboard to head about due north. However, bold alterations of course must take into account other shipping. The French *Eglantine*, sailing northeast up the Dover Strait in dense fog, made such an alteration to starboard to avoid a rogue vessel, the Belgian *Inez*, proceeding in the wrong direction down the TSS. As the *Eglantine* completed the maneuver and started her turn back she bounced off the port side of the Norwegian *Credo* who had been overhauling her about half a mile off. The Norwegian ship ought to have kept well clear of the *Eglantine*, but that failure was matched by the failure of the French vessel to have proper regard for the presence of the overhauling ship. Both vessels were equally liable, but the rogue ship did not escape:

> It would in the circumstances be unjust to hold that *Inez* was less at fault than either of the other two and each vessel would be liable to make good one-third of the damage done.[75]

### If Early Action Is Not Possible or if a Fog Signal Is Heard

Hearing a fog signal apparently forward of the beam or when a close-quarters situation with a vessel ahead cannot be avoided invokes the second level of action required of a vessel navigating in restricted visibility.

[74] The *Roseline* [1981] 2 Lloyd's Rep. 416.
[75] The *Credo* [1989] 1 Lloyd's Rep. 593.

This portion of Rule 19 is closest in meaning to the former fog rule that demanded vessels to "stop engines and navigate with extreme caution," and it can be expected that previous court rulings will have particular relevance.

Rule 19(e) contains the proviso "except where it has been *determined* that a *risk of collision* does *not* exist (emphasis added). This undoubtedly means that, where it is not certain what the position, course, speed, and CPA of the other vessel may be—or to use former terminology "a vessel the position of which is not ascertained"—then the remainder of the rule applies. It was held before the invention of radar that the position of a vessel could only be regarded as ascertained when fog signals placed the matter beyond doubt, but it was rare for the courts to be satisfied that fog signals alone resolved doubt,[76] particularly as the direction and distance of sound signals can be misleading in fog. With the advent of radar, the question of whether the position of a vessel whose fog signal had been heard apparently forward of the beam was "ascertained" when she was visible on the radar screen was soon considered.[77]

Many navigators thought that one good radar range and bearing, or certainly a series of ranges and bearings, constituted "ascertainment" of the other vessel's position. However,

> many of them whose misfortune had brought them into Court were disabused of this idea by the learned judges; evidently a great more was needed.[78]

Apart from distance and bearing, the minimum amount of knowledge required is the other vessel's course and speed[79] and the probable closest point of approach. On deciding on the latter point the court also commented on the likelihood of expecting routine alterations of course at navigational focus areas and that:

> It must be remembered that radar does not foretell intention, and all these are circumstances which must be considered.[80]

Thus, mariners must be very certain indeed that risk of collision does not exist when they find themselves in an unavoidable close-quarters situation with another vessel before they can decide not to come down in speed to bare steerageway. Even with a good radar plot, the possibility that a fog signal they heard may come from a different vessel than the one they are tracking must always be taken into account. The fishing vessels, whose sinkings were mentioned earlier in this chapter, were never seen on radar, although their fog signals were heard.

[76] *See* generally Marsden, *Collisions at Sea*, 536–39.
[77] The *Prins Alexander* [1955] 2 Lloyd's Rep. 1.
[78] F. J. Wylie, *Radar at Sea, Journal of Navigation* 22 (1969), 35.
[79] The *Gunnar Knudsen* [1961] 2 Lloyd's Rep. 437; the *British Aviator* [1964] 2 Lloyd's Rep. 403.
[80] The *Sitala* [1963] 1 Lloyd's Rep. 212.

When the strict proviso of Rule 19(e) cannot be met, then a vessel is required to reduce her speed to the minimum at which she can be kept on her course. This is for either a fog signal heard or for a developing close-quarters situation with another vessel forward of her beam. Such reduction in speed must be made in ample time, without waiting for the close-quarters situation to be reached. The greater the initial safe speed, the earlier, and therefore the greater range, at which speed should be reduced:

> . . . it could then be seen from radar that a close-quarters situation with the *Hagen* was developing and . . . those on board the *Boulgaria* should at this stage have reduced speed further. . . .[81]

Not too rigid an interpretation should be placed on the word "beam," for determining the direction of fog signals is unreliable at best. It was once held that in a case where a whistle was heard abaft the beam twice on the same bearing, the vessel should have stopped.[82] Fog signals heard from astern are not covered by the rule, but in one occasion where a vessel stopped her engines because of running into dense fog, she was faulted for not maintaining steerageway and falling off her course across the stem of an overtaking vessel.[83]

Those in charge of a vessel should not delay in reducing speed because they themselves have not heard the fog signal; they must act on the report of their lookouts.

> I see no excuse for the failure of the master and pilot to act upon the report made to them by the third officer, when he informed them that he had heard the whistle of a vessel ahead. It seems to me that it is no excuse on the part of either pilot or master to say he did not hear it himself.[84]

Previously, on both the high seas and in inland waters, the rules required a power-driven vessel to stop her engines when she heard, apparently forward of her beam, a fog signal of a vessel whose position had not been ascertained or when there was a vessel detected ahead of the beam with which she could not avoid a close-quarters situation. This action is no longer mandatory in the first instance, but having slowed down to bare steerageway in a timely manner, it may still be prudent so to do at a later stage. Indeed, Rule 19(e) continues that "if necessary take all her way off." The hearing of a fog signal close aboard for the first time, or the sighting of a vessel of uncertain course looming out of the fog is an example of when such action is urgently necessary, particularly

---

[81] The *Hagen* [1973] 1 Lloyd's Rep. 265; *see also* the *Nora* [1965] 1 Lloyd's Rep. 625; the *Zaglebie Dabrowski* [1978] 1 Lloyd's Rep. 570.

[82] The *Bremen* (1931) 47 T.L.R. 505.

[83] The *Ring* [1964] 2 Lloyd's Rep. 177.

[84] The *Chuson* [1953] 2 Lloyd's Rep. 151.

if the radar is suspect. The phrase "if necessary" permits no exception, and while the circumstances might permit way to be run off just by stopping engines, the fastest way to take off all headway is to back engines full.

Some discretion, however, should be used in putting engines in the astern mode unnecessarily:

> . . . when there is any question of listening for signals one is creating the worst possible conditions for hearing them by working the engines at full speed astern.[85]

In addition, going astern may cause the ship's head to fall off and present her beam to a vessel approaching from ahead. By keeping the bow end-on, or nearly so, to such a vessel, a smaller target is presented, which may assist avoiding action by the other vessel, as well as increase the likelihood of taking any impact forward of the collision bulkhead.

Alterations of course are usually best avoided if there is a close-quarters situation developing or if a fog signal is heard forward of the beam, unless both the position and track of the other vessel are positively known. Long experience has led to the stricture in Rule 7(c) that assumptions shall not be made on the basis of scanty information. Late alterations of course, in any direction, merely on the faith of a fog signal,[86] or catching an incomplete glimpse of a vessel first looming out of the fog,[87] or as a blind reaction to a close radar contact that was not properly tracked,[88] have been roundly condemned by the courts. A tendency in recent cases has been particularly to fault last-minute alterations of course to port for being contrary to Rule 19(d)(i):

> . . . the action taken by *C.K. Apollo* in putting her wheel hard-to-port was too late and in the wrong direction and was contrary to the express terms of rule 19.[89]

An alteration of course is not always found to be negligent for, as ever, the court will judge the case on the circumstances prevailing. In the *Sedgepool* case two vessels were approaching each other in fog on approximately opposite courses in the Ambrose Channel, New York. One ship held the other on radar on her port bow. Both ships, on hearing the other's fog signals, altered to starboard:

---

[85] The *Monarch* [1953] 2 Lloyd's Rep. 151.

[86] *Miguel de Larrinaga* [1956] 2 Lloyd's Rep. 538.

[87] Crown SS Co. v. Eastern Navigation Co. Ltd. (1918) S.C. 303; the *Koningin Luise* (1922) 12 Ll. L. Rep. 477; the *Devention* (1922) 12 Ll. L. Rep. 484; the *Wear* (1925) 22 Ll. L. Rep. 59; the *Bharatkhand* [1952] 1 Lloyd's Rep. 470.

[88] The *Anna Salem* [1954] 1 Lloyd's Rep. 475; the *Achille Lauro* [1956] 2 Lloyd's Rep. 540; the *British Aviator* [1964] 2 Lloyd's Rep. 403; the *Linde* [1969] 2 Lloyd's Rep. 568.

[89] The *Sanshin Victory* [1980] 2 Lloyd's Rep. 359; *see also* the *Roseline* [1981] 2 Lloyd's Rep. 417.

This was a collision which . . . occurred in a narrow channel, and in those circumstances, I should be very slow to blame a ship which hearing a fog signal from another vessel, altered her course to starboard in an attempt to get more over to her proper side.[90]

## Vessels Must Navigate with Caution

"And in any event navigate with extreme caution," concludes the restricted visibility rule, "until danger of collision is over." There is subtle irony in these closing words to the navigator, already chafing with impatience at the reduced speed and enforced stops, who pushes on too eagerly with the voyage. For the hardest thing to prove in any court after a collision has occurred is that the danger of collision no longer existed. It behooves mariners who have conformed to the law up to this point to practice the most scrupulous care in feeling their way past the other vessel. An occasional kick ahead, enough to keep their vessel on her course, with a change in that course only justified when the master is reasonably certain of the other's position, course, speed, and CPA, and with a prompt and vigorous reversal of engines if the latter decreases or the other's fog signals are steady on the bow, is the action most likely to prevent collision and to win court approval if the worst happens.

Whether in inland waters or on the high seas, it should be remembered that three short blasts must accompany any reversal of the engines if the other vessel is sighted; otherwise, the signal must not be used. Equally, other maneuvering signals are only valid after sighting the vessel that one is feeling one's way past. And then, of course, the regular rules govern, but never when one vessel is not in sight of another.

## Rules in Restricted Visibility Are for Safety and Should Be Obeyed

The new regulations have come a long way in recognizing the practical need of maritime trade to run to a reasonable timetable, which, effectively, means that ships under way need to make way in restricted visibility. The strictures of moderate speed, and hopefully of the half-distance rule, have been exchanged for the more flexible, though more extensive in application, guidelines for safe speed. The rules acknowledge that well-equipped and properly manned ships can avoid close-quarters situations without reducing below safe speed. Further, instead of having no option in certain circumstances but to stop engines, ships may now proceed at steerageway, albeit minimum steerageway. It is, of course, the rapid and major technological advances in ships' equipment, particularly radar, that have allowed this less strait-jacketed approach.

However, with this increased capability to "see" and freedom to act in restricted visibility, there comes increased responsibility to use, and use

---

[90] The *Sedgepool* [1956] 2 Lloyd's Rep. 668.

properly, the greatly expanded amount of information on the safe handling of vessels.

For unto whomsoever much is given, of him shall much be required.[91]

Greater attention is required of mariners, particularly in mastering the new aids, than some have shown hitherto. While there will always be a premium upon the established principles of good seamanship, no longer acceptable are the standards of bygone days.[92] However, not too much trust should be placed in the latest marvels of science, and the reader is reminded of the quotation from the *Fogo* case cited earlier (see note 63).

While the law in restricted visibility now makes greater allowance for the fact that shipping exists for the timely and profitable transport of goods, it is nevertheless apparent that obedience to the rules will occasion some delay if the weather clamps down. In the past, many mariners had a mistaken form of professional pride in getting their ship in on time regardless of weather conditions, and were influenced also by the fear that their owners would not accept fog as an excuse for any considerable prolongation of the voyage. In some cases this fear was by no means groundless, but it should be less so when responsible owners recognize the risks of liability, not only from collision but also arising from pollution. Thus, the law in restricted visibility does not merely suggest but demands that voyages must often be delayed in the interest of safety of life, of property, and the environment. Navigators who know the law and deliberately set themselves above it are likely sooner or later to come to grief and find that their skill in dodging innumerable vessels while they proceed at excessive speed does not excuse them from liability for a final collision. Although written more than a century ago, the following remains valid:

> It is unquestionably the duty of every master of a ship, whether in intense fog or great darkness, to exercise the utmost vigilance, and to put his vessel under command, so as to secure the best chance of avoiding all accidents, *even though such precautions may occasion some delay in the prosecution of the voyage.*[93]

## SUMMARY

This chapter has examined four major areas relating to the law in restricted visibility: sound signals, safe speed, radar, and close-quarters navigation. All four are inextricably interwoven, and it is fortunate that since near-uniformity of rules has been achieved, there are few distinctions between the rules for the high seas and inland waters. Neither set

---

[91] The *Nora* [1956] 1 Lloyd's Rep. 625.
[92] Jacobsen, *Technology and Liability* (1977) 51 T.L.R. 1132.
[93] The *Itinerant* (1844) 2 W. Rob. Adm. 236.

of rules places a finite value on the meaning of the term "restricted visibility," but the key words are "not in sight of each other." Thus, a radar detection at long range comes under this definition, even though visibility might be, say, over 5 miles.

The few minor differences to be found are mostly in the sounding of fog signals, affecting only a small category of vessels. While the rules do not specify the minimum visibility under which fog signals are mandatory, they should be used when visibility first diminishes the effectiveness of sidelights. The time between signals is a maximum interval that can, and should, be decreased when circumstances warrant. Great care should be exercised that the signal of two prolonged blasts is used only when a ship is truly dead in the water. It should be clearly understood that the signal does not necessarily indicate intention of remaining stopped. The use of the inland danger signal is, by the terms of Rule 34(d), intended for use by vessels in sight of each other, though it has been suggested that in certain circumstances the responsibility requirements in Rule 2 would permit a vessel to sound the danger signal in restricted visibility.

Safe speed has a wide application to all conditions and circumstances, but it is in restricted visibility that it comes closest in meaning to the former "moderate speed." However, the previous concomitance of the "half-distance rule" with moderate speed is less valid—a matter no doubt the courts will decide on when and if necessary. A visibility of 5 miles or less should lead to a reconsideration of present safe speed, with, at least, the engines being placed ready for immediate maneuver. As visibility decreases, so should safe speed, the aim being to have time to detect, plot, evaluate, and avoid at long range a potential close-quarters situation. If avoidance is not possible, then safe speed is again reduced, early, to bare steerageway. On hearing a fog signal ahead, unless absolutely certain of the movements of the ship originating it, bare steerageway is again required with, if necessary, all way being taken off.

Radar is now a mandatory requirement for most ships, but it is not a license for excessive speed in fog. Courts may accord an extra knot or so to the safe speed of a ship properly using radar, but always with the caveat that further reductions are necessary when radar information reveals that the circumstances have changed. Both the rules and the courts provide firm guidance as to the proper use of radar. Systematic plotting is essential, a task in which automated aids have the potential, if used by trained personnel, to be of great assistance.

There are two tiers of action for close-quarters navigation: first, mariners should avoid the situation at long range by following the express terms of Rule 19(d); and second, if unable to avoid, they should slow right down, taking all way off if necessary and resisting precipitate course alterations based on scanty information.

Collisions in restricted visibility continue to provide a major source of court cases. The rules recognize that ships have to navigate in fog, and the law has made provision that the means to do so are on board. It is up to mariners to use them intelligently so that they can proceed with their voyage in a timely manner and always in accordance with the rules.

# 10

# Responsible Use of the Rules

### Responsibility

Rule 2 of both the international regulations and the inland rules has the appropriate heading of *Responsibility*—responsibility, that is, to use the rules sensibly. The first part of the rule clearly spells out that there will be no exoneration for mariner or owner who irresponsibly fails to:

• comply with rules;
• take any normal seamanlike precaution;
• take into account any special circumstances evident.

The second part of the rule again mentions special circumstances, along with other general factors that might make a departure from the rules necessary.

In effect Rule 2 enjoins all to know and use the rules but warns against too rigid an interpretation. For it is the responsibility of mariners to take all seamanlike precautions in all situations, including those of "special circumstances," and, when necessary to avoid danger, to take additional measures not included in the rules, or in some cases, to depart from the rules altogether. For the rules offer practical advice and instructions to mariners faced with particular problems; they are not strict rules to be applied literally come what may. Moreover, the courts have always taken an open approach to the rules, construing them in the light of the prevailing circumstances whether they be special or not.

### Good Seamanship Defined in Rules

Seamanship, according to the dictionary, is the skill of a good seaman. The working definition in Rule 2(a) of both the international regulations and the inland rules is simply this: *any precaution which may be required by the ordinary practice of seamen,* and it is one of those things that the mariner may not neglect with impunity. What is required of seamen is ordinary skill and ordinary intelligence; they are not expected to foresee and provide against *every* eventuality. Seamanship of itself does not authorize departure from the rules, but provides:

> a solemn warning that compliance [with the rules] does not terminate the ever present duty of using reasonable skill and care.[1]

What is good seamanship is a question of fact, to be decided on after a consideration of all relevant circumstances.[2]

To the careful student of the rules of the road it is apparent that the lawmakers who formulated the rules—and they included the leading professional seamen of their day—were at great pains to make them definite, specific, and comprehensive. Every possible situation was considered, and what was in the opinion of the delegates the most effective course of action to prevent collision in each case was prescribed. Thus certain crossing, overtaken, and other vessels were designated as having the right-of-way, and vessels encountering them were directed to take all the action necessary to avoid them, with the understanding that such action should be based on the assurance that the stand-on vessel would maintain course and speed. Two vessels meeting end on were both specifically directed to avoid collision by turning to the right. Vessels were required to go at safe speed, to sound fog signals when required, and to reduce to minimum speed on hearing fog signals forward of the beam. It follows that obedience to these rules, which represent the lawmakers' ideas of what is the proper procedure under given circumstances, constitutes the first test of good seamanship; and conversely, disregard of the rules is generally prima facie evidence of bad seamanship. However, though the regulations do represent good seamanship, they do not cover more than a small part of seamanlike practice.

Later in this chapter, it will be pointed out that the responsibility rule allows departure from the other rules when special circumstances and immediate danger exist. Superior to this dispensation, however, is the responsibility to use good seamanship *in all cases;* i.e., an obligation is imposed in all circumstances to act in accordance with the recognized practice of skilled seamen. Such skills are not static, but constantly evolving as technology provides increased capabilities. The obligation might refer to the mariner's conduct leading up to, and perhaps even bringing about, the actual collision situation, or to his conduct in avoiding a collision thrust upon him by the fault of the other vessel, or to his conduct in maneuvering to lessen or to aggravate the damage of a collision after

---

[1] The *Queen Mary* (1949) 82 Ll. L. Rep. 341.
[2] The *Heranger* (1939) A.C. 101; the *Queen Mary* (1949) 82 Ll. L. Rep. 334; the *F.J. Wolfe* (1945) P. 97.

it had become inevitable. In considering the mariner's responsibility in such matters, it must be stressed again that the collision regulations are but one part, and a small part, of the principles of good seamanship. A separate book could be written on the all-encompassing needs of good seamanship, but this chapter will concentrate on those related to collisions.

### Forehandedness Is Essential

The scope of good seamanship is wide, but its practice has one underlying quality—that of forehandedness, or of thinking ahead. Sensible precautions are essential whether they be, to name but a few, the securing of cargo, a reduction of speed, the placing of the upper deck out of bounds, operating the fathometer, tuning a radar, calling extra hands, clearing away anchors, posting lookouts, or mentally working out what to do if something goes wrong.

Subsequent investigation often reveals that accidents usually arise from the adverse conjunction of several root causes each necessary but none sufficient by itself to cause the accident. One contributory cause in collisions can be not just the neglect of short-term measures (outlined in the preceeding paragraph) to meet the needs of the ordinary practice of seamanship or special circumstances but also failure to carry out medium-term measures such as comprehensive passage planning to take into account all hazards, including marine traffic. A rogue ship transgressing a traffic separation scheme usually falls into this category of unseamanlike failure to plan ahead. More recently the scope of accident inquiries has been searching even further back in time at long-term decisions to consider the design, managerial, and organizational sectors.[3] The investigations in the wake of the *Exxon Valdez* grounding in Alaska, the Zeebrugge disaster in Belgium, and the *Marchioness* collision in England have highlighted this development. This is as it should be, for Rule 2 is as applicable to owners as it is mariners.

Mariners who have failed to think ahead have included the inbound ship's pilot who should have been aware of the potential danger of sheering caused by rapid narrowing of the channel beyond an excavation "burrow pit," yet whose negligence in attempting to pass a downbound vessel in the narrow position of the channel was the sole cause of the subsequent collision.[4] Likewise the master of a barge that drifted out of control after having been plucked off the mud by the help from two tugs was found 70 percent at fault for, among other things, abdicating

[3] J. T. Reason, "How to Promote Error Tolerance in Complex Systems in the Context of Ships and Aircraft," *Seaways,* January 1991.

[4] Transorient Nav. v. *Southwind*, 1982 AMC 1085.

responsibility for the freeing operation without any plan or suggestions.[5] Another barge was found negligent for failure to monitor weather forecasts and to heed storm warnings in sufficient time to move to a sheltered location, "spud down," and anchor the barge at bow and stern.[6]

## Presumption against Moving Vessel

It is a matter of seamanship that any vessel under way keeps clear of a vessel not under way. There is a definite presumption, by the courts, in favor of a vessel moored or at anchor, as against the vessel that collides with her—and quite properly, of course, because of the relative helplessness of the fixed vessel to avoid collision. In clear weather, with lights on the anchored vessel at night, the other vessel is practically self-convicted of faulty seamanship, either through improper lookout or bad maneuvering. As frequently held:

> A moving vessel is prima facie in fault for a collision with one which is moored.[7]

A recent case to illustrate the outcome of a collision between one ship at anchor and another under way arose from an incident in the Shatt al Arab. With a following current of about $1\frac{1}{2}$ to 2 knots, and a moderate breeze from aft, the *Ayra Rokh* attempted at a very late stage to cross the bows of the anchored *Aghios Gerassimos*. An unusually good anchor watch was being maintained in the latter ship, but as the *Ayra Rokh* had altered course to starboard across the bow within the last minutes before the collision, it was too late for any effective action to be taken on board the *Aghios Gerassimos*. The court found that

> The collision was not caused by any negligent act or omission on board *Aghios Gerassimos* but by the indecision and wrong action on board *Ayra Rokh* who was alone to blame for the collision.[8]

So strong is presumption of fault against the moving vessel that rare indeed is the case where all the liability is put upon the vessel moored or at anchor. However, a barge moored to the end of a New York pier was damaged by a Cunard liner attempting to make a landing at an adjacent pier. An hour before the steamship's arrival, the barge was given notice to move out of her dangerous position while the liner landed, and was offered the free services of a tug to aid her in moving out of the way and back again. The court held that she refused to move at her peril and dismissed her libel against the steamship.[9]

---

[5] Mosbacher v. La. Makariado, 1981 AMC 1458.

[6] Dion's Yacht Yard v. Hydro-Dredge, 1982 AMC 1657.

[7] The *Banner* (Ala. 1915) 225 F.433.

[8] The *Ayra Rokh* [1980] 1 Lloyd's Rep. 68.

[9] The *Etruria* (N.Y. 1898) 88 F.555; *see also* the *Express* (N.Y. 1892) 49 F.764.

These cases are very rare, however, and ordinarily the best that can be hoped for by the vessel unfortunate enough to strike an anchored or moored vessel in clear weather is a division of damages, on one of four grounds: (1) improper position of the anchored vessel; (2) no lights, or improper lights, on the anchored vessel at night; (3) failure of the anchored vessel to maintain anchor watch where circumstances required; (4) failure of the anchored vessel to take proper steps to avoid the collision.

**Anchored Vessel Liable for Improper Position**

The presumption in favor of an anchored vessel struck by a moving ship arises only when the vessel was anchored in a proper place. An unmanned barge was anchored by the Coast Guard in a navigable channel adjacent to, but beyond, a charted anchorage. The barge was without proper lights and was hit by a fishing boat. The government was found liable.[10] When an underpowered and negligently navigated tug collided with a ship anchored outside the Mississippi River anchorage area, 35 percent of the damage was apportioned to the anchored vessel whose statutory violation precluded reliance on the presumption of fault by the moving vessel.[11] A vessel should not anchor in a fairway unless she has no choice in the matter. If she should anchor in an improper place, she must shift as soon as possible.[12] While awaiting a River Maas pilot, a master was not negligent in deciding to anchor at night in a government-approved anchorage area off the Hook of Holland rather than to risk collision with other vessels while sailing up and down for two hours.[13]

**Anchored Vessel Liable for Improper Lights**

As well as the unmanned barge mentioned above, further examples of ships anchored with improper lights may be found in Chapter 3. In addition, liability for night-time collision by a crew boat with an anchored trawler was apportioned 70 percent against the anchored vessel for failure to maintain proper anchor lights.[14]

**Failure to Maintain Necessary Anchor Watch**

Despite the absence of any specific provision in the international and inland rules, the courts have in the past found that an anchor watch is sometimes required under the rule of good seamanship and no doubt in the future could equally cite the requirement to maintain a lookout at all times. Essentially the requirement for an anchor watch will depend

[10] Gaspart v. U.S., 1979 AMC 2232.
[11] Alama Barge v. Rim Maritime, 1985 AMC 2540.
[12] The *British Holly* (1924) 20 Ll. L. Rep. 237.
[13] General Electric v. *Lady Sophia*, 1979 AMC 2554.
[14] Davis v. Superior Oil, 1981 AMC 2282.

on the circumstances, including the type of vessel involved and the number in her crew.[15] It was held that a small coaster, with a crew of twenty-five, who, while at anchor in the River Thames on a clear, fine night, was struck by a vessel under way, was not expected to maintain a full anchor watch and that, in the prevailing circumstances, the employment of a single lookout was sufficient precaution.[16]

Finally, inasmuch as a vessel is liable for any damage she may do to another vessel by dragging her anchor, whenever weather, current conditions, or poor holding ground are such to indicate that possibility, a competent anchor watch becomes essential to prevent it.[17] This watch must be experienced and have received the master's instructions.[18]

The presumption of fault on the part of a vessel that drags anchor into collision with another ship may be rebutted by proof (1) that the collision could not have been prevented, or (2) that the other ship could have avoided contact. A drifting vessel was found solely liable for collision in a crowded anchorage even though another ship may have failed to post an adequate anchor watch, since the latter was not a contributory cause.[19] Failure to test engines before weighing anchor was unseamanlike conduct.[20]

### Failure of Anchored Vessel to Take Mitigating Action

While a vessel at anchor is relatively unable to maneuver, there are two acts that are required of her under all circumstances, and omission of either of them may involve her in fault for a collision under the rule of good seamanship. In the first place, she must not anchor too close to another vessel, the legal presumption being that the vessel anchored first has a right to ample swinging room, upon which the later arrival must not infringe. Secondly, she must anchor securely—that is, with sufficient chain out—and if heavy weather or a strong current makes it necessary, she must drop a second anchor to prevent dragging into another vessel. Failure to do this has resulted in numerous decisions holding the dragging vessel at fault for collision.[21] In one such case, the steamship *Bragdo*, at anchor off Staten Island in a December gale with 45 fathoms out, dragged across the chain of the steamship *British Isles* and set her adrift. In finding the *Bragdo* at fault, despite the fact that the gale had reached hurricane

[15] The *Gerda Toft* [1953] 1 Lloyd's Rep. 257.
[16] The *Cedartrees* [1957] 1 Lloyd's Rep. 57.
[17] The *Forde* (CCA N.Y. 1919) 262 F.127.
[18] The *Sedulity* [1956] 1 Lloyd's Rep. 510.
[19] Neptune Maritime v. *Essi Camilla*, 1984 AMC 2983.
[20] The *Filiatra Legacy* [1986] 1 Lloyd's Rep. 407.
[21] The *Bertha* (Va. 1917) 244 F.319; the *Djerissa* CCA (1920) 267 F.115; the *Jessie* and the *Zaanland* (1917) P. 138.

strength, the circuit court of appeals cited the rule from Knight's *Seamanship*, recommending a length of cable equal to seven times the depth of water for ordinary circumstances with more if weather conditions cause the vessel to put excessive strain on the chain.[22] It is prima facie evidence of negligence for a vessel to drag her anchor, and all seamanlike precautions have to be taken to prevent it. In the *Velox*, a ship dragged her anchors in weather of unusual severity and collided with another. The relevant sailing directions contained a warning about the holding ground, and it was found that when the weather became bad the *Velox* should have used her engines to prevent initial dragging and to have taken even more drastic action later to arrest the dragging:

> . . . no seaman can be called upon to exercise more than ordinary care: but . . . when a seaman is called upon to face wholly exceptional conditions, ordinary care of itself necessarily demands that exceptional precautions may have to be taken.[23]

If an anchored vessel finds herself threatened by another vessel, whether the latter be under way or not, there are some actions she can take to avoid or reduce the effect of collision. These measures may often be futile, because the need to take them does not become apparent until too late for them to be effective.[24] However, the courts have occasionally found that such measures should have been taken, particularly the working of chain whether it be pulling up on the cable[25] or the more common exigency of veering more chain. If a vessel at anchor can avoid collision by use of her helm, she may be held to blame if, having the opportunity to do so, she did not exercise it.[26] However, she must not take such action until it becomes clear that the ship under way cannot, by her own action, avoid a collision.[27]

In conjunction with working her cable and helm, a ship at anchor with power ready can, and should, use her engines to assist avoiding action. Following a collision in the River Schelde, the *Sabine* was faulted for not paying out more cable and using her engines in order to make more room for the *Ore Prince* to pass.[28]

In uncomfortable circumstances the seamanlike measure is to take one's ship to sea. Following successive collisions in a gale between three ships Mediterranean-moored in Tartous, Syria, the master of the Russian ship *Kapitan Alekseyev* was found guilty of negligence in failing to take

---

[22] The *British Isles* (CCA 1920) 264 F.318.
[23] The *Velox* [1955] 1 Lloyd's Rep. 376.
[24] The *Ceylon Maru* (Md. 1920) 266 F.396; the *Beaverton* (N.Y. 1919) 273 F.539.
[25] The *Prospector* [1958] 2 Lloyd's Rep. 298.
[26] Marsden, *Collisions at Sea*, 607.
[27] The *Viper* (1926) P. 37.
[28] The *Sabine* [1974] 1 Lloyd's Rep. 473.

his vessel, particularly as she was carrying explosives, out of the harbor at an earlier stage. The *Alekseyev* dragged anchors, falling upon the adjacent Singaporean *Nordmark* whose master had done all that could reasonably be expected of him. When *Alekseyev* did sail, her maneuvers resulted in the parting of ropes of a Greek ship *Panagiostis Xilas*, who fell upon some barges. All damages were recoverable from the owners of the *Alekseyev*.[29]

## Standing Too Close to Other Vessels

The same line of reasoning that presumes it bad seamanship to hit a vessel that is moored or at anchor applies when a collision occurs between ships passing too close to each other, as sometimes happens when a vessel with way upon her meets one that is lying dead in the water. This possibly debatable extension of presumption of fault by a moving vessel was early hinted at as follows:

> The obligation on the part of free vessels to avoid risk of collision with those incumbered, or at rest, is imperative, and one that the admiralty courts must enforce, having regard to the perils of navigation and the importance of the rule of the road in respect thereto.[30]

Similarly, off pilot stations where ships may be encountered lying stopped it has been said:

> . . . it was in any event the duty of *Sestriere*, as a matter of good seamanship in the special circumstances of the case . . . to take timely action to keep clear of the *Alonso* who arrived on the scene first. . . .[31]

Both ships had been approaching the drop-off point for disembarking their pilots (see Figure 42). The *Alonso* had arrived first and altered course to a northerly heading at about 3 knots to drop her pilot. The *Sestriere* was approaching from *Alonso*'s port bow and reducing speed to about 1 or 2 knots. Both ships recognized the risk of collision and both sounded the in-doubt signal. The *Alonso* went hard to starboard, but collision was not averted. This action was not excused as being taken in the agony of

**Fig. 42.**

[29] The *Kapitan Alekseyev* [1984] 2 Lloyd's Rep. 173.
[30] The *Shinsei Maru* (Va. 1920) 266 F.548.
[31] The *Sestriere* [1976] 1 Lloyd's Rep. 131.

the moment, and she joined the *Sestriere* in being found equally liable for the bad seamanship: both should have taken way off.

More recently, in the Gulf of Thailand the

> *Thomaseverett* was negligent in adopting her course . . . so as to pass between *Esso Chittagong*, which had been waiting for a pilot, and the pilot vessel, there being no more than a cable clearance on either side.[32]

However, while it may be good seamanship and manners to avoid a vessel stopped in the water on the high seas, it must be made clear that she does not have the privileges of a ship at anchor. She is under way and where risk of collision exists should comply with the regulations as far as she is able.[33]

When slowing down to embark a pilot, sufficient allowance must be made for leeway. A large steamship in light trim had hardly any steerageway when, on embarking the pilot, a squall blew her downwind onto a vessel at anchor. The *William Wilberforce:*

> was alone to blame for the collision . . . which resulted from the inadequate margin of safety which she left.[34]

Even when both vessels are making way, it is unseamanlike to approach so close to one another that, for example: upon that ship's stopping or altering course slightly a collision cannot be avoided;[35] or where insufficient sea room is left for corrective action to overcome a steering casualty;[36] or where there is a narrow stretch of river ahead;[37] or to attempt to squeeze through a narrow gap when the vessel ahead swings in the river.[38]

### Restriction of Speed in Good Visibility

Discussion of safe speed applicable to *any* condition of visibility was given in Chapter 9. Rule 6 of both the international regulations and the inland rules contains a list of factors that must be taken into account, regardless of how good the visibility is, in determining what is a safe speed.

In most canals and in many rivers and harbors, a specific speed limit is fixed by local statute or ordinance, and such a regulation unquestionably has the force of law. When a speed regulation exists, it invariably means speed over the ground, and allowance must therefore be made when the rate is accelerated by a favorable current.[39] One of the important

---

[32] The *Thomaseverett* [1979] 2 Lloyd's Rep. 402.

[33] Marsden, *Collisions at Sea*, 612: but *see also* discussion in Chapter 7, note 31, re the *Devotion II* [1979] 1 Lloyd's Rep. 509.

[34] The *William Wilberforce* (1934) 49 Ll. L. Rep. 219.

[35] The *Kate* (1933) 46 Ll. L. Rep. 348.

[36] The *Frosta* [1973] 2 Lloyd's Rep. 348.

[37] The *Ore Chief* [1974] 2 Lloyd's Rep. 427.

[38] The *Sabine* [1974] 1 Lloyd's Rep. 472.

[39] The *Plymouth* (CCA N.Y. 1921) 271 F.461.

applications of the rule of good seamanship as interpreted by the courts is in the restriction of speed. An examination of the cases shows numerous vessels at fault for excessive speed in inland waters in the absence of any specific speed limit, these speeds ranging all the way from 4 to 17 knots. It may be stated as a general rule that any speed in a harbor or narrow channel is excessive (1) if it causes damage to other property by the vessel's swell, or (2) if it renders the vessel herself unmanageable in maneuvering to avoid collision.

(1) *Damage caused by vessel's swell.* For more than one hundred years now the view has prevailed: namely, that a large power-driven vessel that proceeds at such speed as to create a swell causing injury to another vessel properly in the waters she is navigating and properly handled, is liable for such injury, even if that speed is only 5 or 6 miles an hour.[40] In the case referred to, the offending steamer, with her engines on dead slow ahead, passed within a few feet of a scow loading at an icehouse and was held for failure to stop her engine entirely. In another case the opinion of the court included the following excellent statement of the rule, which still holds:

> Such waters are not to be appropriated to the exclusive use of any class of vessels. We do not mean to hold that ocean steamers are to accommodate their movements to craft unfit to navigate the bay, either from inherent weakness, or overloading, or improper handling, or which are carelessly navigated. But of none of these is there any proof here, and in the absence of such proof we do hold that craft such as the libelant's have the right to navigate there without anticipation of any abnormal dangerous condition, produced solely by the wish of the owners of exceptionally large craft to run them at such a rate of speed as will insure the quickest passage. To hold otherwise would be virtually to exclude smaller vessels, engaged in a legitimate commerce, from navigating the same waters.[41]

In a more recent case, a barge loading on the St. Lawrence River just west of Quebec was injured by pounding on the bottom when she was struck by a heavy swell from the Cunard steamer *Andania*, which passed her at a speed over the ground of about 17 knots, though there is a legal speed limit in that part of the river of 9 knots. Ascertaining the extent of the damage after the barge had completed a voyage to New York, the owner sued the Cunard Line *in personam*, and was met with the interesting defense that the steamship was in charge of a compulsory pilot, and that the company through its agent, the master, was therefore not liable. However, the court held that the master, who was also on the bridge, was negligent in not exercising his superior authority and ordering the pilot to slow down in conformity with the government speed regulation.[42]

[40] The *New York* (N.Y. 1888) 34 F.757.
[41] The *Majestic* (CCA N.Y. 1891) 48 F.730.
[42] The *Emma Grimes* (N.Y. 1933) 2 F. Supp. 319; *see also* the *Hendrick Hudson* (N.Y. 1933) 3 F. Supp. 317.

Excessive speed can also cause damage and death in more open waters where no government speed limits apply. Outside Dover harbor in the English Channel, a pilot was boarding a vessel when his launch rolled violently in a choppy sea and he was crushed. Finding that the wake of a passing ship contributed to the unexpected severity of the roll, the court said

> . . . those in charge of the *Maid of Kent* should have realized from the time of clearing the breakwater in Dover Harbour that, if they passed *Dunedin Star* at a distance of about half a mile and at nearly 20 knots, the wash might create a danger for the pilot launch if it proceeded alongside the *Dunedin Star*.[43]

As a matter of practical seamanship it is well to remember that to reduce the swell of a speeding power-driven vessel, it is necessary to slow down a considerable distance before reaching the vessel it is intended to protect. In a New York case where the passing steamer in a narrow channel did not slow sufficiently or in time, it is reported that the tow was actually broken up by the swell that piled up *ahead* before the steamer had come abeam.[44] A tanker proceeding at full speed in a narrow channel without a proper lookout violated the inland rules and her duty to use due care under the circumstances. Hence, she was liable for the resulting swell damage to a shrimp boat.[45]

Commanding officers of naval vessels who find themselves under the necessity of making high-speed trial or post-repair runs in more or less confined waters will be interested in cases where the following defenses have *not* been accepted by the courts: (1) that a vessel's waves did not render navigation more perilous than would a high wind; (2) that a vessel was navigating at a speed customary for ships of her class;[46] (3) that other vessels passed on that or other similar occasions were not injured;[47] (4) that the vessel injured did not sound a warning signal to the other vessel to slow down;[48] and (5) that the vessel injured might have saved herself by taking unusual precautions.[49]

More recently a U.S. Navy destroyer, proceeding up the Columbia River at more than 21 knots, created a 5-foot wave that was the sole cause of swell damage to a seaworthy river barge in tow of a downbound tug. The destroyer's excessive speed violated Inland Rule 6, and she

---

[43] The *Maid of Kent* [1974] 1 Lloyd's Rep. 435.
[44] The *Luke* (CCA N.Y. 1927) 19 F.2d 925.
[45] Alamia v. Chevron Transport, 1988 AMC 185.
[46] The *New York* (N.Y. 1888) 34 F.757.
[47] The *Asbury Park* (N.Y. 1905) 144 F.553; the *Hendrick Hudson* (N.Y. 1908) 159 F.581.
[48] The *Chester W. Chapin* (N.Y. 1907) 155 F.854.
[49] The *Emma Grimes* (N.Y. 1933) 2 F. Supp. 319.

failed to sustain her *Pennsylvania* Rule burden of proving that this could not have been a contributing cause to the damage.[50]

(2) *Speed excessive under particular conditions.* It has long been held by the Supreme Court that a power-driven vessel in a crowded harbor or river should not be operated at a higher speed than will keep her under perfect control. This is, of course, merely a rule of common sense.

Similarly, in numerous other decisions vessels in collision have been held liable for excessive speed where it was found that they approached other vessels in restricted waters at speeds that the results showed were imprudent. In a collision between two steamships on the Patapsco River near Baltimore on a clear day, one of them, the *Acilia*, was found solely liable for the damage for going at her ordinary cruising speed of 10 knots, the circuit court of appeals remarking that:

> Full speed in these dredged channels when about to pass other vessels is undeniably a fault which increases every risk of navigation.[51]

It is a well-known fact that vessels in shallow water have a tendency to sheer and become unmanageable, and that if they attempt to pass too closely they are likely to be brought into collision by suction. Hence, vessels colliding from either of these causes are often convicted of excessive speed. A typical case occurred at Horeshoe Bend on the Delaware River between the steamship *Saratoga*, going down light, and the steamship *Taunton* coming up from sea. It was a clear day; the vessels saw each other 2 miles apart, signaled a port-to-port meeting when a mile apart, and were about to clear each other in the usual manner, when the *Saratoga* touched a mud bank at the side of the channel, the existence of which was well known and marked, and sheered into the other vessel before she could be stopped. On a showing that the *Taunton* was properly on her own side of the channel, but that the *Saratoga*'s speed of not less than 8 knots caused her to "smell the bottom" as she rounded the buoy, the latter was found solely liable for the collision.[52]

A more recent case of excessive speed in a river was in the Schelde, Belgium, where interaction between two ships passing resulted in the overtaken ship taking the ground.

> It was not seamanlike for *Ore Chief* to overtake *Olympic Torch* . . . because the two ships were large vessels entering a narrow and shallow stretch of river after having made a turn . . . She should have reduced speed for good seamanship required that overtaking should have been postponed. . . .[53]

---

[50] Bernert Towboat v. *Chandler*, 1987 AMC 2919.

[51] The *Acilia* (CCA Md. 1903) 120 F.455.

[52] The *Saratoga* (Pa. 1910) 180 F.620; *see also* Appleby v. the *Kate Irving* (Md. 1880) 2 F.919.

[53] The *Ore Chief* [1974] 2 Lloyd's Rep. 432, 433.

The question of good seamanship is also involved when vessels make their way at too great a speed along a waterfront and fail to keep a safe distance off pierheads. The courts have again and again held vessels at fault that collided with vessels *properly* emerging from their berths. Vessels maneuvering around piers are under special circumstances, and the greatest caution must be observed when there is a possibility of encountering them. It is no defense to a collision a few feet off the piers to argue that the speed was less than the statutory limit.

> A statute imposing a penalty for running along the piers of the East River at a speed exceeding 10 knots does not necessarily render a less rate of speed prudent. The speed must be regulated by the dangers attending the navigation under the particular circumstances of the case.[54]

Equally common prudence requires a vessel entering a crowded harbor to exercise more than ordinary care.[55] Even in less restricted waters, with good weather and no laid-down speed limit, ships can be castigated for excessive speed:

> . . . it was not  . . seamanlike for her to try to work up to full speed while still in the roadstead.[56]

### Vessels Must Undock at Proper Time

Despite the cases mentioned earlier in this chapter, where vessels proceeding along rivers were faulted for unseamanlike speed after colliding with vessels *properly* leaving their berths, it does not follow that vessels undocking can blindly cast off. All ships must dock or undock at a proper time, having any regard to any ship navigating in the stream. Obviously it requires a good lookout,[57] for as has been said:

> . . . it is the duty of the vessel that is docking or undocking to give way to the vessel which is lawfully proceeding up or down river. . . . She has to carry out her operation without embarrassing passing traffic, and that involves that she must choose the proper moment for embarking on the adventure of docking or undocking.[58]

> What is wrong for the vessel entering the main channel from the side is to do so at such a time and in such a manner as to require that upcoming ship to take drastic action.[59]

Equally the vessel in the stream, as we saw before, should be handled with consideration for the difficulties of the undocking vessel. When the *Jan Laurenz,* proceeding downriver, saw the *St. William* undocking close

---

[54] Greenman v. Narragansett (N.Y. 1880) 4 F.244.
[55] D'Shaughnessy v. Besse, 1979 AMC 2479.
[56] The *Savina* [1974] 2 Lloyd's Rep. 325.
[57] The *Aracelio Iglesias* [1968] 1 Lloyd's Rep. 131.
[58] The *Hopper R.G.* [1952] 2 Lloyd's Rep. 352.
[59] The *Adellen* [1954] 1 Lloyd's Rep. 144.

ahead of her, she maintained her speed in what was described as a "race for the viaduct." However, the court also found that:

> *St. William* was to blame for leaving her berth at an improper time . . . and persisting in going down the canal and not holding back.[60]

## Good Seamanship May Require Holding Back at a Bend

It is axiomatic that a good seaman will know the state of the tide and of the current, particularly in rivers and narrow straits. If stemming the current, and the blind-bend signal is heard from another vessel coming downstream, it will often be prudent to wait until the other has passed.[61] However, unless there are local regulations, the duty to wait only applies if a current is actually running at the time.[62] Even then, the duty is not absolute, for it is applicable only when good seamanship decrees it proper to stop and wait, a question that clearly depends on the circumstances of the case.[63] Thus, in a narrow channel with a swift current in one direction, it has been held in several cases that when vessels meet, the one moving with the current is the favored vessel.[64] In a collision between a tug and tow on a long hawser coming down the Hudson River and rounding the sharp bend at West Point, where the current sweeps rapidly toward the opposite bank, and a similar tug and tow coming up the river, this rule was applied in favor of the former and against the latter.[65] It was applied when two steamships met in the Delaware River, in the narrow channel above Horseshoe Buoy, when one of them, running light and stemming the tide, tried to cross the bow of the other, deeply laden and coming with the tide. The former was held solely liable. The Supreme Court, applying it to a collision between a steamer and three barges in a tow that the steamer sank in Hell Gate with the tide running 7 knots, thus definitely stated the rule:

> Where two steamers about to meet are running one with and the other against the tide, if it be necessary that one or the other should stop in order to avoid a collision, the one proceeding against the tide should stop.[66]

Formal recognition of this doctrine exists in local rules throughout the rivers of the world. For U.S. inland waters, it is covered by Inland Rule 9(a)(ii), where downbound vessels in narrow channels or fairways of the Great Lakes, Western Rivers, and other specified waters, have right-of-

---

[60] The *Jan Laurenz* [1972] 1 Lloyd's Rep. 404.
[61] The *Talabot* (1890) 15 P.D. 194; the *Ezardian* (1911) P. 92.
[62] The *Sagaporack* & *Durham Castle* v. Hontestroom (1927) 25 Ll. L. Rep. 377.
[63] The *Backworth* (1927) 43 T.L.R. 644.
[64] The *Marshall* (N.Y. 1882) 12 F.921.
[65] The *Scots Greys* v. the *Santiago de Cuba* (CC Pa. 1883) 19 F.213.
[66] The *Galatea* (N.Y. 1876) 23 L. Ed. 727.

way over upbound vessels and the duty of proposing the manner and place of passing. Although, therefore, geographical limits have been placed on the applicability of the rule, the practice of good seamanship may extend it to other narrow channels. Neither does the requirement to hold back apply only to passing vessels. A tug was found 50 percent at fault for a collision in a narrow channel with a steamship that it attempted to overtake while the steamship was altering course around a bend.[67]

### Vessels Must Be Properly Manned and Operated

Apart from the owner's responsibility to provide properly for and staff a ship, good seamanship requires masters to organize their watchstanders properly and insist that the correct standards are maintained.

> It appeared . . . clear from . . . evidence that the state of discipline on board the ship was inclined to be lax, and that the attitude of those on the bridge to their watchkeeping duties was lacking in a proper sense of responsibility.[68]

In commenting on the general slackness in the running of the ships that were involved in a serious collision in the North Sea, the court said owners should ensure that the masters understood their duties and appreciated that they were to run an efficient ship. The court produced a long list of what factors constituted a well-run ship.[69] In U.S. waters a master's inability to understand his or her vessel's radarscope constituted negligent use of radar and was a proximate cause of collision in fog.[70] In a separate case, it was said that in certain circumstances, such as thick fog and dense traffic:

> . . . if the master . . . needed a rest from the bridge, his place should have been taken by another officer, such as the chief officer.[71]

At all times, there must be a sufficiency of trained crew on board and, when necessary, on watch. A tug was faulted because she could not sound her whistle while the mate on watch was handling the helm and there was no other person available.[72] When a small schooner, moored at New Orleans in a gale, sought to change her position in the absence of the captain, with only a man and a boy to handle her, she was held responsible for her own injuries when impaled on the bow of a steamer and sunk.[73] A fishing boat owner breached his duty to supply an adequate crew by

---

[67] Penn. Tanker v. *Exxon Mass.*, 1981 AMC 1903.
[68] The *Sea Star* [1976] 1 Lloyd's Rep. 122.
[69] "*Eleni V* and the *Roseline*," *Seaways*, August 1981.
[70] Curtis Bay v. *Md. Clipper*, 1979 AMC 2653.
[71] The *Zaglebie Dabrowskie* [1978] 1 Lloyd's Rep. 570.
[72] The *Murdoch* [1953] 1 Lloyd's Rep. 440.
[73] The *Sarah* v. *Bellais* (CCA La. 1892) 52 F.233.

delegating the hiring to the master without imposing any standards of professional competence. Knowledge of this practice precluded the owner from limiting his liability from the boat's collision and subsequent sinking while being navigated by an incompetent deckhand.[74] And similarly, when a vessel in a tow on the Saint Mary's River turned toward an approaching steamer because the helmsman made a mistake in executing the master's orders—putting the wheel hard right instead of hard left—she was found liable for the resulting damage.[75]

It is often necessary to supplement an emergency maneuver with the dropping of one or both anchors. In order to do this, someone must be standing by. As said by a district court:

> In waters well frequented by small tows, a ship must have a competent person standing by in the forecastle ready at a moment's notice to let go the anchors.[76]

However, in one unusual case in a busy river, one ship was:

> . . . not guilty of negligence in failing to let go her anchors because the orders to let them go could not be heard because of the noise of [the other ship's] anchors running out.[77]

### Vessel Should Not Sail with Defective Equipment

Vessels have been found liable for a collision where they have chosen to get under way even though there was a defective compass[78] or lights that were not operating correctly. In some cases vessels have been convicted because a failure occurred a second time, such as a steering failure, and the cause was not determined and corrected after the first failure. An unexpected failure of equipment will not be excused if the equipment has not been submitted to periodic inspection and preventive maintenance.

Every self-propelled vessel of 1,600 or more gross tons must have a marine radar system, an illuminated magnetic steering compass with an up-to-date deviation card, a gyrocompass that the helmsman can read, an illuminated rudder angle indicator in the wheelhouse, an echo-sounder, and equipment on the bridge for plotting relative motion.[79] Similar equipment requirements are laid down internationally in chapter V of the 1974 SOLAS. If during the voyage some equipment fails, the voyage may be completed subject to the nearest CG authority being informed as soon as possible. Similarly, a failure of the bridge-to-bridge radiotelephone should be "given consideration in the navigation of the

---

[74] Ocean Foods, Lim. Procs., 1989 AMC 579.
[75] The *Sitka* (N.Y. 1904) 132 F.861.
[76] River Terminals Corp. v. U.S. (DC La. 1954) 121 F. Supp. 98.
[77] The *Oldekerk* [1974] 1 Lloyd's Rep. 95.
[78] Greater New Orleans Expressway v. Tug *Claribel*, 222 F. Supp. 521 (E.D. La.) 1963.
[79] 33 CFR 164.35 (a)–(j).

vessel."[80] A stationary tug was 25 percent at fault for failing to have an operable bridge-to-bridge radio on board to warn approaching vessels of its position.[81]

### Navigators Must Know Their Vessel and the Conditions to Be Encountered

Particularly in close quarters, navigators must be familiar with the advance and transfer that are characteristic of their vessel for the speed at which they are traveling. They must also be knowledgeable of the effectiveness of a backing bell depending on the speed. Allowance must be made, in both cases, for the effect of wind and current. As expressed by the court:

> A navigator is chargeable with knowledge of the maneuvering capacity of his vessel. He is bound to know the character of his vessel and how she would turn in ordinary conditions.[82]

> The second mate's failure to familiarise himself with the *Sanko's* manoeuvring capabilities is a contributing factor. Had he familiarised himself with this information, he may have taken evasive action sooner and avoided the collision.[83]

A vessel will not be excused for a collision caused by weather conditions if those conditions could have been avoided. As stated by a district court in two different cases:

> Tug's obligation includes responsibility to utilize available weather reports so that it can operate in manner consistent with foreseeable risk and captain of tug is chargeable with knowledge of weather predictions whether he knows them or not.[84]

> Sudden violent and unpredictable winds, known in the Aleutian Islands as "williwahs," must always be taken into account by prudent navigators, and their occurrence will not exonerate the defendant.[85]

Similarly, a vessel cannot be excused for striking a navigational hazard if the cause of the navigator's ignorance is failure to carry up-to-date charts or if he or she goes against the considered advice of the pilot and harbor master.[86] The importance of keeping charts up to date was highlighted when a tanker drew up courses that did not allow for either new anchorages or a fairway, and she collided with another returning to the anchorage.[87] Equally, ignorance is no excuse for failure to comply

[80] 33 USC 1205 (Supp V 1975).
[81] G & L v. *Capt Wilfred*, 1980 AMC 566.
[82] City of New York v. Morania No. 12 Inc. (1973) 357 F. Supp. 234.
[83] Rich Ocean Car Carriers v. *Sanko Diamond*, 1989 AMC 226.
[84] M. P. Howlett Inc. v. Tug *Dalzellido* (DC N.Y. 1971) 324 F. Supp. 912.
[85] Nehus v. Alaska Marine, 1983 AMC 2681.
[86] Texada Mines v. *AFOVOS* [1974] 2 Lloyd's Rep. 175.
[87] The *Golden Mistral* [1986] 1 Lloyd's Rep. 407.

with a traffic separation scheme, even though in the past it was not binding on the particular flag-state's ships:

> Her master should have known of the scheme and obeyed it as a matter of good seamanship.[88]

IMO-adopted traffic separation schemes are now, of course, binding to all ships on the high seas. Even when some distance from them, a ship can be afffected by failure to take into account the implications to traffic flow:

> Good seamanship required *Garden City* to steer a more westerly course so as to line herself up on the entrance to the southbound traffic route and avoid unnecessary encounters with ships proceeding northwards in the other traffic route.[89]

## Leniency Toward Salvagers

Damages arising from salvage efforts are regarded leniently. In the *St. Blane* case, it was not accepted that the collision that occurred while going alongside the disabled yacht *Ariadne* was due to negligent seamanship, though the master of the *St. Blane* was guilty of negligence in failing to take all reasonable care to avoid further damage to the yacht after the crew had been taken off.

> It is well established that the Court takes a lenient view of the conduct of salvors or would be salvors, and is slow to find that those who try their best, in good faith, to save life or property in peril at sea, and make mistakes, or errors of judgement in doing so, have been guilty of negligence . . . salvors should not in general be criticized if, faced with an actual or potential conflict between saving life on the one hand, and preserving property on the other, they err on the side of the former at the expense of the latter.[90]

Thus, despite the loss of the *Ariadne* and the unseamanlike precautions to minimize damage when the two vessels were alongside each other, the *St. Blane* was not found liable.

## First Rule of Good Seamanship

In the final analysis, good seamanship becomes a factor in collision prevention insofar as the navigator exercises it, by observing the rules of the road, and by conducting his or her vessel where it is safe, when it is safe, and in the manner of a prudent seaman. Such is the test placed upon a navigator by the courts, as typically expressed by the circuit court of appeals:

> No man is infallible, and there are certain errors for which the law does not hold a navigator liable; but he is liable for an error of judgment *which a careful and prudent navigator would not have made.*[91]

---

[88] The *Genimar* [1977] 2 Lloyd's Rep. 17.
[89] The *Zaglebie Dabrowskie* [1978] 1 Lloyd's Rep. 571.
[90] The *St. Blane* [1974] 1 Lloyd's Rep. 563.
[91] The *Old Reliable* (CCA Pa. 1921) 269 F.725.

## When Departure from the Rules May Be Necessary

The second part of the Responsibility Rule allows for the lawful departure from the rules themselves when hazards and special circumstances justify a departure to avoid immediate danger. Such criteria might seem to justify a wholesale abandonment of the rules every time danger threatened. However, common sense, and not selfish interest, clearly requires that safety is attained by the uniform and exact observance of the rules, a situation that the vast majority of encounters permits. Thus, the mariner should never depart from the regulations except when absolutely necessary, even though the rules were never envisaged as a strait-jacket. The whole point of the rules is to avoid collision, indeed risk of collision, and therefore the regulations should not be so applied as to bring this about. The duty to avoid collision is higher than slavish compliance to the rules, and for that purpose, departure may be made. Neither is a ship bound to take a course of action that, if she obeyed the rules, would place her into greater danger.

> Where there was one and only one chance of escape from collision, a seaman was justified in taking the benefit of that chance, although it necessitated a departure from the regulations.[92]

Naturally, to justify a departure from the regulations there must be clear proof that adherence to them would have caused an immediate danger and that the departure was adopted to avoid such danger.

## Rule 2(b) Not Substitute at Will for Other Rules

The foregoing makes it very plain to the mariner that Rule 2(b) is far from being a mere substitute at will for the requirements of the other rules. The United States Supreme Court has explicitly limited the application of the special circumstance rule in three well-known decisions:

> It applies only where there is some special cause rendering a departure necessary to avoid immediate danger such as the nearness of shallow water, or a concealed rock, the approach of a third vessel, or something of that kind.[93]

> Nevertheless it is true that there may be extreme cases where departure from their requirements is rendered necessary to avoid impending peril, but only to the extent that such danger demands.[94]

> Exceptions to these rules, though provided for . . . should be admitted with great caution, and only when imperatively required by the special circumstances of the case.[95]

---

[92] The *Queen Mary* (1949) 82 Ll. L. Rep. 341.
[93] The *Maggie J. Smith* (1887) 123 U.S., 349, 31 L. Ed. 175.
[94] Belden v. Chase (1893) 150 U.S. 674, 37 L. Ed. 1218.
[95] The *Oregon* (1895) 158 U.S. 186, 39 L. Ed. 943.

Referring to the above opinions of the court of last resort in the *H. F. Dimock,* the circuit court of appeals remarks that, taking it altogether, these expressions go little, if any, beyond applying the rule of in extremis.[96]

## Cases Held Not Justifying Departure

It may serve to clear up in the reader's mind what the courts recognize as special circumstances if we first consider a number of situations that the courts have held are *not* special circumstances within the meaning of the rule or to a degree entitling a vessel to disregard the ordinary requirements. We have pointed out that there is no such special circumstance if an impending danger is too distant to be considered immediate. A further illustration of this point was the case in the River Plate Estuary where an outbound vessel, the *Sagittarius,* attempted to excuse her failure, in contravention of the local rules, to hold back at a bend by pleading that she would have been unable to comply with them in relation to the other ships following the first inbound vessel. The court ruled that the international regulations, which were co-applicable with the local ones:

> authorize departures from the other rules only when these are necessary in order to avoid immediate danger. The potential difficulties in relation to other ships did not . . . give rise to immediate danger within the meaning of these rules. On the contrary the immediate danger was that of passing the *Schwarzburg* at a prohibited place.[97]

A meeting place of several navigational channels is not necessarily an area where special circumstances allow departure from the rules. In the *Homer* case, it was held that the normal, in this case crossing, rules applied at the junction of the channels when two ships met with no other vessels involved.[98]

## Cases Held to Justify Departure

Turning now to the more positive aspect of this rule we shall consider a sample of decisions where special circumstances have been held to justify a departure from the ordinary rules. They may be said to fall into four groups: (1) where the situation is in extremis; (2) where other conditions make obedience to the ordinary rules impracticable; (3) when the ordinary rules must be modified because of the presence of a third or more vessels, and (4) where one of two vessels proposes a departure and the other assents.

---

[96] The *H.F. Dimock* (CCA 1896) 77 F.226.
[97] The *Schwarzburg* [1967] 1 Lloyd's Rep. 38.
[98] The *Homer* [1972] 1 Lloyd's Rep. 429.

**Situations in Extremis**

Whenever two moving vessels approach each other so closely that collision is inevitable unless action is taken by both vessels to prevent it, the situation is in extremis. Except in thick weather without radar, or in confined waters, obedience to the rules will generally prevent vessels from coming into dangerous proximity, it being the intent of the rules to prevent not only collision itself but risk of collision. Hence, it will be found almost invariably that when two vessels reach a situation where collision is imminent, one or both of them has violated the rules. This may be illustrated in the crossing situation. If the give-way vessel fails to give way and both hold on long enough, collision will inevitably occur. It has never been the intent of the rules that the stand-on vessel, which is under a specific requirement to maintain course and speed, should hold that course and speed right through the other vessel. On the contrary, as soon as the vessels reach a position where collision is so imminent that it cannot be avoided by the give-way vessel alone, it immediately becomes not only the right but the expressed duty of the stand-on vessel to take such action as will, in the judgment of her commanding officer, best aid to avert collision. Rule 17(b) is a statutory provision to that effect, applying not only in the crossing situation but in every situation where one vessel is privileged and the other is burdened. As stated by the circuit court of appeals in a collision between two tugs at Charleston, South Carolina:

> There is no right of way on which a vessel is entitled to insist when it is obvious that it will result in danger of collision.[99]

And as held by the circuit court of appeals in a collision of two ferry-boats in New York harbor, where the stand-on vessel maintained course and speed after it was manifest that departure therefrom could alone prevent collision:

> When a collision is imminent, each vessel must do all in her power to avert it, no matter what may have been the previous faults, or which may have the right of way.[100]

A similar opinion was stated by the district court in a later case in which a sailing vessel in tow of two tugs collided with an ocean steamship on Puget Sound in foggy weather:

> Even improper navigation of another vessel does not excuse adherence to a definite rule, when such adherence plainly invites collision, and stubborn adherence to rule is sometimes culpable fault.[101]

Under the current rules, both on the high seas and in inland waters, the stand-on vessel *may* "take action to avoid collision by her maneuver alone, as soon as it becomes apparent to her that the vessel required to

[99] The *Hercules* (S.C. 1892) 51 F.452.
[100] The *Mauch Chunk* (N.Y. 1907) 154 F.182.
[101] The *Kaga Maru* (Wash. 1927) 18 F.2d 295.

keep out of the way is not taking appropriate action in compliance with these rules." Thus, the stand-on vessel is no longer held to stand on into the jaws of collision if she can determine the other vessel is not giving way at an early stage. However, if this permissive action is not taken at a relatively long range, then the stand-on vessel continues to be bound to maintain course and speed until in extremis.

It is always difficult for the navigators of stand-on ships to choose the right moment for taking action in extremis. In many cases they are in a dilemma in that, if they act too early, they may frustrate the belated action by the give-way ship to keep out of the way, while if they act too late, the action taken may be ineffective. Because of these difficulties the courts are slow to criticize a navigator merely because it can be shown, after the event, that the action that he or she took was either too early or too late. Navigators are only criticized if, in taking action at the time they did, they did not exercise the ordinary skill and care that could reasonably be expected from a mariner faced with a situation of that kind.[102]

## Two Kinds of Situations in Extremis

The courts make a distinction here in favor of the vessel that is brought into a situation in extremis solely through the fault of another vessel. It is true that she cannot invoke special circumstance to excuse a violation or an improper action unless she comes into court with clean hands. Where there have been statutory violations prior to in extremis, then there is a burden on a vessel to prove that her fault could not have been a cause of collision. Should this be the case, then almost time without number the courts have agreed with an opinion expressed by the circuit court of appeals ninety years ago:

> Where the master of a vessel, who is a navigator of experience and good judgment, is confronted with a sudden peril, caused by the action of another vessel, so that he is justified in believing that collision is inevitable, and he exercises his best judgment in the emergency, his action, even though unwise, cannot be imputed to his vessel as a fault.[103]

A long line of decisions, many quoted in earlier editions of this book, have found vessels excused for action taken in haste when faced with an emergency situation caused by another vessel. As pointed out by both a district court and a circuit court of appeals in two decisions some seventy years ago:

> If one vessel places another in a position of extreme danger through wrongful navigation, the other is not to be held in fault if she is not navigated with perfect skill and presence of mind.[104]

[102] The *Martin Fierro* [1974] 2 Lloyd's Rep. 209.
[103] The *Queen Elizabeth* (CCA 1903) 122 F.406.
[104] The *Lafayette* (CCA N.Y. 1920) 269 F.917.

The master of a vessel acting *in extremis* is not held to an exercise of that cool and deliberate judgment which facts later developed show would have been a better course.[105]

It is indeed not "perfect skill and presence of mind" or "cool and deliberate judgment" that the courts are looking for, but, as said earlier, "ordinary skill and care." In a case of a ship in a channel moving suddenly across the bows of an outbound ship, it was said of the latter:

> In judging the conduct of the master of the *Troll River*, it is necessary to bear in mind that he was placed in an extremely difficult position by the negligence of the *Shavit*, and the Court should not be too astute to find faults in the action he took in good faith to try and cope with the emergency so created.[106]

Equally, where a ship, on meeting another who was on the wrong side of a channel, took action that was aimed to mitigate the seriousness of the collision, she was not criticized for:

> putting her wheel to port, or not immediately reversing her engines, when she saw what the *City of Leeds* was doing, for a serious collision by then was inevitable and different action might have made the damage resulting from it greater rather than less.[107]

Even if there should be a delay, albeit slight, in the reaction of a ship confronted with a collision situation, she will not necessarily be found negligent and may escape liability for the collision:

> . . . the master, in waiting about one minute before taking avoiding action, made what can now in retrospect be seen to have been an error of judgement, but that he was not in all the circumstances negligent . . .[108]

Moreover, even when the action was thought to be wrong, as suggested in the above quote, it is often regarded as less contributory towards collision and may significantly reduce the apportionment of blame:

> . . . this fault was therefore causative but as it was taken when the vessels were at very close quarters and perhaps too hastily it was less blameworthy than a wrong decision taken with ample time for consideration.[109]

However, it must not be considered that any action in extremis is necessarily going to be excused by the courts, particularly if it is taken far too late.

> While making all reasonable allowances for the difficulty facing the master of the *Olympian* . . . he was at fault in that he waited too long before taking starboard wheel action . . . and the effort to avoid collision did not succeed.[110]

[105] Sullivan v. Pittsburgh SS. Co. (1925) 230 Mich 414, 203 NW 126.

[106] The *Troll River* [1974] 2 Lloyd's Rep. 188.

[107] The *City of Leeds* [1978] 2 Lloyd's Rep. 356.

[108] The *Avance* [1979] 1 Lloyd's Rep. 153.

[109] The *Sanshin Victory* [1980] 2 Lloyd's Rep. 359; *see also* the *Estrella* [1977] 1 Lloyd's Rep. 526.

[110] The *Nowy Sacz* [1976] 2 Lloyd's Rep. 696; *see also* the *Auriga* [1977] 1 Lloyd's Rep. 395.

Neither, as was said earlier in Chapter 9, is precipitate action excused.

> The *Fierro* was only at fault in that, faced with a situation of danger entirely of the *Naya*'s making, she did not take the right action in time to avoid or mitigate a collision . . . for putting her wheel to hard to port in the face of an up-coming ship without sufficient evidence of her intentions, does not involve too high a standard of skill and care.[111]

To conclude this point, it may be said that special circumstances exist and vessels are in extremis regardless of the cause, whenever the situation becomes one in which, because of the proximity of the vessels, adherence to the normal rules is reasonably certain to cause collision. While the courts adopt an understanding attitude to action departing from the rules in these circumstances, they still must be convinced that such action was that of a mariner of ordinary care and was instigated to avert or minimize a collision.

### When Conditions Make Conformance to the Rules Impracticable

It is not an easy thing to claim that conditions allowed Rule 2(b) to be invoked, when application of good seamanship in Rule 2(a) could have adjusted the encounter to more favorable circumstances! In the main, the ordinary rules do allow for most physical conditions, but the concurrence of several can lead to special circumstances excusing conformance to the rules. In fog, near a notorious sand bank with strong tidal currents, a vessel in a crowded traffic route was excused for not stopping engines on hearing repeated fog signals forward of her beam, because it would have been dangerous for her to do so.[112] Similarly, although an upbound vessel violated the half-distance rule by proceeding at half-speed in heavy fog, the need to make a turn and avoid the downbound vessel was a "special circumstance" justifying the violation.[113] However, one vessel in the horns of a dilemma was blamed for not choosing the risk of going aground in preference to a risk of collision with its more serious probable consequences.[114]

### Presence of More Than Two Vessels

It frequently happens, of course, in crowded harbors, in straits, and off headlands, that more than two vessels are involved in approaching each other. Special circumstances may, but not necessarily, arise on such occasions. The test is can the normal rules be obeyed or not? If the latter is the case then special circumstances exist.

---

[111] The *Martin Fierro* [1974] 2 Lloyd's Rep. 209.
[112] The *Mount Athos* [1962] 1 Lloyd's Rep. 97.
[113] Cottesbrooke v. *Beishu Maru* 1979 AMC 1205.
[114] The *Durhambrook* [1962] 1 Lloyd's Rep. 104; *see also* the *Whitby Abbey* [1962] 1 Lloyd's Rep. 110.

A point to remember is that when special circumstances exist every vessel must, at the first evidence of confusion, be prompt to reduce her headway or to take any other steps necessary to avoid collision. It is a situation where the unpardonable sin is to maintain a dangerous rate of speed on the theory of a preconceived right-of-way that would apply were there only two vessels involved. As a precaution on the other side, the situation is not one of special circumstances if the relative distances apart and speeds are such that obedience to the ordinary rules will cause the vessels to encounter each other two at a time; in that case, these rules must be followed. Thus, where there were other vessels in the vicinity that were alleged to have hampered the movement of the stand-on vessel, but they were not close enough to prevent her compliance with the steering rules, there was not a case of special circumstances.[115]

The situation of three vessels may be further complicated if additional vessels are involved, and of course the greater the number of vessels the greater the necessity of caution by each one. In general the same principle applies: that special circumstances must be deemed to exist until the regular rules can be obeyed with safety.

### Departure from Rules by Agreement

In two of the three possible approaching situations between power-driven vessels, the manner of passing is prescribed by the rules. An overtaking vessel may choose the side on which to pass, but a meeting vessel is required to go to starboard and a crossing vessel must comply with the rules of stand-on and give-way. The dangers and the occasional advisability of being a party to a departure from the usual procedure in the crossing situation have been discussed in Chapter 7. In a crossing collision in New York harbor the stand-on vessel proposed a two-blast signal, the give-way vessel assented with two blasts, and a collision followed. In finding both vessels at fault the circuit court of appeals pointed out that:

> The situation in this circuit, after the agreement, is one of special circumstances.[116]

The disastrous 1986 collision between two Soviet ships in the Black Sea, aspects of which were discussed in chapters 8 and 9, had its origin in an agreed departure from the rules. On a clear night, the two ships agreed by radiotelephone that the normal roles in a crossing situation would be reversed: the stand-on *Petr Vasev* would give way to the passenger ship *Admiral Nakhimov* who was on the former's port bow. In the event the bulk carrier maintained course, believing from her ARPA solu-

---

[115] The *Morristown* (CCA N.Y. 1922) 278 F.714.
[116] The *Interstate* (N.Y. 1922) 280 F.446.

tion that she would pass ahead of the passenger liner who, however, not only failed to maintain her original speed (she continued to pick up speed) but made some minor alterations of course to port. This unfortunate combination of circumstances resulted in collision. Nonetheless, this did not render invalid the agreement reached by radio, for such negotiations are permissible to meet special circumstances under Rule 2. Whether special circumstances were truly present in these waters at that time is a matter of opinion, but having come to the agreement both ships failed to abide by it, and ignored the ordinary practice of good seamanship. Sufficient time and water existed for the *Petr Vasev* to take bolder avoiding action (Rule 16) and, when she did not, for the *Admiral Nakhimov* to bail out of the situation under Rules 17(a)(ii) and 17(b). While described as an ARPA-assisted collision, uncertainty was truly the dominant cause, brought about, it is suggested, by not unambiguously deciding the method of passing when the departure from the rules was first agreed.

The same arguments apply when two vessels meet head-on and one of them proposes a starboard-to-starboard passing, contrary to the statute both in inland waters and on the high seas. As a concluding statement, these arguments may be summarized as follows:

• A proposal to proceed contrary to law is not binding upon the other vessel.

• Unless and until such proposal is assented to by the other, both vessels must proceed in accordance with the rules.

• When such proposal is assented to by the other, neither vessel thereafter has the right-of-way, but both are equally bound to proceed with caution under the rule of special circumstances.

## SUMMARY

Good seamanship as defined in the rules of the road means taking every precaution that may be required by the ordinary practice of seamen. The first test of good seamanship is obedience to the rules, but it must be remembered that:

> The Collision Regulations do not contain the whole wisdom of the sea . . .[117]

Timely preparation and insistence on proper standards, allied to fore-handedness, are the mark of a good seaman and so often can avert the situation that would otherwise lead to disaster.

Under the rule of good seamanship there is always a presumption of fault against a vessel anchored improperly; against a moving vessel that collides with a vessel moored or at anchor; and sometimes against a vessel going up a swift stream that collides with a vessel going downstream.

---

[117] The *Hardwick Grange* (1940) 67 Ll. L. Rep. 359.

A vessel may be held at fault for damage done by her swell, or for maintaining such a speed that, because of the proximity of piers or of crowded traffic, collision results. Nonetheless, it is the responsibility of the vessel departing to ensure she undocks at a proper time. It is an obligation of good seamanship, indeed of seaworthiness, that a vessel be properly equipped, staffed, and operated, including to be prepared to let go the anchors at short notice under certain conditions. A vessel must not leave the dock with essential equipment that is defective, and a navigator is charged with knowledge of the maneuvering characteristics of his or her vessel, the weather, and information from up-to-date publications and charts. To repeat, good seamanship is a factor in collision prevention as it influences the mariners' observing of the rules of the road, and in conducting their vessel where it is safe, when it is safe, and in a prudent manner.

Rule 2(a) suggests that special circumstances may require action in addition to a full observance of the ordinary rules. Rule 2(b) provides for a departure from the ordinary rules when special circumstances make this necessary to avoid immediate danger.

The Supreme Court has said that the rule of special circumstances "applies only where there is some special cause rendering a departure necessary to avoid immediate danger such as the nearness of shallow water, or a concealed rock, the approach of a third vessel, or something of that kind." It is characteristic of the special circumstance rule that when it is properly invoked, *neither vessel thereafter has the right-of-way and both are required to navigate with extreme caution.*

The rule of special circumstances applies: (1) whenever an approaching situation reaches the condition in extremis; (2) when physical conditions that should be apparent to both vessels prevent compliance with the ordinary rules; (3) when an approaching situation simultaneously involves more than two vessels; and (4) when action contrary to the rules is proposed by a signal of one vessel and accepted by a signal of the other. In regard to the last, it should be remembered that such a proposal by one vessel is not binding on the other; that unless and until such proposal is assented to, both vessels are bound to proceed in accordance with the rules; and that after such assent both vessels are burdened, under the rule of special circumstances, to the extent that they must then proceed with caution.

# 11

# A Proper Lookout

**Requirement of Proper Lookout Positive**

The admonition of Rule 5, international and inland rules, to maintain a proper lookout at all times applies to every vessel. Despite this some 58 percent of the collision cases considered for this edition involved a failure, to some degree, to keep such a lookout, often in clear weather. Yet nothing could be more positive than the obligation to keep a proper lookout laid down by the rules: failure to do so is castigated by the courts. As held in a collision between two small vessels on a clear night many years ago:

> The failure to keep a lookout is a violation of the general rule to prevent collisions between vessels, and nothing can exonerate a vessel from such failure, unless it should appear that the collision would have occurred notwithstanding such failure. This rule is undoubtedly as applicable to the boats of the motor class as to ocean vessels.[1]

The obligation should be regarded as applying at all times when under way, day or night, and even, under some circumstances, when at anchor. For while the rules do not specify a watch on a vessel at anchor, it is a seamanlike action to check anchor lights, anchor bearings, the onset of restricted visibility (with its concomitant need to sound a fog signal) and to provide for a capability to warn off an approaching vessel. Though the onus was on the other vessel involved, such a warning from the anchored *Coral I,* whose circumstances will be described later in this chapter, might have avoided a collision. As ever, the time to take a seamanlike precaution, such as posting a lookout while at anchor, is before it is needed.

---

[1] The *Brindle* v. the *Eagle* (Alaska 1922) 6 Alaska 503.

## Lookout Defined

A lookout has been defined by the federal court as a person who is specially charged with the duty of observing the lights, sounds, echoes, or any obstruction to navigation with the thoroughness that the circumstances permit.[2] The words *specially charged* imply that such person shall have no other duties that detract in any way from the keeping of a proper lookout. Thus, it has been held in numerous cases that because the lookout must devote his or her attention to this duty, the officer of the deck or the helmsman cannot properly serve as lookout.[3] Clearly, then, the duties of the lookout and helmsman are separate, and the helmsman should not be considered the person on lookout while steering, other than in the smallest of vessels where an all-round view is provided at the steering position. Whoever is keeping a lookout must be able to give full attention to that task, and no duties should be assigned or undertaken that would interfere with keeping a proper lookout.

## Lookout Interpreted

*Lookout* has been interpreted to mean "an appreciation of what is taking place."[4] It is axiomatic that in order to avoid a danger, then its existence must be known. Information about dangers can be received from a wide variety of sources both in the planning and execution phases of any voyage. Failure in the planning stage—for example, in using out-of-date charts—can expose a ship to unnecessary close-quarters situations, apart from creating the wrong impression of what the situation is in the watch keeper's mind: the seeds of many a collision are sown long before ships close each other. Nonetheless, it is action on receipt of more immediate intelligence that can prevent a close-quarters situation from arising and leading to a collision. Historically, mariners have relied on their sight and hearing to provide this intelligence. Both remain most important but are supplemented these days by a variety of aids, notably radar and radio. Hence a good lookout:

> involves not only a visual lookout, and not only the use of ears but it also involves the intelligent interpretation of the data received by way of . . . various scientific instruments.[5]

No one source of data disposes of any other, though varying degrees of importance can attach to each depending on the circumstances of every case and, indeed, some may have to be augmented by provision of additional personnel or equipment. Be that as it may, the collection

---

[2] The *Tillicum* (Wash. 1914) 217 F.976.
[3] The *Kaga Maru* (Wash. 1927) 18 F.2d 295; the *Donau* (Wash. 1931) 49 F.2d 799.
[4] The *Santander* [1966] 2 Lloyd's Rep. 77.
[5] The *Homer* [1973] 1 Lloyd's Rep. 501.

and interpretation of data acquired in keeping a proper lookout are, in most instances, a team effort. The number on watch may be small, as in passage on a clear night on the open sea, or greater when in restricted visibility in confined waters, but a coordinated team it must be if it is to be effective. The failure to pass on a sighting or a radio message, as in the case of the *Speedlink Vanguard* discussed later, can lead to an incomplete picture being held by the decision maker, namely the watch keeper or master. An indispensable member of the team is the person appointed as the lookout.

**Absence of Lookout**

Absence of key personnel from the bridge will invariably lead to a charge of improper lookout. Thus, the *Statue of Liberty* was at fault for her bad lookout one night with clear visibility, when for twelve minutes before the collision, only the second officer was on her bridge.[6] And the other ship, the *Andulo*, was faulted for not taking more accurate observations of compass bearings, which constituted inadequate lookout. Similarly:

> The fault of the *Horta Barbosa* was due to a most serious defect of lookout on board her, amounting virtually to an abdication of responsibility by her second officer, who was absent from the bridge 6–7 minutes before the collision.[7]

Even when a bridge team is posted, many collisions in clear weather have been found to have an underlying theme of bad lookout that led to a poor appreciation of the situation. The *Homer* was at fault for bad aural and visual lookout, because she did not hear two separate sound signals or observe the other ship's alteration of course to starboard.[8] In another collision, at night in clear weather where both ships were again cited for bad lookout, one, the *Ziemia:*

> . . . did not appreciate what lights *Djerada* was carrying, or what course she was on, until one minute before the collision . . . that could have only been due to his extremely bad lookout.[9]

In a case mentioned in Chapter 8, the approach of the *Cinderella* to the waters in the vicinity of the Kiel Buoy was to be expected as was that of the *Achilleus* who was also approaching. A close-quarters situation was inevitable and justifiable, but that did not excuse a totally inadequate

---

[6] The *Statue of Liberty* [1971] 2 Lloyd's Rep. 277.

[7] The *Sea Star* [1976] 2 Lloyd's Rep. 478; the *Devotion II* [1979] 1 Lloyd's Rep. 513; "*Johanna O.D.18,*" *Lloyd's Maritime and Commercial Law Quarterly*, February 1980, 97.

[8] The *Homer* [1973] 1 Lloyd's Rep. 50; the *Troll River* [1974] 2 Lloyd's Rep. 181; the *Glenfalloch* [1979] 1 Lloyd's Rep. 255; the *Stella Antares* [1978] 1 Lloyd's Rep. 52; the *City of Leeds* [1978] 2 Lloyd's Rep. 356.

[9] The *Djerada* [1976] 1 Lloyd's Rep. 56; the *Sestriere* [1976] 1 Lloyd's Rep. 1; the *Auriga* [1977] 1 Lloyd's Rep. 396; the *Savina* [1975] 2 Lloyd's Rep. 141.

lookout; no one on the bridge of *Cinderella* appeared to have appreciated that *Achilleus* had headway and was going to cross ahead. While the latter bore the greater portion of the blame for this collision, *Cinderella* still took 30 percent for her poor lookout.[10]

Under present-day watch keeping standards, a lookout's brief absence from his or her post while the vessel is in open waters *may* not be contrary to sound navigational practices. However, the lookout's absence must be approved by the watch officer who must take into account prevailing circumstances before authorizing it. Also, there may be circumstances in which the officer of the watch can safely be the sole lookout in daylight. Once again, this practice should only be followed after the situation has been carefully assessed *on each occasion* and it has been established without doubt it is safe to do so. Clearly assistance must be immediately available should circumstances change.[11]

### Lookout in Confined Waters

Two ships weighed anchor in the Great Bitter Lake, one to join a north-bound and the other to join a southbound convoy through the Suez Canal. The southerly ship, the Spanish cargo vessel *Frigo Las Palmas*, turned to port and collided with the Saudi Arabian tanker *Petroship B*, which had turned to starboard. The cargo carrier concentrated her look-out to starboard and no proper lookout was maintained on the port bow, on which bow lay the tanker. The latter attracted 75 percent of the blame for putting her engines full speed ahead when the ships were at close quarters, but the *Frigo Las Palmas* bore the remaining 25 percent for her failure to maintain a proper lookout.[12]

It was the duty of a vessel having embarked on a turning maneuver to keep a good lookout for any vessel going down or coming upriver.[13] Two ships arriving at a pilot vessel were equally to blame for not seeing each other, at night in fair visibility, until 300 yards apart.[14] In an overtaking situation in the Khor Musa, the faster ship was faulted for failing to watch a slower ship very close on her port side.[15] Failure to sound a warning signal, because no proper lookout was kept, led to a stand-on ship in a crossing situation, where the give-way vessel failed to give way, taking 40 percent of the fault.[16]

[10] The *Achilleus* [1985] 2 Lloyd's Rep. 338.

[11] International Convention on Standards of Training, Certification and Watchkeeping for Seafarers.

[12] The *Petroship B* [1986] 2 Lloyd's Rep. 252.

[13] The *Francis Nullo* [1973] 1 Lloyd's Rep. 72; the *Sabine* [1974] 1 Lloyd's Rep. 465; the *Bokslaw Chrobry* [1974] 2 Lloyd's Rep. 308.

[14] The *Lucile Bloomfield* [1967] 1 Lloyd's Rep. 341.

[15] The *Iran Torch* [1988] 2 Lloyd's Rep. 38.

[16] *Stena Freighter* v. *Seirya*, 1982 AMC 913.

## All Available Means Appropriate

In addition to maintaining "a proper lookout by sight and hearing," the rules also require a proper lookout "by all available means appropriate in the prevailing circumstances and conditions so as to make a full appraisal of the situation and of the risk of collision." The expression "all available means appropriate" means that effective use must be made of suitable instruments and equipment and is not confined to the use of radar only to supplement a visual and aural watch. Binoculars should be used, not only by the lookout, but by the bridge personnel, and if necessary, used on the bridge wing or through an open window.

> It is difficult, in my view, in any event, to understand why he did not use binoculars on seeing the approaching *Gorm*. Apparently he remained behind closed windows in the wheelhouse.[17]

Clear visibility does not dispense with the need to keep a radar lookout. In the United States courts, ships have been found at fault for not using radar as a general lookout at night, after colliding with offshore oil-drilling rigs, even though the visibility was clear.

Other courts have ruled similarly:

> . . . it was clear that those on board *Kylix* had made wholly erroneous estimates of both the relative course and the distance of *Rustringen* and that those errors arose primarily from their relying solely on visual observations and estimates instead of making use of radar which was available to them. The pilot and master both said that, since it was a clear night, there was no need to use the radar. The advice . . . which I accept, is that radar should have been used.[18]

Again near the Suez Canal, this time in the Suez Bay area, an incoming vessel struck an anchored vessel on a clear, dark night. The anchored Liberian tanker *Coral I* was in lightened condition and only her forward anchor light was visible to the approaching Greek tanker *Neil Armstrong*. The latter was on a steady course at what was judged an excessive speed. For at least ten minutes the other vessel's anchor light would have been dead ahead against a solid black backgound. Nonetheless, the dark mass of *Coral I* was not seen until at a distance of about 50 meters, too late to avoid a collision. It was clear that *Neil Armstrong*'s lookout was defective, and if an efficient radar watch had been maintained, the echo of *Coral I* would have been seen dead ahead in plenty of time to avoid the collision. However, the failure of *Coral I* to exhibit proper anchor lights (she was using oil lamps, having run out of fuel for the generator) meant that the *Neil Armstrong* was able to recover 60 percent of her damages.[19]

---

[17] The *Gorm* [1961] 1 Lloyd's Rep. 196.
[18] The *Kylix* [1979] 1 Lloyd's Rep 139.
[19] The *Coral I* [1982] 1 Lloyd's Rep. 442.

In a collision off Singapore between the Indonesian tanker *Andhika Patra* and the Liberian bulk carrier *Golden Mistral* in good visibility after sunset, each vessel had ample opportunity to see the other vessel in sufficient time to take proper avoiding action (see Figure 43). Neither vessel had any excuse for not having seen the other vessel until they were less than one cable distant from each other; on both sides, that was the overriding cause of the collision. The master of *Andhika Patra* was using a chart that had not been brought up to date and did not show the nearby anchorage that was *Golden Mistral's* destination. The latter's error in putting the wheel the wrong way on sighting the tanker less than a minute before the collision was a reaction taken in haste as a result of the total failure to keep a proper lookout; if the movement of ships could not be observed, or even if it *possibly* could not be observed, by those on the bridge of the *Golden Mistral* by reason of background lights ashore, then it was the duty of the *Golden Mistral* to keep a radar watch. Both vessels were equally to blame for this collision.[20]

However, in another case, the admiralty court found that

> *Esso Chittagong* was also negligent in failing to observe the course change of *Thomaseverett* but her failure to make radar observations was not negligent in that *Thomaseverett* had been seen and visibility was good.[21]

Clearly, whether radar should be used to supplement a proper visual lookout will depend on the circumstances and the adequacy of the lookout. Sometimes, a vessel is not obliged to use radar, even in restricted visibility, if it is not working properly, though active efforts should be made to have repairs completed as soon as possible.

> There might well be times when the continued use of radar by a navigator who was uncertain of the results he was observing and unwilling to place reliance thereon might well be foolhardy and hazardous.[22]

However, Judge Medina in the U.S. Appeals Court, when reviewing this case in 1959, gave the following caution:

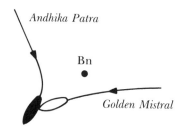

*Andhika Patra*

Bn

*Golden Mistral*

**Fig. 43.**

[20] The *Golden Mistral* [1986] 1 Lloyd's Rep. 408.
[21] The *Thomaseverett* [1981] 1 Lloyd's Rep. 1.
[22] The Pocahontas Steamship Co. v. *Esso Aruba* (1950).

This does not mean that, in the face of the fact that a properly functioning radar will give useful and necessary information, the master had a discretion to decide that it will not give such information and turn off his radar. A master has no more discretion to disrgard this aid to navigation than he has to disregard the use of charts, current tables and soundings where the circumstances require the use thereof.

The use of a radar as a general lookout does not dispense with the need to maintain a visual lookout:

> The question . . . on this occasion was: "Was it seamanlike for the *Arietta* to rely on relative motion radar observation only and to have no visual look-out?" and the answer was. "No." [23]

Where shore-based radar stations are operating, it has been held that use should be made of them:

> . . . these facilities of radar advice are made and supplied and established for the greater safety of shipping in general and for greater accuracy in navigation. . . . A vessel which deliberately disregards such an aid when available is exposing not only herself, but other shipping to undue risks, that is, risks which with seamanlike prudence could, and should, be eliminated. . . . There is a duty upon shipping to use such aids when readily available—and if they elect to disregard such aids they do so at their own risk. [24]

### VHF: An Aid to Proper Lookout

In addition to keeping a radar lookout, vessels should not neglect to listen to the radio:

> I find that the *Antonio Carlos* was at fault for bad look-out in the broadest sense; namely, faulty appreciation of VHF information and total absence of radar look-out. [25]

Confusion on the bridge of the U.S. Coast Guard training ship *Cuyahoga,* conducting officer-candidate training, led to a collision with the Argentinian dry bulk carrier *Santa Cruz II* in which eleven lives were lost. There was an inexperienced complement of personnel on board, inadequate to perform the duties of the vessel, and the commanding officer was suffering from a lack of sleep. He formed the misperception he was traveling in the same direction as the Argentinian and turned left across the other vessel's bow when they were only a mile apart. The cargo vessel was found not to be in breach of a statutory duty under the Bridge-to-Bridge Radiotelephone Act to maintain a listening watch and if necessary transmit navigational information on VHF. Her pilot had no duty to radio a warning to the approaching Coast Guard vessel, which

---

[23] The *Arietta* [1970] 1 Lloyd's Rep. 70; *see also* the *Annaliese* [1970] 1 Lloyd's Rep 36; the *Miguel de Larringa* [1956] 2 Lloyd's Rep. 538.

[24] The *Vechtstroom* [1964] 1 Lloyd's Rep. 118.

[25] The *Bovenkerk* [1973] 1 Lloyd's Rep. 70; the *Anco Princess* [1978] 1 Lloyd's Rep. 296.

was so small that she was not required to have a radiotelephone under the Act.[26]

An overtaking Mexican tanker *Jose Colomo* did not embarrass the navigation of the Israeli bulk carrier *En Gedi* in international waters of the Gulf of Mexico or contribute to the latter being rammed by the crossing Liberian *Acadia Forest*. Visual contact on a clear night was a more than adequate form of communication, and the Israeli did not violate the Bridge-to-Bridge Radiotelephone Act by failing to use her radio to alert the oncoming ship, a burdened vessel in a crossing situation.[27]

However, failure of her personnel to maintain a radio listening watch as required by the Act, plus not having on board the current Notice to Mariners for the area, resulted in a tug being found 75 percent at fault for bringing towed barges into collision with a dredger's unmarked discharge line in the navigable area of the ship channel.[28] In August 1989, another dredger, the *Bowbelle*, ran down at night a pleasure steamer, the *Marchioness*, as they proceeded under the arch of a bridge in the River Thames. The subsequent inquiry found inter alia that the ability to maintain a proper lookout by ear and eye in both ships was severely impaired by design and operating faults: the dredger's bows blocked vision ahead and the pleasure steamer disco-dance floor's lights and music obscured vision aft and raised noise levels.[29]

Failure to absorb the information available from VHF was a factor in the collision between two ferries off Harwich. To recount, the *European Gateway* was shaping to cross the dredged channel ahead of inbound *Speedlink Vanguard*, while the latter thought she would round to starboard into the dredged channel for a routine port-to-port passing. The *European Gateway* had declared her intention on VHF to the harbor authorities by stating, "Cork Spit outward will be keeping north of the channel." This was heard on *Speedlink Vanguard*'s bridge by the combined helmsman/lookout but not relayed to the master.[30] Thus was set the scene for a tragic misunderstanding.

### Standard Marine Vocabulary

The growing importance of radio communications in many aspects of maritime endeavor has promoted the use of a common language. IMO's

---

[26] Makin v. Empress Lineas, 1987 AMC 1017.

[27] Zim Israel v. Special Carriers, 1986 AMC 2016.

[28] Higman Towing v. Tom James, 1987 AMC 909.

[29] The Report of the Chief Inspector of Marine Accidents regarding the collision between the passenger launch *Marchioness* and the motor vessel *Bowbelle*, Department of Transport, London, 1991.

[30] "*European Gateway/Speedlink Vanguard* Collision: Results of the Formal Investigation," *Seaways*, October 1984.

Standards of Training, Certification and Watchkeeping (STCW) lays down that an officer in charge of a navigational watch on ships of 200 gross registered tons or more shall have an adequate knowledge of the English language and the ability to express him- or herself clearly in his communications with other ships or coast stations; even, or perhaps especially, with English, some words can have a different meaning to different listeners. Add to this the complication of different accents or dialects and there is ample room for confusion. Consequently, IMO has drawn up a Standard Marine Navigational Vocabulary,[31] the aim of which is to standardize the language used in communications across the whole spectrum of navigation at sea. It is hoped that use of the vocabulary will become second nature to those using it, so that the terms and procedures will come without effort and mean the same thing to the listener and the speaker. Under STCW the ability to understand and use the vocabulary is required for the certification of officers in charge of a navigational watch of ships covered by that convention. *Sea Speak* is a teaching and training manual based on that vocabulary.

## Lookout Is All-Encompassing

The term *lookout* comprises not only the proper use of sight and hearing, augmented by equipment such as radar, but also a proper appreciation of a situation by the person in charge of the watch. The officer of the deck must be alert to what is happening in his or her own vessel, checking the steering, the correct functioning of equipment, and, not least, seeing that the correct lights continue to be shown at night. Several collisions in recent years have occurred due to dilatory discovery of equipment defects.

> Where, in my judgement, she was at fault, was in having a very bad look-out, and a bad look-out in every possible sense of the term. It seems to me that it comes within the term "bad look-out" when I say that she was at fault for failing to take proper precautions to meet the situation in the event of the compass breaking down again, as it in fact did. It was, in my judgement, bad look-out on the part of this young third officer in failing to appreciate, long before he did appreciate it, what was happening, namely that his vessel was falling off to starboard, and in failing to appreciate what the probable cause of the falling off was. It was bad look-out on the part of the quartermaster, when he knew perfectly well that the compass had stuck again, not to report the matter at once to the officer in charge. It was bad look-out on the part of the officer to take no steps himself, whether by going to the standard compass or otherwise, to check up on what was happening and what was the course of his vessel.[32]

[31] IMO Resolution A 380(X) 14 November 1977.

[32] The *Staffordshire* (1948) 81 Ll. L. Rep. 141; *also* the *Anna Salem* [1954] 1 Lloyd's Rep. 488.

Many similar judgments have followed in subsequent cases.[33] The advent of modern aids in ships seems sometimes to lead to an unfounded belief in their reliability and a too-casual attitude toward keeping a proper lookout. In the Mediterranean, in 1964, the cargo ship *Trentbank* suffered a failure of her automatic steering as she was overtaking the tanker *Fogo* and swung across the bow of the latter.

> I ought not to leave this part of the case without observing how lamentable was the attitude of the master of the *Trentback* and her chief officer towards the system of automatic steering. The master had given no orders to ensure that somebody was on the look-out all the time. The chief officer, according to his own story, saw nothing wrong in undertaking a clerical task and giving only an occasional glance forward when he knew that there was other shipping about and that he was the only man on board his ship who was keeping any semblance of a look-out at all. Automatic steering is a most valuable invention if properly used. It can lead to disaster when it is left to look after itself while vigilance is relaxed. It is on men that safety at sea depends and they cannot make a greater mistake than to suppose that machines can do all their work for them.[34]

The previously mentioned International Convention on Standards of Training, Certification and Watchkeeping (STCW) adopted by IMO in 1978 contains inter alia basic principles to be observed in keeping a navigational watch. This convention came into force on 28 April 1984 but has yet to be ratified by the United States, though the *Exxon Valdez* oil spill may have added impetus to such a move.[35] Nonetheless, the provisions of STCW played a de facto role in the recently completed USCG project to overhaul certification for merchant mariners, as well as Public Law 98–89 which modified some of the navigation laws relating to seamen and vessels.[36] All told, the principles enunciated in the convention and the law distill much of the wisdom the courts have pronounced over the years on keeping a safe watch and a proper lookout.

It was a violation of a basic principle to make sure that the direction of an intended alteration of course was clear of other shipping that was the underlying cause for a collision at night between a tanker and a motor vessel off Bombay (see Figure 44). The inbound *Capulonix*, carrying 48,000 tons of Iranian crude, was on the starboard bow of the outbound *State of Himachal Pradesh*. The latter was on the port side of the exit channel to drop her pilot, with her speed down to about 2 knots. Neither ship need have been troubled by the presence of the other. *Capulonix*, inward bound, was gradually altering her course to port in order to keep

---

[33] The *Chusan* [1955] 2 Lloyd's Rep. 685; the *Esso Plymouth* [1955] 1 Lloyd's Rep. 429; the *Indus* [1957] 1 Lloyd's Rep. 335; the *Greathope* [1957] 2 Lloyd's Rep. 197; the *British Tenacity* [1963] 2 Lloyd's Rep. 1; the *Salaverry* [1968] 1 Lloyd's Rep. 53.

[34] The *Trentback* [1967] 2 Lloyd's Rep. 208.

[35] *Lloyd's List*, 5 April 1989.

[36] J. Drahos, "U.S. and Them," *Seaways*, August 1989.

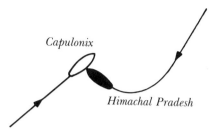

**Fig. 44.**

in the deepest water. *Pradesh* was about ahead of her showing a green light well open, with plenty of water in which to maneuver. As *Pradesh* was bound for Cochin she could, after disembarking the pilot, have shaped a safe course to have allowed the ships to pass safely starboard to starboard while both ships were outside the narrow channel. Nonetheless, she altered course to starboard some 90 degrees, a deliberate maneuver that was, without any doubt, the predominant cause of the collision. No explanation was given for this unseamanlike maneuver, but the judge concluded:

> I can only think that this manoeuvre was carried out because of an extremely bad lookout aboard *Pradesh*. After Pilot . . . had disembarked from *Pradesh,* her master ought personally to have taken a careful look all round the horizon before increasing speed and altering course. If he had taken that simple precaution I feel sure that he would not have given the orders which he gave. It is apparent from his evidence that after the pilot has disembarked Captain . . . was more concerned with saluting the pilot vessel which was on his port side than observing the tanker approaching on his starboard bow.[37]

Thus, the situation of complete safety that prevailed when the pilot of *Pradesh* was disembarked was changed into one of danger by the action of *Pradesh* in increasing her speed and turning to starboard with the intention of crossing ahead of *Capulonix;* that action was inexcusable and blameworthy to a high degree. Further, *Pradesh* could have steadied or come back to port at any time until two minutes before the collision and thus have avoided it. The blameworthiness of the master of *Capulonix* in failing to react correctly to the emergency thrust upon her was of a lower order: *Pradesh* bore 85 percent of the blame.

### Immaterial Absence of Proper Lookout Not a Fault

It is not meant to imply that whenever two vessels collide, the mere proof of improper lookout on either vessel, in the technical sense, will ipso facto condemn that vessel for the collision. On the contrary, it has been

---

[37] The *State of Himachal Pradesh* [1985] 2 Lloyd's Ship Rep. 577.

held by the Supreme Court that the absence of a lookout is unimportant when the approaching vessel was seen long before the collision occurred;[38] that it is immaterial when it does not appear that the collision could in any way be attributed to a lookout's absence;[39] and that the absence of a lookout stationed where he or she should be will not render a vessel in fault for a collision when she was navigated exactly as she should have been had there been a lookout reporting the situation.[40] As said by the circuit court of appeals in a later case, where an overtaking vessel rammed the vessel ahead:

> Absence of a lookout is not entitled to weight in cases where the proof is satisfactory that the vessel in fault saw the other in time to have taken every precaution it was its duty to take, and which, if taken, would have avoided the collision.[41]

But the difficulty in practice is, of course, to overcome the presumption of fault that the absence of a proper lookout entails and to furnish such satisfactory proof. It is only when it can be made clear that the lack of a lookout could not have contributed to the collision that it will be excused.[42]

Notwithstanding such occasional exceptions, the navigator should always adhere to the general admiralty rule that:

> The strict performance of a vessel's duty to maintain proper lookout is required and failure to do so, especially when other craft are known to be in the vicinity, is culpable negligence.[43]

Many court decisions on the subject indicate that the strict performance referred to means, at least in most circumstances, not only that lookouts shall be free from other duties but that they shall be (1) qualified by a certain amount of experience as seamen, (2) vigilant and alert, (3) properly stationed, and (4) in such numbers as circumstances require in order that the vessel may avoid risk of collision.

### Lookout Should Be Experienced Seaman

No definite minimum experience requirement has been laid down by the courts as qualifying someone for duty as lookout, but several decisions have shown the necessity of some attention to this point. The general theme of these findings is that lookouts must have some knowledge of their responsibilities that comes with experience:

[38] The *Dexter* (Md. 1875) 23 L. Ed. 84: the *George W. Elder* (CCA 1918) 249 F.9656.
[39] The *Tacoma* (Wash. 1888) 36 L. Ed. 469.
[40] Elcoate v. the *Plymothian* (Va. 1897) 42 L. Ed. 519.
[41] The *M. J. Rudolph* (N.Y. 1923) 292 F.740; the *Lehigh* (N.Y. 1935) 12 F. Supp. 75.
[42] The *Titan* (CC 1885) 23 F.413; *see also* Dion v. United States (D. Me. 1961) 199 F. Supp. 707.
[43] The *Kaga Maru* (Wash. 1927) 18 F.2d 295.

The failure of the lookout of a steamer to report a vessel when discovered is negligence, though the master and pilot were on the bridge.[44]

A lookout's duty is to report as soon as he sees any vessel with which there is danger of collision or which in any way may affect the navigation of his own; and he cannot speculate on the probabilities of collision, such responsibility being for the master.[45]

This does not suggest that lookouts should report everything they see; in crowded waters they could not be expected to cope. In such a case consideration should be given to placing additional lookouts. Certainly the courts will take into account the number of seamen available on board when considering whether a proper lookout was maintained.[46] Even if this is done, the lookouts must use their discretion to some extent in reporting what they see. As was said in one case:

You cannot report every light you see in the River Thames. You have to watch until you see a light, which perhaps, you have seen before, becoming material, because if you are going to report every light in Gravesend Reach when coming up the Thames the confusion would be something appalling to those in charge of the navigation; but you have to have a look-out to report every material light as soon as it becomes material.[47]

This heightens the need for lookouts to be experienced, well trained, and thoroughly briefed on every occasion before taking up their duty.

It should go without saying that the choice of a competent lookout is only half the requirement, the other half being an insistence by the officer of the deck that reports be made to him or her promptly and correctly, at times of good visibility as well as bad, so that in darkness or in thick weather they will be rendered as a matter of habit.

IMO has laid down mandatory minimum requirements for personnel forming as part of a navigational watch. While not those for the certification of able seaman, the requirements specify minimum age, sea experience, and training, and include the

ability to keep a proper look-out by sight and hearing and report the approximate bearing of a sound signal, light or other object in degrees or points.[48]

The experience, service, or training must be carried out under the direct supervision of the master, the officer in charge of the navigational watch, or a qualified rating.

---

[44] The *Hansa* (CCA N.Y. 1870) Fed. Case No. 6,036.

[45] The *Madison* (CCA N.Y. 1918) 250 F.850.

[46] The *Spirality* [1954] 2 Lloyd's Rep. 59; also the *Saxon Queen* [1954] 2 Lloyd's Rep. 286, the *Mode* [1954] 2 Lloyd's Rep. 26.

[47] The *Shakkeborg* (1911) Sh. Gaz. Apr. 11.

[48] Standards of Training, Certification and Watchkeeping for Seafarers.

**Lookout Should Be Vigilant**

That a high degree of vigilance is constantly required of the lookout is evident from the findings in numerous past cases, but not an unreasonable degree exceeding that of the ordinary practice of seamen. In earlier days the need for alertness and vigilance was self-evident to even the most junior seaman in an era when eyes and ears were the only means of detecting another ship: the lookout knew that much depended on him. Today, except in hostilities, the human lookout is often perceived as playing second fiddle to the electronic lookout, radar. Too often vigilance in the human lookout is allowed to atrophy. It has in some ships come to be regarded as an unpleasant and boring chore. Not surprisingly, performance of lookouts in such ships has declined. Worse still, the posting of lookouts, to judge from some of the cases in this book, is not necessarily any longer the ordinary practice of some seamen.

Yet no other duty takes precedence over this simple requirement to keep watch while on watch. To overcome this perceived devaluation of the lookout's role brought about by radar, it is necessary for watch officers to motivate their lookouts. A sense of participation, the feeling of being a member of a team, the regular interchange of information, thoughtful briefings, alternating with the helmsman, and regular training, illustrated with examples of failures of lookout, will all help maintain interest and vigilance.

This vigilance is needed today as much as it ever was. Radar may give the early warning of approaching vessels, but it is the alert lookout who gives that warning when a yacht, small craft, or debris is sighted at short range, particularly in rough weather. Equally, it is the well-briefed vigilant lookout who first sees signs of another ship altering course, perhaps while the watch officer is momentarily distracted on his or her many other duties. In every ship there must always be at least one pair of eyes actively searching outwards for danger at *all* times.

The advent of the world's first ship with a bridge designed specifically for one-person operation[49] raises concerns about the vigilance of her lookout, particularly if operations are ever permitted at night. Nonetheless, the desire for one-person-operated ships should do much to further the case for bridge ergonomics: increased efficiency here might permit more time for lookout.

**Lookout Specially Necessary in Fog**

The degree of vigilance required is, of course, greatly increased under way in foggy weather, and absence or insufficiency of a lookout under

---

[49] 84,000 tdw products carrier *Petrobulk Mars*, first of a class of five, Lloyd's List 2 December 1988.

such conditions under way can never be justified by the plea that visibility was so low as to render a lookout useless. If lookouts cannot see, at least they can hear. Under the general admiralty rules it is the duty of every vessel, when navigating in a fog, to maintain a lookout in a proper position, who shall be charged with no other duty.[50] A local custom cannot excuse a vessel from observing this rule.[51] As said by the circuit court of appeals:

> The denser the fog and the worse the weather are greater cause for vigilance, and a vessel cannot excuse failure to maintain lookout on the ground that the weather was so thick that another vessel could not be seen until actually in collision.[52]

A lookout should have been posted, in addition to the officer of the watch and the helmsman, when a ship encountered heavy rain in the South China Sea.[53] Similarly, a tug that violated Inland Rules 5 and 7 by failing to post a lookout during conditions of restricted visibility was solely at fault for a collision with a moored vessel that was not obstructing the channel of the Gulf Intracoastal Waterway.[54]

However, as brought out by the circuit court in the collision of the *Bailey Gatzert* with a Columbia River dredge, this injunction apparently does not apply with the same force to a vessel at anchor in fog, provided she is making proper fog signals.[55] However, a vessel at anchor in fog would be advised to keep a lookout on radar if so fitted. The *Kwai*, a Hong Kong naptha gas carrier, came to anchor in the Bay of Algeciras in visibility of between two and three cables. She was struck by the American container ship *St Louis*, who attempted to claim that collision could have been avoided if the *Kwai*, who had been keeping watch on radar, had sounded three blasts earlier. The *St Louis* was outbound from Algeciras harbor, and her master had a firm conviction that there was no ship ahead, so much so that he ignored the information available on his radar sets. In fact, for about seven minutes, the *Kwai* had been lying in the water dead ahead of the *St Louis*, clearly detectable by radar. Not until the three blasts were heard did realization dawn, but too late to avoid collision. The *St Louis* was found solely at fault.[56]

For ships under way, not only must visual and aural lookouts be posted in restricted visibility, but so must a proper radar lookout be maintained:

> *John C. Pappas* was at fault because she took no special precaution by way of extra look-outs on encountering fog, while the *Almizar* was guilty of poor

[50] The *Wilbert L. Smith* (Wash. 1914) 217 F.981.
[51] The *Tillicum* (Wash. 1914) 217 F.976.
[52] The *Sagamore* (Mass. 1917) 247 F.743.
[53] The *E. R. Wallonia* [1987] 2 Lloyd's Rep. 485.
[54] Self-Towing v. Brown Marina, 1987 AMC 1968.
[55] The *Bailey Gatzert* (CCA Ore. 1910) 179 F.44.
[56] The *Kwai* [1986] 2 Lloyd's Rep. 126.

radar look-out and should have realized that radar echo was of a large vessel on a steady bearing. *John C. Pappas* was also at fault for not hearing fog signals forward of her beam.[57]

Time and time again, ships have been faulted for a bad radar lookout and faulty appreciation of the information available.

> . . . if a proper radar lookout had been kept during the approach period, it should have been appreciated that a close-quarters situation with risk of collision was developing. Both ships were guilty of defective appreciation of radar.[58]

Following a U.S. Coast Guard investigation, a mariner's license was suspended after a Liberian bulk carrier collided at full speed with an offshore production platform in international waters off Louisiana. The causes of the casualty were the failures to adequately assess the position of the ship and to post a proper lookout: only the chief mate and the bosun (on the helm) were on the bridge in hurricane winds with near-zero visibility.[59] In an unusual reversal of roles, the suggestion that a Dutch general cargo vessel was to blame for a collision with a racing yacht in dense fog in the English Channel was rejected when it was shown that a proper watch had been kept: the yacht was solely to blame for seriously negligent navigation, not the least of which was the replacing of the prescribed masthead radar reflector with a stocking filled with crumpled aluminum foil.[60]

### Lookout Should Be Properly Stationed

The rules are silent as to the specific location of the lookout. The options available are usually in the bows, on the bridge, and, in a very few specialized ships these days, in the crow's nest. The choice, to be consciously made by the mariner, must depend on the characteristics of the ship and the circumstances she finds herself in. As said by the circuit court of appeals:

> He is required by good navigation to be placed at the point best suited for the purpose alike of hearing and observing the approach of objects likely to be brought into collision with the vessel, having regard to the circumstances of the case and the conditions of the weather.[61]

A long line of court decisions has well established that the lookout's normal position should be as low down and as far forward in the ship

---

[57] The *Almizar* [1971] 2 Lloyd's Rep. 290.

[58] The *Ercole* [1979] 1 Lloyd's Rep. 539; also the *Hagen* [1973] 1 Lloyd's Rep. 257; the *Elazig* [1972] 1 Lloyd's Rep. 355; the *Bovenkerk* [1973] 1 Lloyd's Rep. 62; the *Zaglebie Dabrowskie* [1978] 1 Lloyd's Rep. 571.

[59] The *Vomar*, Lloyd's List, 12 September 1988.

[60] The *St. Michael*, Lloyd's List, 20 July 1988.

[61] The *Vedamore* (1905) 137 F.844.

as conditions allow. Clearly in preradar days this put lookouts in the place where they would most likely be the first to hear and see another vessel, particularly in fog. This judicial attitude was once summarized:

> The courts have been rigid in holding vessels to maintaining lookout as far forward and as near the water as possible. Especially where the water is dark, with otherwise a fairly clear night, it is important that the lookout should be as near it as possible, in order that his eye may follow the surface, and thus be in position to detect anything low down which may be approaching.[62]

And rigidly upheld it was. For example, a United States submarine was held solely at fault for sinking a small schooner near the western end of the Cape Cod Canal shortly after World War I, on a clear night with a smooth sea and all lights burning brightly, a charge of improper lookout being sustained. In its decision, the court recognized the extremely limited space available for a lookout on the bow of an R-boat, but declared that every moving vessel must maintain a competent, careful, and efficient lookout stationed on the forward part of the vessel, and that the rule applied with equal force to submarines or other vessels of special construction in the absence of statutory exception.[63] Of course, when sea conditions were unsuitable, a lookout was not expected forward of the bridge. An ocean tug whose lookout was in the pilothouse because green seas were sweeping over the bow, and a steamship navigating the Atlantic on a clear night with her lookout on the bridge because of the coldness of the weather and the freezing spray forward were both absolved from blame.[64]

If the weather is clear and the lookouts sufficiently vigilant, it really matters little where they are stationed provided they have unobstructed visibility ahead and on both bows. If the weather is not clear, they should be in a place where their hearing is unimpaired as much as possible by noise from the engines, exhausts, and fog signals of their own ship.[65] In either case lookouts should not be subjected to distractions, such as conversation on the bridge,[66] and should be as well protected from the weather as their duties permit.

The tendency in these days of radar is routinely to station the lookout on the bridge—not inside, but on the wings. Provided the view is unobstructed, this can often be a place where the lookout can best aid the watch officer and be integrated into the watch team. But when conditions

---

[62] Eastern Dredging Co. v. *Winnisimmet* (1908) 162 F.860.
[63] U.S. v. Black (CCA 1936) 82 F.2d 394.
[64] The *Caro* (N.Y. 1884) 23 F.734; the *Kaiserin Marie Theresa* (CCA N.Y. 1906) 147 F.97.
[65] The *Cabo Santo Tome* (1933) 46 Ll. L. Rep. 165.
[66] The *British Confidence* (1951) 2 Lloyd's Rep. 621.

are not routine, such as in fog or in congested waters, then the situation should be reviewed, the lookout repositioned as necessary, and the watch team augmented. Despite today's reduced manning standards, the modern equivalent of calling the watch below should always be considered when an enhanced lookout is prudent. Most recent court findings comment on the adequacy of a ship's overall lookout rather than the technical position of a single lookout. The number of people in a crew, whether on watch or not, could be a factor in determining whether a proper lookout was kept or not.

While the normal duty of a lookout is to keep watch in the ahead sector, there are circumstances that require a lookout also at the stern. Clearly, when making a sternboard is an obvious case. Less clear, perhaps, is when there is a possibility of being overtaken, notably in confined waters or in traffic separation schemes. While the overtaking ship is always required to keep clear, it does seem prudent of any vessel liable to be overtaken to cast a look aft before altering course or speed.

> While a man stationed at the stern as a lookout is not at all times necessary, no vessel should change her course materially without having first made such an observation in all directions as will enable her to know how what she is about to do will affect others in her immediate vicinity.[67]

Although this is an old case, there continues to be a number of similar incidents where ships liable to be overtaken are all too often unaware of what is coming up from astern.

## Lookouts Must Be Adequate for Circumstances

Providing he or she is experienced, vigilant, and properly stationed, a single lookout with that exclusive duty will ordinarily be sufficient. Under some circumstances, however, more than one lookout is required. As alluded to above, when conditions are unusual, then the watch team should be augmented, including the positioning of additional lookouts, possibly in the bows and the stern. So too must the overall lookout be enhanced, particularly on the bridge where additional qualified personnel should close up on the radar and, where appropriate, the radio. To invite the watch officer to undertake all these tasks, in addition to controlling the lookouts and attending to the safe navigation of the ship, is to ask too much of one person. At stake is the safety of the ship and all on board for which the loss of rest in calling off-watch personnel is a small price to pay. The law contemplates that every vessel under way shall exercise vigilance that is continuous and unbroken. Nothing less will do.

---

[67] The *Illinois* (1881) 26 L. Ed. 563; *see also* the *Iran Torch* [1988] 2 Lloyd's Rep. 38.

## Importance of Lookouts

From the standpoint of the navigator who is interested in avoiding liability for collision, which usually means avoiding the collision itself, perhaps there could be no more appropriate conclusion to these remarks on a proper lookout than the words of the United States Supreme Court, delivered in a case that arose out of a collision between a steamship and a brig outside New York harbor on a foggy night in 1865. Although it may be said that the requirement for strict adherence to the unequivocal language of this decision has been somewhat mitigated by the advances of radar, there can be no mistaking the good advice inherent in the intent of the following words:

> The duty of the lookout is of the highest importance. Upon nothing else does the safety of those concerned so much depend. A moment's negligence on his part may involve the loss of his vessel with all the property and the lives of all on board. The same consequence may ensue to the vessel with which his shall collide. In the performance of this duty the law requires indefatigable care and sleepless vigilance. . . . It is the duty of all courts charged with the administration of this branch of our jurisprudence to give it the fullest effect whenever the circumstances are such as to call for its application. Every doubt as to the performance of the duty and the effect of nonperformance, should be resolved against the vessel sought to be inculpated until she vindicates herself by testimony to the contrary.[68]

## SUMMARY

A lookout has been defined by the federal court as a person who is specially charged with the duty of observing the lights, sounds, echoes, or any obstruction to navigation with that thoroughness that the circumstances permit. Any neglect to keep a proper lookout has caused the courts to hold a vessel in collision without a proper lookout at fault unless it can be proved that the other vessel was discovered as soon as a proper lookout would have discovered her. As technology progressed, the concept of lookout expanded to include not only the person keeping a visual and aural lookout, but the entire bridge team and particularly that competent person who maintained a continuous surveillance with radar as well as monitoring VHF radio. All the data received from various instruments must be intelligently interpreted, and this interpretation constitutes part of keeping a good lookout.

Numerous court decisions have built up a considerable doctrine with reference to what constitutes a proper lookout. Such a lookout must have no other duties, such as conning or steering the vessel; he or she must be constantly alert and vigilant, must have had a reasonable amount of

---

[68] The *Ariadne* (13 Wall) 475 (1872).

experience as a seaman; must report what he or she sees or hears to the officer of the watch; and must ordinarily be stationed as low down and as far forward on the vessel as circumstances permit. In conditions of crowded traffic and in thick weather, enough lookouts must be posted to detect the approach of another vessel from any direction. What is required is the maintenance of sufficient lookout—visually, aurally, and by radar—when circumstances warrant.

# APPENDIX

# Navigation Rules

*International—Inland*

---

*International*

*Inland*

## PART A—GENERAL

*RULE 1*

*Application*

(a) These Rules shall apply to all vessels upon the high seas and in all waters connected therewith navigable by seagoing vessels.

(b) Nothing in these Rules shall interfere with the operation of special rules made by an appropriate authority for roadsteads, harbors, rivers, lakes or inland waterways connected with the high seas and navigable by seagoing vessels. Such special rules shall conform as closely as possible to these Rules.

(c) Nothing in these Rules shall interfere with the operation of any special rules made by the Government of any State with respect to additional station of signal lights, shapes or whistle

## PART A—GENERAL

*RULE 1*

*Application*

(a) These Rules apply to all vessels upon the inland waters of the United States, and to vessels of the United States on the Canadian waters of the Great Lakes to the extent that there is no conflict with Canadian law.

(b)(i) These Rules constitute special rules made by an appropriate authority within the meaning of Rule 1(b) of the International Regulations

(ii) All vessels complying with the construction and equipment requirements of the International Regulations are considered to be in compliance with these Rules.

(c) Nothing in these Rules shall interfere with the operation of any special rules made by the Secretary of the Navy with respect to additional station or signal lights and shapes or whistle

*International*

signals for ships of war and vessels proceeding under convoy, or with respect to additional station or signal lights or shapes for fishing vessels engaged in fishing as a fleet. These additional station or signal lights, shapes or whistle signals shall, so far as possible, be such that they cannot be mistaken for any light, shape or signal authorized elsewhere under these Rules.[1]

(d) Traffic separation schemes may be adopted by the Organization for the purpose of these Rules.

(e) Whenever the Government concerned shall have determined that a vessel of special construction or purpose cannot comply fully with the provisions of any of these Rules with respect to the number, position, range or arc of visibility of lights or shapes, as well as to the disposition and characteristics of sound-signalling appliances, such vessel shall comply with such other provisions in regard to the number, position, range or arc of visibility of lights or shapes, as well as to the disposition and characteristics of sound-signalling appliances, as her Government shall have determined to be the closest possible compliance with these Rules in respect to that vessel.

*Inland*

signals for ships of war and vessels proceeding under convoy, or by the Secretary with respect to additional station or signal lights and shapes for fishing vessels engaged in fishing as a fleet. These additional station or signal lights and shapes or whistle signals shall, so far as possible, be such that they cannot be mistaken for any light, shape, or signal authorized elsewhere under these Rules. Notice of such special rules shall be published in the Federal Register and, after the effective date specified in such notice they shall have effect as if they were a part of these Rules.[1]

(d) Vessel traffic service regulations may be in effect in certain areas.

(e) Whenever the Secretary determines that a vessel or class of vessels of special construction or purpose cannot comply fully with the provisions of any of these Rules with respect to the number, position, range, or arc of visibility of lights or shapes, as well as to the disposition and characteristics of sound-signalling appliances, without interfering with the special function of the vessel, the vessel shall comply with such other provisions in regard to the number, position, range, or arc of visibility of lights or shapes, as well as to the disposition and characteristics of sound-signalling appliances, as the Secretary shall have determined to be the closest possible compliance with these Rules. The Secretary may issue a certificate of alternative compliance for a

---

[1] Submarines may display, as a distinctive means of identification, an intermittent flashing amber (yellow) beacon with a sequence of operation of one flash per second for three (3) seconds followed by a three (3) second off-period. Other special rules made by the Secretary of the Navy with respect to additional station and signal lights are found in Part 707 of Title 32, Code of Federal Regulations (32 CFR 707).

*International*

*Inland*

vessel or class of vessels specifying the closest possible compliance with these Rules. The Secretary of the Navy shall make these determinations and issue certificates of alternative compliance for vessels of the Navy.

(f) The Secretary may accept a certificate of alternative compliance issued by a contracting party to the International Regulations if he determines that the alternative compliance standards of the contracting party are substantially the same as those of the United States.

*RULE 2*
*Responsibility*

(a) Nothing in these Rules shall exonerate any vessel, or the owner, master or crew thereof, from the consequences of any neglect to comply with these Rules or of the neglect of any precaution which may be required by the ordinary practice of seamen, or by the special circumstances of the case.

(b) In construing and complying with these Rules due regard shall be had to all dangers of navigation and collision and to any special circumstances, including the limitations of the vessels involved, which may make a departure from these Rules necessary to avoid immediate danger.

*RULE 3*
*General Definitions*

For the purpose of these Rules, except where the context otherwise requires:

(a) The word "vessel" includes every description of water craft, including nondisplacement craft and seaplanes, used or capable of being used as a means of transportation on water.

(b) The term "power-driven vessel" means any vessel propelled by machinery.

*RULE 2*
*Responsibility*

(a) Nothing in these Rules shall exonerate any vessel, or the owner, master, or crew thereof, from the consequences of any neglect to comply with these Rules or of the neglect of any precaution which may be required by the ordinary practice of seamen, or by the special circumstances of the case.

(b) In construing and complying with these Rules due regard shall be had to all dangers of navigation and collision and to any special circumstances, including the limitations of the vessels involved, which may make a departure from these Rules necessary to avoid immediate danger.

*RULE 3*
*General Definitions*

For the purpose of these Rules and this Act, except where the context otherwise requires:

(a) The word "vessel" includes every description of water craft, including nondisplacement craft and seaplanes, used or capable of being used as a means of transportation on water;

(b) The term "power-driven vessel" means any vessel propelled by machinery;

*International*

(c) The term "sailing vessel" means any vessel under sail provided that propelling machinery, if fitted, is not being used.

(d) The term "vessel engaged in fishing" means any vessel fishing with nets, lines, trawls or other fishing apparatus which restrict maneuverability, but does not include a vessel fishing with trolling lines or other fishing apparatus which do not restrict maneuverability.

(e) The word "seaplane" includes any aircraft designed to maneuver on the water.

(f) The term "vessel not under command" means a vessel which through some exceptional circumstance is unable to maneuver as required by these Rules and is therefore unable to keep out of the way of another vessel.

(g) The term "vessel restricted in her ability to maneuver" means a vessel which from the nature of her work is restricted in her ability to maneuver as required by these Rules and is therefore unable to keep out of the way of another vessel.

The term 'vessels restricted in their ability to maneuver' shall include but not be limited to:

(i) a vessel engaged in laying, servicing or picking up a navigation mark, submarine cable or pipeline;

(ii) a vessel engaged in dredging, surveying or underwater operations;

(iii) a vessel engaged in replenishment or transferring persons, provisions or cargo while underway;

(iv) a vessel engaged in the launching or recovery of aircraft;

(v) a vessel engaged in mineclearance operations;

(vi) a vessel engaged in a towing operation such as severely restricts the

*Inland*

(c) The term "sailing vessel" means any vessel under sail provided that propelling machinery, if fitted, is not being used;

(d) The term "vessel engaged in fishing" means any vessel fishing with nets, lines, trawls, or other fishing apparatus which restricts maneuverability, but does not include a vessel fishing with trolling lines or other fishing apparatus which do not restrict maneuverability;

(e) The word "seaplane" includes any aircraft designed to maneuver on the water;

(f) The term "vessel not under command" means a vessel which through some exceptional circumstance is unable to maneuver as required by these Rules and is therefore unable to keep out of the way of another vessel;

(g) The term "vessel restricted in her ability to maneuver" means a vessel which from the nature of her work is restricted in her ability to maneuver as required by these Rules and is therefore unable to keep out of the way of another vessel; vessels restricted in their ability to maneuver include, but are not limited to:

(i) a vessel engaged in laying, servicing or picking up a navigation mark, submarine cable, or pipeline;

(ii) a vessel engaged in dredging, surveying, or underwater operations;

(iii) a vessel engaged in replenishment or transferring persons, provisions, or cargo while underway;

(iv) a vessel engaged in the launching or recovery of aircraft;

(v) a vessel engaged in mineclearance operations; and

(vi) a vessel engaged in a towing operation such as severely restricts the

*International*

towing vessel and her tow in their ability to deviate from their course.

(h) The term "vessel constrained by her draft" means a power-driven vessel which, because of her draft in relation to the available depth and width of navigable water is severely restricted in her ability to deviate from the course she is following.

(i) The word "underway" means that a vessel is not at anchor, or made fast to the shore, or aground.

(j) The words "length" and "breadth" of a vessel means her length overall and greatest breadth.

(k) Vessels shall be deemed to be in sight of one another only when one can be observed visually from the other.

(l) The term "restricted visibility" means any condition in which visibility is restricted by fog, mist, falling snow, heavy rainstorms, sandstorms or any other similar causes.

*Inland*

towing vessel and her tow in their ability to deviate from their course.

(h) The word "underway" means that a vessel is not at anchor, or made fast to the shore, or aground;

(i) The words "length" and breadth" of a vessel means her length overall and greatest breadth;

(j) Vessels shall be deemed to be in sight of one another only when one can be observed visually from the other;

(k) The term "restricted visibility" means any condition in which visibility is restricted by fog, mist, falling snow, heavy rainstorms, sandstorms, or any other similar causes;

(l) "Western Rivers" means the Mississippi River, its tributaries, South Pass, and Southwest Pass, to the navigational demarcation lines dividing the high seas from harbors, rivers, and other inland waters of the United States, and the Port Allen-Morgan City Alternate Route, and that part of the Atchafalaya River above its junction with the Port Allen-Morgan City Alternate Route including the Old River and the Red River;

(m) "Great Lakes" means the Great Lakes and their connecting and tributary waters including the Calumet River as far as the Thomas J. O'Brien Lock and Controlling Works (between mile 326 and 327), the Chicago River as far as the east side of the Ashland Avenue Bridge (between mile 321 and 322), and the Saint Lawrence River as far east as the lower exit of Saint Lambert Lock;

(n) "Secretary" means the Secretary of the department in which the Coast Guard is operating;

*International*

*Inland*

(o) "Inland Waters" means the navigable waters of the United States shoreward of the navigational demarcation lines dividing the high seas from harbors, rivers, and other inland waters of the United States and the waters of the Great Lakes on the United States side of the International Boundary;

(p) "Inland Rules" or "Rules" mean the Inland Navigational Rules and the annexes thereto, which govern the conduct of vessels and specify the lights, shapes, and sound signals that apply on inland waters; and

(q) "International Regulations" means the International Regulations for Preventing Collisions at Sea, 1972, including annexes currently in force for the United States.

**PART B—STEERING AND SAILING RULES**

**Section I—Conduct of Vessels in Any Condition of Visibility**

*RULE 4*
*Application*

Rules in this Section apply to any condition of visibility.

*RULE 5*
*Look-out*

Every vessel shall at all times maintain a proper look-out by sight and hearing as well as by all available means appropriate in the prevailing circumstances and conditions so as to make a full appraisal of the situation and of the risk of collision.

*RULE 6*
*Safe Speed*

Every vessel shall at all times proceed at a safe speed so that she can take

**PART B—STEERING AND SAILING RULES**

**Subpart I—Conduct of Vessels in Any Condition of Visibility**

*RULE 4*
*Application*

Rules in this subpart apply in any condition of visibility.

*RULE 5*
*Look-out*

Every vessel shall at all times maintain a proper look-out by sight and hearing as well as by all available means appropriate in the prevailing circumstances and conditions so as to make a full appraisal of the situation and of the risk of collision.

*RULE 6*
*Safe Speed*

Every vessel shall at all times proceed at a safe speed so that she can take

*International*

proper and effective action to avoid collision and be stopped within a distance appropriate to the prevailing circumstances and conditions.

In determining a safe speed the following factors shall be among those taken into account:

(a) By all vessels:

(i) the state of visibility;

(ii) the traffic density including concentrations of fishing vessels or any other vessels;

(iii) the maneuverability of the vessel with special reference to stopping distance and turning ability in the prevailing conditions;

(iv) at night the presence of background light such as from shore lights or from back scatter of her own lights;

(v) the state of wind, sea and current, and the proximity of navigational hazards;

(vi) the draft in relation to the available depth of water.

(b) Additionally, by vessels with operational radar:

(i) the characteristics, efficiency and limitations of the radar equipment;

(ii) any constraints imposed by the radar range scale in use;

(iii) the effect on radar detection of the sea state, weather and other sources of interference;

(iv) the possibility that small vessels, ice and other floating objects may not be detected by radar at an adequate range;

(v) the number, location and movement of vessels detected by radar;

(vi) the more exact assessment of the visibility that may be possible when radar is used to determine the range of vessels or other objects in the vicinity.

*Inland*

proper and effective action to avoid collision and be stopped within a distance appropriate to the prevailing circumstances and conditions.

In determining a safe speed the following factors shall be among those taken into account:

(a) By all vessels:

(i) the state of visibility;

(ii) the traffic density including concentration of fishing vessels or any other vessels;

(iii) the maneuverability of the vessel with special reference to stopping distance and turning ability in the prevailing conditions;

(iv) at night the presence of background light such as from shore lights or from back scatter of her own lights;

(v) the state of wind, sea, and current, and the proximity of navigational hazards;

(vi) the draft in relation to the available depth of water.

(b) Additionally, by vessels with operational radar:

(i) the characteristics, efficiency and limitations of the radar equipment;

(ii) any constraints imposed by the radar range scale in use;

(iii) the effect on radar detection of the sea state, weather, and other sources of interference;

(iv) the possibility that small vessels, ice and other floating objects may not be detected by radar at an adequate range;

(v) the number, location, and movement of vessels detected by radar; and

(vi) the more exact assessment of the visibility that may be possible when radar is used to determine the range of vessels or other objects in the vicinity.

*International*

*Inland*

## RULE 7
*Risk of Collision*

(a) Every vessel shall use all available means appropriate to the prevailing circumstances and conditions to determine if risk of collision exists. If there is any doubt such risk shall be deemed to exist.

(b) Proper use shall be made of radar equipment if fitted and operational, including long-range scanning to obtain early warning of risk of collision and radar plotting or equivalent systematic observation of detected objects.

(c) Assumptions shall not be made on the basis of scanty information, especially scanty radar information.

(d) In determining if risk of collision exists the following considerations shall be among those taken into account:

(i) such risk shall be deemed to exist if the compass bearing of an approaching vessel does not appreciably change;

(ii) such risk may sometimes exist even when an appreciable bearing change is evident, particularly when approaching a very large vessel or a tow or when approaching a vessel at close range.

## RULE 8
*Action to Avoid Collision*

(a) Any action taken to avoid collision shall, if the circumstances of the case admit, be positive, made in ample time and with due regard to the observance of good seamanship.

(b) Any alteration of course and/or speed to avoid collision shall, if the circumstances of the case admit, be large enough to be readily apparent to another vessel observing visually or by radar; a succession of small alterations of course and/or speed should be avoided.

## RULE 7
*Risk of Collision*

(a) Every vessel shall use all available means appropriate to the prevailing circumstances and conditions to determine if risk of collision exists. If there is any doubt such risk shall be deemed to exist.

(b) Proper use shall be made of radar equipment if fitted and operational, including long-range scanning to obtain early warning of risk of collision and radar plotting or equivalent systematic observation of detected objects.

(c) Assumptions shall not be made on the basis of scanty information, especially scanty radar information.

(d) In determining if risk of collision exists the following considerations shall be among those taken into account:

(i) such risk shall be deemed to exist if the compass bearing of an approaching vessel does not appreciably change; and

(ii) such risk may sometimes exist even when an appreciable bearing change is evident, particularly when approaching a very large vessel or a tow or when approaching a vessel at close range.

## RULE 8
*Action to Avoid Collision*

(a) Any action taken to avoid collision shall, if the circumstances of the case admit, be positive, made in ample time and with due regard to the observance of good seamanship.

(b) Any alteration of course or speed to avoid collision shall, if the circumstances of the case admit, be large enough to be readily apparent to another vessel observing visually or by radar; a succession of small alterations of course or speed should be avoided.

*International*

(c) If there is sufficient sea room, alteration of course alone may be the most effective action to avoid a close-quarters situation provided that it is made in good time, is substantial and does not result in another close-quarters situation.

(d) Action taken to avoid collision with another vessel shall be such as to result in passing at a safe distance. The effectiveness of the action shall be carefully checked until the other vessel is finally past and clear.

(e) If necessary to avoid collision or allow more time to assess the situation, a vessel shall slacken her speed or take all way off by stopping or reversing her means of propulsion.

(f)(i) A vessel which, by any of these rules, is required not to impede the passage or safe passage of another vessel shall, when required by the circumstances of the case, take early action to allow sufficient sea room for the safe passage of the other vessel.

(ii) A vessel required not to impede the passage or safe passage of another vessel is not relieved of this obligation if approaching the other vessel so as to involve risk of collision and shall, when taking action, have full regard to the action which may be required by the rules of this part.

(iii) A vessel, the passage of which is not to be impeded remains fully obliged to comply with the rules of this part when the two vessels are approaching one another so as to involve risk of collision.

## RULE 9
*Narrow Channels*

(a) A vessel proceeding along the course of a narrow channel or fairway shall keep as near to the outer limit of

*Inland*

(c) If there is sufficient sea room, alteration of course alone may be the most effective action to avoid a close-quarters situation provided that it is made in good time, is substantial and does not result in another close-quarters situation.

(d) Action taken to avoid collision with another vessel shall be such as to result in passing at a safe distance. The effectiveness of the action shall be carefully checked until the other vessel is finally past and clear.

(e) If necessary to avoid collision or allow more time to assess the situation, a vessel shall slacken her speed or take all way off by stopping or reversing her means of propulsion.

## RULE 9
*Narrow Channels*

(a)(i) A vessel proceeding along the course of a narrow channel or fairway shall keep as near to the outer limit of

*International*

the channel or fairway which lies on her starboard side as is safe and practicable.

(b) A vessel of less than 20 meters in length or a sailing vessel shall not impede the passage of a vessel which can safely navigate only within a narrow channel or fairway.

(c) A vessel engaged in fishing shall not impede the passage of any other vessel navigating within a narrow channel or fairway.

(d) A vessel shall not cross a narrow channel or fairway if such crossing impedes the passage of a vessel which can safely navigate only within such channel or fairway. The latter vessel may use the sound signal prescribed in Rule 34(d) if in doubt as to the intention of the crossing vessel.

(e)(i) In a narrow channel or fairway when overtaking can take place only if the vessel to be overtaken has to take action to permit safe passing, the vessel intending to overtake shall indicate her intention by sounding the appropriate signal prescribed in Rule 34(c)(i). The vessel to be overtaken shall, if in agreement, sound the appropriate signal prescribed in Rule 34(c)(ii) and take steps to permit safe passing. If in doubt she may sound the signals prescribed in Rule 34(d).

*Inland*

the channel or fairway which lies on her starboard side as is safe and practicable.

(ii) Notwithstanding paragraph (a)(i) and Rule 14(a), a power-driven vessel operating in narrow channels or fairways on the Great Lakes, Western Rivers, or waters specified by the Secretary, and proceeding downbound with a following current shall have the right-of-way over an upbound vessel, shall propose the manner and place of passage, and shall initiate the maneuvering signals prescribed by Rule 34(a)(i), as appropriate. The vessel proceeding upbound against the current shall hold as necessary to permit safe passing.

(b) A vessel of less than 20 meters in length or a sailing vessel shall not impede the passage of a vessel that can safely navigate only within a narrow channel or fairway.

(c) A vessel engaged in fishing shall not impede the passage of any other vessel navigating within a narrow channel or fairway.

(d) A vessel shall not cross a narrow channel or fairway if such crossing impedes the passage of a vessel which can safely navigate only within that channel or fairway. The latter vessel shall use the danger signal prescribed in Rule 34(d) if in doubt as to the intention of the crossing vessel.

(e)(i) In a narrow channel or fairway when overtaking, the vessel intending to overtake shall indicate her intention by sounding the appropriate signal prescribed in Rule 34(c) and take steps to permit safe passing. The overtaken vessel, if in agreement, shall sound the same signal. If in doubt she shall sound the danger signal prescribed in Rule 34(d).

*International*

(ii) This Rule does not relieve the overtaking vessel of her obligation under Rule 13.

(f) A vessel nearing a bend or an area of a narrow channel or fairway where other vessels may be obscured by an intervening obstruction shall navigate with particular alertness and caution and shall sound the appropriate signal prescribed in Rule 34(e).

(g) Any vessel shall, if the circumstances of the case admit, avoid anchoring in a narrow channel.

## RULE 10
### Traffic Separation Schemes

(a) This rule applies to traffic separation schemes adopted by the Organization and does not relieve any vessel of her obligation under any other rule.

(b) A vessel using a traffic separation scheme shall:

(i) proceed in the appropriate traffic lane in the general direction of traffic flow for that lane;

(ii) so far as practicable keep clear of a traffic separation line or separation zone;

(iii) normally join or leave a traffic lane at the termination of the lane, but when joining or leaving from either side shall do so at as small an angle to the general direction of traffic flow as practicable.

(c) A vessel shall, so far as practicable, avoid crossing traffic lanes but if obliged to do so shall cross on a heading as nearly as practicable at right angles to the general direction of traffic flow.

(d)(i) A vessel shall not use an inshore traffic zone when she can safely use the appropriate traffic lane within the adjacent traffic separation scheme. However, vessels of less than 20 metres in length, sailing vessels and vessels en-

*Inland*

(ii) This Rule does not relieve the overtaking vessel of her obligation under Rule 13.

(f) A vessel nearing a bend or an area of a narrow channel or fairway where other vessels may be obscured by an intervening obstruction shall navigate with particular alertness and caution and shall sound the appropriate signal prescribed in Rule 34(e).

(g) Every vessel shall, if the circumstances of the case admit, avoid anchoring in a narrow channel.

## RULE 10
### Vessel Traffic Services

Each vessel required by regulation to participate in a vessel traffic service shall comply with the applicable regulations.

*International*                    *Inland*

gaged in fishing may use the inshore traffic zone.

(ii) Notwithstanding subparagraph (d)(i), a vessel may use an inshore traffic zone when en route to or from a port, offshore installation or structure, pilot station or any other place situated within the inshore traffic zone or to avoid immediate danger.

(e) A vessel other than a crossing vessel or a vessel joining or leaving a lane shall not normally enter a separation zone or cross a separation line except:

(i) in cases of emergency to avoid immediate danger;

(ii) to engage in fishing within a separation zone.

(f) A vessel navigating in areas near the terminations of traffic separation schemes shall do so with particular caution.

(g) A vessel shall so far as practicable avoid anchoring in a traffic separation scheme or in areas near its terminations.

(h) A vessel not using a traffic separation scheme shall avoid it by as wide a margin as is practicable.

(i) A vessel engaged in fishing shall not impede the passage of any vessel following a traffic lane.

(j) A vessel of less than 20 meters in length or a sailing vessel shall not impede the safe passage of a power-driven vessel following a traffic lane.

(k) A vessel restricted in her ability to maneuver when engaged in an operation for the maintenance of safety of navigation in a traffic separation scheme is exempted from complying with this Rule to the extent necessary to carry out the operation.

(l) A vessel restricted in her ability to maneuver when engaged in an oper-

*International*

ation for the laying, servicing or picking up of a submarine cable, within a traffic separation scheme, is exempted from complying with this Rule to the extent necessary to carry out the operation.

## Section II—Conduct of Vessels in Sight of One Another

*RULE 11*
*Application*

Rules in this Section apply to vessels in sight of one another.

*RULE 12*
*Sailing Vessels*

(a) When two sailing vessels are approaching one another, so as to involve risk of collision, one of them shall keep out of the way of the other as follows:

(i) when each has the wind on a different side, the vessel which has the wind on the port side shall keep out of the way of the other;

(ii) when both have the wind on the same side, the vessel which is to windward shall keep out of the way of the vessel which is to leeward;

(iii) if a vessel with the wind on the port side sees a vessel to windward and cannot determine with certainty whether the other vessel has the wind on the port or on the starboard side, she shall keep out of the way of the other.

(b) For the purposes of this Rule the windward side shall be deemed to be the side opposite to that on which the mainsail is carried or, in the case of a square-rigged vessel, the side opposite to that on which the largest fore-and-aft sail is carried.

*Inland*

## Subpart II—Conduct of Vessels in Sight of One Another

*RULE 11*
*Application*

Rules in this subpart apply to vessels in sight of one another.

*RULE 12*
*Sailing Vessels*

(a) When two sailing vessels are approaching one another, so as to involve risk of collision, one of them shall keep out of the way of the other as follows:

(i) when each has the wind on a different side, the vessel which has the wind on the port side shall keep out of the way of the other;

(ii) when both have the wind on the same side, the vessel which is to windward shall keep out of the way of the vessel which is to leeward; and

(iii) if a vessel with the wind on the port side sees a vessel to windward and cannot determine with certainty whether the other vessel has the wind on the port or on the starboard side, she shall keep out of the way of the other.

(b) For the purpose of this Rule the windward side shall be deemed to be the side opposite to that on which the mainsail is carried or, in the case of a square-rigged vessel, the side opposite to that on which the largest fore-and-aft sail is carried.

*International*

*Inland*

## RULE 13
*Overtaking*

(a) Notwithstanding anything contained in the Rules of Part B, Sections I and II any vessel overtaking any other shall keep out of the way of the vessel being overtaken.

(b) A vessel shall be deemed to be overtaking when coming up with another vessel from a direction more than 22.5 degrees abaft her beam, that is, in such a position with reference to the vessel she is overtaking, that at night she would be able to see only the sternlight of that vessel but neither of her sidelights.

(c) When a vessel is in any doubt as to whether she is overtaking another, she shall assume that this is the case and act accordingly.

(d) Any subsequent alteration of the bearing between the two vessels shall not make the overtaking vessel a crossing vessel within the meaning of these Rules or relieve her of the duty of keeping clear of the overtaken vessel until she is finally past and clear.

## RULE 14
*Head-on Situation*

(a) When two power-driven vessels are meeting on reciprocal or nearly reciprocal courses so as to involve risk of collision each shall alter her course to starboard so that each shall pass on the port side of the other.

(b) Such a situation shall be deemed to exist when a vessel sees the other ahead or nearly ahead and by night she could see the masthead lights of the other in a line or nearly in a line and/or both sidelights and by day she observes the corresponding aspect of the other vessel.

## RULE 13
*Overtaking*

(a) Notwithstanding anything contained in Rules 4 through 18, any vessel overtaking any other shall keep out of the way of the vessel being overtaken.

(b) A vessel shall be deemed to be overtaking when coming up with another vessel from a direction more than 22.5 degrees abaft her beam; that is, in such a position with reference to the vessel she is overtaking, that at night she would be able to see only the sternlight of that vessel but neither of her sidelights.

(c) When a vessel is in any doubt as to whether she is overtaking another, she shall assume that this is the case and act accordingly.

(d) Any subsequent alteration of the bearing between the two vessels shall not make the overtaking vessel a crossing vessel within the meaning of these Rules or relieve her of the duty of keeping clear of the overtaken vessel until she is finally past and clear.

## RULE 14
*Head-on Situation*

(a) Unless otherwise agreed, when two power-driven vessels are meeting on reciprocal or nearly reciprocal courses so as to involve risk of collision each shall alter her course to starboard so that each shall pass on the port side of the other.

(b) Such a situation shall be deemed to exist when a vessel sees the other ahead or nearly ahead and by night she could see the masthead lights of the other in a line or nearly in a line or both sidelights and by day she observes the corresponding aspect of the other vessel.

*International*

(c) When a vessel is in any doubt as to whether such a situation exists she shall assume that it does exist and act accordingly.

## RULE 15
*Crossing Situation*

When two power-driven vessels are crossing so as to involve risk of collision, the vessel which has the other on her own starboard side shall keep out of the way and shall, if the circumstances of the case admit, avoid crossing ahead of the other vessel.

## RULE 16
*Action by Give-way Vessel*

Every vessel which is directed to keep out of the way of another vessel shall, so far as possible, take early and substantial action to keep well clear.

## RULE 17
*Action by Stand-on Vessel*

(a)(i) Where one of two vessels is to keep out of the way the other shall keep her course and speed.

(ii) The latter vessel may however take action to avoid collision by her ma-

*Inland*

(c) When a vessel is in any doubt as to whether such a situation exists she shall assume that it does exist and act accordingly.

(d) Notwithstanding paragraph (a) of this Rule, a power-driven vessel operating on the Great Lakes, Western Rivers, or waters specified by the Secretary, and proceeding downbound with a following current shall have the right-of-way over an upbound vessel, shall propose the manner of passage, and shall initiate the maneuvering signals prescribed by Rule 34(a)(i), as appropriate.

## RULE 15
*Crossing Situation*

(a) When two power-driven vessels are crossing so as to involve risk of collision, the vessel which has the other on her starboard side shall keep out of the way and shall, if the circumstances of the case admit, avoid crossing ahead of the other vessel.

(b) Notwithstanding paragraph (a), on the Great Lakes, Western Rivers, or water specified by the Secretary, a vessel crossing a river shall keep out of the way of a power-driven vessel ascending or descending the river.

## RULE 16
*Action by Give-way Vessel*

Every vessel which is directed to keep out of the way of another vessel shall, so far as possible, take early and substantial action to keep well clear.

## RULE 17
*Action by Stand-on Vessel*

(a)(i) Where one of two vessels is to keep out of the way, the other shall keep her course and speed.

(ii) The latter vessel may however, take action to avoid collision by her ma-

*International*

neuver alone, as soon as it becomes apparent to her that the vessel required to keep out of the way is not taking appropriate action in compliance with these Rules.

(b) When, from any cause, the vessel required to keep her course and speed finds herself so close that collision cannot be avoided by the action of the give-way vessel alone, she shall take such action as will best aid to avoid collision.

(c) A power-driven vessel which takes action in a crossing situation in accordance with subparagraph (a)(ii) of this Rule to avoid collision with another power-driven vessel shall, if the circumstances of the case admit, not alter course to port for a vessel on her own port side.

(d) This Rule does not relieve the give-way vessel of her obligation to keep out of the way.

*RULE 18*
*Responsibilities Between Vessels*

Except where Rules 9, 10 and 13 otherwise require:

(a) A power-driven vessel underway shall keep out of the way of:

(i) a vessel not under command;

(ii) a vessel restricted in her ability to maneuver;

(iii) a vessel engaged in fishing;

(iv) a sailing vessel.

(b) A sailing vessel underway shall keep out of the way of:

(i) a vessel not under command;

(ii) a vessel restricted in her ability to maneuver;

(iii) a vessel engaged in fishing.

(c) A vessel engaged in fishing when underway shall, so far as possible, keep out of the way of:

(i) a vessel not under command;

*Inland*

neuver alone, as soon as it becomes apparent to her that the vessel required to keep out of the way is not taking appropriate action in compliance with these Rules.

(b) When, from any cause, the vessel required to keep her course and speed finds herself so close that collision cannot be avoided by the action of the give-way vessel alone, she shall take such action as will best aid to avoid collision.

(c) A power-driven vessel which takes action in a crossing situation in accordance with subparagraph (a)(ii) of this Rule to avoid collision with another power-driven vessel shall, if the circumstances of the case admit, not alter course to port for a vessel on her own port side.

(d) This Rule does not relieve the give-way vessel of her obligation to keep out of the way.

*RULE 18*
*Responsibilities Between Vessels*

Except where Rules 9, 10 and 13 otherwise require:

(a) A power-driven vessel underway shall keep out of the way of:

(i) a vessel not under command;

(ii) a vessel restricted in her ability to maneuver;

(iii) a vessel engaged in fishing; and

(iv) a sailing vessel.

(b) A sailing vessel underway shall keep out of the way of:

(i) a vessel not under command;

(ii) a vessel restricted in her ability to maneuver; and

(iii) a vessel engaged in fishing.

(c) A vessel engaged in fishing when underway shall, so far as possible, keep out of the way of:

(i) a vessel not under command;

*International*

(ii) a vessel restricted in her ability to maneuver.

(d)(i) Any vessel other than a vessel not under command or a vessel restricted in her ability to maneuver shall, if the circumstances of the case admit, avoid impeding the safe passage of a vessel constrained by her draft, exhibiting the signals in Rule 28.

(ii) A vessel constrained by her draft shall navigate with particular caution having full regard to her special condition.

(e) A seaplane on the water shall, in general, keep well clear of all vessels and avoid impeding their navigation. In circumstances, however, where risk of collision exists, she shall comply with the Rules of this Part.

## Section III—Conduct of Vessels in Restricted Visibility

*RULE 19*
*Conduct of Vessels in*
*Restricted Visibility*

(a) This Rule applies to vessels not in sight of one another when navigating in or near an area of restricted visibility.

(b) Every vessel shall proceed at a safe speed adapted to the prevailing circumstances and conditions of restricted visibility. A power-driven vessel shall have her engines ready for immediate maneuver.

(c) Every vessel shall have due regard to the prevailing circumstances and conditions of restricted visibility when complying with the Rules of Section I of this Part.

(d) A vessel which detects by radar alone the presence of another vessel shall determine if a close-quarters situation is developing and/or risk of colli-

*Inland*

(ii) a vessel restricted in her ability to maneuver.

(d) A seaplane on the water shall, in general, keep well clear of all vessels and avoid impeding their navigation. In circumstances, however, where risk of collision exists, she shall comply with the Rules of this Part.

## Subpart III—Conduct of Vessels in Restricted Visibility

*RULE 19*
*Conduct of Vessels in*
*Restricted Visibility*

(a) This Rule applies to vessels not in sight of one another when navigating in or near an area of restricted visibility.

(b) Every vessel shall proceed at a safe speed adapted to the prevailing circumstances and conditions of restricted visibility. A power-driven vessel shall have her engines ready for immediate maneuver.

(c) Every vessel shall have due regard to the prevailing circumstances and conditions of restricted visibility when complying with Rules 4 through 10.

(d) A vessel which detects by radar alone the presence of another vessel shall determine if a close-quarters situation is developing or risk of collision

*International*

sion exists. If so, she shall take avoiding action in ample time, provided that when such action consists of an alteration of course, so far as possible the following shall be avoided:

(i) an alteration of course to port for a vessel forward of the beam, other than for a vessel being overtaken;

(ii) an alteration of course towards a vessel abeam or abaft the beam.

(e) Except where it has been determined that a risk of collision does not exist, every vessel which hears apparently forward of her beam the fog signal of another vessel, or which cannot avoid a close-quarters situation with another vessel forward of her beam, shall reduce her speed to the minimum at which she can be kept on her course. She shall if necessary take all her way off and in any event navigate with extreme caution until danger of collision is over.

## PART C—LIGHTS AND SHAPES

*RULE 20*
*Application*

(a) Rules in this Part shall be complied with in all weathers.

(b) The Rules concerning lights shall be complied with from sunset to sunrise, and during such times no other lights shall be exhibited, except such lights as cannot be mistaken for the lights specified in these Rules or do not impair their visibility or distinctive character, or interfere with the keeping of a proper look-out.

(c) The lights prescribed by these Rules shall, if carried, also be exhibited from sunrise to sunset in restricted visibility and may be exhibited in all other circumstances when it is deemed necessary.

*Inland*

exists. If so, she shall take avoiding action in ample time, provided that when such action consists of an alteration of course, so far as possible the following shall be avoided:

(i) an alteration of course to port for a vessel forward of the beam, other than for a vessel being overtaken; and

(ii) an alteration of course toward a vessel abeam or abaft the beam.

(e) Except where it has been determined that a risk of collision does not exist, every vessel which hears apparently forward of her beam the fog signal of another vessel, or which cannot avoid a close-quarters situation with another vessel forward of her beam, shall reduce her speed to the minimum at which she can be kept on course. She shall if necessary take all her way off and, in any event, navigate with extreme caution until danger of collision is over.

## PART C—LIGHTS AND SHAPES

*RULE 20*
*Application*

(a) Rules in this Part shall be complied with in all weathers.

(b) The Rules concerning lights shall be complied with from sunset to sunrise, and during such times no other lights shall be exhibited, except such lights as cannot be mistaken for the lights specified in these Rules or do not impair their visibility or distinctive character, or interfere with the keeping of a proper look-out.

(c) The lights prescribed by these Rules shall, if carried, also be exhibited from sunrise to sunset in restricted visibility and may be exhibited in all other circumstances when it is deemed necessary.

*International*

(d) The Rules concerning shapes shall be complied with by day.

(e) The lights and shapes specified in these Rules shall comply with the provisions of Annex I to these Regulations.

## RULE 21
### Definitions

(a) "Masthead light" means a white light placed over the fore and aft centerline of the vessel showing an unbroken light over an arc of the horizon of 225 degrees and so fixed as to show the light from right ahead to 22.5 degrees abaft the beam on either side of the vessel.

(b) "Sidelights" means a green light on the starboard side and a red light on the port side each showing an unbroken light over an arc of the horizon of 112.5 degrees and so fixed as to show the light from right ahead to 22.5 degrees abaft the beam on its respective side. In a vessel of less than 20 meters in length the sidelights may be combined in one lantern carried on the fore and aft centerline of the vessel.

(c) "Sternlight" means a white light placed as nearly as practicable at the stern showing an unbroken light over an arc of the horizon of 135 degrees and so fixed as to show the light 67.5 degrees from right aft on each side of the vessel.

(d) "Towing light" means a yellow light having the same characteristics as

*Inland*

(d) The Rules concerning shapes shall be complied with by day.

(e) The lights and shapes specified in these Rules shall comply with the provisions of Annex I of these Rules.

## RULE 21
### Definitions

(a) "Masthead light" means a white light placed over the fore and aft centerline of the vessel showing an unbroken light over an arc of the horizon of 225 degrees and so fixed as to show the light from right ahead to 22.5 degrees abaft the beam on either side of the vessel, except that on a vessel of less than 12 meters in length the masthead light shall be placed as nearly as practicable to the fore and aft centerline of the vessel.

(b) "Sidelights" mean a green light on the starboard side and a red light on the port side each showing an unbroken light over an arc of the horizon of 112.5 degrees and so fixed as to show the light from right ahead to 22.5 degrees abaft the beam on its respective side. On a vessel of less than 20 meters in length the sidelights may be combined in one lantern carried on the fore and aft centerline of the vessel, except that on a vessel of less than 12 meters in length the sidelights when combined in one lantern shall be placed as nearly as practicable to the fore and aft centerline of the vessel.

(c) "Sternlight" means a white light placed as nearly as practicable at the stern showing an unbroken light over an arc of the horizon of 135 degrees and so fixed as to show the light 67.5 degrees from right aft on each side of the vessel.

(d) "Towing light" means a yellow light having the same characteristics as

*International*

the "sternlight" defined in paragraph (c) of this Rule.

(e) "All-round light" means a light showing an unbroken light over an arc of the horizon of 360 degrees.

(f) "Flashing light" means a light flashing at regular intervals at a frequency of 120 flashes or more per minute.

*Inland*

the "sternlight" defined in paragraph (c) of this Rule.

(e) "All-round light" means a light showing an unbroken light over an arc of the horizon of 360 degrees.

(f) "Flashing light" means a light flashing at regular intervals at a frequency of 120 flashes or more per minute.

(g) "Special flashing light" means a yellow light flashing at regular intervals at a frequency of 50 to 70 flashes per minute, placed as far forward and as nearly as practicable on the fore and aft centerline of the tow and showing an unbroken light over an arc of the horizon of not less than 180 degrees nor more than 225 degrees and so fixed as to show the light from right ahead to abeam and no more than 22.5 degrees abaft the beam on either side of the vessel.

*RULE 22*
*Visibility of Lights*

The lights prescribed in these Rules shall have an intensity as specified in Section 8 of Annex I to these Regulations so as to be visible at the following minimum ranges:

(a) In vessels of 50 meters or more in length:
—a masthead light, 6 miles;
—a sidelight, 3 miles;
—a sternlight, 3 miles;
—a towing light, 3 miles;
—a white, red, green or yellow all-round light, 3 miles.

(b) In vessels of 12 meters or more in length but less than 50 meters in length;
—a masthead light, 5 miles; except that where the length of the vessel is less than 20 meters, 3 miles;
—a sidelight, 2 miles;

*RULE 22*
*Visibility of Lights*

The lights prescribed in these Rules shall have an intensity as specified in Annex I to these Rules, so as to be visible at the following minimum ranges:

(a) In a vessel of 50 meters or more in length:
—a masthead light, 6 miles;
—a sidelight, 3 miles;
—a sternlight, 3 miles;
—a towing light, 3 miles;
—a white, red, green or yellow all-round light, 3 miles; and
—a special flashing light, 2 miles.

(b) In a vessel of 12 meters or more in length but less than 50 meters in length:
—a masthead light, 5 miles; except that where the length of the vessel is less than 20 meters, 3 miles;
—a sidelight, 2 miles;

## International

—a sternlight, 2 miles;
—a towing light, 2 miles;
—a white, red, green or yellow all-round light, 2 miles.

(c) In vessels of less than 12 meters in length:
—a masthead light, 2 miles;
—a sidelight, 1 mile;
—a sternlight, 2 miles;
—a towing light, 2 miles;
—a white, red, green or yellow all-round light, 2 miles.

(d) In inconspicuous, partly submerged vessels or objects being towed:
—a white all-round light, 3 miles.

### RULE 23
*Power-driven Vessels Underway*

(a) A power-driven vessel underway shall exhibit:
(i) a masthead light forward;

(ii) a second masthead light abaft of and higher than the forward one; except that a vessel of less than 50 meters in length shall not be obliged to exhibit such light but may do so;
(iii) sidelights;
(iv) a sternlight.
(b) An air-cushion vessel when operating in the nondisplacement mode shall, in addition to the lights prescribed in paragraph (a) of this Rule, exhibit an all-round flashing yellow light.
(c)(i) A power-driven vessel of less than 12 meters in length may in lieu of the lights prescribed in paragraph (a) of this Rule exhibit an all-round white light and sidelights;

## Inland

—a sternlight, 2 miles;
—a towing light, 2 miles;
—a white, red, green or yellow all-round light, 2 miles; and
—a special flashing light, 2 miles.
(c) In a vessel of less than 12 meters in length:
—a masthead light, 2 miles;
—a sidelight, 1 mile;
—a sternlight, 2 miles;
—a towing light, 2 miles;
—a white, red, green or yellow all-round light, 2 miles; and
—a special flashing light, 2 miles.
(d) In an inconspicuous, partly submerged vessel or object being towed;
—a white all-round light, 3 miles.

### RULE 23
*Power-driven Vessels Underway*

(a) A power-driven vessel underway shall exhibit:
(i) a masthead light forward; except that a vessel of less than 20 meters in length need not exhibit this light forward of amidships but shall exhibit it as far forward as is practicable;
(ii) a second masthead light abaft of and higher than the forward one; except that a vessel of less than 50 meters in length shall not be obliged to exhibit such light but may do so;
(iii) sidelights; and
(iv) a sternlight.
(b) An air-cushion vessel when operating in the nondisplacement mode shall, in addition to the lights prescribed in paragraph (a) of this Rule, exhibit an all-round flashing yellow light where it can best be seen.
(c) A power-driven vessel of less than 12 meters in length may, in lieu of the lights prescribed in paragraph (a) of this Rule, exhibit an all-round white light and sidelights.

*International*

(ii) a power-driven vessel of less than 7 meters in length whose maximum speed does not exceed 7 knots may in lieu of the lights prescribed in paragraph (a) of this Rule exhibit an all-round white light and shall, if practicable, also exhibit sidelights;

(iii) the masthead light or all-round white light on a power-driven vessel of less than 12 meters in length may be displaced from the fore and aft centerline of the vessel if centerline fitting is not practicable, provided that the sidelights are combined in one lantern which shall be carried on the fore and aft centerline of the vessel or located as nearly as practicable in the same fore and aft line as the masthead light or the all-round white light.

*Inland*

(d) A power-driven vessel when operating on the Great Lakes may carry an all-round white light in lieu of the second masthead light and sternlight prescribed in paragraph (a) of this Rule. The light shall be carried in the position of the second masthead light and be visible at the same minimum range.

*RULE 24*
*Towing and Pushing*

(a) A power-driven vessel when towing shall exhibit:

(i) instead of the light prescribed in Rule 23(a)(i) or (a)(ii), two masthead lights in a vertical line. When the length of the tow, measuring from the stern of the towing vessel to the after end of the tow exceeds 200 meters, three such lights in a vertical line;

(ii) sidelights;

(iii) a sternlight;

(iv) a towing light in a vertical line above the sternlight;

*RULE 24*
*Towing and Pushing*

(a) A power-driven vessel when towing astern shall exhibit:

(i) instead of the light prescribed either in Rule 23(a)(i) or 23(a)(ii), two masthead lights in a vertical line. When the length of the tow, measuring from the stern of the towing vessel to the after end of the tow exceeds 200 meters, three such lights in a vertical line;

(ii) sidelights;

(iii) a sternlight;

(iv) a towing light in a vertical line above the sternlight; and

*International*

(v) when the length of the tow exceeds 200 meters, a diamond shape where it can best be seen.

(b) When a pushing vessel and a vessel being pushed ahead are rigidly connected in a composite unit they shall be regarded as a power-driven vessel and exhibit the lights prescribed in Rule 23.

(c) A power-driven vessel when pushing ahead or towing alongside, except in the case of a composite unit, shall exhibit:

(i) instead of the light prescribed in Rule 23(a)(i) or (a)(ii), two masthead lights in a vertical line;

(ii) sidelights;

(iii) a sternlight.

(d) A power-driven vessel to which paragraph (a) or (c) of this Rule apply shall also comply with Rule 23(a)(ii).

(e) A vessel or object being towed, other than those mentioned in paragraph (g) of this Rule, shall exhibit:

(i) sidelights;

(ii) a sternlight;

(iii) when the length of the tow exceeds 200 meters, a diamond shape where it can best be seen.

(f) Provided that any number of vessels being towed alongside or pushed in a group shall be lighted as one vessel:

(i) a vessel being pushed ahead, not being part of a composite unit, shall exhibit at the forward end, sidelights;

(ii) a vessel being towed alongside shall exhibit a sternlight and at the forward end, sidelights.

(g) An inconspicuous, partly submerged vessel or object, or combination of such vessels or objects being towed, shall exhibit:

*Inland*

(v) when the length of the tow exceeds 200 meters, a diamond shape where it can best be seen.

(b) When a pushing vessel and a vessel being pushed ahead are rigidly connected in a composite unit they shall be regarded as a power-driven vessel and exhibit the lights prescribed in Rule 23.

(c) A power-driven vessel when pushing ahead or towing alongside, except as required by paragraphs (b) and (i) of this Rule, shall exhibit:

(i) instead of the light prescribed either in Rule 23(a)(i) or 23(a)(ii), two masthead lights in a vertical line;

(ii) sidelights; and

(iii) two towing lights in a vertical line.

(d) A power-driven vessel to which paragraphs (a) or (c) of this Rule apply shall also comply with Rule 23(a)(i) and 23(a)(ii).

(e) A vessel or object other than those referred to in paragraph (g) of this Rule being towed shall exhibit:

(i) sidelights;

(ii) a sternlight; and

(iii) when the length of the tow exceeds 200 meters, a diamond shape where it can best be seen.

(f) Provided that any number of vessels being towed alongside or pushed in a group shall be lighted as one vessel:

(i) a vessel being pushed ahead, not being part of a composite unit, shall exhibit at the forward end sidelights, and a special flashing light; and

(ii) a vessel being towed alongside shall exhibit a sternlight and at the forward end sidelights.

(g) An inconspicuous, partly submerged vessel or object being towed shall exhibit:

## International

(i) if it is less than 25 meters in breadth, one all-round white light at or near the forward end and one at or near the after end except that dracones need not exhibit a light at or near the forward end;

(ii) if it is 25 meters or more in breadth, two additional all-round white lights at or near the extremities of its breadth;

(iii) if it exceeds 100 meters in length, additional all-round white lights between the lights prescribed in subparagraphs (i) and (ii) so that the distance between the lights shall not exceed 100 meters;

(iv) a diamond shape at or near the aftermost extremity of the last vessel or object being towed and if the length of the tow exceeds 200 meters an additional diamond shape where it can best be seen and located as far forward as is practicable.

(h) Where from any sufficient cause it is impracticable for a vessel or object being towed to exhibit the lights or shapes prescribed in paragraph (e) or (g) of this Rule, all possible measures shall be taken to light the vessel or object towed or at least to indicate the presence of such vessel or object.

(i) Where from any sufficient cause it is impracticable for a vessel not normally engaged in towing operations to display the lights prescribed in paragraph (a) or (c) of this Rule, such vessel shall not be required to exhibit those lights when engaged in towing another vessel in distress or otherwise in need of assistance. All possible measures shall be taken to indicate the nature of the relationship between the towing vessel and the vessel being towed as authorized by Rule 36, in particular by illuminating the towline.

## Inland

(i) if it is less than 25 meters in breadth, one all-round white light at or near each end;

(ii) if it is 25 meters or more in breadth, four all-round white lights to mark its length and breadth;

(iii) if it exceeds 100 meters in length, additional all-round white lights between the lights prescribed in subparagraphs (i) and (ii) so that the distance between the lights shall not exceed 100 meters: *Provided,* That any vessels or objects being towed alongside each other shall be lighted as one vessel or object;

(iv) a diamond shape at or near the aftermost extremity of the last vessel or object being towed; and

(v) the towing vessel may direct a searchlight in the direction of the tow to indicate its presence to an approaching vessel.

(h) Where from any sufficient cause it is impracticable for a vessel or object being towed to exhibit the lights prescribed in paragraph (e) or (g) of this Rule, all possible measures shall be taken to light the vessel or object towed or at least to indicate the presence of the unlighted vessel or object.

(i) Notwithstanding paragraph (c), on the Western Rivers (except below the Huey P. Long Bridge on the Mississippi River) and on waters specified by the Secretary, a power-driven vessel when pushing ahead or towing alongside, except as paragraph (b) applies, shall exhibit:

(i) sidelights; and

(ii) two towing lights in a vertical line.

*International*

*Inland*

(j) Where from any sufficient cause it is impracticable for a vessel not normally engaged in towing operations to display the lights prescribed by paragraph (a), (c) or (i) of this Rule, such vessel shall not be required to exhibit those lights when engaged in towing another vessel in distress or otherwise in need of assistance. All possible measures shall be taken to indicate the nature of the relationship between the towing vessel and the vessel being assisted. The searchlight authorized by Rule 36 may be used to illuminate the tow.

*RULE 25*
*Sailing Vessels Underway and Vessels Under Oars*

(a) A sailing vessel underway shall exhibit:
　(i) sidelights;
　(ii) a sternlight.

(b) In a sailing vessel of less than 20 meters in length the lights prescribed in paragraph (a) of this Rule may be combined in one lantern carried at or near the top of the mast where it can best be seen.

(c) A sailing vessel underway may, in addition to the lights prescribed in paragraph (a) of this Rule, exhibit at or near the top of the mast, where they can best be seen, two all-round lights in a vertical line, the upper being red and the lower green, but these lights shall not be exhibited in conjunction with the combined lantern permitted by paragraph (b) of this Rule.

(d)(i) A sailing vessel of less than 7 meters in length shall, if practicable, exhibit the lights prescribed in paragraph (a) or (b) of this Rule, but if she does not, she shall have ready at hand an electric torch or lighted lantern

*RULE 25*
*Sailing Vessels Underway and Vessels Under Oars*

(a) A sailing vessel underway shall exhibit:
　(i) sidelights; and
　(ii) a sternlight.

(b) In a sailing vessel of less than 20 meters in length the lights prescribed in paragraph (a) of this Rule may be combined in one lantern carried at or near the top of the mast where it can best be seen.

(c) A sailing vessel underway may, in addition to the lights prescribed in paragraph (a) of this Rule, exhibit at or near the top of the mast, where they can best be seen, two all-round lights in a vertical line, the upper being red and the lower green, but these lights shall not be exhibited in conjunction with the combined lantern permitted by paragraph (b) of this Rule.

(d)(i) A sailing vessel of less than 7 meters in length shall, if practicable, exhibit the lights prescribed in paragraph (a) or (b) or this Rule, but if she does not, she shall have ready at hand an electric torch or lighted lantern

*International*

showing a white light which shall be exhibited in sufficient time to prevent collision.

(ii) A vessel under oars may exhibit the lights prescribed in this Rule for sailing vessels, but if she does not, she shall have ready at hand an electric torch or lighted lantern showing a white light which shall be exhibited in sufficient time to prevent collision.

(e) A vessel proceeding under sail when also being propelled by machinery shall exhibit forward where it can best be seen a conical shape, apex downwards.

*RULE 26*
*Fishing Vessels*

(a) A vessel engaged in fishing, whether underway or at anchor, shall exhibit only the lights and shapes prescribed in this Rule.

(b) A vessel when engaged in trawling, by which is meant the dragging through the water of a dredge net or other apparatus used as a fishing appliance, shall exhibit:

(i) two all-round lights in a vertical line, the upper being green and the lower white, or a shape consisting of two cones with their apexes together in a vertical line one above the other; a vessel of less than 20 meters in length may instead of this shape exhibit a basket;

(ii) a masthead light abaft of and higher than the all-round green light; a vessel of less than 50 meters in length shall not be obliged to exhibit such a light but may do so;

(iii) when making way through the water, in addition to the lights prescribed in this paragraph, sidelights and a sternlight.

*Inland*

showing a white light which shall be exhibited in sufficient time to prevent collision.

(ii) A vessel under oars may exhibit the lights prescribed in this Rule for sailing vessels, but if she does not, she shall have ready at hand an electric torch or lighted lantern showing a white light which shall be exhibited in sufficient time to prevent collision.

(e) A vessel proceeding under sail when also being propelled by machinery shall exhibit forward where it can best be seen a conical shape, apex downward. A vessel of less than 12 meters in length is not required to exhibit this shape, but may do so.

*RULE 26*
*Fishing Vessels*

(a) A vessel engaged in fishing, whether underway or at anchor, shall exhibit only the lights and shapes prescribed in this Rule.

(b) A vessel when engaged in trawling, by which is meant the dragging through the water of a dredge net or other apparatus used as a fishing appliance, shall exhibit;

(i) two all-round lights in a vertical line, the upper being green and the lower white, or a shape consisting of two cones with their apexes together in a vertical line one above the other; a vessel of less than 20 meters in length may instead of this shape exhibit a basket;

(ii) a masthead light abaft of and higher than the all-round green light; a vessel of less than 50 meters in length shall not be obliged to exhibit such a light but may do so; and

(iii) when making way through the water, in addition to the lights prescribed in this paragraph, sidelights and a sternlight.

*International*

(c) A vessel engaged in fishing, other than trawling, shall exhibit;

(i) two all-round lights in a vertical line, the upper being red and the lower white, or a shape consisting of two cones with apexes together in a vertical line one above the other; a vessel of less than 20 meters in length may instead of this shape exhibit a basket;

(ii) when there is outlying gear extending more than 150 meters horizontally from the vessel, an all-round white light or a cone apex upwards in the direction of the gear;

(iii) when making way through the water, in addition to the lights prescribed in this paragraph, sidelights and a sternlight.

(d) A vessel engaged in fishing in close proximity to other vessels engaged in fishing may exhibit the additional signals described in Annex II to these Regulations.

(e) A vessel when not engaged in fishing shall not exhibit the lights or shapes prescribed in this Rule, but only those prescribed for a vessel of her length.

*RULE 27*
*Vessels Not Under Command or*
*Restricted in Their Ability*
*to Maneuver*

(a) A vessel not under command shall exhibit:

(i) two all-round red lights in a vertical line where they can best be seen;

(ii) two balls or similar shapes in a vertical line where they can best be seen;

(iii) when making way through the water, in addition to the lights prescribed in this paragraph, sidelights and a sternlight.

(b) A vessel restricted in her ability to maneuver, except a vessel engaged

*Inland*

(c) A vessel engaged in fishing, other than trawling, shall exhibit:

(i) two all-round lights in a vertical line, the upper being red and the lower white, or a shape consisting of two cones with apexes together in a vertical line one above the other; a vessel of less than 20 meters in length may instead of this shape exhibit a basket;

(ii) when there is outlying gear extending more than 150 meters horizontally from the vessel, an all-round white light or a cone apex upward in the direction of the gear; and

(iii) when making way through the water, in addition to the lights prescribed in this paragraph, sidelights and a sternlight.

(d) A vessel engaged in fishing in close proximity to other vessels engaged in fishing may exhibit the additional signals described in Annex II to these Rules.

(e) A vessel when not engaged in fishing shall not exhibit the lights or shapes prescribed in this Rule, but only those prescribed for a vessel of her length.

*RULE 27*
*Vessels Not Under Command*
*or Restricted in Their Ability*
*to Maneuver*

(a) A vessel not under command shall exhibit:

(i) two all-round red lights in a vertical line where they can best be seen;

(ii) two balls or similar shapes in a vertical line where they can best be seen; and

(iii) when making way through the water, in addition to the lights prescribed in this paragraph, sidelights and a sternlight.

(b) A vessel restricted in her ability to maneuver, except a vessel engaged

*International*

in mineclearance operations, shall exhibit:

(i) three all-round lights in a vertical line where they can best be seen. The highest and lowest of these lights shall be red and the middle light shall be white;

(ii) three shapes in a vertical line where they can best be seen. The highest and lowest of these shapes shall be balls and the middle one a diamond;

(iii) when making way through the water, a masthead light or lights, sidelights and a sternlight, in addition to the lights prescribed in subparagraph (i);

(iv) when at anchor, in addition to the lights or shapes prescribed in subparagraphs (i) and (ii), the light, lights or shape prescribed in Rule 30.

(c) A power-driven vessel engaged in a towing operation such as severely restricts the towing vessel and her tow in their ability to deviate from their course shall, in addition to the lights or shapes prescribed in Rule 24(a), exhibit the lights or shapes prescribed in subparagraphs (b)(i) and (ii) of this Rule.

(d) A vessel engaged in dredging or underwater operations, when restricted in her ability to maneuver, shall exhibit the lights and shapes prescribed in subparagraphs (b)(i), (ii) and (iii) of this Rule and shall in addition, when an obstruction exists, exhibit:

(i) two all-round red lights or two balls in a vertical line to indicate the side on which the obstruction exists;

(ii) two all-round green lights or two diamonds in a vertical line to indicate the side on which another vessel may pass;

(iii) when at anchor, the lights or shapes prescribed in this paragraph instead of the lights or shape prescribed in Rule 30.

*Inland*

in mineclearance operations, shall exhibit:

(i) three all-round lights in a vertical line where they can best be seen. The highest and lowest of these lights shall be red and the middle light shall be white;

(ii) three shapes in a vertical line where they can best be seen. The highest and lowest of these shapes shall be balls and the middle one a diamond;

(iii) when making way through the water, masthead lights, sidelights and a sternlight, in addition to the lights prescribed in subparagraph (b)(i); and

(iv) when at anchor, in addition to the lights or shapes prescribed in subparagraphs (b)(i) and (ii), the light, lights or shapes prescribed in Rule 30.

(c) A vessel engaged in a towing operation which severely restricts the towing vessel and her tow in their ability to deviate from their course shall, in addition to the lights or shapes prescribed in subparagraphs (b)(i) and (ii) of this Rule, exhibit the lights or shape prescribed in Rule 24.

(d) A vessel engaged in dredging or underwater operations, when restricted in her ability to maneuver, shall exhibit the lights and shapes prescribed in subparagraphs (b)(i), (ii), and (iii) of this Rule and shall in addition, when an obstruction exists, exhibit:

(i) two all-round red lights or two balls in a vertical line to indicate the side on which the obstruction exists;

(ii) two all-round green lights or two diamonds in a vertical line to indicate the side on which another vessel may pass; and

(iii) when at anchor, the lights or shape prescribed by this paragraph, instead of the lights or shapes prescribed in Rule 30 for anchored vessels.

*International*

(e) Whenever the size of a vessel engaged in diving operations makes it impracticable to exhibit all lights and shapes prescribed in paragraph (d) of this Rule, the following shall be exhibited:

(i) three all-round lights in a vertical line where they can best be seen. The highest and lowest of these lights shall be red and the middle light shall be white;

(ii) a rigid replica of the International Code flag "A" not less than 1 meter in height. Measures shall be taken to ensure its all-round visibility.

(f) a vessel engaged in mineclearance operations shall in addition to the lights prescribed for a power-driven vessel in Rule 23 or to the lights or shape prescribed for a vessel at anchor in Rule 30 as appropriate, exhibit three all-round green lights or three balls. One of these lights or shapes shall be exhibited near the foremast head and one at each end of the fore yard. These lights or shapes indicate that it is dangerous for another vessel to approach within 1000 meters of the mineclearance vessel.

(g) Vessels of less than 12 meters in length, except those engaged in diving operations, shall not be required to exhibit the lights and shapes prescribed in this Rule.

(h) The signals prescribed in this Rule are not signals of vessels in distress and requiring assistance. Such signals are contained in Annex IV to these Regulations.

*RULE 28*
*Vessels Constrained by Their Draft*

A vessel constrained by her draft may, in addition to the lights prescribed for power-driven vessels in Rule 23, exhibit where they can best be seen three

*Inland*

(e) Whenever the size of a vessel engaged in diving operations makes it impracticable to exhibit all lights and shapes prescribed in paragraph (d) of this Rule, the following shall instead be exhibited:

(i) Three all-round lights in a vertical line where they can best be seen. The highest and lowest of these lights shall be red and the middle light shall be white;

(ii) A rigid replica of the International Code flag "A" not less than 1 meter in height. Measures shall be taken to insure its all-round visibility.

(f) A vessel engaged in mineclearance operations shall in addition to the lights prescribed for a power-driven vessel in Rule 23 or to the lights or shape prescribed for a vessel at anchor in Rule 30 as appropriate, exhibit three all-round green lights or three balls. One of these lights or shapes shall be exhibited near the foremast head and one at each end of the fore yard. These lights or shapes indicate that it is dangerous for another vessel to approach within 1000 meters of the mineclearance vessel.

(g) A vessel of less than 12 meters in length, except when engaged in diving operations, is not required to exhibit the lights or shapes prescribed in this Rule.

(h) The signals prescribed in this Rule are not signals of vessels in distress and requiring assistance. Such signals are contained in Annex IV to these Rules.

*RULE 28*
*[Reserved]*

*International*

*Inland*

all-round red lights in a vertical line,
or a cylinder.

## RULE 29
*Pilot Vessels*

(a) A vessel engaged on pilotage
duty shall exhibit:

(i) at or near the masthead, two all-
round lights in a vertical line, the upper
being white and the lower red;

(ii) when underway, in addition,
sidelights and a sternlight;

(iii) when at anchor, in addition to
the lights prescribed in subparagraph
(i), the light, lights or shape prescribed
in Rule 30 for vessels at anchor.

(b) A pilot vessel when not engaged
on pilotage duty shall exhibit the lights
or shapes prescribed for a similar vessel
of her length.

## RULE 30
*Anchored Vessels and*
*Vessels Aground*

(a) A vessel at anchor shall exhibit
where it can best be seen:

(i) in the fore part, an all-round
white light or one ball;

(ii) at or near the stern and at a
lower level than the light prescribed in
subparagraph (i), an all-round white
light.

(b) A vessel of less than 50 meters in
length may exhibit an all-round white
light where it can best be seen instead
of the lights prescribed in paragraph
(a) of this Rule.

(c) A vessel at anchor may, and a
vessel of 100 meters and more in length
shall, also use the available working or
equivalent lights to illuminate her
decks.

(d) A vessel aground shall exhibit
the lights prescribed in paragraph (a)

## RULE 29
*Pilot Vessels*

(a) A vessel engaged on pilotage
duty shall exhibit:

(i) at or near the masthead, two all-
round lights in a vertical line, the upper
being white and the lower red;

(ii) when underway, in addition,
sidelights and a sternlight; and

(iii) when at anchor, in addition to
the lights prescribed in subparagraph
(i), the anchor light, lights, or shape
prescribed in Rule 30 for anchored
vessels.

(b) A pilot vessel when not engaged
on pilotage duty shall exhibit the lights
or shapes prescribed for a vessel of her
length.

## RULE 30
*Anchored Vessels and*
*Vessels Aground*

(a) A vessel at anchor shall exhibit
where it can best be seen:

(i) in the fore part, an all-round
white light or one ball; and

(ii) at or near the stern and at a
lower level than the light prescribed in
subparagraph (i), an all-round white
light.

(b) A vessel of less than 50 metres in
length may exhibit an all-round white
light where it can best be seen instead
of the lights prescribed in paragraph
(a) of this Rule.

(c) A vessel at anchor may, and a
vessel of 100 metres or more in length
shall, also use the available working or
equivalent lights to illuminate her
decks.

(d) A vessel aground shall exhibit
the lights prescribed in paragraph (a)

*International*

or (b) of this Rule and in addition, where they can best be seen:
  (i) two all-round red lights in a vertical line;
  (ii) three balls in a vertical line.

(e) A vessel of less than 7 meters in length, when at anchor, not in or near a narrow channel, fairway, or anchorage, or where other vessels normally navigate, shall not be required to exhibit the lights or shape prescribed in paragraphs (a) and (b) of this Rule.

(f) A vessel of less than 12 meters in length, when aground, shall not be required to exhibit the lights or shapes prescribed in subparagraphs (d)(i) and (ii) of this Rule.

*RULE 31*
*Seaplanes*

Where it is impracticable for a seaplane to exhibit lights and shapes of the characteristics or in the positions prescribed in the Rules of this Part she shall exhibit lights and shapes as closely similar in characteristics and position as is possible.

**PART D—SOUND AND LIGHT SIGNALS**

*RULE 32*
*Definitions*

(a) The word "whistle" means any sound signaling appliance capable of producing the prescribed blasts and which complies with the specifications in Annex III to these Regulations.

*Inland*

or (b) of this Rule and in addition, if practicable, where they can best be seen:
  (i) two all-round red lights in a vertical line; and
  (ii) three balls in a vertical line.

(e) A vessel of less than 7 metres in length, when at anchor, not in or near a narrow channel, fairway, anchorage, or where other vessels normally navigate, shall not be required to exhibit the lights or shape prescribed in paragraphs (a) and (b) of this Rule.

(f) A vessel of less than 12 metres in length when aground shall not be required to exhibit the lights or shapes prescribed in subparagraphs (d)(i) and (ii) of this Rule.

(g) A vessel of less than 20 metres in length, when at anchor in a special anchorage area designated by the Secretary, shall not be required to exhibit the anchor lights and shapes required by this Rule.

*RULE 31*
*Seaplanes*

Where it is impracticable for a seaplane to exhibit lights and shapes of the characteristics or in the positions prescribed in the Rules of this Part she shall exhibit lights and shapes as closely similar in characteristics and position as is possible.

**PART D—SOUND AND LIGHT SIGNALS**

*RULE 32*
*Definitions*

(a) The word "whistle" means any sound signaling appliance capable of producing the prescribed blasts and which complies with the specifications in Annex III to these Rules.

*International*

(b) The term "short blast" means a blast of about one second's duration.

(c) The term "prolonged blast" means a blast of from four to six seconds' duration.

## RULE 33
### Equipment for Sound Signals

(a) A vessel of 12 meters or more in length shall be provided with a whistle and a bell and a vessel of 100 meters or more in length shall, in addition, be provided with a gong, the tone and sound of which cannot be confused with that of the bell. The whistle, bell and gong shall comply with the specifications in Annex III to these Regulations. The bell or gong or both may be replaced by other equipment having the same respective sound characteristics, provided that manual sounding of the prescribed signals shall always be possible.

(b) A vessel of less than 12 meters in length shall not be obliged to carry the sound signalling appliances prescribed in paragraph (a) of this Rule but if she does not, she shall be provided with some other means of making an efficient sound signal.

## RULE 34
### Maneuvering and Warning Signals

(a) When vessels are in sight of one another, a power-driven vessel underway, when maneuvering as authorized or required by these Rules, shall indicate that maneuver by the following signals on her whistle:

—one short blast to mean "I am altering my course to starboard";

—two short blasts to mean "I am altering my course to port";

—three short blasts to mean "I am operating astern propulsion".

*Inland*

(b) The term "short blast" means a blast of about 1 second's duration.

(c) The term "prolonged blast" means a blast of from 4 to 6 seconds' duration.

## RULE 33
### Equipment for Sound Signals

(a) A vessel of 12 meters or more in length shall be provided with a whistle and a bell and a vessel of 100 meters or more in length shall, in addition, be provided with a gong, the tone and sound of which cannot be confused with that of the bell. The whistle, bell and gong shall comply with the specifications in Annex III to these Rules. The bell or gong or both may be replaced by other equipment having the same respective sound characteristics, provided that manual sounding of the prescribed signals shall always be possible.

(b) A vessel of less than 12 meters in length shall not be obliged to carry the sound signaling appliances prescribed in paragraph (a) of this Rule but if she does not, she shall be provided with some other means of making an efficient sound signal.

## RULE 34
### Maneuvering and Warning Signals

(a) When power-driven vessels are in sight of one another and meeting or crossing at a distance within half a mile of each other, each vessel underway, when maneuvering as authorized or required by these Rules:

(i) shall indicate that maneuver by the following signals on her whistle: one short blast to mean "I intend to leave you on my port side"; two short blasts to mean "I intend to leave you on my starboard side"; and three short

*International*

*Inland*

blasts to mean "I am operating astern propulsion".

(ii) upon hearing the one or two blast signal of the other shall, if in agreement, sound the same whistle signal and take the steps necessary to effect a safe passing. If, however, from any cause, the vessel doubts the safety of the proposed maneuver, she shall sound the danger signal specified in paragraph (d) of this Rule and each vessel shall take appropriate precautionary action until a safe passing agreement is made.

(b) Any vessel may supplement the whistle signals prescribed in paragraph (a) of this Rule by light signals, repeated as appropriate, whilst the maneuver is being carried out:

(i) these light signals shall have the following significance;

—one flash to mean "I am altering my course to starboard";

—two flashes to mean "I am altering my course to port";

—three flashes to mean "I am operating astern propulsion";

(ii) the duration of each flash shall be about one second, the interval between flashes shall be about one second, and the interval between successive signals shall be not less than ten seconds;

(iii) the light used for this signal shall, if fitted, be an all-round white light, visible at a minimum range of 5 miles, and shall comply with the provisions of Annex I to these Regulations.

(b) A vessel may supplement the whistle signals prescribed in paragraph (a) of this Rule by light signals:

(i) These signals shall have the following significance: one flash to mean "I intend to leave you on my port side"; two flashes to mean "I intend to leave you on my starboard side"; three flashes to mean "I am operating astern propulsion";

(ii) The duration of each flash shall be about 1 second; and

(iii) The light used for this signal shall, if fitted, be one all-round white or yellow light, visible at a minimum range of 2 miles, synchronized with the whistle, and shall comply with the provisions of Annex I to these Rules.

(c) When in sight of one another in a narrow channel or fairway:

(i) a vessel intending to overtake another shall in compliance with Rule 9(e)(i) indicate her intention by the following signals on her whistle:

(c) When in sight of one another:

(i) a power-driven vessel intending to overtake another power-driven vessel shall indicate her intention by the following signals on her whistle: one

*International*

—two prolonged blasts followed by one short blast to mean "I intend to overtake you on your starboard side";

—two prolonged blasts followed by two short blasts to mean "I intend to overtake you on your port side".

(ii) the vessel about to be overtaken when acting in accordance with Rule 9(e)(i) shall indicate her agreement by the following signal on her whistle:

—one prolonged, one short, one prolonged and one short blast, in that order.

(d) When vessels in sight of one another are approaching each other and from any cause either vessel fails to understand the intentions or actions of the other, or is in doubt whether sufficient action is being taken by the other to avoid collision, the vessel in doubt shall immediately indicate such doubt by giving at least five short and rapid blasts on the whistle. Such signal may be supplemented by a light signal of at least five short and rapid flashes.

(e) A vessel nearing a bend or an area of a channel or fairway where other vessels may be obscured by an intervening obstruction shall sound one prolonged blast. Such signal shall be answered with a prolonged blast by any approaching vessel that may be within hearing around the bend or behind the intervening obstruction.

(f) If whistles are fitted on a vessel at a distance apart of more than 100 meters, one whistle only shall be used for giving maneuvering and warning signals.

*Inland*

short blast to mean "I intend to overtake you on your starboard side"; two short blasts to mean "I intend to overtake you on your port side"; and

(ii) the power-driven vessel about to be overtaken shall, if in agreement, sound a similar sound signal. If in doubt she shall sound the danger signal prescribed in paragraph (d).

(d) When vessels in sight of one another are approaching each other and from any cause either vessel fails to understand the intentions or actions of the other, or is in doubt whether sufficient action is being taken by the other to avoid collision, the vessel in doubt shall immediately indicate such doubt by giving at least five short and rapid blasts on the whistle. This signal may be supplemented by a light signal of at least five short and rapid flashes.

(e) A vessel nearing a bend or an area of a channel or fairway where other vessels may be obscured by an intervening obstruction shall sound one prolonged blast. This signal shall be answered with a prolonged blast by any approaching vessel that may be within hearing around the bend or behind the intervening obstruction.

(f) If whistles are fitted on a vessel at a distance apart of more than 100 meters, one whistle only shall be used for giving maneuvering and warning signals.

(g) When a power-driven vessel is leaving a dock or berth, she shall sound one prolonged blast.

(h) A vessel that reaches agreement with another vessel in a meeting, crossing, or overtaking situation by using

*International*

*Inland*

the radiotelephone as prescribed by the Bridge-to-Bridge Radiotelephone Act (85 Stat. 165; 33 U.S.C. 1207), is not obliged to sound the whistle signals prescribed by this Rule, but may do so. If agreement is not reached, then whistle signals shall be exchanged in a timely manner and shall prevail.

*RULE 35*
*Sound Signals in Restricted Visibility*

In or near an area of restricted visibility, whether by day or night, the signals prescribed in this Rule shall be used as follows:

(a) A power-driven vessel making way through the water shall sound at intervals of not more than 2 minutes one prolonged blast.

(b) A power-driven vessel underway but stopped and making no way through the water shall sound at intervals of not more than 2 minutes two prolonged blasts in succession with an interval of about 2 seconds between them.

(c) A vessel not under command, a vessel restricted in her ability to maneuver, a vessel constrained by her draft, a sailing vessel, a vessel engaged in fishing and a vessel engaged in towing or pushing another vessel shall, instead of the signals prescribed in paragraphs (a) or (b) of this Rule, sound at intervals of not more than 2 minutes three blasts in succession, namely one prolonged followed by two short blasts.

(d) A vessel engaged in fishing, when at anchor, and a vessel restricted in her ability to maneuver when carrying out her work at anchor, shall instead of the signals prescribed in paragraph (g) of this Rule sound the

*RULE 35*
*Sound Signals in Restricted Visibility*

In or near an area of restricted visibility, whether by day or night, the signals prescribed in this Rule shall be used as follows:

(a) A power-driven vessel making way through the water shall sound at intervals of not more than 2 minutes one prolonged blast.

(b) A power-driven vessel underway but stopped and making no way through the water shall sound at intervals of not more than 2 minutes two prolonged blasts in succession with an interval of about 2 seconds between them.

(c) A vessel not under command; a vessel restricted in her ability to maneuver, whether underway or at anchor; a sailing vessel; a vessel engaged in fishing, whether underway or at anchor; and a vessel engaged in towing or pushing another vessel shall, instead of the signals prescribed in paragraphs (a) or (b) of this Rule, sound at intervals of not more than 2 minutes, three blasts in succession; namely, one prolonged followed by two short blasts.

(d) A vessel towed or if more than one vessel is towed the last vessel of the tow, if manned, shall at intervals of not more than 2 minutes sound four blasts in succession; namely, one prolonged followed by three short blasts. When

*International*

signal prescribed in paragraph (c) of this Rule.

(e) A vessel towed or if more than one vessel is towed the last vessel of the tow, if manned, shall at intervals of not more than 2 minutes sound four blasts in succession, namely one prolonged followed by three short blasts. When practicable, this signal shall be made immediately after the signal made by the towing vessel.

(f) When a pushing vessel and a vessel being pushed ahead are rigidly connected in a composite unit they shall be regarded as a power-driven vessel and shall give the signals prescribed in paragraphs (a) or (b) of this Rule.

(g) A vessel at anchor shall at intervals of not more than one minute ring the bell rapidly for about 5 seconds. In a vessel of 100 meters or more in length the bell shall be sounded in the forepart of the vessel and immediately after the ringing of the bell the gong shall be sounded rapidly for about 5 seconds in the after part of the vessel. A vessel at anchor may in addition sound three blasts in succession, namely one short, one prolonged and one short blast, to give warning of her position and of the possibility of collision to an approaching vessel.

(h) A vessel aground shall give the bell signal and if required the gong signal prescribed in paragraph (g) of this

*Inland*

practicable, this signal shall be made immediately after the signal made by the towing vessel.

(e) When a pushing vessel and a vessel being pushed ahead are rigidly connected in a composite unit they shall be regarded as a power-driven vessel and shall give the signals prescribed in paragraphs (a) or (b) of this Rule.

(f) A vessel at anchor shall at intervals of not more than 1 minute ring the bell rapidly for about 5 seconds. In a vessel of 100 meters or more in length the bell shall be sounded in the forepart of the vessel and immediately after the ringing of the bell the gong shall be sounded rapidly for about 5 seconds in the after part of the vessel. A vessel at anchor may in addition sound three blasts in succession; namely, one short, one prolonged and one short blast, to give warning of her position and of the possibility of collision to an approaching vessel.

(g) A vessel aground shall give the bell signal and if required the gong signal prescribed in paragraph (f) of this Rule and shall, in addition, give three separate and distinct strokes on the bell immediately before and after the rapid ringing of the bell. A vessel aground may in addition sound an appropriate whistle signal.

(h) A vessel of less than 12 meters in length shall not be obliged to give the above-mentioned signals but, if she

*International*

Rule and shall, in addition, give three separate and distinct strokes on the bell immediately before and after the rapid ringing of the bell. A vessel aground may in addition sound an appropriate whistle signal.

(i) A vessel of less than 12 meters in length shall not be obliged to give the above-mentioned signals but, if she does not, shall make some other efficient sound signal at intervals of not more than 2 minutes.

(j) A pilot vessel when engaged on pilotage duty may in addition to the signals prescribed in paragraphs (a), (b) or (g) of this Rule sound an identity signal consisting of four short blasts.

*Inland*

does not, shall make some other efficient sound signal at intervals of not more than 2 minutes.

(i) A pilot vessel when engaged on pilotage duty may in addition to the signals prescribed in paragraphs (a), (b) or (f) of this Rule sound an identity signal consisting of four short blasts.

(j) The following vessels shall not be required to sound signals as prescribed in paragraph (f) of this Rule when anchored in a special anchorage area designated by the Secretary:

(i) a vessel of less than 20 meters in length; and

(ii) a barge, canal boat, scow, or other nondescript craft.

## RULE 36
### Signals to Attract Attention

If necessary to attract the attention of another vessel, any vessel may make light or sound signals that cannot be mistaken for any signal authorized elsewhere in these Rules, or may direct the beam of her searchlight in the direction of the danger, in such a way as not to embarrass any vessel. Any light to attract the attention of another vessel shall be such that it cannot be mistaken for any aid to navigation. For the purpose of this Rule the use of high intensity intermittent or revolving lights, such as strobe lights, shall be avoided.

## RULE 36
### Signals to Attract Attention

If necessary to attract the attention of another vessel, any vessel may make light or sound signals that cannot be mistaken for any signal authorized elsewhere in these Rules, or may direct the beam of her searchlight in the direction of the danger, in such a way as not to embarrass any vessel.

## RULE 37
### Distress Signals

When a vessel is in distress and requires assistance she shall use or exhibit the signals described in Annex IV to these Regulations.

## RULE 37
### Distress Signals

When a vessel is in distress and requires assistance she shall use or exhibit the signals described in Annex IV to these Rules.

*International*

**PART E—EXEMPTIONS**

*RULE 38*

*Exemptions*

Any vessel (or class of vessels) provided that she complies with the requirements of the International Regulations for Preventing Collisions at Sea, 1960, the keel of which is laid or which is at a corresponding stage of construction before the entry into force of these Regulations may be exempted from compliance therewith as follows:

(a) The installation of lights with ranges prescribed in Rule 22, until four years after the date of entry into force of these Regulations.

(b) The installation of lights with color specifications as prescribed in Section 7 of Annex I to these Regulations, until four years after the date of entry into force of these Regulations.

(c) The repositioning of lights as a result of conversion from imperial to metric units and rounding off measurement figures, permanent exemption.

*Inland*

**PART E—EXEMPTIONS**

*RULE 38*

*Exemptions*

Any vessel or class of vessels, the keel of which is laid or which is at a corresponding stage of construction before the date of enactment of this Act, provided that she complies with the requirements of—

(a) The Act of June 7, 1897 (30 Stat. 96), as amended (33 U.S.C. 154–232) for vessels navigating the waters subject to that statute;

(b) Section 4233 of the Revised Statutes (33 U.S.C. 301–356) for vessels navigating the waters subject to that statute;

(c) The Act of February 8, 1895 (28 Stat. 645), as amended (33 U.S.C. 241–295) for vessels navigating the waters subject to that statute; or

(d) Sections 3, 4, and 5 of the Act of April 25, 1940 (54 Stat. 163), as amended (46 U.S.C. 526 b, c, and d) for motorboats navigating the waters subject to that statute; shall be exempted from compliance with the technical Annexes to these Rules as follows;

(i) the installation of lights with ranges prescribed in Rule 22, until 4 years after the effective date of these Rules, except that vessels of less than 20 meters in length are permanently exempt;

(ii) the installation of lights with color specifications as prescribed in Annex I to these Rules, until 4 years after the effective date of these Rules, except that vessels of less than 20 meters in length are permanently exempt;

(iii) the repositioning of lights as a result of conversion to metric units and rounding off measurement figures are permanently exempt; and

*International*

(d)(i) The repositioning of masthead lights on vessels of less than 150 meters in length, resulting from the prescriptions of Section 3(a) of Annex I to these Regulations, permanent exemption.

(ii) The repositioning of masthead lights on vessels of 150 meters or more in length, resulting from the prescriptions of Section 3(a) of Annex I to these Regulations, until 9 years after the date of entry into force of these Regulations.

(e) The repositioning of masthead lights resulting from the prescriptions of Section 2(b) of Annex I to these Regulations, until 9 years after the date of entry into force of these Regulations.

(f) The repositioning of sidelights resulting from the prescriptions of Sections 2(g) and 3(b) of Annex I to these Regulations, until 9 years after the date of entry into force of these Regulations.

(g) The requirements for sound signal appliances prescribed in Annex III to these Regulations, until 9 years after the date of entry into force of these Regulations.

(h) The repositioning of all-round lights resulting from the prescription of Section 9(b) of Annex I to these Regulations, permanent exemption.

*ANNEX I*
*Positioning and Technical Details of Lights and Shapes*

**1. Definition**
The term "height above the hull" means height above the uppermost continuous deck. This height shall be measured from the position vertically beneath the location of the light.

*Inland*

(iv) the horizontal repositioning of masthead lights prescribed by Annex I to these Rules:
(1) on vessels of less than 150 meters in length, permanent exemption.
(2) on vessels of 150 meters or more in length, until 9 years after the effective date of these Rules.

(v) the restructuring or repositioning of all lights to meet the prescriptions of Annex I to these Rules, until 9 years after the effective date of these Rules;

(vi) power-driven vessels of 12 meters or more but less than 20 meters in length are permanently exempt from the provisions of Rule 23(a)(i) and 23 (a)(iv) provided that, in place of these lights, the vessel exhibits a white light aft visible all round the horizon; and

(vii) the requirements for sound signal appliances prescribed in Annex III to these Rules, until 9 years after the effective date of these Rules.

*ANNEX I*
*Positioning and Technical Details of Lights and Shapes*

**§ 84.01 Definitions.**
(a) The term "height above the hull" means height above the uppermost continuous deck. This height shall be measured from the position vertically beneath the location of the light.

(b) The term "practical cut-off" means, for vessels 20 meters or more in length, 12.5 percent of the minimum

*International*

*Inland*

luminous intensity (Table 84.15(b)) corresponding to the greatest range of visibility for which the requirements of Annex I are met.

(c) The term "Rule" or "Rules" means the Inland Navigation Rules contained in Sec. 2 of the Inland Navigational Rules Act of 1980 (Pub. L. 96–591, 94 Stat. 3415, 33 U.S.C. 2001, December 24, 1980) as amended.

**2. Vertical positioning and spacing of lights**

(a) On a power-driven vessel of 20 meters or more in length the masthead lights shall be placed as follows:

(i) the forward masthead light, or if only one masthead light is carried, then that light, at a height above the hull of not less than 6 meters, and, if the breadth of the vessel exceeds 6 meters, then at a height above the hull not less than such breadth, so however that the light need not be placed at a greater height above the hull than 12 meters;

(ii) when two masthead lights are carried the after one shall be at least 4.5 meters vertically higher than the forward one.

(b) The vertical separation of masthead lights of power-driven vessels shall be such that in all normal conditions of trim the after light will be seen over and separate from the forward light at a distance of 1000 meters from the stem when viewed from sea level.

(c) The masthead light of a power-driven vessel of 12 meters but less than 20 meters in length shall be placed at a height above the gunwale of not less than 2.5 meters.

(d) A power-driven vessel of less than 12 meters in length may carry the uppermost light at a height of less than 2.5 meters above the gunwale. When however a masthead light is carried in

**§ 84.03 Vertical positioning and spacing of lights.**

(a) On a power-driven vessel of 20 meters or more in length the masthead lights shall be placed as follows:

(1) The forward masthead light, or if only one masthead light is carried, then that light, at a height above the hull of not less than 5 meters, and, if the breadth of the vessel exceeds 5 meters, then at a height above the hull not less than such breadth, so however that the light need not be placed at a greater height above the hull than 8 meters;

(2) When two masthead lights are carried the after one shall be at least 2 meters vertically higher than the forward one.

(b) The vertical separation of masthead lights of power-driven vessels shall be such that in all normal conditions of trim the after light will be seen over and separate from the forward light at a distance of 1000 meters from the stem when viewed from water level.

(c) The masthead light of a power-driven vessel of 12 meters but less than 20 meters in length shall be placed at a height above the gunwale of not less than 2.5 meters.

(d) The masthead light, or the all-round light described in Rule 23(c), of a power-driven vessel of less than 12 meters in length shall be carried at least one meter higher than the sidelights.

*International*

addition to sidelights and a sternlight or the all-round light prescribed in rule 23(c)(i) is carried in addition to sidelights, then such masthead light or all-round light shall be carried at least 1 meter higher than the sidelights.

(e) One of the two or three masthead lights prescribed for a power-driven vessel when engaged in towing or pushing another vessel shall be placed in the same position as either the forward masthead light or the after masthead light; provided that, if carried on the aftermast, the lowest after masthead light shall be at least 4.5 meters vertically higher than the forward masthead light.

(f)(i) The masthead light or lights prescribed in Rule 23(a) shall be so placed as to be above and clear of all other lights and obstructions except as described in subparagraph (ii).

(ii) When it is impracticable to carry the all-round lights prescribed by Rule 27(b)(i) or Rule 28 below the masthead lights, they may be carried above the after masthead light(s) or vertically in between the forward masthead light(s) and after masthead light(s), provided that in the latter case the requirement of Section 3(c) of this Annex shall be complied with.

(g) The sidelights of a power-driven vessel shall be placed at a height above the hull not greater than three quarters of that of the forward masthead light. They shall not be so low as to be interfered with by deck lights.

(h) The sidelights, if in a combined lantern and carried on a power-driven vessel of less than 20 meters in length, shall be placed not less than 1 meter below the masthead light.

*Inland*

(e) One of the two or three masthead lights prescribed for a power-driven vessel when engaged in towing or pushing another vessel shall be placed in the same position as either the forward masthead light or the after masthead light, provided that the lowest after masthead light shall be at least 2 meters vertically higher than the highest forward masthead light.

(f)(1) The masthead light or lights prescribed in Rule 23(a) shall be so placed as to be above and clear of all other lights and obstructions except as described in paragraph (f)(2) of this section.

(2) When it is impracticable to carry the all-round lights prescribed in Rule 27(b)(i) below the masthead lights, they may be carried above the after masthead light(s) or vertically in between the forward masthead light(s) and after masthead light(s), provided that in the latter case the requirement of § 84.05(d) shall be complied with.

(g) The sidelights of a power-driven vessel shall be placed at least one meter lower than the forward masthead light. They shall not be so low as to be interfered with by deck lights.

(h) [Reserved]

*International*

(i) When the Rules prescribe two or three lights to be carried in a vertical line, they shall be spaced as follows:

(i) on a vessel of 20 meters in length or more such lights shall be spaced not less than 2 meters apart, and the lowest of these lights shall, except where a towing light is required, be placed at a height of not less than 4 meters above the hull;

(ii) on a vessel of less than 20 meters in length such lights shall be spaced not less than 1 meter apart and the lowest of these lights shall, except where a towing light is required, be placed at a height of not less than 2 meters above the gunwale;

(iii) when three lights are carried they shall be equally spaced.

(j) The lower of the two all-round lights prescribed for a vessel when engaged in fishing shall be at a height above the sidelights not less than twice the distance between the two vertical lights.

(k) The forward anchor light prescribed in Rule 30(a)(i), when two are carried, shall not be less than 4.5 meters above the after one. On a vessel of 50 meters or more in length this forward anchor light shall be placed at a height of not less than 6 meters above the hull.

**3. Horizontal positioning and spacing of lights**

(a) When two masthead lights are prescribed for a power-driven vessel, the horizontal distance between them shall not be less than one half of the length of the vessel but need not be more than 100 meters. The forward light shall be placed not more than one quarter of the length of the vessel from the stem.

*Inland*

(i) When the Rules prescribe two or three lights to be carried in a vertical line, they shall be spaced as follows:

(1) On a vessel of 20 meters in length or more such lights shall be spaced not less than 1 meter apart, and the lowest of these lights shall, except where a towing light is required, be placed at a height of not less than 4 meters above the hull;

(2) On a vessel of less than 20 meters in length such lights shall be spaced not less than 1 meter apart and the lowest of these lights shall, except where a towing light is required, be placed at a height of not less than 2 meters above the gunwale;

(3) When three lights are carried they shall be equally spaced.

(j) The lower of the two all-round lights prescribed for a vessel when engaged in fishing shall be at a height above the sidelights not less than twice the distance between the two vertical lights.

(k) The forward anchor light prescribed in Rule 30(a)(i), when two are carried, shall not be less than 4.5 meters above the after one. On a vessel of 50 meters or more in length this forward anchor light shall be placed at a height of not less than 6 meters above the hull.

**§ 84.05 Horizontal positioning and spacing of lights**

(a) Except as specified in paragraph (b) of this section, when two masthead lights are prescribed for a power-driven vessel, the horizontal distance between them shall not be less than one quarter of the length of the vessel but need not be more than 50 meters. The forward light shall be placed not more than one half of the length of the vessel from the stem.

*International*

*Inland*

(b) On power-driven vessels 50 meters but less than 60 meters in length operated on the Western Rivers, and those waters specified in §89.25, the horizontal distance between masthead lights shall not be less than 10 meters.

(b) On a power-driven vessel of 20 meters or more in length the sidelights shall not be placed in front of the forward masthead lights. They shall be placed at or near the side of the vessel.

(c) On a power-driven vessel of 20 meters or more in length the sidelights shall not be placed in front of the forward masthead lights. They shall be placed at or near the side of the vessel.

(c) When the lights prescribed in Rule 27(b)(i) or Rule 28 are placed vertically between the forward masthead light(s) and the after masthead light(s) these all-round lights shall be placed at a horizontal distance of not less than 2 meters from the fore and aft centerline of the vessel in the athwartship direction.

(d) When the lights prescribed in Rule 27(b)(i) are placed vertically between the forward masthead light(s) and the after masthead light(s) these all-round lights shall be placed at a horizontal distance of not less than 2 meters from the fore and aft centerline of the vessel in the athwartship direction.

**4. Details of location of direction-indicating lights for fishing vessels, dredgers and vessels engaged in underwater operations**

**§ 84.07 Details of location of direction-indicating lights for fishing vessels, dredgers and vessels engaged in underwater operations**

(a) The light indicating the direction of the outlying gear from a vessel engaged in fishing as prescribed in Rule 26(c)(ii) shall be placed at a horizontal distance of not less than 2 meters and not more than 6 meters away from the two all-round red and white lights. This light shall be placed not higher than the all-round white light prescribed in Rule 26(c)(i) and not lower than the sidelights.

(a) The light indicating the direction of the outlying gear from a vessel engaged in fishing as prescribed in Rule 26(c)(ii) shall be placed at a horizontal distance of not less than 2 meters and not more than 6 meters away from the two all-round red and white lights. This light shall be placed not higher than the all-round white light prescribed in Rule 26(c)(i) and not lower than the sidelights.

(b) The lights and shapes on a vessel engaged in dredging or underwater operations to indicate the obstructed side and/or the side on which it is safe to pass, as prescribed in Rule 27(d)(i) and (ii), shall be placed at the maximum practical horizontal distance, but in no case less than 2 meters, from the lights or shapes prescribed in Rule 27(b)(i)

(b) The lights and shapes on a vessel engaged in dredging or underwater operations to indicate the obstructed side and/or the side on which it is safe to pass, as prescribed in Rule 27(d)(i) and (ii), shall be placed at the maximum practical horizontal distance, but in no case less than 2 meters, from the lights or shapes prescribed in Rule 27(b)(i)

*International*

*Inland*

and (ii). In no case shall the upper of these lights or shapes be at a greater height than the lower of the three lights or shapes prescribed in Rule 27(b)(i) and (ii).

**5. Screens for sidelights**

The sidelights of vessels of 20 meters or more in length shall be fitted with inboard screens painted matt black, and meeting the requirements of Section 9 of this Annex. On vessels of less than 20 meters in length the sidelights, if necessary to meet the requirements of Section 9 of this Annex, shall be fitted with inboard matt black screens. With a combined lantern, using a single vertical filament and a very narrow division between the green and red sections, external screens need not be fitted.

**6. Shapes**

(a) Shapes shall be black and of the following sizes:

(i) a ball shall have a diameter of not less than 0.6 meter;

(ii) a cone shall have a base diameter of not less than 0.6 meter and a height equal to its diameter;

(iii) a cylinder shall have a diameter of at least 0.6 meter and a height of twice its diameter;

(iv) a diamond shape shall consist of two cones as defined in (ii) above having a common base.

(b) The vertical distance between shapes shall be at least 1.5 meter.

(c) In a vessel of less than 20 meters in length shapes of lesser dimensions but commensurate with the size of the

and (ii). In no case shall the upper of these lights or shapes be at a greater height than the lower of the three lights or shapes prescribed in Rule 27(b)(i) and (ii).

**§ 84.09 Screens**

(a) The sidelights of vessels of 20 meters or more in length shall be fitted with mat black inboard screens and meet the requirements of § 84.17. On vessels of less than 20 meters in length, the sidelights, if necessary to meet the requirements of § 84.17, shall be fitted with mat black inboard screens. With a combined lantern, using a single vertical filament and a very narrow division between the green and red sections, external screens need not be fitted.

(b) On power-driven vessels less than 12 meters in length constructed after July 31, 1983, the masthead light, or the all round light described in Rule 23(c) shall be screened to prevent direct illumination of the vessel forward of the operator's position.

**§ 84.11 Shapes**

(a) Shapes shall be black and of the following sizes:

(1) A ball shall have a diameter of not less than 0.6 meter;

(2) A cone shall have a base diameter of not less than 0.6 meter and a height equal to its diameter;

(3) A diamond shape shall consist of two cones (as defined in Paragraph (a)(2) of this section) having a common base.

(b) The vertical distance between shapes shall be at least 1.5 meter.

(c) In a vessel of less than 20 meters in length shapes of lesser dimensions but commensurate with the size of the

*International*

vessel may be used and the distance apart may be correspondingly reduced.

### 7. Color specification of lights

The chromaticity of all navigation lights shall conform to the following standards, which lie within the boundaries of the area of the diagram specified for each color by the International Commission on Illumination (CIE).

The boundaries of the area for each color are given by indicating the corner coordinates, which are as follows:

(i)  *White:*
    x  0.525  0.525  0.452  0.310  0.310  0.443
    y  0.382  0.440  0.440  0.348  0.283  0.382

(ii)  *Green:*
    x  0.028  0.009  0.300  0.203
    y  0.385  0.723  0.511  0.356

(iii)  *Red:*
    x  0.680  0.660  0.735  0.721
    y  0.320  0.320  0.265  0.259

(iv)  *Yellow:*
    x  0.612  0.618  0.575  0.575
    y  0.382  0.382  0.425  0.406

### 8. Intensity of lights

(a) The minimum luminous intensity of lights shall be calculated by using the formula:

$$I = 3.43 \times 10^6 \times T \times D^2 \times K^{-D}$$

where I is luminous intensity in candelas under service conditions,

T is threshold factor $2 \times 10^{-7}$ lux,

D is range of visibility (luminous range) of the light in nautical miles,

*Inland*

vessel may be used and the distance apart may be correspondingly reduced.

### § 84.13 Color specification of lights

(a) The chromaticity of all navigation lights shall conform to the following standards, which lie within the boundaries of the area of the diagram specified for each color by the International Commission on Illumination (CIE), in the "Colors of Light Signals", which is incorporated by reference. It is Publication CIE No. 2.2. (TC–1.6), 1975, and is available from the Illumination Engineering Society, 345 East 47th Street, New York, NY 10017. It is also available for inspection at the Office of the Federal Register, Room 8401, 1100 L Street N.W., Washington, D.C. 20408. This incorporation by reference was approved by the Director of the Federal Register.

(b) The boundaries of the area for each color are given by indicating the corner coordinates, which are as follows:

(1)  *White:*
    x  0.525  0.525  0.452  0.310  0.310  0.443
    y  0.382  0.440  0.440  0.348  0.283  0.382

(2)  *Green:*
    x  0.028  0.009  0.300  0.203
    y  0.385  0.723  0.511  0.356

(3)  *Red:*
    x  0.680  0.660  0.735  0.721
    y  0.320  0.320  0.265  0.259

(4)  *Yellow:*
    x  0.612  0.618  0.575  0.575
    y  0.382  0.382  0.425  0.406

### § 84.15 Intensity of lights

(a) The minimum luminous intensity of lights shall be calculated by using the formula:

$$I = 3.43 \times 10^6 \times T \times D^2 \times K^{-D}$$

where I is luminous intensity in candelas under service conditions,

T is threshold factor $2 \times 10^{-7}$ lux,

D is range of visibility (luminous range) of the light in nautical miles,

*International*

K is atmospheric transmissivity. For prescribed lights the value of K shall be 0.8, corresponding to a meteorological visibility of approximately 13 nautical miles.

(b) A selection of figures derived from the formula is given in the following table:

| Range of visibility (luminous range) of light in nautical miles D | Luminous intensity of light in candelas for K = I 0.8 |
|---|---|
| 1 | 0.9 |
| 2 | 4.3 |
| 3 | 12 |
| 4 | 27 |
| 5 | 52 |
| 6 | 94 |

*Note:* The maximum luminous intensity of navigation lights should be limited to avoid undue glare. This shall not be achieved by a variable control of the luminous intensity.

**9. Horizontal sectors**

(a)(i) In the forward direction, side-lights as fitted on the vessel shall show the minimum required intensities. The intensities shall decrease to reach practical cut-off between 1 degree and 3 degrees outside the prescribed sectors.

(ii) For sternlights and masthead lights and at 22.5 degrees abaft the beam for sidelights, the minimum required intensities shall be maintained over the arc of the horizon up to 5 degrees within the limits of the sectors prescribed in Rule 21. From 5 degrees within the prescribed sectors the intensity may decrease by 50 percent up to the prescribed limits; it shall decrease steadily to reach practical cut-off at not

*Inland*

K is atmospheric transmissivity. For prescribed lights the value of K shall be 0.8, corresponding to a meteorological visibility of approximately 13 nautical miles.

(b) A selection of figures derived from the formula is given in Table 84.15(b).

Table 84.15(b)

| Range of visibility (luminous range) of light in nautical miles D | Minimum luminous intensity of light in candelas for K = 0.8 I |
|---|---|
| 1 | 0.9 |
| 2 | 4.3 |
| 3 | 12 |
| 4 | 27 |
| 5 | 52 |
| 6 | 94 |

**§ 84.17 Horizontal sectors**

(a)(1) In the forward direction, side-lights as fitted on the vessel shall show the minimum required intensities. The intensities shall decrease to reach practical cut-off between 1 and 3 degrees outside the prescribed sectors.

(2) For sternlights and masthead lights and at 22.5 degrees abaft the beam for sidelights, the minimum required intensities shall be maintained over the arc of the horizon up to 5 degrees within the limits of the sectors prescribed in Rule 21. From 5 degreees within the prescribed sectors the intensity may decrease by 50 percent up to the prescribed limits; it shall decrease steadily to reach practical cut-off at not

*International*

more than 5 degrees outside the pre-scribed sectors.

(b) All-round lights shall be so lo-cated as not to be obscured by masts, topmasts or structures within angular sectors of more than 6 degrees, except anchor lights prescribed in Rule 30, which need not be placed at an imprac-ticable height above the hull.

**10. Vertical sectors**

(a) The vertical sectors of electric lights as fitted, with the exception of lights on sailing vessels underway shall ensure that:

(i) at least the required minimum intensity is maintained at all angles from 5 degrees above to 5 degrees be-low the horizontal;

(ii) at least 60 percent of the re-quired minimum intensity is main-tained from 7.5 degrees above to 7.5 degrees below the horizontal.

(b) In the case of sailing vessels un-derway the vertical sectors of electric lights as fitted shall ensure that:

(i) at least the required minimum intensity is maintained at all angles from 5 degrees above to 5 degrees be-low the horizontal;

(ii) at least 50 percent of the re-quired minimum intensity is main-tained from 25 degrees above to 25 de-grees below the horizontal.

(c) In the case of lights other than electric these specifications shall be met as closely as possible.

*Inland*

more than 5 degrees outside the pre-scribed sectors.

(b) All-round lights shall be so lo-cated as not to be obscured by masts, topmasts or structures within angular sectors of more than 6 degrees, except anchor lights prescribed in Rule 30, which need not be placed at an imprac-ticable height above the hull, and the all-round white light described in Rule 23(d), which may not be obscured at all.

**§ 84.19 Vertical sectors**

(a) The vertical sectors of electric lights as fitted, with the exception of lights on sailing vessels underway and on unmanned barges, shall ensure that:

(1) At least the required minimum intensity is maintained at all angles from 5 degrees above to 5 degrees be-low the horizontal;

(2) At least 60 percent of the re-quired minimum intensity is main-tained from 7.5 degrees above to 7.5 degrees below the horizontal.

(b) In the case of sailing vessels un-derway the vertical sectors of electric lights as fitted shall ensure that:

(1) At least the required minimum intensity is maintained at all angles from 5 degrees above to 5 degrees be-low the horizontal;

(2) At least 50 percent of the re-quired minimum intensity is main-tained from 25 degrees above to 25 de-grees below the horizontal.

(c) In the case of unmanned barges the minimum required intensity of electric lights as fitted shall be main-tained on the horizontal.

(d) In the case of lights other than electric lights these specifications shall be met as closely as possible.

*International*

**11. Intensity of non-electric lights**

Non-electric lights shall so far as practicable comply with the minimum intensities, as specified in the Table given in Section 8 of this Annex.

**12. Maneuvering light**

Notwithstanding the provisions of paragraph 2(f) of this Annex the maneuvering light described in Rule 34(b) shall be placed in the same fore and aft vertical plane as the masthead light or lights and, where practicable, at a minimum height of 2 meters vertically above the forward masthead light, provided that it shall be carried not less than 2 meters vertically above or below the after masthead light. On a vessel where only one masthead light is carried the maneuvering light, if fitted, shall be carried where it can best be seen, not less than 2 meters vertically apart from the masthead light.

**13. Approval**

The construction of lights and shapes and the installation of lights on board the vessel shall be to the satisfaction of the appropriate authority of the State whose flag the vessel is entitled to fly.

*ANNEX II*
*Additional Signals for Fishing Vessels Fishing in Close Proximity*

**1. General**

The lights mentioned herein shall, if exhibited in pursuance of Rule 26(d), be placed where they can best be seen. They shall be at least 0.9 meter apart but at a lower level than lights prescribed in Rule 26(b)(i) and (c)(i). The lights shall be visible all around the horizon at a distance of at least 1 mile but at a lesser distance than the lights prescribed by these Rules for fishing vessels.

*Inland*

**§ 84.21 Intensity of non-electric lights**

Non-electric lights shall so far as practicable comply with the minimum intensities, as specified in the Table given in § 84.15.

**§ 84.23 Maneuvering light**

Notwithstanding the provisions of § 84.03(f), the maneuvering light described in Rule 34(b) shall be placed approximately in the same fore and aft vertical plane as the masthead light or lights and, where practicable, at a minimum height of one-half meter vertically above the forward masthead light, provided that it shall be carried not less than one-half meter vertically above or below the after masthead light. On a vessel where only one masthead light is carried the maneuvering light, if fitted, shall be carried where it can best be seen, not less than one-half meter vertically apart from the masthead light.

**§ 84.25 Approval.** [Reserved]

*ANNEX II*
*Additional Signals for Fishing Vessels Fishing in Close Proximity*

**§ 85.1. General**

The lights mentioned herein shall, if exhibited in pursuance of Rule 26(d), be placed where they can best be seen. They shall be at least 0.9 meter apart but at a lower level than lights prescribed in Rule 26(b)(i) and (c)(i) contained in the Inland Navigational Rules Act of 1980. The lights shall be visible all around the horizon at a distance of at least 1 mile but at a lesser distance than the lights prescribed by these Rules for fishing vessels.

*International*

**2. Signals for trawlers**

(a) Vessels when engaged in trawling, whether using demersal or pelagic gear, may exhibit:

(i) when shooting their nets: two white lights in a vertical line;

(ii) when hauling their nets: one white light over one red light in a vertical line;

(iii) when the net has come fast upon an obstruction: two red lights in a vertical line.

(b) Each vessel engaged in pair trawling may exhibit:

(i) by night, a searchlight directed forward and in the direction of the other vessel of the pair;

(ii) when shooting or hauling their nets or when their nets have come fast upon an obstruction, the lights prescribed in 2(a) above.

**3. Signals for purse seiners**

Vessels engaged in fishing with purse seine gear may exhibit two yellow lights in a vertical line. These lights shall flash alternately every second and with equal light and occultation duration. These lights may be exhibited only when the vessel is hampered by its fishing gear.

*ANNEX III*
*Technical Details of Sound*
*Signal Appliances*

**1. Whistles**

(a) **Frequencies and range of audibility.** The fundamental frequency of the signal shall lie within the range 70–700 Hz.

The range of audibility of the signal from a whistle shall be determined by those frequencies, which may include the fundamental and/or one or more higher frequencies, which lie within the range 180–700 Hz (± 1 percent) and

*Inland*

**§ 85.3 Signals for trawlers**

(a) Vessels when engaged in trawling, whether using demersal or pelagic gear, may exhibit:

(1) When shooting their nets: two white lights in a vertical line;

(2) When hauling their nets: one white light over one red light in a vertical line;

(3) When the net has come fast upon an obstruction: two red lights in a vertical line.

(b) Each vessel engaged in pair trawling may exhibit:

(1) By night, a searchlight directed forward and in the direction of the other vessel of the pair;

(2) When shooting or hauling their nets or when their nets have come fast upon an obstruction, the lights prescribed in paragraph (a) above.

**§ 85.5 Signals for purse seiners**

Vessels engaged in fishing with purse seine gear may exhibit two yellow lights in a vertical line. These lights shall flash alternately every second and with equal light and occultation duration. These lights may be exhibited only when the vessel is hampered by its fishing gear.

*ANNEX III*
*Technical Details of Sound*
*Signal Appliances*

**Subpart A—Whistles**

**§ 86.01 Frequencies and range of audibility.**

The fundamental frequency of the signal shall lie within the range 70–525 Hz. The range of audibility of the signal from a whistle shall be determined by those frequencies, which may include the fundamental and/or one or more higher frequencies, which lie within the frequency ranges and pro-

*International*

which provide the sound pressure levels specified in paragraph 1(c) below.

(b) **Limits of fundamental frequencies.** To ensure a wide variety of whistle characteristics, the fundamental frequency of a whistle shall be between the following limits:

(i) 70–200 Hz, for a vessel 200 meters or more in length;

(ii) 130–350 Hz, for a vessel 75 meters but less than 200 meters in length;

(iii) 250–700 Hz, for a vessel less than 75 meters in length.

(c) **Sound signal intensity and range of audibility.** A whistle fitted in a vessel shall provide, in the direction of maximum intensity of the whistle and at a distance of 1 meter from it, a sound pressure level in at least one ⅓-octave band within the range of frequencies 180–700 Hz (± 1 percent) of not less than the appropriate figure given in the table below.

*Inland*

vide the sound pressure levels specified in § 86.05.

**§ 86.03 Limits of fundamental frequencies.**

To ensure a wide variety of whistle characteristics, the fundamental frequency of a whistle shall be between the following limits:

(a) 70–200 Hz, for a vessel 200 meters or more in length;

(b) 130–350 Hz, for a vessel 75 meters but less than 200 meters in length;

(c) 250–525 Hz, for a vessel less than 75 meters in length.

**§ 86.05 Sound signal intensity and range of audibility.**

A whistle on a vessel shall provide, in the direction of the forward axis of the whistle and at a distance of 1 meter from it, a sound pressure level in at least one ⅓-octave band of not less than the appropriate figure given in Table 86.05 within the following frequency ranges (± 1 percent):

(a) 130–1200 Hz, for a vessel 75 meters or more in length;

(b) 250–1600 Hz, for a vessel 20 meters but less than 75 meters in length;

(c) 250–2100 Hz, for a vessel 12 meters but less than 20 meters in length.

*International*

*Inland*

Table 86.05

| Length of vessel in meters | 1/3-octave band level at 1 meter in dB referred to $2 \times 10^{-5}$ N/m | Audible range in nautical miles |
|---|---|---|
| 200 or more | 143 | 2 |
| 75 but less than 200 | 138 | 1.5 |
| 20 but less than 75 | 130 | 1 |
| Less than 20 | 120 | 0.5 |

| Length of vessel in meters | Fundamental frequency range (Hz) | For measured frequencies (Hz) | 1/3-octave band level at 1 meter in dB referred to $2 \times 10^{-5}$ N/m | Audible range in nautical miles |
|---|---|---|---|---|
| 200 or more | 70–200 | 130–180 | 145 | |
| | | 180–250 | 143 | 2 |
| | | 250–1200 | 140 | |
| 75 but less than 200 | 130–350 | 130–180 | 140 | |
| | | | | 1.5 |
| | | 180–250 | 138 | |
| | | 250–1200 | 134 | |
| 20 but less than 75 | 250–525 | 250–450 | 130 | |
| | | | | 1.0 |
| | | 450–800 | 125 | |
| | | 800–1600 | 121 | |
| 12 but less than 20 | 250–525 | 250–450 | 120 | |
| | | | | 0.5 |
| | | 450–800 | 115 | |
| | | 800–2100 | 111 | |

The range of audibility in the table above is for information and is approximately the range at which a whistle may be heard on its forward axis with 90 percent probability in conditions of still air on board a vessel having average background noise level at the listening posts (taken to be 68 dB in the octave band centered on 250 Hz and 63 dB in the octave band centered on 500 Hz).

In practice the range at which a whistle may be heard is extremely variable and depends critically on weather conditions; the values given can be regarded as typical but under conditions of strong wind or high ambient noise level at the listening post the range may be much reduced.

*Note:* The range of audibility in the table above is for information and is approximately the range at which a whistle may usually be heard on its forward axis in conditions of still air on board a vessel having average background noise level at the listening posts (taken to be 68 dB in the octave band centered on 250 Hz and 63 dB in the octave band centered on 500 Hz).

In practice the range at which a whistle may be heard is extremely variable and depends critically on weather conditions; the values given can be regarded as typical but under conditions of strong wind or high ambient noise level at the listening post the range may be much reduced.

*International*

(d) **Directional properties.** The sound pressure level of a directional whistle shall be not more than 4 dB below the prescribed sound pressure level on the axis at any direction in the horizontal plane within ± 45 degrees of the axis. The sound pressure level at any other direction in the horizontal plane shall be not more than 10 dB below the prescribed sound pressure level on the axis, so that the range in any direction will be at least half the range on the forward axis. The sound pressure level shall be measured in that one-third octave band which determines the audibility range.

(e) **Positioning of whistles.** When a directional whistle is to be used as the only whistle on a vessel, it shall be installed with its maximum intensity directed straight ahead.

A whistle shall be placed as high as practicable on a vessel, in order to reduce interception of the emitted sound by obstructions and also to minimize hearing damage risk to personnel. The sound pressure level of the vessel's own signal at listening posts shall not exceed 110 dB (A) and so far as practicable should not exceed 100 dB (A).

(f) **Fitting of more than one whistle.** If whistles are fitted at a distance apart of more than 100 meters, it shall be so arranged that they are not sounded simultaneously.

(g) **Combined whistle systems.** If due to the presence of obstructions the sound field of a single whistle or of one of the whistles referred to in paragraph 1(f) above is likely to have a zone of greatly reduced signal level, it is recommended that a combined whistle system

*Inland*

**§ 86.07 Directional properties.**

The sound pressure level of a directional whistle shall be not more than 4 dB below the sound pressure level specified in § 86.05 in any direction in the horizontal plane within ± 45 degrees of the forward axis. The sound pressure level of the whistle at any other direction in the horizontal plane shall not be more than 10 dB less than the sound pressure level specified for the forward axis, so that the range of audibility in any direction will be at least half the range required on the forward axis. The sound pressure level shall be measured in that one-third octave band which determines the audibility range.

**§ 86.09 Positioning of whistles.**

(a) When a directional whistle is to be used as the only whistle on the vessel and is permanently installed, it shall be installed with its forward axis directed forward.

(b) A whistle shall be placed as high as practicable on a vessel, in order to reduce interception of the emitted sound by obstructions and also to minimize hearing damage risk to personnel. The sound pressure level of the vessel's own signal at listening posts shall not exceed 110 dB (A) and so far as practicable should not exceed 100 dB (A).

**§ 86.11 Fitting of more than one whistle.**

If whistles are fitted at a distance apart of more than 100 meters, they shall not be sounded simultaneously.

**§ 86.13 Combined whistle systems.**

(a) A combined whistle system is a number of whistles (sound emitting sources) operated together. For the purposes of the Rules a combined whistle system is to be regarded as a single whistle.

*International*

be fitted so as to overcome this reduction. For the purposes of the Rules a combined whistle system is to be regarded as a single whistle. The whistles of a combined system shall be located at a distance apart of not more than 100 meters and arranged to be sounded simultaneously. The frequency of any one whistle shall differ from those of the others by at least 10 Hz.

*Inland*

(b) The whistles of a combined system shall—

(1) Be located at a distance apart of not more than 100 meters.

(2) Be sounded simultaneously,

(3) Each have a fundamental frequency different from those of the others by at least 10 Hz, and

(4) Have a tonal characteristic appropriate for the length of vessel which shall be evidenced by at least two-thirds of the whistles in the combined system having fundamental frequencies falling within the limits prescribed in § 86.03, or if there are only two whistles in the combined system, by the higher fundamental frequency falling within the limits prescribed in § 86.03.

*Note:* If due to the presence of obstructions the sound field of a single whistle or of one of the whistles referred to in § 86.11 is likely to have a zone of greatly reduced signal level, a combined whistle system should be fitted so as to overcome this reduction.

**§ 86.15 Towing vessel whistles.**

A power-driven vessel normally engaged in pushing ahead or towing alongside may, at all times, use a whistle whose characteristic falls within the limits prescribed by § 86.03 for the longest customary composite length of the vessel and its tow.

**2. Bell or gong**

(a) **Intensity of signal.** A bell or gong, or other device having similar sound characteristics shall produce a sound pressure level of not less than 110 dB at a distance of 1 meter from it.

(b) **Construction.** Bells and gongs shall be made of corrosion-resistant material and designed to give a clear tone. The diameter of the mouth of the

**Subpart B—Bell or gong**

**§ 86.21 Intensity of signal.**

A bell or gong, or other device having similar sound characteristics shall produce a sound pressure level of not less than 110 dB at 1 meter.

**§ 86.23 Construction.**

Bells and gongs shall be made of corrosion-resistant material and designed to give a clear tone. The diame-

*International*

bell shall be not less than 300 mm for vessels of 20 meters or more in length, and shall be not less than 200 mm for vessels of 12 meters or more but of less than 20 meters in length. Where practicable, a power-driven bell striker is recommended to ensure constant force but manual operation shall be possible. The mass of the striker shall be not less than 3 percent of the mass of the bell.

### 3. Approval

The construction of sound signal appliances, their performance and their installation on board the vessel shall be to the satisfaction of the appropriate authority of the State whose flag the vessel is entitled to fly.

*ANNEX IV*
*Distress Signals*

### 1. Need of assistance

The following signals, used or exhibited either together or separately, indicate distress and need of assistance:

(a) a gun or other explosive signal fired at intervals of about a minute;

(b) a continuous sounding with any fog-signalling apparatus;

(c) rockets or shells, throwing red stars fired one at a time at short intervals;

(d) a signal made by radiotelegraphy or by any other signaling method consisting of the group . . . — — — . . . (SOS) in the Morse Code;

(e) a signal sent by radiotelephony consisting of the spoken word "Mayday";

(f) the International Code Signal of distress indicated by N.C.;

(g) a signal consisting of a square flag having above or below it a ball or anything resembling a ball;

*Inland*

ter of the mouth of the bell shall be not less than 300 mm for vessels of more than 20 meters in length, and shall be not less than 200 mm for vessels of 12 to 20 meters in length. The mass of the striker shall be not less than 3 percent of the mass of the bell. The striker shall be capable of manual operation.

*Note:* When practicable, a power-driven bell striker is recommended to ensure constant force.

**Subpart C—Approval**
**§ 86.31 Approval.** [Reserved]

*ANNEX IV*
*Distress Signals*

### § 87.1 Need of assistance.

The following signals, used or exhibited either together or separately, indicate distress and need of assistance:

(a) A gun or other explosive signal fired at intervals of about a minute;

(b) A continuous sounding with any fog-signalling apparatus;

(c) Rockets or shells, throwing red stars fired one at a time at short intervals;

(d) A signal made by radiotelegraphy or by any other signaling method consisting of the group . . . — — — . . . (SOS) in the Morse Code;

(e) A signal sent by radiotelephony consisting of the spoken word "Mayday";

(f) The International Code Signal of distress indicated by N.C.;

(g) A signal consisting of a square flag having above or below it a ball or anything resembling a ball;

*International*

(h) flames on the vessel (as from a burning tar barrel, oil barrel, etc.);

(i) a rocket parachute flare or a hand flare showing a red light;

(j) a smoke signal giving off orange-colored smoke;

(k) slowly and repeatedly raising and lowering arms outstretched to each side;

(l) the radiotelegraph alarm signal;

(m) the radiotelephone alarm signal;

(n) signals transmitted by emergency position-indicating radio beacons.

(o) approved signals transmitted by radiocommunication systems.

2. The use or exhibition of any of the foregoing signals except for the purpose of indicating distress and need of assistance and the use of other signals which may be confused with any of the above signals is prohibited.

3. Attention is drawn to the relevant sections of the International Code of Signals, the Merchant Ship Search and Rescue Manual and the following signals:

(a) a piece of orange-colored canvas with either a black square and circle or other appropriate symbol (for identification from the air);

(b) a dye marker.

*Inland*

(h) Flames on the vessel (as from a burning tar barrel, oil barrel, etc.);

(i) A rocket parachute flare or a hand flare showing a red light;

(j) A smoke signal giving off orange-colored smoke;

(k) Slowly and repeatedly raising and lowering arms outstretched to each side;

(l) The radiotelegraph alarm signal;

(m) The radiotelephone alarm signal;

(n) Signals transmitted by emergency position-indicating radio beacons;

(o) Signals transmitted by radiocommunication systems.

(p) A high intensity white light flashing at regular intervals from 50 to 70 times per minute.

**§ 87.3 Exclusive use.**

The use or exhibition of any of the foregoing signals except for the purpose of indicating distress and need of assistance and the use of other signals which may be confused with any of the above signals is prohibited.

**§ 87.5 Supplemental signals.**

Attention is drawn to the relevant sections of the International Code of Signals, the Merchant Ship Search and Rescue Manual, the International Telecommunication Union Regulations, and the following signals:

(a) A piece of orange-colored canvas with either a black square and circle or other appropriate symbol (for identification from the air);

(b) A dye marker.

*ANNEX V*
*Pilot Rules*

**§ 88.01 Purpose and applicability.**

This Part applies to all vessels operating on United States inland waters

*International*

*Inland*

and to United States vessels operating on the Canadian waters of the Great Lakes to the extent there is no conflict with Canadian law.

**§ 88.03 Definitions.**

The terms used in this part have the same meaning as defined in the Inland Navigational Rules Act of 1980.

**§ 88.05 Copy of Rules.**

After January 1, 1983, the operator of each self-propelled vessel 12 meters or more in length shall carry on board and maintain for ready reference a copy of the Inland Navigation Rules.

**§ 88.09 Temporary exemption from light and shape requirements when operating under bridges.**

A vessel's navigation lights and shapes may be lowered if necessary to pass under a bridge.

**§ 88.11 Law enforcement vessels.**

(a) Law enforcement vessels may display a flashing blue light when engaged in direct law enforcement or public safety activities. This light must be locatd so that it does not interfere with the visibility of the vessel's navigation lights.

(b) The blue light described in this section may be displayed by law enforcement vessels of the United States and the States and their political subdivisions.

**§ 88.12 Public safety activities.**

(a) Vessels engaged in government sanctioned public safety activities, and commercial vessels performing similar functions, may display an alternately flashing red and yellow light signal. This identification light signal must be located so that it does not interfere with the visibility of the vessel's navigation lights. The identification light signal may be used only as an identification

*International*

*Inland*

signal and conveys no special privilege. Vessels using the identification light signal during public safety activities must abide by the Inland Navigation Rules, and must not presume that the light or the exigency gives them precedence or right of way.

(b) Public safety activities include but are not limited to patrolling marine parades, regattas, or special water celebrations; traffic control; salvage; firefighting; medical assistance; assisting disabled vessels; and search and rescue.

## § 88.13 Lights on barges at bank or dock.

(a) The following barges shall display at night and, if practicable, in periods of restricted visibility the lights described in paragraph (b) of this section—

(1) Every barge projecting into a buoyed or restricted channel.

(2) Every barge so moored that it reduces the available navigable width of any channel to less than 80 meters.

(3) Barges moored in groups more than two barges wide or to a maximum width of over 25 meters.

(4) Every barge not moored parallel to the bank or dock.

(b) Barges described in paragraph (a) shall carry two unobstructed white lights of an intensity to be visible for at least one mile on a clear dark night, and arranged as follows:

(1) On a single moored barge, lights shall be placed on the two corners farthest from the bank or dock.

(2) On barges moored in group formation, a light shall be placed on each of the upstream and downstream ends of the group on the corners farthest from the bank or dock.

*International*

*Inland*

(3) Any barge in a group, projecting from the main body or group toward the channel, shall be lighted as a single barge.

(c) Barges moored in any slip or slough which is used primarily for mooring purposes are exempt from the lighting requirements of this section.

(d) Barges moored in well-illuminated areas are exempt from the lighting requirements of this section. These areas are as follows:

*Chicago Sanitary Ship Canal*

(1) Mile 293.2 to 293.9
(3) Mile 295.2 to 296.1
(5) Mile 297.5 to 297.8
(7) Mile 298 to 298.2
(9) Mile 298.6 to 298.8
(11) Mile 299.3 to 299.4
(13) Mile 299.8 to 300.5
(15) Mile 303 to 303.2
(17) Mile 303.7 to 303.9
(19) Mile 305.7 to 305.8
(21) Mile 310.7 to 310.9
(23) Mile 311 to 311.2
(25) Mile 312.5 to 312.6
(27) Mile 313.8 to 314.2
(29) Mile 314.6
(31) Mile 314.8 to 315.3
(33) Mile 315.7 to 316
(35) Mile 316.8
(37) Mile 316.85 to 317.05
(39) Mile 317.5
(41) Mile 318.4 to 318.9
(43) Mile 318.7 to 318.8
(45) Mile 320 to 320.3
(47) Mile 320.6
(49) Mile 322.3 to 322.4
(51) Mile 322.8
(53) Mile 322.9 to 327.2

*Calumet Sag Channel*

(61) Mile 316.5

*Little Calumet River*

(71) Mile 321.2
(73) Mile 322.3

*International*

*Inland*

*Calumet River*
(81) Mile 328.5 to 328.7
(83) Mile 329.2 to 329.4
(85) Mile 330, west bank to 330.2
(87) Mile 331.4 to 331.6
(89) Mile 332.2 to 332.4
(91) Mile 332.6 to 332.8

*Cumberland River*
(101) Mile 126.8
(103) Mile 191

**§ 88.15 Lights on dredge pipelines.**

Dredge pipelines that are floating or supported on trestles shall display the following lights at night and in periods of restricted visibility.

(a) One row of yellow lights. The lights must be—

(1) Flashing 50 to 70 times per minute,

(2) Visible all around the horizon,

(3) Visible for at least 2 miles on a clear dark night,

(4) Not less than 1 and not more than 3.5 meters above the water,

(5) Approximately equally spaced, and

(6) Not more than 10 meters apart where the pipeline crosses a navigable channel. Where the pipeline does not cross a navigable channel the lights must be sufficient in number to clearly show the pipeline's length and course.

(b) Two red lights at each end of the pipeline, including the ends in a channel where the pipeline is separated to allow vessels to pass (whether open or closed). The lights must be—

(1) Visible all around the horizon, and

(2) Visible for at least 2 miles on a clear dark night, and

(3) One meter apart in a vertical line with the lower light at the same height above the water as the flashing yellow light.

*International*

## INTERPRETATIVE RULES
Sec.
82.1 Purpose.
82.3 Pushing vessel and vessel being pushed: Composite unit.
  AUTHORITY 33 U.S.C. 180, 30 Stat. 98; 49 CFR 1.46(c)(2); 28 Stat. 647, 33 U.S.C. 258; 49 CFR 1.46(c)(3); sec. 4233 R.S., 33 U.S.C. 322.

### § 82.1 Purpose.
(a) This part contains the interpretative rules concerning the 72 COLREGS that are adopted by the Coast Guard for the guidance of the public.

### § 82.3 Pushing vessel and vessel being pushed: Composite unit.
Rule 24(b) of the 72 COLREGS states that when a pushing vessel and a vessel being pushed ahead are rigidly connected in a composite unit, they are regarded as a power-driven vessel and must exhibit the lights under Rule 23. A "composite unit" is interpreted to be a pushing vessel that is rigidly connected by mechanical means to a vessel being pushed so they react to sea and swell as one vessel. "Mechanical means" does not include the following:
  (a) Lines.
  (b) Hawsers.
  (c) Wires.
  (d) Chains.
[CGD 76-133. 42 FR 35792, July 11, 1977. Redesignated by CGD 81-017, 46 FR 28154, May 26, 1981]

*Inland*

## INTERPRETATIVE RULES
Sec.
90.1 Purpose.
90.3 Pushing vessel and vessel being pushed. Composite unit.
  AUTHORITY: 33 U.S.C. 2071, 49 CFR 1.46(n)(14).

### § 90.1 Purpose.
(a) This part contains the interpretative rules for the Inland Rules. These interpretative rules are intended as a guide to assist the public and promote compliance with the Inland Rules.

### § 90.3 Pushing vessel and vessel being pushed: Composite unit.
Rule 24(b) of the Inland Rules states that when a pushing vessel and a vessel being pushed ahead are rigidly connected in a composite unit, they are regarded as a power-driven vessel and must exhibit the lights prescribed in Rule 23. A "composite unit" is interpreted to be the combination of a pushing vessel and a vessel being pushed ahead that are rigidly connected by mechanical means so they react to sea and swell as one vessel. Mechanical means does not include lines, wires, hawsers, or chains.
[CGD 83-011, 48 FR 51621, Nov. 10, 1983]

# Index of Cases

# Index

# About the Author

Capt. Richard A. Smith, RN, is a graduate of the Britannia Royal Navy College, Dartmouth, the Royal Naval College, Greenwich, the U.S. Armed Forces Staff College, Norfolk, Virginia, and the NATO Defence College, Rome. After joining the Royal Navy in 1958, he served at sea in frigates, destroyers, minesweepers, carriers, and landing ships, mainly in navigational and command appointments. Ashore, he ran the navigational desk at the Ministry of Defence level and, later, held responsibilities as Queen's Harbour Master for the busiest stretches of inshore waters in the United Kingdom. One of the Younger Brethren of Trinity House—the organization responsible for England's maritime navigational aids—Captain Smith is also a Fellow of both the Nautical Institute and the Royal Institute of Navigation. While an exchange officer at the U.S. Naval Academy in 1975, he was selected chairman of the navigational department, becoming the first foreign officer to head any department in the academy's history.

The **Naval Institute Press** is the book-publishing arm of the U.S. Naval Institute, a private, nonprofit society for sea service professionals and others who share an interest in naval and maritime affairs. Established in 1873 at the U.S. Naval Academy in Annapolis, Maryland, where its offices remain, today the Naval Institute has more than 100,000 members worldwide.

Members of the Naval Institute receive the influential monthly magazine *Proceedings* and discounts on fine nautical prints, ship and aircraft photos, and subscriptions to the quarterly *Naval History* magazine. They also have access to the transcripts of the Institute's Oral History Program and get discounted admission to any of the Institute-sponsored seminars offered around the country.

The Naval Institute's book-publishing program, begun in 1898 with basic guides to naval practices, has broadened its scope in recent years to include books of more general interest. Now the Naval Institute Press publishes more than sixty titles each year, ranging from how-to books on boating and navigation to battle histories, biographies, ship and aircraft guides, and novels. Institute members receive discounts on the Press's nearly 400 books in print.

Full-time students are eligible for special half-price membership rates. Life memberships are also available.

For a free catalog describing Naval Institute Press books currently available, and for further information about U.S. Naval Institute membership, please write to:

Membership & Communications Department
U.S. Naval Institute
118 Maryland Avenue
Annapolis, Maryland 21402-5035

Or call, toll-free, (800) 233-USNI.